THE MAKING OF

AMERICAN CALIFORNIA

A PROVIDENTIAL APPROACH

by Dorothy Dimmick

Recorder of the Providential steps necessary
for the Making of American California.

Written for the American Christian in California.

ISBN 1-893103-12-9

Printed in the United States of America

Published by Beautiful Feet Books, Inc.
139 Main Street
Sandwich, MA 02563

www.bfbooks.com
508.833.8626

"One generation shall praise Thy works to another,

and shall declare thy mighty acts."

(Psalm 145:4)

DEDICATION

The first edition (1977) of THE MAKING OF AMERICAN CALIFORNIA
was dedicated to my husband, Walter Franklin Dimmick.

The second edition (1990) was dedicated to my friend and teacher,
Verna Marie Hall (1912-1987).

The third edition (1996) is dedicated to my beloved family,
Walter Franklin Dimmick, husband
David Wilson Dimmick, son
Kevin Craig Dimmick, son
and to the memory of
Walter Scott Dimmick, son (1950-1994)

Dorothy Dimmick

VERNA MARIE HALL (1912–1987)

"A Lady with a lamp shall stand in
the great history of our land,
A noble type of good Heroic Womanhood."
(Santa Filomena, Stanza 10, Longfellow, 1858)

Miss Verna Hall was introduced to me by a mutual friend about 1943. Later, Verna invited me to join a group of people in San Francisco interested in studying the Constitution of the United States and related subjects. The "related subjects" came from their delving into old book stores for books prior to 1850, the year they believed socialism had crept into every avenue of our society in America. They were digging into the Christian roots of our country.

Since I lived and worked in Berkeley at that time, transportation was difficult for me so I declined her invitation. However, I attended her lectures on the subject of the Constitution whenever possible. I also purchased her prototype book, called THE HISTORIC ORIGIN OF THE CONSTITUTION OF THE UNITED STATES, published in 1959, a volume of 435 pages.

I believe Verna Hall was a very special individual. She was pleasant to be with, had a delightful sense of humor, and an infinite capacity for work. But there was a depth of understanding of things spiritual within her that attracted. She was an avid Bible student, devoted to a search of the Scriptures and their relation to the historic origins of the Constitution of the United States. She was a genius at analyzing the trends of history from a Christian providential perspective.

Verna's brilliant work on THE CHRISTIAN HISTORY OF THE CONSTITUTION OF THE UNITED STATES OF AMERICA began to make an impact on the Christian community when she became associated with Miss Rosalie June Slater, the American Christian Educator. As the CHRISTIAN HISTORY needed to be taught, Miss Slater, through her book, TEACHING AND LEARNING AMERICA'S CHRISTIAN HISTORY, provided the necessary tools by which the ordinary Christian could begin to comprehend and put into practice the philosophy that Christianity must be lived in every avenue of life, including that of civil government.

Believing that Christianity is the master principle, the Biblical origin and foundation of our American Constitution, Miss Hall chronicled the pilgrimage of the Christian Idea of Man and Government from the Ten Commandments to the Constitution of the United States. It was her concern that America was fast becoming imbued with doctrines antagonistic to those that maintain a Christian Constitutional Republic. It was her goal to educate Americans out of the wilderness of ignorance about their heritage and help us "remember" God's saving grace to this nation through the study of a providential chain of historic events and people, which she called THE CHAIN OF CHRISTIANITY.

In working with Miss Hall upon the Index of the material of the future volumes she had planned to publish, I learned that one of her favorite Bible passages was Psalm 114:1-7:

"When Israel went out of Egypt, the house of Jacob
from a people of strange language; Judah was
his sanctuary, and Israel his dominion.
The sea saw it, and fled: Jordan was driven back.
The mountains skipped like rams, and
the little hills like lambs.
What ailed thee, O thou sea, that thou fleddest?
thou Jordan, that thou was driven back?
Ye mountains, that ye skipped like rams; and
ye little hills, like lambs?
Tremble, thou earth, at the presence of the Lord,
at the presence of the God of Jacob."

Miss Hall equated the character of men like George Washington to the mountains; the little hills to those of lesser character, but none-the-less contributors to the Liberty of the individual which is guaranteed in our nation through our Constitution.

Through a study of her works, we find Verna Marie Hall, from the highest mountain, calling us to remember who we are, God's creatures, created in the image and likeness of God, showing forth His Glory through the free and independent man.

I pray that through Miss Hall's works, and the American Christian education of Miss Slater, our nation will come out from the *strange language* of socialism; that we will find our sanctuary and dominion through the precepts and principles of our Lord and Saviour, Jesus Christ.

"The mountains shall bring peace to the people,
and the little hills, by righteousness."

(Psalm 72:3)

"No people can be bound to acknowledge and adore the invisible hand,

which conducts the Affairs of men more than

the People of the United States.

Every step, by which they have advanced to the character

of an independent nation, seems to have been

distinguished by some token

of <u>providential</u> agency."

George Washington

INAUGURAL ADDRESS

THE MAKING OF AMERICAN CALIFORNIA:

A PROVIDENTIAL APPROACH

"PROVIDENTIAL: Effected by the providence of God; proceeding from divine direction or superintendence..."(Noah Webster, AN AMERICAN DICTIONARY OF THE ENGLISH LANGUAGE, First Edition, 1828)

How does California relate to the whole providential purpose of America?

AMERICA:

From THE CHRISTIAN HISTORY OF THE AMERICAN REVOLUTION: CONSIDER AND PONDER, page 47, we read: "A land in North America, discovered in the tenth century by the Scandinavians, only to be hidden away again till the time should be ripe for its settlement by a people providentially prepared for its occupancy." The people God chose to occupy this land had the Word of God in their hands to reason from and to relate its principles to all areas of their lives including the area of civil government. The result was America, the world's first Christian Republic.

CALIFORNIA:

As America grew stronger in its Biblical principles and character, firmly establishing its Constitutional Government for the protection and liberty of the individual, God preserved the land of California for a people providentially prepared to occupy it, a people willing to carry westward the Christian idea of man and government. Through many steps, California became the Child of America, an American Commonwealth based upon American Common Law, and a Link in the Chain of Christianity moving westward.

The following is the Preface to the First Edition, 1977, of THE MAKING OF AMERICAN CALIFORNIA. The present edition is essentially the same but it has been expanded.

Personal
Testimony

For many years I have watched the continued progress and unfoldment of the educational program for the Christian school, the Christian home, and the Christian church based upon THE CHRISTIAN HISTORY OF THE CONSTITUTION OF THE UNITED STATES OF AMERICA by Verna M. Hall, Compiler, and its companion volume, TEACHING AND LEARNING AMERICA'S CHRISTIAN HISTORY by Rosalie J. Slater. It was natural that my thoughts should turn to this program when I was searching for a constructive activity in my life.

Our three sons were out of college; there was just so much housekeeping and gardening I could do; I had returned to college for a teaching credential which was interesting but not enough to satisfy; and my husband and I were not really world travelers or "social butterflies." There is nothing wrong with those activities; they just did not fill the void in my family-oriented everyday life. I decided to offer my clerical services to THE FOUNDATION FOR AMERICAN CHRISTIAN EDUCATION in San Francisco. Their answer was a complete surprise, and one which I immediately started to work upon. It was: Why don't you research the history of California from a Christian perspective?

On both sides of our families, our children are fourth generation native Californians, so my interest in California goes very deep. I also knew that none of us had had a satisfactory education in the history of California. There was something missing, especially from the Christian point-of-view. I am most grateful for the beautiful concepts of California's history which have unfolded since undertaking my investigation.

My research revealed that the Christian history of California is distinct from any other story of California for two reasons:

California,
Child of America

First, while we acknowledge our debt to Spain and other countries for the discovery and colonization of California, there is no doubt that California is the Child of America. Our first California State Constitution was built upon American Christian principles. Through this work, I believe the reader will be able to appreciate that fact.

California,
Link in Chain of
Christianity

Second, my research confirmed that California is another link in the Chain of Christianity moving westward.

Principle Approach
to Christian History

This history of the background of California up to 1850, THE MAKING OF AMERICAN CALIFORNIA, was written for the Christian day-school student and teacher. In order to give the student a continual appreciation of his State from the primary grades through high school, it is suggested that this portion of California's history be divided into three grades using The Principle Approach developed by Miss Slater in TEACHING AND LEARNING AMERICA'S CHRISTIAN HISTORY:

Suggestions

a) For the primary grades (4th, 5th, or 6th): A brief study of how California was discovered, explored, named, and settled; an understanding of the events which freed California from a mandatory Church-State law, with most of the emphasis on the early American pioneers and how they entered California;

b) For the junior high school student (7th or 8th): A study of the Mexican-American war; with emphasis upon the gold discovery with all its attendant glitter, and how it became providentially a fact after the United States obtained California from Mexico;

c) For the high school student (preferably, the 11th grade): A study of how American law was set up in California, guaranteeing her the American institutions which have made her such a great State.

Gratitude

I am most grateful for encouragement in this work by Miss Hall, Miss Slater, and Mr. James B. Rose, Headmaster of the American Heritage Christian Schools in Hayward, California.

(Mr. Rose is now President of The American Christian History Institute, and author of A GUIDE TO AMERICAN CHRISTIAN EDUCATION FOR THE HOME AND SCHOOL: THE PRINCIPLE APPROACH. This book may be obtained from: A.C.H.I., P.O. Box 648, Palo Cedro, California 96073.)

Christian Character

The "end" of Christian education is the growth in Christian character. *"Train up a child in the way that he should go, and when he is old, he will not depart from it."* (Prov. 22:6) It takes the character of a Christian to support a Republic, a Christian's understanding of responsibility, or our response to God's ability.

Nation's Firm Foundation

"Liberty Under Law" was the tone of our country's Founding Fathers when they struggled to give us the Republican form of Government. To them it was an experiment in government, but our United States Constitution has proven to be reliable, steadfast, strong, and protective of the individual's rights. Our nation stands today, a giant among nations, in spite of the decline in the American Christian's character and the destructive attacks of humanism, communism, and other "isms," all of which have taken their toll.

Our nation has a Christian foundation but requires Christians knowledgeable of its Biblical principles to keep it on course. In the last two hundred years, the American Christians have gradually forgotten their nation's unique history and their responsibility for its proper operation, hence America is floundering. It is up to us as American Christians to find our way back to a firm republican, truly representative basis of government, and the best way is to investigate our "beginnings," within our nation and within each state.

How important is a State?

National and Federal

Did you know that our Constitution, the "miracle" created in Philadelphia in 1787, was mostly an extension of the thirteen <u>state</u> constitutions already in effect? Most of the delegates to the Constitutional Convention were familiar with the successes and the pitfalls of their respective <u>state</u> laws. This put them in a position to use the best aspects of their state constitutions when creating our national constitution. The Constitution of the United States was to be the law, not only for the thirteen states then in existence, but for the future states carved out of the vast North American Continent. It had to be Continental in scope. It was assumed the unknown West would someday be occupied by Americans who would then form themselves into more states.

California, September 9, 1850

And so it was. However, it took sixty-three years (1787-1850) before California, the farthest western state, was added to our Union. When California was invited to join the United States, it did so in 1850 as a full-fledged State, with a State Constitution, already having had a meeting of its First Legislature. This is demonstrable of the Christian qualities of faith, energy, perseverance, and patience amongst its founders.

Search for Truth

Since each State has an interesting story to tell, part of Christ's Story, I would like to record for the Christian reader, the MAKING OF AMERICAN CALIFORNIA, A PROVIDENTIAL APPROACH. I wish to show God's Providence in California's background up to 1850 and the marvelous way in which God worked to bring this distant western land under the wing of the United States, instead of allowing it to be under Spain, Russia, or England. We have always been taught that everything California was, and is, we owe to the Spanish-Catholic nation. This is partially true, but it is the whole truth that changes our view.

In THE CHRISTIAN HISTORY OF THE AMERICAN REVOLUTION, CONSIDER AND PONDER, Miss Hall states:

Obstacles Overcome

"Mountains are either obstacles or opportunities. Christian civil government is either an obstacle, a 'stumbling/block' or an opportunity to prove the power of Christ in the life of the individual. Let us be like the early pioneers moving west to settle California. After struggling for months across the vast plains and desert, they saw these seemingly impassable mountains. But instead of being defeated by them (as the Spanish thought they would be), they used them as an opportunity to prove the power of Christ in their lives and bring California into the Union the farthest westward land for Christianity at that time."

Not to be deterred, our pioneers pulled wagons over those mighty, craggy mountains and across the dusty, dry deserts, enduring much hardship. Yet these liberty-loving Americans trudged on to establish homes in what was then a foreign land under foreign laws. Through God's Providence they were finally assured of living under the protection of the laws of the United States from which most of them had come.

Teach Them

The vast forces at work to allow California to enter the growing Union of States were indeed providential. These forces should be known to the youth of California. They should learn to appreciate the efforts of past pioneers in establishing the foundations of their state, the thirty-first State of the Union.

Inspire Them

How better to inspire youth to great achievements through Christ than to view the Hand of God in its immensity - at work for them. Americans and Californians, how better than through our young people to find our way back *"to the liberty wherewith Christ hath made us free, and be not entangled again with the yoke of bondage."* (Gal. 5:1)

Note: Among the many mechanical steps which are necessary in bringing this material to you the Reader, the Teacher, the Student, is that of proofreading. I wish to express my thanks to Mrs. Beulah B. Macdonald, a dear friend, for her efficient help in proofing these pages, and for her loving encouragement along the way.

I also thank Mrs. Desta Garrett for her work in the final preparation of the manuscript for printing, and the Foundation for American Christian Education for the use of their equipment.

XII

PREFACE, 1996

"I will overturn, overturn, overturn, it; and it shall be no more, until he come whose right it is; and I will give it him."   (Ezekiel 21:27)

"For unto us a child is born, unto us a son is given, and the government shall be upon his shoulder..." (Isaiah 9:6)

The subtle errors in our American society and government that have been hidden from us for so long are now beginning to reach the surface, to be destroyed. God will continue to overturn the darkness to make way for the light of Christ's Christianity in every avenue of life. *"...he placed at the east of the garden of Eden Cherubims, and a flaming sword which turned every which way, to keep the way of the tree of life."* (Genesis 3:24) "The flaming sword" of Truth is destined to predominate, not only in our beloved California, but in all the world. *"I have sworn by myself, the word is gone out of my mouth in righteousness, and shall not return, That unto me every knee shall bow, every tongue shall swear."* (Isaiah 45:23) This is God's promise to us. This is our heritage! But in the meantime, we must WATCH and pray. *"Take ye heed, watch and pray; for ye know not when the time is."* (Mark 13:33) *"And what I say unto you I say unto all, WATCH."* (Mark 13:37)

It has been gratifying to me to have seen hundreds of mothers and fathers and children rededicate their lives to a true knowledge of history through the Christian home-schooling phenomena which has taken root in this country. Parents are obliged to learn in order to teach their children, and children must learn that the source of all knowledge comes from the Bible.

After our United States Constitution was firmly established, from "the cradle of liberty" the Westward Movement marched across our land to California. However, we took our God-given individual liberty for granted. We should remember that "eternal vigilance is the price of liberty," as ours is a remarkable Republic established under the Providence of God.

We have, through neglect, slid into a socialistic state which claims government can do all for the people. But God is in control. The return to righteousness may be slow and painful as more people return to the precepts of Christianity in their lives and in their government.

When one studies the historic origins of this country, we learn that the American people were educated in Self-government, especially during the ten years prior to the American Revolutionary War. How? By sermons from the pulpits of America. Today it takes courage on the part of our preachers and ministers to stand for the Constitution of the United States of America, and to conserve the liberties of the children of God.

As we work our way out of the dark morass of ignorance and out from under the mass media of lies, we shall demand and get the rewards of God's free children. *"No man can serve two masters; either he will hate the one, and love the other; or else he will hold to the one, and despise the other. Ye cannot serve God and mammon."* (Matthew 6:24)

I have watched the results of the Christian home-schooling movement with interest. It takes dedication and hard work. The results, however, are the establishment of Christian character in the lives of a new generation.

I hope I have contributed in some degree through emphasizing the Christian character of the discoverers of California mentioned in this book. Governmentally, I hope the reader realizes that the foundations creating our United States Republic are the same foundations which came into and were adopted by California. It has amazed me when I learn how many lives have been touched through teaching the things about California that have never been taught in the public schools. Providentially, California is the Child of America.

CONTENTS

INTRODUCTION

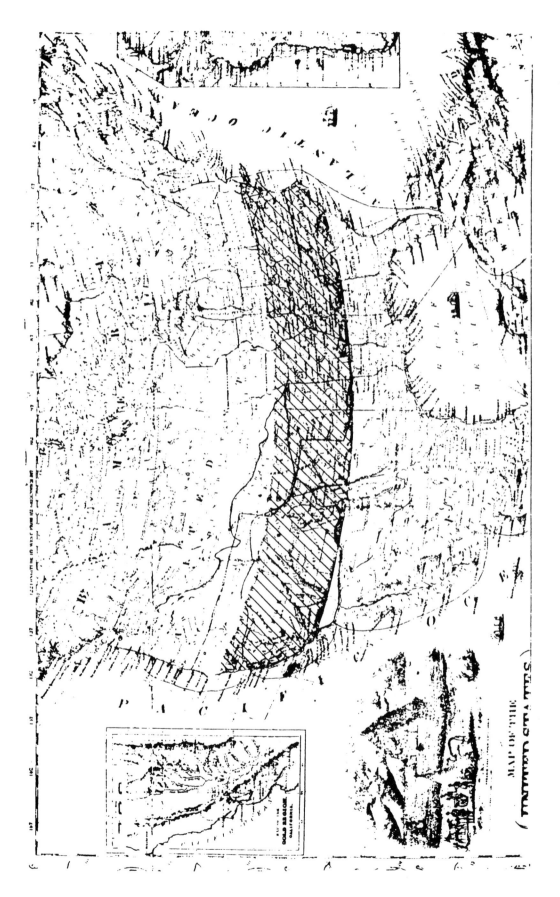

Portion of "Map of the U.S., The British Provinces, Mexico & C., Showing the Routes of the U.S. Mail Steam Packets to California and a Plan of the Gold Region. Published by J. H. Colton, 86 Cedar Street, New York, 1849." From Foreword by Joseph A. Sullivan, editor, PETER BURNETT, FIRST GOVERNOR OF THE STATE OF CALIFORNIA, AN OLD PIONEER.

INTRODUCTION

"The Lord of hosts hath sworn, saying, Surely as I have thought, so shall it come to pass; and as I have purposed, so shall it stand." (Isa. 14:24)

One Nation
Under God

From the beginning of our nation, from the landing of the colonists at Jamestown in 1607 and the landing of the little group of Pilgrims on the shores of New England in 1620, our North American continent from coast to coast was meant to contain "one nation under God." From the Atlantic Ocean to the Pacific Ocean, the Chain of Christianity was to cross our land from the pioneering of William Bradford to the pioneering of Jedediah Smith.

The grants by England to our original colonies of Virginia and Massachusetts included practically the whole of the North American Continent. When considering the size of the little group of Pilgrims who landed on the shores of New England in 1620, it was rather presumptuous of England to grant them the entire Continent. Looking back upon that seed planted on the coast of New England, however, the grants were providential.

Look at the Colton Map on page 2. Here is pictured the territory covered by the Virginia, Massachusetts and Carolina grants.

On the west coast of California, the closing of these English grants to our original colonies of Virginia and Massachusetts took place when Lt. Joseph Warren Revere, grandson of our Revolutionary war hero, Paul Revere, removed the California Bear Flag in Sonoma in 1846 and raised the United States Flag over Mexican Territory. According to God's plan, our American Christian principles had traveled the breadth of the North American Continent. Some call this Manifest Destiny, but who can question the Hand of God in history when we remember: *"That all the people of the earth might know the hand of the Lord, that it is mighty...."* (Joshua 4:24)

With the movement of the Chain of Christianity from Massachusetts to California, from "sea-to-shining-sea," we see that the Christian idea of man and government has formed these United States into "one nation under God." California was part of God's Plan.

SOURCE MATERIAL

Books published
by F.A.C.E.

Since you are being introduced to concepts perhaps new to you, listed are the Christian History books which have been used as source material.[1]

The following books were compiled by Miss Verna Hall:

THE CHRISTIAN HISTORY OF THE CONSTITUTION OF THE UNITED STATES OF AMERICA: CHRISTIAN SELF-GOVERNMENT, Volume I;

THE CHRISTIAN HISTORY OF THE CONSTITUTION OF THE UNITED STATES OF AMERICA: SELF-GOVERNMENT WITH UNION, Volume II;

THE CHRISTIAN HISTORY OF THE AMERICAN REVOLUTION: CONSIDER AND PONDER.

The following book was written by Miss Rosalie Slater:

TEACHING AND LEARNING AMERICA'S CHRISTIAN HISTORY: THE PRINCIPLE APPROACH.

THE BIBLE AND THE CONSTITUTION OF THE UNITED STATES OF AMERICA, written by Miss Hall and Miss Slater.

INTRODUCTION DIVIDED INTO FOUR SECTIONS:

Overview, Chain of Christianity

1. As California is another Link in the Chain of Christianity moving westward, the reader is given an Overview of the Chain of Christianity leading to the providential founding of our American Christian Nation. The complete text is to be found in Volume I of THE CHRISTIAN HISTORY OF THE CONSTITUTION.

Overview, Background of California

2. Since California was providentially prepared to receive the Christian principles of American Christian Constitutional Government, an Overview is presented of the background of California's history up to 1850 when she became a State. California is the Child of America, and we document the steps which providentially made her so.

Church and State

3. As there seems to be some confusion as to the correct American position on the question of Church to State, and State to Church, and because it was so important to the history of California, included is an excerpt from THE CHRISTIAN HISTORY OF THE CONSTITUTION, Volume II, pages 35-40.

TEACHING AND LEARNING

4. The setting for the study of THE MAKING OF AMERICAN CALIFORNIA is derived from the American Christian Philosophy of Education, first identified by Miss Rosalie Slater in TEACHING AND LEARNING AMERICA'S CHRISTIAN HISTORY. In accordance with that philosophy, three Leading Ideas are given to help the student as he reads the text of THE MAKING OF AMERICAN CALIFORNIA.

PART I: OVERVIEW OF THE CHAIN OF CHRISTIANITY

From THE CHRISTIAN HISTORY OF THE CONSTITUTION, Volume I, pages 1 and 2, compiled by Miss Hall, is the providential purpose of recording for American Christians the Chain of Christianity, California being one of its Links:

America's
Stewardship

"This nation has in its keeping 'the last word in human political institutions,' - the Republican form of government.

America, awaiting
spirit of new
civilization

The vast region which the flag of the United States protects was, two centuries and a half ago (written in 1890), the roaming ground of tribes of Indians...It was virtually a waste awaiting, in the order of Providence, the magic influence of an incoming race, imbued with the spirit of a new civilization. The period referred to was an epoch in which there had been <u>a providential preparation for great events in the Old World</u>. It was an era of wonderful discovery in the heavens and in the earth.

European
Reformation
through inquiry
from Church to
State

It was also the period of the Reformation. This, in its essence, was the assertion of the principle of individuality, or of true spiritual freedom; and in the beginning, not by Protestants alone, of whom Luther was the great exponent, but by Catholics also, represented in the polished and profound Reuchlin. Though first occupied with subjects not connected with political speculation, yet it was natural and inevitable, that <u>inquiry should widen out from the realm of the Church into that of the State</u>. Then a fresh impetus was given to the transformation of society, which began when Christianity - the basis of the good, permanent, and progressive in modern civilization - first appeared in the world.

Pagan Idea of Man

Domination by State

At that time, social order rested on the assumed natural inequality of men. The individual was regarded as of value only as he formed a part of the political fabric, and was able to contribute to its uses, as though it were the end of his being to aggrandize the State. This was the <u>pagan idea of man</u>. The wisest philosophers of antiquity could not rise above it. Its influence imbued the pagan world. The State regarded as of paramount importance, not the man, but the citizen whose physical and intellectual forces it absorbed. If this tended to foster lofty civic virtues and splendid individual culture in the classes whom the State selected as the recipients of its favors, it bore hard on those whom the State virtually ignored, - on the laboring men, mechanics, the poor, captives in war, slaves, and woman. This low view of man was exerting its full influence when Rome was at the height of its power and glory.

CHAIN OF CHRISTIANITY MOVES WESTWARD

WITH "SIGNS FOLLOWING"

"RELIGION STANDS ON TIP-TOE IN OUR LAND, READIE TO PASS TO THE AMERICAN STRAND."
—George Herbert

HENRY HELWYS 1612
JOHN MILTON 1608
RICHARD MATHER 1596
WILLIAM BRADFORD 1590
JOHN WINTHROP 1588
THOMAS HOOKER 1586
HUGO GROTIUS 1583
JOHN ROBINSON 1575
WILLIAM BREWSTER 1563
GENEVA BIBLE 1557

PRELUDE TO AMERICA

RICHARD HOOKER 1554?
GASPARD DE COLIGNY 1519
JOHN FOX 1516
JOHN CALVIN 1509
JOHN KNOX 1505?
WILLIAM TYNDALE 1494
MILES COVERDALE 1488
HUGH LATIMER 1485
ULRICH ZWINGLI 1484
MARTIN LUTHER 1483
JOHANN GUTENBERG 1396
JOHN HUSS 1369
WYCLIFFE 1324?

MORNING STARS OF REFORMATION

MAGNA CHARTA 1215

IRELAND—PATRICK 389
AUGUSTINE 354
JEROME 340

FOURTH CENTURY

GERMANY
BRITAIN
SPAIN
FRANCE—FRANKS (GAUL)

SECOND CENTURY

ROME
GREECE
EUROPE—LYDIA (ACTS 16)

FIRST WESTWARD PLANTING OF SEEDS OF CHRISTIANITY

FIRST CENTURY

AMERICA'S PLANTING
JAMESTOWN 1607
KING JAMES BIBLE 1611
MAYFLOWER COMPACT 1620

APOSTLES AND DISCIPLES
PAUL'S MISSIONARY JOURNEYS

JESUS CHRIST AND GOSPEL—GRACE
MOSES AND TEN COMMANDMENTS—LAW

PILGRIMS LAND AT PLYMOUTH 1620
PETITION OF RIGHT 1628
JOHN BUNYAN 1628

WILLIAM PENN 1644
BILL OF RIGHTS 1689
LOCKE'S TREATISE ON GOVERNMENT 1689

CHRISTOPHER DOCK 1698
JONATHAN EDWARDS 1703
JOHN AND CHARLES WESLEY 1703, 1707

GEORGE WHITEFIELD 1714
MONTESQUIEU 'THE SPIRIT OF LAWS' 1748
BLACKSTONE'S "COMMENTARIES" 1765

THE DECLARATION OF INDEPENDENCE 1776

A NEW NATION
THE CONSTITUTION OF THE UNITED STATES OF AMERICA 1787

NINETEENTH CENTURY
THE MONROE DOCTRINE 1823

"'TIS WESTERN COURSE THROUGH CHINA AND JAPAN IS IMPEDED . . . BY MODERNISM."
—Abraham Kuyper, 1898, Princeton

WESTWARD THE COURSE OF EMPIRE
"WESTWARD THE COURSE OF EMPIRE TAKES ITS WAY, THE FIRST FOUR ACTS ALREADY PAST, A FIFTH SHALL CLOSE THE DRAMA WITH THE DAY; TIME'S NOBLEST OFFSPRING IS THE LAST."
— Berkeley

Note: This list of names, events, and nations is not intended to be exhaustive, but rather indicative of the fact that God used men and nations through Christ to bring forth America and her form of government, for His glory and for all the nations of the earth.

From THE CHRISTIAN HISTORY OF THE CONSTITUTION OF THE UNITED STATES OF AMERICA, Vol. I, by Verna M. Hall

Christianity then appeared with its central doctrine, that man was created in the Divine image, and destined for immortality; pronouncing, that, in the eye of God, all men are equal. This asserted for the individual an independent value. It occasioned the great inference, that <u>man is superior to the State, which ought to be fashioned for his use</u>. This was the advent of a new spirit and a new power in the world..."

The writer goes on to say:

"This historical judgement is applicable to a line of illustrious characters, who grasped <u>the Christian idea of man</u>; and, because of the brilliancy of their service in behalf of human rights they deserve a place among the morning stars of the American constellation."

Briefly, let us review this "period of providential preparation" and some of these "illustrious characters" who carried forth the Chain of Christianity, westward, from Asia through Europe and England to America.

THE THREE HISTORICAL NATIONS

From TEACHING AND LEARNING, page 160:

"(These are) the three great historical nations (which) had to contribute, each in its own peculiar way, to <u>prepare the soil</u> for the planting of Christianity, - the Jews on the side of the religious element; the Greeks on the side of science and art; the Romans, as masters of the world, on the side of the political element. When the fulness of time was arrived, and Christ appeared, - then the goal of history had thus been reached, - then it was, that through him, and by the power of the spirit that proceeded from him, -the might of Christianity, - all the threads, hitherto separated, of human development, were to be brought together and interwoven in one web."

THE JEWS

The first significant event in this "preparation" was the Hebrew Decalogue, which gave the Hebrew a set of laws allowing him the greatest amount of individual freedom he had been able to attain since the time of his captivity in Egypt. Moses' recording of the Law on tablets of stone gave the Israelites rules to act within the law, not outside of it.

The Old Testament records the ascending thought of man's concept of individual liberty until we come to the New Testament. Jesus Christ came with grace and truth to fulfill the law, and to define the law. When asked by a lawyer, which is the great commandment in the law, Jesus answered:

7

Matthew 5:17

"Thou shalt love the Lord thy God with all thy heart, and with all thy soul, and with all thy mind. This is the first and great commandment. And the second is like unto it, Thou shalt love thy neighbour as thyself. On these two commandments hang all the law and the prophets." (Matthew 22:37-40) Jesus gave us in his Sermon on the Mount, man's highest sense of individual liberty with responsibility and the Christian idea of man. This idea was not extended into civil government until we bring His Story to America.

THE GREEKS

From Europe: Cultural Preparation

The Greeks became masters of learning, of culture, science, and art. Through trade and colonization they carried their philosophy on ships to the seas of Asia Minor. In this manner they spread the Greek language so that the New Testament was written in Greek.

Governmentally, Greece lacked Union

Years of struggle for the ascendancy of the ancient (430 B.C.) Greek states of Athens, Sparta, and Thebes had brought no results toward the creation of a federal system of government. The governments were sovereign over the citizen; there was no distribution of powers of government between the central government and the original states. Their exhaustion became indifference and opened the way for the complete conquest of Greece by the barbaric military monarchy of Philip of Macedon. For the next two hundred years the Greeks became prey for a foreign aggressor.

Spread of Greek Culture

It was the son of King Philip of Macedon, Alexander the Great, whose tremendous conquests included the whole of the Mediterranean area. He was responsible for the diffusion of the Greek civilization over Asia and the East by means of Greek colonies. Greek elements, such as temples, statues, theaters, porticos, ceremonies, festivals in the Greek manner, especially the Greek language and literature, were infused into and mingled with the settlements and monarchies which Alexander's empire broke up.

Greek Language

Alexander the Great was a pagan and imbued with the pagan idea of man, with its attendant conquest and tyranny. The Chain of Christianity moved westward with Christian principles, but as God uses men and nations for His purposes, so He used the energy of Alexander to spread the Greek language around the eastern Mediterranean, thereby making the work of Paul easier.

Center of Greek Culture

Alexander the Great founded the City of Alexandria in 332 B.C. Its situation made it a commercial center for all the nations lying around the Mediterranean and a communicating link with the wealth and civilizations of the East. Under the Ptolemies, it became the center of culture. There the great library was built, which housed the complete library of Aristotle; its museums developed into a Greek university; there the Septuagint was produced. It became a center of Hellenism, and of Semitism, being the greatest Jewish city in the world at that time. From 306 B.C. to 30 B.C. was the foundation of the Ptolemaic dynasty; from 30 B.C., it was subjugated by the Romans until 642 A.D. when Alexandria was destroyed by the Arabs.

8

In TEACHING AND LEARNING, page 161, we read:

Acts 14:11, 12

"Among the numberless lessons which we may derive from the study of Grecian history, is...the error of ascribing to arts, to literature, and the politeness, that power of softening and correcting the human heart, which is, in truth, the exclusive prerogative of religion. Really to mend the heart, and purify the principle, is a deeper work than the most finished cultivation of the taste has ever been able to effect."

THE ROMANS

Political Preparation: Rome added Roman Citizen

Acts 22:25-29

Along the Chain of Christianity, Rome added the Roman citizen. Militarily and politically, Rome conquered the whole Mediterranean world. From CHRISTIAN HISTORY, Volume I, page 12, we read:

"The secret of Rome's wonderful strength lay in the fact that she incorporated the vanquished peoples into her own body politic... Never before had so many people been brought under one government without making slaves of most of them...Roman citizens (were) protected by Roman law, sharing in the material and spiritual benefits of Roman civilization."

No Representation

However, it was conquest with incorporation but without representation. Rome's principle of government joined a degree of liberty with union, but crushed local self-government.

"The old Roman world knew nothing of representative assemblies...The Roman's only notion of delegated power was that of authority delegated by the government to its generals and prefects who discharged at a distance its military and civil functions. When, therefore, the Roman popular government, originally adapted to a single city, had come to extend itself over a large part of the world, it lacked the one institution by means of which government could be carried on over so vast an area without degenerating into despotism..."

Preparation for The Messiah

The providential aspect of Rome's conquest lay in the disbursement of the Greek language, which prepared the people to receive the doctrine of Christ. From TEACHING AND LEARNING,[1] Miss Slater states:

"It should be remembered in the first place, that the Romans had already become Greek to some considerable extent, before they were the political masters of those eastern countries where the language, mythology and literature of Greece had become more or less familiar...When all parts of the civilized world were bound together in one empire, - when one common organization pervaded the whole, - when channels of communication were

9

everywhere opened - when new facilities of travelling were provided, - then was 'the fulness of time' (Gal. 4:4), then the Messiah came. The Greek language had already been prepared as a medium for preserving and transmitting the doctrine; the Roman government was now prepared to help the progress even of that religion which it persecuted."

"Then saith he unto them, Render therefore unto Caesar the things which are Caesar's; and unto God the things that are God's." (Matthew 22:21)

ENGLAND

England added Principle of Representation

It is from England that we have obtained the Teutonic or English method of nation making, which contains the Principle of Representation.

"By the thirteenth century the increasing power and pretentions of the crown, as the unification of English nationality went on, brought about a result unlike anything known on the continent of Europe; it brought about a resistless coalition between the great nobles, the rural gentry and yeomanry, and the burghers of the towns, for the purpose of curbing royalty, arresting the progress of centralization, and setting up representative government on a truly national scale..."[2]

Magna Charta, 1215

The outcome was, of course, a challenge to monarchy and resulted in the Magna Charta, which marked "the transition from the age of traditional rights, preserved in the nation's memory...to the age of written legislation."[3]

"MAGNA CHARTA: 1. The great charter, so called, obtained by the English barons from King John, A.D. 1215; 2. A fundamental constitution which guaranteed rights and privileges."[4]

CHRISTIAN RIGHTS AND ENGLISH LAW TRANSFERRED TO AMERICA

"The Magna Charta marked a landmark in the limitation of monarchy and represented a <u>limitation</u> of the power of government. To the American Christian who recognized sovereignty as 'found in the free and independent man,' the God-given Rights of the individual were to be <u>preserved</u> by government."[5]

The English people fought hard for their Rights. THE CHRISTIAN HISTORY OF THE CONSTITUTION chronicles the following moving incident:

English Petition of Right

"On the fifth day of June, 1628, the House of Commons presented the most extraordinary spectacle, perhaps in all its history. The famous Petition of Right had been passed by both Houses, and the royal answer had just been received. Its tone was that of gracious assent, but it omitted the necessary legal formalities, and

10

the Commons well knew what this meant. They were to be tricked with sweet words, and the petition was not to acquire the force of a statute. How was it possible to deal with such a slippery creature?...(The House) was deprived of all constitutional methods of redress. 'Let us sit in silence,' quoth Sir Dudley Digges, 'we are miserable, we know not what to do.' 'Nay,' cried Sir Nathaniel Rich, 'we must now speak, or forever hold our peace.' Then did grim Mr. Prynne and Sir Edward Coke mingle their words with sobs, while there were few dry eyes in the House. Presently they found their voices, and used them in a way that rung from the startled king his formal assent to the Petition of Right."[6]

TEACHING AND LEARNING has this to say about the right to petition:

"The right to petition against grievances and encroachments upon individual liberty became a method of constitutional redress. As specific rights became part of the law of the land, men resorted to further clarification through written legislation - as opposed to political action which might merely exchange external sovereigns. Gradually sovereignty - the power of government -was transferred to 'the free and independent man' and appeared finally in the republican form of government of the United States of America."[7]

The background of America's Christian constitutional form of government lies principally in England.

"The Sidneys, and Miltons, and Lockes of England were teachers in America as well as in their native land, and more effectual, because their instructions fell in a readier...The spirit was kindled in England; it went with Robinson's congregation to Holland; it landed with them at Plymouth; it was the basis of the first constitution..."[8]

THE BIBLE IN ENGLISH

Let us go back to the very foundation of our study, the steps necessary to the Bible having been written in the English language, starting with John Wycliffe.

One hundred and sixty-seven years after the establishment of the Magna Charta, the Scriptures were made available to the individual man when John Wycliffe, the "Morning Star of the Reformation," translated the Holy Bible from Latin into English.

"Prior to the middle of the fourteenth century, none of the translating work with the Bible in England was 'designed to make the

11

Word of God accessible to the mass of the people, and to spread scriptural knowledge among them. The only object which was kept in view was partly to furnish aid to the clergy and to render service to the educated class.'"[9]

JOHN WYCLIFFE (1320-1384)

Earliest Break with Latin Christianity

"With Wycliffe's first beams in a dark age of anti-Christian idolatry occurred the 'earliest break' with Latin Christianity.

Wycliffe resolved to introduce the laymen directly to the Christian Bible by translating the great basis of their faith - the original revelation from God, as they had been taught to believe and did believe - into the vernacular, into the language in which every layman might read it for himself...Before the beginning of the fifteenth century every Englishman who could read was in a position to know whether what his priest was telling him had the warrant of the great revelation upon which all claimed to rest.[10]

To Wycliffe the translation of the Bible was not an end in itself, but only a means to an end - that end being to place the Bible in the hands of his own countrymen, and to bring home the Word of God to the hearts of the English people. For this purpose copies of it were now made and circulated, not only of the whole Bible, but also of portions, and even of single books...[11]

The Bible being thus made a comparatively familiar book, great stress was laid upon the exposition of its contents by preaching. Staff in hand, the preachers journeyed on foot from place to place, and paused wherever they could obtain hearing from gentle or simple...The preaching was in English...Besides these open-air gatherings, assemblies were convened in halls and cottages, in chapels, in gardens. Here and there a little company would assemble to converse on Divine things, to build one another up in faith and knowledge. At such meetings the Bible in Wycliffe's translation would be read aloud...Even the art of reading would be taught on such occasions...[12]

God gave Wycliffe...the vision of the relation of the Bible to all spheres of the individual's life... including civil and the State."[13]

THE HISTORY OF THE ENGLISH BIBLE

On the Chain of Christianity the development of the English Bible was a necessary "preparation" to our American Christian Constitutional form of government:

"To learn of salvation through Jesus Christ, and how to live the Christian life, the Bible must be open to the individual. Therefore the history of the Bible in the hands of the individual is the history of Christian civil government. Also, because the church is the assembly or congregation of believers, whatever is reasoned from Scripture regarding church polity or government, is the precursor of civil polity or government. Thus it also can be said that the history of church government is the history of Christian civil government."[14]

Let us look at the development of the English Bible:

1382 Wycliffe translated the Old and New Testaments from Latin into English;

1525 Tyndale is the father of our present English Bible. Our Bibles retain 80% of Tyndale's work in the Old Testament; 90% in the New Testament. His work was translated from the original Hebrew;

1536-1538 The English King commanded "one boke of the whole Bible" be set up in each of the 11,000 parishes in England;

1539 The first edition of Tyndale's Great Bible, a huge unwieldy folio, appeared. It was a "magnificent specimen" of the art of printing, the frontispiece having been designed by Hans Holbein;

1560 The Geneva Bible divided the text into verses. It was of comfortable size and moderate price. It had great appeal as the habit of Bible-reading steadily grew;

1611 With the accession to the throne of England of James I, the King James Bible appeared as a result in 1604 of a petition to the throne by the Puritan section of the national church for a Bible to replace their "corrupted" translation. Nine-tenths of the words in the Authorized Version are of Saxon origin, not of Latin origin.

King James Bible

"Most important was the fact...that this was the freest and purest of Bible translations since Wycliffe's first work. This edition had no notes and 'the interpretation of it was therefore left perfectly free.' A Bible relying wholly on the power of the Word to reveal its holy message![15]

The last decade of the sixteenth century had witnessed an outburst of genius, whether in poetry, in the drama, or in prose, to which it would indeed be difficult to find a parallel. The names of Shakespeare, Marlow, Spenser, Hooker, Chapman, Bacon, Jonson, Sidney,...form a galaxy of greatness before which we can only bow our heads...The world of literature was seen bursting into loveliest blossom, and the national language clothing itself in strength, in richness, and in power...It was in some such air as this that the translators of the King's Bible lived and moved and had their being."[16]

LUTHER AND CALVIN

Two Lights in the Darkness

Along the Chain of Christianity, we see how God used men and nations to advance the concept of man's individual liberty on a scriptural basis. During the period of the "dark ages" in Europe when every semblance of individual liberty had fled, there appeared two lights, two men, Martin Luther and John Calvin.

MARTIN LUTHER (1482-1546)

"Martin Luther, an Augustine monk, denouncing indulgences, introduced a schism in religion.[17]

Luther challenged the Papacy

Luther appealed to the authority of the Scriptures to challenge the divine right of papacy at the Diet of Worms in 1521."[18]

It is to the Council that he uttered these famous words: "'...unless my conscience is thus bound by the Word of God, I cannot and will not retract; for it is unsafe and injurious to act against one's own conscience, Here I stand, I can do no other: may God help me!! Amen!'"[18]

Lutheran Bible, 1534

Man of Germany

"By far the most important task, however, which occupied his leisure, was the translation of the Bible...The work of the translation was completed at Wittenberg, until at length, in 1534, the complete Lutheran Bible was given to the people... It is true that other translations into the vernacular had preceded this of Luther. But...none were so true at once to the German and to the original...As David was the man of Israel, so Luther was the man of Germany.[18]

Liberty of Conscience

Spiritual and Physical Reformation necessary to American History

Neither the wonderful art of printing, nor the discovery of this transatlantic continent (America), had aroused with such mighty energy the mind of christendom, as did the discovery of a new world in theology by Luther, and the sudden reformation in religion which sprung up in Germany, and swiftly extended through Northern Europe...A free church, free education, free association, the right to speak and to write, - these are the consequences of the liberty of conscience proclaimed by the Reformers... These two events (The Reformation and the Discovery of America), therefore, the most important in modern times, are intimately connected in their bearing on American history. God timed the physical and the spiritual discovery to each other."[19]

14

JOHN CALVIN (1509-1564)

"The times of Luther were followed by those of Calvin. He, like his great predecessor, undertook to search the Scriptures, and in them found the same truth and the same life; but a different character distinguishes his work.

Calvin's
Renovation

The renovation of the individual, of the Church, and of the human race, is his theme...The liberty which the Truth brings is not for individuals only: it affects the whole of society. Calvin's work of renovation, in particular, which was doubtless first of all an internal work, was afterwards destined to exercise a great influence over nations.

A Bible for
French Protestants

In intellect, Calvin was undoubtedly one of the most remarkable men of the sixteenth century...He assisted in preparing the translation of the Bible which passed into general use among the French Protestants, though his work in this line was of much less significance than that of Luther...'No writing of the Reformation era was more feared by Roman Catholics, more zealously fought against and more hostilely pursued, than Calvin's Institutes'... Geneva, under his hand, became a citadel and an arena, a refuge to which the fugitive might flee from persecution, and a training-school in which he might be equipped for heroic service.[20]

The Republic
of Geneva

...the characteristic element of the Genevese Reform is liberty...It is in this small republic that we find men remarkable for their devotion to liberty, for their attachment to law, for the boldness of their thoughts, the firmness of their character, and the strength of their energy...

Calvin's Liberty of
Conscience passed
on to Pilgrims

The 'pilgrims' who left their country in the reign of James I and, landing on the barren shores of New England, founded populous and mighty colonies, are his (Calvin's) sons, his direct and legitimate sons; and that American nation which we have seen growing so rapidly boasts as its father the humble reformer on the shores of the Leman."[21]

PILGRIMS AND PURITANS

The way was slow;
the price was steep

It took hundreds of years for the Christian idea of the civil and religious liberty of the individual to actually take the form of law in America. It was to the Pilgrims that we are indebted to a break from absolute tyrannical government to a Bible-based form of Christian government. They took a stand, and America was born.

In our study of the Pilgrims, we note the difference between the Puritans and the Pilgrims, or Separatists, as they were called:

Puritan desired to
stay within Church
of England

"In the old world on the other side of the ocean, the Puritan was a Nationalist, believing that a Christian nation is a Christian church, and demanding that the Church of England should be thoroughly reformed; while the Pilgrim was a Separatist, not only from the Anglican Prayer-book and Queen Elizabeth's episcopacy, but from all national churches. Between them there was a sharp contention...The Pilgrim wanted liberty for himself and his wife and little ones, and for his brethren, to walk with God in a Christian life as the rules and motives of such a life were revealed to him from God's Word. For that he went into exile; for that he crossed the ocean; for that he made his home in a wilderness. The Puritan's idea was not liberty, but right government in church and state - such government as should not only permit him but also compel other men to walk in the right way."[22]

It had taken centuries for God to raise up a people providentially prepared to bring the Christian idea of man and government together. He had preserved the land "hidden away," but the Christian character of the individual had to be readied to occupy that land. Little-by-little, Christ's story has unfolded in the minds and hearts of men and nations.

"The Puritan (including the Pilgrim) searched the Bible, not only for principles and rules, but for mandates, - and, when he could find none of these, for analogies, - to guide him in precise arrangements of public administration, and in the minutest points of individual conduct."[23]

Reasoning from their study of the Bible, which had been translated into English by Wycliffe one hundred years earlier, the English Pilgrims were convinced they were not governed according to the Word of God. Their story is familiar. They left Plymouth, England; after a stay in Holland, sailed on the MAYFLOWER and landed on the shores of America in the winter of 1620.

"At the moment of their landing...they possessed institutions of government, and institutions of religion: and friends and families, and social and religious institutions, framed by consent, founded on choice and preference...

The morning that beamed on the first night of their repose saw the Pilgrims already at home in their country. There were political institutions, and civil liberty, and religious worship. Poetry has fancied nothing, in the wanderings of heroes, so distinct and characteristic. Here was man, indeed, unprotected, and unprovided for, on the shore of a rude and fearful wilderness; but it was politic, intelligent, and educated man. Everything was civilized but the physical world. Institutions, containing in

16

substance all that ages had done for human government, were organized in a forest.

First Foundations
Christian

Cultivated mind was to act on uncultivated nature... a government and a country were to commence, with the very first foundations laid under the divine light of the Christian religion."[24]

Qualities needed
in Wilderness Expe-
rience

The study of the Bible molded the character of the Pilgrims to <u>stay</u> on the harsh, forested, eastern coast of America where they were so isolated from civilization. We liken their character to that of the sweet chamomile: "God's children are like stars that shine brightest in the darkest skies; like the chamomile, which, the more it is trodden down, the faster it spreads and grows."[25]

Pilgrim Endurance
Two-fold

The fact that "not one turned back" is important in our history for the significance of the Pilgrim endurance was two-fold as stated in CHRISTIAN HISTORY OF THE CONSTITUTION, Volume I, page 182:

"Had Plymouth been deserted by the Pilgrim Fathers in 1621-22, Massachusetts Bay would have remained desolate, and even Virginia would doubtless have been abandoned. Then, before new colonization could be organized, France would have made good her claim by pushing down our Atlantic coast until she met Spain descending from the south, – unless, indeed, Holland had retained her hold at the centre... Sir Thomas Hutchinson...spoke of them in his History: 'These were the founders of the Colony at New Plymouth. The settlement of this Colony occasioned the settlement of Massachusetts Bay, which was the source of all the other Colonies in New England. Virginia was in a dying state, and seemed to revive and flourish from the example of New England.'"

MAYFLOWER COMPACT

First Civil
Body Politic

Before they occupied the land, the Pilgrims created the Mayflower Compact, the first civil body politic of America.

With Mayflower
Compact, Christian
form of civil
government
begins to appear
in America

In TEACHING AND LEARNING AMERICA'S CHRISTIAN HISTORY, page 179, we read: "The tradition of Christian self-government which the Pilgrims on the Mayflower carried with them, culminated in America's first document of Christian self-government – the Mayflower Compact... It was the first written document of American representative government..." Hence, the Christian form of government began to appear in America with the Mayflower Compact of the Pilgrims.

"Much can be taught and much can be learned from the courageous story of our Pilgrims as they considered themselves 'stepping stones' for those who would come after. Their adventures

17

were sometimes exciting – sometimes they had just 'daily dullness' – but the real thrill comes from perceiving the <u>qualities</u> which enabled them to 'stay firm for, of those who lived in the first year, <u>not one went back</u>.' And those who lived – lived to a wonderful age in the Lord: 'God, it seems, would have all men to behold and observe such mercies and works of his providence as these are towards his people.'

The account in CHRISTIAN HISTORY, pages 185-207 of William Bradford's HISTORY OF PLIMOTH PLANTATION should be cherished by Christians in America of whatever generation. It is truly the 'Christian heritage' of their Pilgrim and Puritan forefathers who carried the seed of Christian life and Christian character and Christian government into all the activities of this first Christian settlement on our shores.[26]

The seed of Christian self-government, formed in the first century of Christianity, came to these shores with the tiny settlement of the Mayflower Pilgrims." (See TEACHING AND LEARNING, pages 216-224.)

Voluntary Union and Local Self-Government

It was the Pilgrim that made the Christian form of government work in America, that of Voluntary Union and Local Self-Government, through the Mayflower Compact. The result was the 150 years of self-government from the landing of the Pilgrims to the Declaration of Independence. Because of them, today we enjoy our written Constitution guaranteeing the individual man his rights under law, and a culmination of the <u>Christian idea of man</u> as stated at the beginning of THE CHRISTIAN HISTORY OF THE CONSTITUTION OF THE UNITED STATES OF AMERICA, Volume I.

Christian Idea of Man

LOCKE, BLACKSTONE, MONTESQUIEU

Aided American Colonists to write American Christian Constitution

There are many men along the Chain of Christianity whom God used to bring forth the Christian idea of man in government. There are three that I will deal with to give you an idea of their momentous contributions to the liberty of the individual which we enjoy in America today under the protection of our written Constitution.

JOHN LOCKE (1632-1704)

Locke, Philosopher of American Revolution

John Locke is called the Philosopher of the American Revolution. It is said our Founding Fathers walked around with the Bible in one pocket and John Locke in the other. He lived in England, contemporary with the Pilgrims.

In CHRISTIAN HISTORY OF THE CONSTITUTION, page 51, under the heading "Locke's Influence," we read:

"Locke, in particular, was the authority to whom the Patriots paid greatest deference. He was the most famous of seventeenth century democratic theorists, and his ideas had their due weight with the colonists. Almost every writer seems to have been influenced by him, many quoted his words, and the argument of others shows the unmistakable imprint of his philosophy. The first great speech of Otis was wholly based upon Locke's ideas; Samuel Adams, on the 'Rights of the Colonists as Men and as British Subjects', followed the same model. Many of the phrases of the Declaration of Independence may be found in Locke's Treatise; there is hardly any important writer of this time who does not openly refer to Locke, or tacitly follow the lead he had taken. The argument in regard to the limitations upon Parliament was taken from Locke's reflections on the 'supreme legislature' and the necessary restrictions upon its authority. No one stated more strongly than did he the basis for the doctrine that 'taxation without representation is tyranny'. No better epitome of the Revolutionary theory could be found than in John Locke on civil government."

OF CIVIL
GOVERNMENT

OF CIVIL GOVERNMENT by John Locke is considered so important to our study of the background of our American Christian Constitution that CHRISTIAN HISTORY OF THE CONSTITUTION, Volume I, Pages 57-125, contain that Essay for our study.

Giving us an insight into his religious beliefs and character, we read from his ESSAY CONCERNING HUMAN UNDERSTANDING:[27]

"In 1695 Mr. Locke published his treatise of 'the Reasonableness of Christianity,' in which he has proved that the Christian Religion, as delivered in the scriptures, and free from all corrupt mixtures, is the most reasonable institution in the world...The last fourteen or fifteen years of his life Mr. Locke spent chiefly at Oates...During this agreeable retirement, he applied himself to the study of the scriptures...He admired the wisdom and goodness of God in the method found out for the salvation of mankind: and when he thought upon it, he could not forbear crying out, 'O the depth of the riches of the goodness and knowledge of God.'"

From CHRISTIAN HISTORY, Page 2:

"John Locke...was so successful in catching and expressing the liberal spirit of his age, in his work on Civil Government, that it became the platform of a great political party, and gradually widened out into an influence that operated far beyond the thought or the theory of its adherents; so that, Hallam says 'while silently spreading its fibres from its roots over Europe and America, it prepared the way for theories hardly bolder in their

19

announcements but expressed with more passionate ardor, from which the last and present age have sprung.' This historical judgement is applicable to a line of illustrious characters, who grasped the Christian idea of man; and, because of the brilliancy of their service in behalf of human rights, they deserve a place among the morning stars of the American constellation."

SIR WILLIAM BLACKSTONE (1723-1780)

Blackstone codified
English Laws

In a thumbnail sketch of William Blackstone, Miss Slater states: "Widely studied in America his COMMENTARIES ON THE LAWS OF ENGLAND reaffirmed God as the source of law and man's obligation to write human laws in accord with God's laws."[28]

From CHRISTIAN HISTORY:[29]

"Among those who have risen to eminence by the profession of the law, none have obtained a more extended and durable reputation than Sir William Blackstone.

He formed the design of reducing into system the common law, which had hitherto lain in scattered fragments in the reports, or in large masses in the Institutes of Coke...of treating with elegance a subject on which the graces of composition had never before been bestowed - of teaching, in a place where it had never before been taught, a science which no one there desired to learn...Too much gratitude cannot be paid to him by lawyers, for this gratuitous and invaluable present to his profession.

COMMENTARIES

In 1765 appeared the first volume of the Commentaries... It may be inferred that he was no enthusiastic either in religion or in politics; in the former he was a sincere believer in Christianity, from a profound investigation of its evidence; in the latter he was what would be called a Conservative, friendly to mild but authoritative government, inimical to the agitations of pretended patriots..."

From TEACHING AND LEARNING:[30]

"Blackstone's COMMENTARIES ON THE LAWS OF ENG-LAND represented the first collection of the common law of England with detailed explanations as to how this law functioned specifically in a constitutional monarchy with its heritage of Magna Charta, Petition of Rights and the Bill of Rights. This digest of English common law represented also a remarkable commentary on the philosophy of law, particularly as it related to the rights of individuals in society. Blackstone is specific and detailed in his analysis, and thus became a basic part of the study of the course of law by English and American students.

He propounds in terms the doctrine that municipal or positive laws derive their validity from their conformity to the so-called law of nature or law of God. 'No human laws,' he says, 'are of any validity if contrary to this.'[31]

We find, through Locke, Montesquieu, and Blackstone, the establishment of a Christian philosophy of government and law, which aided our American colonists to write an American Christian Constitution."[32]

CHARLES DE MONTESQUIEU (1689-1755)

"Christianity," says Montesquieu, "is a stranger to despotic power."[33]

James Madison observed:

Montesquieu, Separation of Powers

"'...the three great departments of power should be separate and distinct. The oracle who is always consulted and cited on this subject is the celebrated Montesquieu...'"[34]

Montesquieu's SPIRIT OF LAWS, in which he expresses these separations of power, is his great work.

SPIRIT OF LAWS

"Although the success of the 'Spirit of Laws' was not immediate in France, it was not long in doubt. In England, intelligent opinion immediately seized upon the work, and received it with enthusiasm. This was due in a great measure to the fact that the author, had been a close student and admirer of the British Constitution, had adopted the shortest road to the British heart by his intelligent tribute to the superiority of that vague, shadowy and unwritten charter of British liberty.[35]

He delves at the roots of History to learn how from general causes events have grown. He is no believer in chance; there is a Philosophy of History with its rule and principles and they must be studied and found before we can know the nature and reason of Things.[36]

Upon this theory, he has examined symptoms to ascertain causes, and has, with a beauty of style that well became the dignity of his subject, first taught men that the records of the past might be found to contain sermons as well as traditions, lessons as well as facts, and materials for prophecy mingled with the dust of ages.[37]

The foundation of the work (SPIRIT OF LAWS) was the attempt to find those common principles and emotions which, operating upon men of every climate and degree of civilization, produce certain results. He was satisfied that those principles existed, and if found, would afford scientific explanation of what without their aid would seem to be chaotic and inexplicable. Or, to come nearer to his own language, he rejoiced to find 'in the nature of things' the explanation of so many different laws and customs.[38]

Montesquieu, as did Locke, relates law to its primary source - God. In his opening statements of THE SPIRIT OF LAWS he states: 'God is related to the universe, as Creator and Preserver; the laws by which He created all things are those by which He preserves them.'"[39]

Here are a few excerpts from THE SPIRIT OF LAWS:

"In every government there are three sorts of power: The legislative; the executive in respect to things dependent on the law of nations; and the executive in regard to matters that depend on the civil law...By the third, he punishes criminals, or determines the disputes that arise between individuals. The latter we shall call the judiciary power..."[40]

...When the legislative and executive powers are united in the same person, or in the same body of magistrates, there can be no liberty...Again, there is no liberty, if the judiciary power be not separated from the legislative and executive..."[41]

BEGINNING OF LOCAL SELF-GOVERNMENT IN AMERICA

Unity with Diversity

To bring local self-government into the American colonies, we look at the two types of Parent Colonies, the Virginia Colony (1607) and the New England Colony (1620).

Virginia Colony: Episcopal Form of Government

The Virginia Colony was founded primarily as a commercial venture. "Virginia was a continuation of English society...a love for England and English institutions..."[42] It eventually promoted the Episcopal form of government. Large plantations, aristocratic land-owners, slaves, and government from "the top-down" characterized this type of American government.

New England Colony: Congregational Form of Government

The New England Colony was begun by the Pilgrims who came to America primarily for religious and civil liberty. Alexander Hamilton wrote: "The settlement of New England...was instigated by a detestation of civil and ecclesiastical tyranny..."[43] Their Biblically-based desire for the Christian idea of man and government took the Congregational form of government. It began with the local township and county.

From CHRISTIAN HISTORY:[44]

"Of the various kinds of government to be found in the United States, we may begin by considering that of the New England township...It is a principle of all known forms of government the oldest as well as the simplest. Let us observe how the New England township grew up.

When people from England first came to dwell in the wilderness of Massachusetts Bay, they settled in groups upon small irregular-shaped patches of land, which soon came to be known as townships. There were several reasons why they settled thus in small groups, instead of scattering about over the country and carving out broad estates for themselves.

In the first place, their principal reason for coming to New England was their dissatisfaction with the way in which church affairs were managed in the old country. They wished to bring about a reform in the church, in such ways that the members of a congregation should have more voice than formerly in the church government...Hence it was quite natural that they should come in congregations, led by the favorite ministers...This migration, therefore, was a movement not of individuals or of separate families, but of church congregations, and it continued to be so as the settlers made their way inland and westward. The first river towns of Connecticut were founded by congregations coming from Dorchester, Cambridge, and Watertown. This kind of settlement was favoured by the government of Massachusetts, which made grants of land, not to individuals but to companies of people who wished to live together and attend the same church.

...Most of the people lived on small farms, each family raising but little more than enough food for its own support; and the small size of the farms made it possible to have a good many in a compact neighborhood... Thus the early settlers of New England came to live in townships.

...In a New England Township the people directly govern themselves; the government is the people...The New England town is a legal corporation...[45]

We have seen what a great part taxation plays in the business of government, and we shall presently have to treat of county, state, and federal governments, all of them wider in their sphere than the town government. In the course of history, as nations have gradually been built up, these wider governments have been apt to absorb or supplant and crush the narrower governments, such as the parish or township...There is one way of escaping it, and that is to give the little government of the town some real share in making up the great government of the state...The people who speak the English language have been the most successful, and the device by which they have overcome the difficulty is REPRESENTATION."[46]

Again, from CHRISTIAN HISTORY:[47]

Republics not necessarily small

"...It came to be one of the commonplace assumptions of political writers that republics must be small, that free government is practicable only in a confined area, and that the only strong and durable government, capable of maintaining order throughout a vast territory, is some form of absolute monarchy. It was quite natural that people should formerly have held this opinion, and it is indeed not yet quite obsolete, but its fallaciousness will become more and more apparent as American history is better understood.

Our experience has now so far widened that we can see that despotism is not the strongest but wellnigh the weakest form of government; that centralized administrations, like that of the Roman Empire, have fallen to pieces, not because of too much but because of too little freedom; and that the only perdurable government must be that which succeeds in achieving national unity on a grand scale, without weakening the sense of personal and local independence."

CONCLUSION TO CHAIN OF CHRISTIANITY

Contribution of Miss Verna Hall

This overview is but a small sample of the wealth of information about the Christian history of our land. Miss Verna Hall, in her series of books, has painstakingly, brilliantly, and lovingly brought to our attention the Chain of Christianity and our very own heritage, "hidden away" for so long amongst various old books, and files of the Library of Congress. We owe her a great deal of gratitude for helping us "remember" that Christianity is no stranger to civil government and that ours is indeed a Christian nation, built upon the precepts of Jesus Christ.

Contribution of Miss Rosalie Slater

Miss Rosalie Slater, having written the companion volume to CHRISTIAN HISTORY, further helps us by bringing all of Miss Hall's writings into our homes through educating our children. These are works for all generations. Those of us who have missed this in our schooling will find it in schooling our children, and we will be twice blest.

"...Jesus...said unto them, Suffer the little children to come unto me, and forbid them not: for of such is the kingdom of God." (Mark 10:14)

24

PART II: OVERVIEW OF CALIFORNIA'S BACKGROUND TO 1850

To determine the steps which were needed to make California the Child of America, is the purpose of this work. Let us briefly recount the background of the history of California up to Statehood in 1850 to better understand her place in history as the Child of America and a link in the Chain of Christianity moving westward.

STEPS TO DISCOVERY

God used Men and Nations for His Purpose

As we gradually trace the mainstream of history, we observe that "Westward the course of empire takes its way." As early as 1292 the Italian Marco Polo brought evidence of the enticing riches of the Eastern Orient west to Europe. The fact that his experiences were preserved in writing is in itself the Hand of God.

Influence of Marco Polo, 1292

Marco Polo's elaborate descriptions of the eastern empires of "Chin" and "Cipangu" (China and Japan) were to influence explorers and fortune seekers for the next two hundred years. Christopher Columbus was one of those influenced by Polo's stories. God had raised up the character of Christopher Columbus to break through the mesmeric fears and superstitions of his time. It took a mighty deep faith and conviction to allow him to pursue his dream of finding a path across the Atlantic Ocean to what he believed was the rich Orient. Traveling west in 1492, he reached the islands of the Caribbean, thereby opening up a new continent, unbeknown to Columbus.

Columbus: A new continent, 1492

Papal Decree, 1493

Upon Spain's request, Pope Alexander VI issued a Papal Decree stating that all lands discovered west of his Line of Demarcation should belong to Spain; east of the Line, discoveries should be owned by Portugal. With one sweep he had divided their world into the hands of two of the strongest exploring nations, primarily of the Catholic faith.

GEOGRAPHIC PREPARATION

India reached: Da Gama, 1498

In 1498, the Portuguese navigator Da Gama reached India by the Cape of Good Hope, farthest point off the tip of Africa, a very long, tedious and dangerous voyage. A western route was still needed.

South America: Vespucius, 1501

An Italian, Amerigo Vespucius, extended knowledge farther west, after Columbus' successful voyages, and in 1501 discovered that South America was a new continent. He may have inspired the name "America." There is much controversy about this name.

Pacific Ocean: Balboa, 1513; South America: Magellan, 1519

In 1513, Balboa discovered the Pacific Ocean, and in 1519 Magellan, first to circumnavigate the Earth, sailed west from Lisbon through the Straits of Magellan, to find South America a separate continent. Geographically, the earth was unfolding its form.

It was in 1519, too, that a land expedition under Cortes entered the eastern coast of Mexico and marching west, conquered Montezuma's Aztec Indians. He established Mexico as the capital of "New Spain" and may have given "California" its name.

It was one of Cortes' captains, Jimenez, who discovered Baja (Lower) California, northwest of Mexico, in 1533. Then in 1542, it was the Cabrillo-Ferrelo expedition which discovered Alta (Upper) California, including San Diego and Monterey Bays.

Westward bound, the explorers of Spain and Portugal were mainly responsible for the discovery, little-by-little, of North and South America and of conquering the two vast oceans. But in 1579, a challenge to Spain's sea supremacy, and to the Papal Decree, was put forth by an Englishman, Sir Francis Drake. He was a daring navigator, who landed at New Albion (New England) on the northern coast of California. He had great influence on the English monarchy and its far-reaching results.

In 1595, Cermenho, sailing for Spain, had an incredible experience on the coast of California. He was barely able to return to Mexico City. It was then obvious that Spain needed decent harbors on the coast of California and sent out Vizcaino to find such an harbor. Vizcaino entered Monterey Bay in 1602 and his descriptions of it were to mislead Father Serra and Captain Portola in the years to come. From Vizcaino in 1602 to Serra and Portola, who invaded the shores of San Diego in 1769, history records 167 years of inactivity in neglected Alta California.

COLONIZATION OF CALIFORNIA

Colonization of California began with Father Serra, carrying the cross of Catholic Spain, and Captain Portola, wearing the sword of Spanish military might. They were responsible for the beginning of the mission system in California. Twenty missions were established in California by Spain until 1822 when Mexico revolted against Spanish rule. For the next twenty-four years, California was under Mexico.

Now we come to a most interesting and providential part of California's background. Here is a concept which is practically ignored by the secular field but which is actually pivotal in the history of California.

It was under Mexico that the twenty-first and last mission, San Francisco Solano at Sonoma in northern California, was founded in 1823. It was also under Mexico that the missions were secularized in 1834 and the influential padres were forced to put their missions into the hands of local administrators. The greatest influence of Spain and Mexico in California, the state-supported Catholic church, had been curtailed.

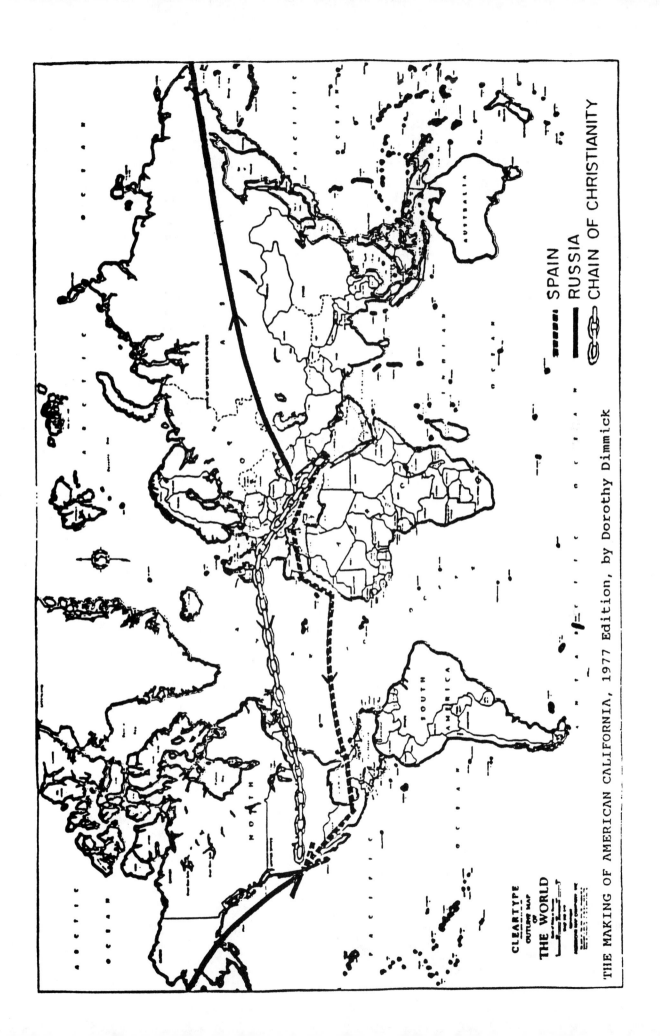

THE MAKING OF AMERICAN CALIFORNIA, 1977 Edition, by Dorothy Dimmick

SPAIN

RUSSIA

CHAIN OF CHRISTIANITY

CLEARTYPE
OUTLINE MAP
OF
THE WORLD

Russians withdrew, 1841

Another threat for many years to the civil government of California was the Russian colony which had been established on the northern coast of California in 1812. They were trappers of the sea otter. When the fur supply became limited, and the United States had issued the Monroe Doctrine in 1823 to discourage foreign advancement into the North American continent, the Russians withdrew in 1841. Russia, with its Russian Orthodox Church, was no longer a threat to California.

Hand of God in California History

Here is an example of the Hand of God in California's history. Here we witness the elimination of two threats of a Church-State situation by Spain's Roman Catholic Church or by Russia's Orthodox Church. Had either country firmly held California, a mandatory religion would have been inevitable for the people of California.

THE MOUNTAIN MEN, EXPLORERS, AND PIONEERS

Matthew 9:17

Protestant thrust: Smith, 1826

When the last of the Spanish missions was secularized in 1834, and the Russian settlement at Fort Ross withdrew in 1841, this seeming void in California had already been filled when "reformed religion" entered the scene with young Jedediah "Bibletoter" Smith in 1826. He was an early mountain man and the first American to blaze the overland trail to California and to Oregon.

Pathmarker: Fremont, 1843

Smith was termed the "Pathfinder," while John C. Fremont, sent by the United States government into California as a topographical engineer in 1843, was called the "Pathmarker." Fremont marked and explored the overland trail to California later used by thousands of home-seeking emigrants and gold-seeking argonauts.

Christian character of pioneers

The mountain men and explorers were quickly followed by pioneers looking for new homes, new fields to plow, and new opportunities for their families. They amazed the Mexicans as they crossed the hot "invincible" plains and scaled the "impassable" icy Sierras. Having walked two thousand miles for four months, one can visualize their joy at beholding the lush and beautiful Sacramento Valley. One of the early wagon trains recalled that upon arriving at the end of the California Trail, the emigrants fell to their knees with this prayer from Deuteronomy (Deut. 8:7-9):

> *"For the Lord thy God bringeth thee into a good land, a land of brooks of water, of fountains and depths that spring out of valleys and hills; a land of wheat, and barley and vines, and fig trees, and pomegranates; a land of oil olive, and honey; a land wherein thou shalt eat bread without scarceness; thou shalt not lack anything in it."*

First wagons: Bidwell, 1841

Before the discovery of gold in 1848, the home-seekers and those young men interested in adventure or bettering their lot, sifted into California. John Bidwell was one of those pioneering young men. He entered California in 1841 with the first organized wagon train, and eventually became one of California's most distinguished citizens. A writer has compared his Christian character to the solidarity of Mt. Shasta, guardian of the gateway to Northern California.

AMERICAN ACQUISITION OF CALIFORNIA

Mexican-American
War, 1846-1847

When Fremont made his Third Expedition to the West, he became involved in the Mexican-American war in California in 1846. The American settlers in California, tired of Mexican harassment, had formed the Bear Flag Republic in Sonoma. War between Mexico and the United States was declared over territory along the Rio Grande claimed by both Mexico and the United States in 1846. It was then that Lt. Joseph Warren Revere lowered the Bear Flag in Sonoma and raised the American Flag. The conflict lasted until 1847 with a victory for the United States.

California obtained
by U.S., 1847

As a result of the war, the Mexican province called Alta California was ceded to the United States by Mexico, for which the United States paid $15,000,000 as part of the terms of peace. The United States acquired what is now California, Nevada, Utah, Arizona, a corner of Wyoming, and parts of New Mexico and Colorado west of what was not already claimed by Texas. The problem of whether to make California a state or a territory was to be decided by the Congress of the United States.

DISCOVERY OF GOLD

Gold discovered,
January, 1848

The discovery of gold in California on January 24, 1848, was providential. For years, the Spanish and Mexicans had searched in vain for the famous Golden Cities of Cibola in North America. Had gold been discovered before the American acquisition of California, the Latin countries, or others, would have no doubt, put up a tremendous fight for this El Dorado.

Settlers needed
organized law

The mania for gold gave California a great increase in immigration, trade, and commerce. The influx of population; the utter confusion of having to do business under Mexican laws; the drain upon law and order as the gold fields attracted even law officials; and the frustration of living under a military government while Congress was debating what to do with California, were reasons why American settlers felt a great need for organized law.

A CONSTITUTION FOR CALIFORNIA

Congress divided on
slave issue, 1848

No legal steps toward organizing California as a state or territory had been taken by Congress as the question of slavery was the uppermost political question in the United States. In 1848, the slave states and the free states were numerically equal. How should California be admitted to the Union? As a free state? As a slave state? The debates in Congress raged over three sessions.

No disposition of
California, 1849

The war was over early in 1847 and in 1849 Congress adjourned having made no provisions for a government in California. California had been governed by

29

existing Mexican law in the meantime and the highest ranking military United States officer acted as governor.

Plans for a California Constitution, June, 1849

With demands from the settlers and upon advice of the President and Secretaries of War and State, on June 3, 1849, Acting Military Governor General Riley issued a Proclamation that an election would be held to call a convention for the purpose of drawing up a constitution for California, and electing delegates to that convention.

First Constitutional Convention, Sept.- Oct., 1849

California's First Constitutional Convention met in Colton Hall in Monterey from September 1 to October 12, 1849. The delegates to that Convention were not intellectuals. Most of them were lawyers, not particularly educated in government, but dedicated to making a State of California. They had great faith they were doing God's will, like Moses: (Exod. 4:2,3,4)

"And the Lord said unto him, What is that in thine hand? And he said, A rod. And he said, Cast it on the ground. And he cast it on the ground, and it became a serpent; and Moses fled from before it.

And the Lord said unto Moses, Put forth thine hand, and take it by the tail. And he put forth his hand, and caught it, and it became a rod in his hand."

Californians drew up a constitution which remained the State's highest law for thirty years. Peter Burnett was California's First Governor. California's First Legislature was held December 20, 1849.

The Memorial

In January of 1850, Senators Gwin and Fremont, and Representatives Gilbert and Wright, took a Memorial to Washington to convince Congress of California's immense desire to be accepted as a full-fledged state.

THE COMPROMISE OF 1850 RESULTED IN STATEHOOD

Compromise in Congress, 1850

Congress finally came to a conclusion regarding California with a "compromise." California was to be admitted as a free state, as written into her Constitution, but the territories of Utah and New Mexico were to be organized without the ban of the Wilmot Proviso against slavery, which prohibited slavery in all territory acquired from Mexico. When the South had been further mollified by a strong new law regulating return of slaves who had escaped into Northern states, the Great Compromise was approved.

Admission Day, September 9, 1850

California was admitted into the United States on September 9, 1850. She had voluntarily made herself into a State, elected her governor and officials, and held her first Legislature before being invited to join the Union. Thus, on our California State Seal, as adopted by the Constitutional Convention, is featured the figure of Minerva, who in Greek mythology, emerged full-grown

State Seal

from the brain of Jupiter, symbolizing the State which entered the Union fully-organized. This is a prime example of "Self-government with Union."

An American
Commonwealth

The influence of the American political principles of government can be most clearly seen in California during the debates of its constitutional convention, and in the debates of its first legislature. Our American political principles were brought into California by the American pioneers, men who were accustomed to living under such principles and institutions in their American homes. They brought them across the mountains and plains and onto the floor of the Convention in Colton Hall. There they created an American Commonwealth.

TO THE AMERICAN CHRISTIAN IN CALIFORNIA

California,
A Link in the Chain
of Christianity

The purpose in assembling this historical information is not to write a California history book, as thousands of words have already been compiled into histories of California, but to record for American Christians the on-going story of California's background as a link in the Chain of Christianity. We realize that the rights of religion, liberty, conscience, property, and education that we enjoy as individuals today in California are due to the groundwork our Christian ancestors laid.

Crumbling the
Foundations

Our framework of law and order has brought our nation through some devastating times. We have gone through wars, Revolutionary, 1812, Civil, World Wars I and II, Korean, Viet Nam, and still we exist. However, the inroads into our political system have been fierce. And the inroads into our religious convictions need reassessing. Generally, the basis of judgment is no longer from the Bible. The trends today are away from American Christian education, American Christian respect for conscience and property, away from American individual liberty. The State is slowly replacing God and the "good of the masses" is slowly replacing Christ's admonitions to the individual.

One may argue, why do we need such re-evaluation; look how clever we are. We have such technical skill and knowledge; we have probed the deepest oceans and the highest skies; we are ready to extend our knowledge into the vast space we look out upon; we can control matter from the tiniest atom to the biggest atomic explosion. Can you discredit that?

Return to Biblical
Law of Liberty!

No, the American has indeed achieved great technological skill within the framework of a system of liberty long ago developed to allow him to do just that. If, however, he falls farther away from Christian principles, away from the American system of law and order established under God, can we then expect him to continue to enjoy his individual liberty? Daniel Webster warned us: "It is difficult to conceive how there can remain morality in the government when it shall cease to exist among the people..."[1] The decision as to whether or not we can alter the current trend away from our Christian premise, is yours.

Always Westward

Because California is an extension of America, she has the stewardship of extending the Chain of Christianity farther westward. God reserved and prepared California as a Link in that Chain. From California, the Chain must continue westward. American Christian rights and American Christian law must progress. Can we accept this stewardship?

First, we must restore integrity and honesty, Christian characteristics, into politics and civil government in California, starting at the local level. Then, we can be a light to our neighbors overseas.

Where are you?

Where do you start? Right where you are! As a good citizen of California and a good citizen of America, you are part of the Chain of Christianity. Learn your state's historical background and learn your country's background. Learn it is due to Christian principles that in America man has constitutionally guaranteed to him the most liberty he has ever known. We are stewards of that liberty.

> "Well indeed has it been said that eternal vigilance is the price of liberty. God never meant that in this world in which He placed us we should earn our salvation without steadfast labor."[2] And,

> "'Knowledge is power,' when wisely applied, and a more accurate acquaintance with their government and its history will enable American citizens to mould it more wisely still, to correct all defects of administration, and to speedily reach that minimum of governmental interference with the efforts and interests of the citizens which shall give them the fullest liberty consistent with security and surrender the whole round of human life, as completely as possible to the beneficent action of natural law."[3]

PART III. AMERICAN POSITION ON CHURCH AND STATE

Providentially,
California inherited
religious liberty
from America

Part of our Introduction is to find out how California was affected by our American position on church and state. There seems to be confusion today as to church's relationship to government and government's relationship to the church. To help clarify this point is the reason for this section, particularly because it was so important in California's history.

California freed
from mandatory
state religion

It was through God's Providence that California did not ally itself to a nation where there was a mandatory state religion. It was a critical period for California when the English, the Russians, and even the French showed designs on this Mexican Province. These were countries all with national religions. It is because the United States of America has its position on church and state that California has enjoyed religious liberty. Our religious liberty has traditionally been respected by the government, legally and morally. In return, our government needs the prayerful support by our churches, and participation in civic affairs by our individual church members. We enjoy "freedom in religion," not "freedom from religion," as we shall see.

Our traditional American position on the question of the relationship between church and state, we learn from Philip Schaaf in CHURCH AND STATE IN THE UNITED STATES (1888), found in CHRISTIAN HISTORY OF THE CONSTITUTION, SELF-GOVERNMENT WITH UNION:[1]

"The American relation of church and state differs from all previous relationships in Europe and in the colonial period of our history; and yet it rests upon them and reaps the benefit of them all...

Position of
Government

In America the government protects the church in her property and rights without interfering with her internal affairs...

Position of Church

It confines the church to her proper spiritual vocation, and leaves the state independent in all the temporal affairs of the nation...

In America, the state has no right whatever to interfere with the affairs of the church, her doctrine, discipline, and worship, and the appointment of ministers. It would be great calamity if religion were to become subject to our ever-changing politics.

No such thing as
The American
Church

The American system differs from the system of toleration...In America there are no such distinctions, but only churches or denominations on a footing of perfect equality before the law. To talk about any particular denomination as THE CHURCH, or THE AMERICAN CHURCH, has no meaning, and betrays ignorance or conceit...The American laws know no such institution as 'the church,' but only separate and independent organizations...

33

**American
Separation of
Church and State**

The American system differs radically and fundamentally from the infidel and red-republican theory of religious freedom. The word freedom is one of the most abused words in the vocabulary. True liberty is a positive force, regulated by law; false liberty is a negative force, a release from restraint. True liberty is the moral power of self-government; the liberty of infidels and anarchists is carnal licentiousness. The American separation of church and state rests on respect for the church; the infidel separation, on indifference and hatred of the church, and of religion itself.

**Civil Liberty
requires support of
Religious Liberty**

The infidel theory was tried and failed in the first Revolution of France. It began with toleration and ended with the abolition of Christianity, and with the reign of terror, which in turn prepared the way for military despotism as the only means of saving society from anarchy and ruin. Our infidels and anarchists would reenact this tragedy if they should ever get the power. They openly profess their hatred and contempt of our Sunday laws, our Sabbaths, our churches, and all our religious institutions and societies. Let us beware of them! The American system grants freedom also to irreligion and infidelity, but only within the limits of the order and safety of morality and the ruin of the state. Civil liberty requires for its support religious liberty, and cannot prosper without it. Religious liberty is not an empty sound, but an orderly exercise of religious duties and enjoyment of all its privileges. It is freedom <u>IN</u> religion, not freedom <u>FROM</u> religion; as true civil liberty is freedom <u>IN</u> law, and not freedom <u>FROM</u> law...

**Christianity,
Pillar of American
Institutions**

Destroy our churches, close our Sunday-schools, abolish the Lord's Day, and our republic would become an empty shell, and our people would tend to heathenism and barbarism. Christianity is the most powerful factor in our society and the pillar of our institutions. It regulates the family; it enjoins private and public virtue; it builds up moral character; it teaches us to love God supremely, and our neighbor as ourselves; it makes good men and useful citizens; it denounces every vice; it encourages every virtue; it promotes and serves the public welfare; it upholds peace and order. Christianity is the only possible religion for the American people, and with Christianity are bound up all our hopes for the future."

CHURCH AND STATE IN 1776

What was the attitude of our Founding Fathers' generation toward the relationship of church and state? Reverend John Witherspoon preached a sermon on May 17, 1776, which was a Fast Day called for by the Continental Congress, in which he said:[2]

34

"Upon the whole, I beseech you to make a wise improvement of the present threatening aspect of public affairs and to remember that your duty to God, to your country, to your families, and to yourselves is the same. True religion is nothing else but an inward temper and outward conduct suited to your state and circumstance in Providence at any time. And as peace with God and conformity to Him, adds to the sweetness of created comforts while we possess them, so in times of difficulty and trial, it is in the man of piety and inward principle that we may expect to find the uncorrupted patriot, the useful citizen, and the invincible soldier, - God grant that in America true religion and civil liberty may be inseparable, and the unjust attempts to destroy the one, may in the issue tend to the support and establishment of both."

CHURCH AND STATE IN 1848: CALIFORNIA

To illustrate the feeling in our country toward church and state in 1848, the following excerpts are presented.

In November of 1848, a group of young men from Boston organized the BOSTON AND CALIFORNIA JOINT STOCK MINING AND TRADING COMPANY. Before venturing into California, this was the advice given them from the President of Harvard University, and from the Secretary of State of the United States Government, and from the Secretary of the State of Massachusetts:

"Reverend Mr. Kirk of the Asburton-Place Orthodox Church, one Sunday evening delivered a special discourse before the company or such as chose to attend. He said we were going to a far-off country, where all were in ignorance and sin, and that we should take our Bibles in one hand, and our great New England civilization in the other and conquer all the wickedness that stood in our path or obstructed our course. We promised to follow his advice.

Dr. Abbe...whose two sons were members of the company, gave to each of us a Bible. He told us when the good books were presented, that we were going to a strange wild and immoral country, and that we must take our Bibles in one hand, and our New England civilization in the other and implant our principles upon the soil. Honorable Edward Everett, then President of Harvard College, made us a present of one hundred volumes, and, in his letter conveying the gift, said: 'You are going to a strange country. Take the Bible in one hand and your New England civilization in the other, and make your mark upon the people and the country.'

The United States Secretary of State...sent us charts and reports of the gold discoveries and told us that we must take our Bibles, guns, and our great New England civilization with us, and act as pioneers of Christianity. They sent for us at the State House and the Secretary of State solemnly gave us State passports (didn't charge anything for them, for a wonder) and said to each of us: 'You are going to a strange country, and will meet many desperate people. You must overcome them. Take your Bibles in one hand, and your great New England civilization in the other and always remember that you are Christians, and carry light into darkness.'"[3]

RELIGION AND OUR AMERICAN CHRISTIAN REPUBLIC

The following quotations are from THE CHRISTIAN HISTORY OF THE CONSTITUTION:[4]

"Church" means
All Denominations

"The United States will embosom all the religious sects or denominations in Christendom. Here they may all enjoy their whole respective systems of worship and church government complete...And who can tell how extensive a blessing this American Joseph may become to the whole human race, although once despised by his brethren, exiled, and sold into Egypt? How applicable that in Genesis xlix. 22.26:

Gen. 49:22-24,26

'Joseph is a fruitful bough, even a fruitful bough by a well; whose branches run over the wall. The archers have sorely grieved him, and shot at him, and hated him. But his bow abode in strength; the arms of his hands were made strong by the arms of the mighty God of Jacob. The blessings of thy father have prevailed above the blessings of my progenitors, unto the utmost bound of the everlasting hills; they shall be on the head of Joseph, and on the crown of the head of him that was separated from his brethren.'

True Religion
to be found
in our American
Christian Republic

Little would civilians have thought ages ago that the world should ever look to America for models of government and polity; little did they think of finding this most perfect polity among the poor outcasts, the contemptible people of New England, and particularly in the long despised civil polity of Connecticut - a polity conceived by the sagacity and wisdom of a Winthrop, a Ludlow, Hynes, Hopkins, Hooker, and the other first settlers of Hartford, in 1636. And while Europe and Asia may hereafter learn that the most liberal principles of law and civil polity are to be found on this side of the Atlantic, they may also find the true religion here depurated from the rust and corruption of ages, and learn from us to reform and restore the church to its primitive purity.

John 12:32

...thus the American Republic, by illuminating the world with truth and liberty, would be exalted and made high among nations, in praise and in name, and in honor.

Holiness ought to be end of all civil government

...her system of dominion must receive its finishing from religion; or, that from the diffusion of virtue among the people of any community would arise their greatest secular happiness; all which will terminate in this conclusion: that holiness ought to be the end of all civil government - *'that thou mayest be an holy people unto the Lord thy God.'"*

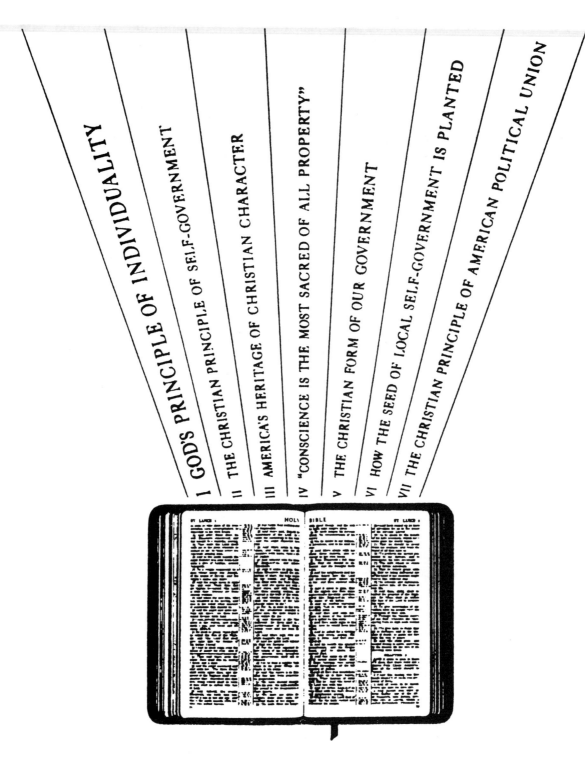

I GOD'S PRINCIPLE OF INDIVIDUALITY

II THE CHRISTIAN PRINCIPLE OF SELF-GOVERNMENT

III AMERICA'S HERITAGE OF CHRISTIAN CHARACTER

IV "CONSCIENCE IS THE MOST SACRED OF ALL PROPERTY"

V THE CHRISTIAN FORM OF OUR GOVERNMENT

VI HOW THE SEED OF LOCAL SELF-GOVERNMENT IS PLANTED

VII THE CHRISTIAN PRINCIPLE OF AMERICAN POLITICAL UNION

Expanding Principles
of America's Christian History

From TEACHING AND LEARNING AMERICA'S CHRISTIAN HISTORY,
by Rosalie J. Slater

38

PART IV: SUGGESTIONS FOR STUDY: PRINCIPLES

"Study to show thyself approved unto God, a workman that needeth not to be ashamed, rightly dividing the word of truth." (II Tim. 2:15)

Biblical principles
for all aspects
of life

On Page 111 of TEACHING AND LEARNING AMERICA'S CHRISTIAN HISTORY, we are given seven minimal principles, derived from the Bible, which are needed to teach the foundations of constitutional government, both for the nation and for the state. They are:

I	God's Principle of Individuality
II	The Christian Principle of Self-Government
III	America's Heritage of Christian Character
IV	"Conscience is the Most Sacred of All Property"
V	The Christian Form of our Government
VI	How the Seed of Local Self-Government is Planted
VII	The Christian Principle of American Political Union

It should be understood that history is used merely to explain how these Principles may be used in building <u>any</u> subject at <u>any</u> level. In fact, they apply to all aspects of life and living, and are particularly helpful in building Christian character in our young people, and in creating a sense of patriotism and pride in America and in California. Why? Because they are based on the Word of God.

"Principle"

Let us turn to WEBSTER'S 1828 DICTIONARY and look up the word PRINCIPLE:

1. In a general sense, the cause, source or origin of anything; that from which a thing proceeds;

2. Ground; foundation; that which supports an assertion, an action or a series of actions or of reasoning;

3. A general truth; a law comprehending many subordinate truths.

Principles give us dominion over the facts.

Miss Slater's
Comments

Miss Rosalie Slater, author of TEACHING AND LEARNING AMERICA'S CHRISTIAN HISTORY, states:

California,
completion of
Pilgrim migration

"The setting for the study of THE MAKING OF AMERICAN CALIFORNIA is in the researching of those Leading Ideas and Principles which unfolded God's Providential Preparation for America as 'the last word in human political institutions,' the world's first Christian Constitutional Republic. California was in effect the completing of the Pilgrim migration from the Old World to the New which landed on the east coast and then, by

39

virtue of the extension of character and Biblical principles of government, reached the west coast of America.

Teachers and students will be able to work from the Leading Ideas and Principles of constitutional character and government, as they appeared in the Christian era. They will be able to trace them historically, and REASON from a Biblical perspective. They will also be able to RELATE these same ideas, ideals, and principles to their own lives in our nation today. As their study leads them to RECORD the results of their research, both Biblical and historical, we pray that their individual NOTEBOOK RECORD will lead them to prepare to leave a RECORD of their own individual contribution to our nation."

The 4 R's

Mr. James B. Rose, author of A GUIDE TO AMERICAN CHRISTIAN EDUCATION FOR THE HOME AND SCHOOL: THE PRINCIPLE AP-PROACH, paraphrases the Bible's Four R's:

"RESEARCHING: studying God's Word to identify basic principles of life and living, and those principles which govern the "how" and "what" in teaching.

REASONING: reasoning from these Biblical principles so as to identify them for the student in each subject of the curriculum.

RELATING: expounding to each student the Bible Truth in the subjects of the curriculum; relating the truths of God's Word to individual Christian character, self-government and stewardship of God's gifts.

RECORDING: the use of writing, by both teacher and student, to account for and elucidate the way in which these principles are being applied to life and living, as well as to a given subject."[1]

THREE LEADING IDEAS

Let us make this Principle Approach philosophy practical by using THE MAKING OF AMERICAN CALIFORNIA as an example.

Within the study of a leading idea, the student should look for more than one Biblical Principle for each leading idea. It is also recommended that Webster's 1828 AMERICAN DICTIONARY OF THE ENGLISH LANGUAGE be used throughout the student's research.

The following are RECORDINGS of three Leading Ideas of THE MAKING OF AMERICAN CALIFORNIA for the student to ponder as he reads the text:

California,
Child of America

I. **LEADING IDEA:** Providentially, California became the Child of America.

PRINCIPLE: We begin to see how the seed of <u>local self-government</u>, developed in America, was planted in California.

BIBLE: *"Where the Spirit of the Lord is, there is Liberty."*
(II Cor. 3:17)

REASONING from the above Biblical principle, governmentally, what made California the Child of America?

AMERICA

In America, the Spirit of the Lord is reflected governmentally by the Constitution of the United States of America. It is the Christian concept of man, versus the pagan concept of man, represented lawfully in our nation by the Republican form of government, which includes the concepts of individual liberty and <u>local self-government</u>.

(The RESEARCH and documentation of this is found in the CHRISTIAN HISTORY OF THE CONSTITUTION series of books compiled by Miss Hall. Miss Slater, in TEACHING AND LEARNING AMERICA'S CHRISTIAN HISTORY, fully explains the Biblical Principles.)

CALIFORNIA

RELATING California to America, the Christian idea of man and government, contained in our United States Constitution, and upon which the American institutions of home, church, and <u>local self-government</u> are based, <u>came to the West to California</u> with the mountain men, the explorers, and the pioneers. These people were prepared, not only physically but spiritually, to create a new state from a sparsely-settled land, setting forth the American Christian principle of self-government they had been living under in America.

Consequently, in California our pioneer Fathers founded an American Commonwealth with a California Constitution built upon American Common Law. Thus the "Spirit of the Lord," represented by the Christian idea of man and the Christian concept of individual liberty, and governmentally by the principle of self-government, providentially was brought into California from America by our pioneer Forefathers. California became the Child of America.

California,
Link in Chain
of Christianity

II.   LEADING IDEA: Providentially, California became a Link
in the Chain of Christianity moving Westward.

PRINCIPLE: The Christian Form of California's Government,
based upon the American Constitution, made California a Link
in the Chain of Christianity.

THE BIBLE: *"Ye are the light of the world. A city that is set
on an hill cannot be hid... Let your light so shine before men,
that they may see your good works, and glorify your Father
which is in heaven."* (Matt. 5:14,16)

REASONING from the above Biblical Principle, how did God
use America as a Link in the historic Chain of Christianity
moving Westward?

AMERICA

"...God used men and nations through Christ to bring forth America and
her form of government for His glory and for all the nations of the earth."[2]
Over a long period, many nations and individuals carried to America the seeds
of the Christian idea of man and government - always traveling westward. It
was people and events, imbued with the doctrine of Christianity, who provided
the links, spiritually, geographically, physically, and governmentally, from Asia
through Europe to America, the "flower of civilization."

It was the Christian character of the Pilgrims traveling from England and
Holland west to Massachusetts, along with their interpretation of the English
Bible regarding faith, steadfastness, and perseverance, who provided the
American consciousness with fundamental principles of government, home, and
education. In Christ-centered America was established our highest sense of
Constitutional government with liberty and protection for the individual.

CALIFORNIA

How does America, as a Link in the Chain of Christianity, RELATE to
California, another Link in the Chain?

Through God's providence and direction, Americans migrated west to
California, bringing with them those seeds of Christian self-government which
had blossomed into a nation such as the world had not before witnessed. The
members of the California Constitutional Convention patterned the principles of
the California Constitution after those of America. They carefully planned that
California join the Union of States as a full-fledged member. This was to be a
spiritual as well as a physical union, one born of the Spirit of Christianity, of the
First and Second Commandments, one which was voluntarily created by their

love for America. Thus, California herself became a "light unto the world," and another Link in the Chain of Christianity constantly moving westward.

THIRD LEADING IDEA

III. LEADING IDEA: California was providentially reserved by God for America.

PRINCIPLE: The Christian Principle of <u>American Political Union</u>.

THE BIBLE: *"Behold, I send an Angel before thee, to keep thee in the way, and to bring thee into the place which I have <u>prepared</u>."* (Exod. 23:20)

REASONING from the above Principle, why was it necessary for God to <u>prepare</u> a place for His people?

AMERICA

"The tendency of the true Gospel principles is to bring the most absolute despotism under the limits of law; to imbue limited monarchies more and more with the spirit of popular institutions; to <u>prepare</u> the people to govern them-selves; and finally to establish everywhere the spirit and the reality, if not the very forms of a republic."[3]

RESEARCH shows us that the American people were self-governed for 150 years before they established a Christian Constitutional Republic. Self-government was the culmination of centuries of Christians seeking the "spirit and the reality" of the Christian idea of man and civil government. After the Americans finalized their Republic with the Christian form of Constitution, and their institutions were firmly established, by 1830 they had reached their farthest outpost in Missouri. The pioneer spirit was calling them to a new land, a land being <u>prepared</u> for them by God.

CALIFORNIA

RELATING California to America, how was California being providentially <u>prepared</u> for Americans to enter California?

1. Geographic Preparation: Land: "...God used men and nations through Christ..." as explorers and discoverers of North America; North America was entered through Mexico; Baja and Alta California were discovered. The Catholic nations were used by God to seek out and identify the new land until such time as God had a people ready.

2. Colonization: The Catholic mission system was established. However, the Catholic religion did not furnish the providential preparation for self-government, nor the character, needed to found and govern colonies, hence the mission system deteriorated.

3. Religious Preparation: The Spanish Missions were secularized. Compulsory Catholic religion was no longer a threat.

    The Russians withdrew from the California coast. Compulsory religion of Russian Orthodox Church was no longer a threat to California.

    The void was filled by the Protestant thrust of Pathfinder Jedediah Smith, and Pathmarker John C. Fremont.

    God held both Spain and Russia from possessing California so that, in effect, it was reserved for a people providentially prepared.

4. A People Providentially Prepared by God: The sturdy stock of pioneers from America entered California by land and sea. They possessed the Christian characteristics to extend Christian constitutional government into California. As we shall see, they possessed a recognition of and appreciation for the value of the individual; the ability to express local self-government; faith; diligence; steadfastness; Brotherly Love, and Christian care; industry; Liberty of Conscience; supporters of a Republican form of government; and voluntary union.

5. Historic Preparation: At the end of the Mexican-American War, 1846-1847, America acquired California before gold was discovered.

6. Providential Preparation: Gold was discovered in 1848. It acted as a magnet drawing to California thousands of Americans who had lived under a Christian Constitutional Republic.

7. Political Union with America: Through her California Constitution of 1849, California voluntarily made herself into a State of the United States of America. Through California's First Legislature, they chose the adjudication of their courts to be by American Common Law. Providentially prepared, California became an American State on September 9, 1850.

CONCLUSION TO INTRODUCTION

"I am the true vine, and my Father is the husbandman."

"I am the vine, ye are the branches: He that abideth in me, and I in him, the same bringeth forth much fruit..." (John 15:1,5)

Christian Idea
of Man blossomed
in America

From the "true vine," Jesus Christ our Lord and Saviour, has blossomed America, a fruitful bough. Here is found the Christian idea of the free and independent man.

> "Christianity then appeared with its central doctrine, that man was created in the Divine image, and destined for immortality; pronouncing, that, in the eye of God, all men are equal. This asserted for the individual an independent value."[4]

The Chain of Christianity carried the Christian idea of man, as opposed to the pagan idea of man, to the fruitful places of America and California to establish a Christian Constitutional Republic.

Your author has endeavored to give a very brief idea of the length of time, the circumstances, and some of the people involved in working out the Chain of Christianity. In CHRISTIAN HISTORY OF THE CONSTITUTION, CONSIDER AND PONDER, Miss Hall states:

Freedom for the
Individual: Result
of Christianity's
March Westward

> "The phrase 'America's Christian History' and the title THE CHRISTIAN HISTORY OF THE AMERICAN REVOLUTION is based upon the conviction that America's civil freedom, i.e. freedom for the individual, came from God through His Son, Jesus Christ, and is the result or effect of Christianity's development and westward march from Asia, through Europe and England to America.

> The cause and timing of events which led to the War for American Independence, the raising up of civil and military leaders and the willingness of a diversified people to be self-governed - the cause of these aspects and many more - is attributed to the fulfillment of the promises of God to those who obey His precepts in His Word, obey His Law of Liberty in all aspects of their lives - including civil government."[5]

Result: American
Documents

As a result of obedience to God's Law of Liberty, we have our American documents: From A Declaration by the Representatives of the United States of America, THE DECLARATION OF INDEPENDENCE, 1776:

> "We hold these Truths to be self-evident, that all Men are created equal, that they are endowed by their Creator with certain unalienable Rights, that among these are Life, Liberty, and the

45

Pursuit of Happiness – that to secure these Rights, Governments are instituted among Men..."

The external, divine document, which guards the freedom and the rights of Americans today, states:

"We the people of the United States, in order to form a more perfect union, establish justice, insure domestic tranquility, provide for the common defence, promote the general welfare, and secure the blessings of liberty to ourselves and our posterity, do ordain and establish THE CONSTITUTION FOR THE UNITED STATES OF AMERICA."

Let us remember: "Eternal vigilance is the price of liberty!"

Remember, religious character of our origin

"Finally, let us not forget the religious character of our origin. Our fathers were brought hither by their high veneration for the Christian religion. They journeyed by its light, and labored in its hope. They sought to incorporate its principles with the elements of their society, and to diffuse its influence through all their institutions, civil, political, or literary. Let us cherish these sentiments, and extend this influence still more widely; in the full convictions, that that is the happiest society which partakes in the highest degree of the mild and peaceful spirit of Christianity."[6]

And from THE BIBLE AND THE CONSTITUTION OF THE UNITED STATES OF AMERICA:

Prophetic Vision

"A few miles south of the Puritan settlement, at Plymouth Plantation, Governor William Bradford, Pilgrim historian, looked back over the first ten years from 1620-1630, when the tiny colony had stood alone depending upon the Providence of God and the individual response of Christian character. With prophetic vision in that year of our Lord, 1630, he glimpsed the power of the Pilgrim testimony of faith and steadfastness, brotherly love and Christian care, diligence and industry, and liberty of conscience. What had begun so meekly as the first expression of self-government with union, the precursor of American Federalism, would extend its influence from Cape Cod to the Golden Gate, ever Westward."[7]

Westward to California

Now, it is my privilege to carry this Chain of Christianity, by way of historic documentation, Westward into San Francisco's Golden Gate.

"Now He that ministereth seed to the sower, both minister bread for your food, and multiply your seed sown, and increase the fruits of your righteousness; Being enriched in every thing to all bountifulness, which causeth through us thanksgiving to God." (II Cor. 9:10,11)

REFERENCES TO INTRODUCTION

SOURCE MATERIAL

1. These source books may be obtained by writing to:
   Foundation for American Christian Education,
   P.O. Box 27035, San Francisco, California 94127.

PART I: OVERVIEW OF CHAIN OF CHRISTIANITY

ROME

1. Slater, Rosalie J. TEACHING AND LEARNING, pp. 164, 165.

ENGLAND

2. Hall, Verna M. CHRISTIAN HISTORY, Vol. I, p. 15.
3. Ibid., p. 38. (For more details on the Magna Charta, see CHRISTIAN HISTORY, Vol. I, pp. 38-41.)
4. Webster, Noah. AN AMERICAN DICTIONARY OF THE ENGLISH LANGUAGE, First Edition, 1828.
5. Slater, Rosalie J. TEACHING AND LEARNING, p. 174.
6. Hall, Verna M. CHRISTIAN HISTORY, Vol. I, p. 41.
7. Slater, Rosalie J. TEACHING AND LEARNING, p. 174.
8. Hall, Verna M. CHRISTIAN HISTORY, Vol. I, p. 37.

THE BIBLE IN ENGLISH

9. Hall, Verna M. CONSIDER AND PONDER, p. XXIV.
10. Hall, Verna M. CHRISTIAN HISTORY, Vol. II, p. 186.
11. Slater, Rosalie J. TEACHING AND LEARNING, p. 166.
12. Ibid., p. 168.
13. Hall, Verna M. CONSIDER AND PONDER, p. XXIV.
14. Ibid., p. XXIV.
15. Slater, Rosalie J. TEACHING AND LEARNING, p. 173.
16. Hall, Verna M. CHRISTIAN HISTORY, Vol. I, p. 36.

LUTHER AND CALVIN

17. Hall, Verna M. CHRISTIAN HISTORY, Vol. I, p. 47.
18. Slater, Rosalie J. TEACHING AND LEARNING, pp. 169, 170.
19. Hall, Verna M. CONSIDER AND PONDER, pp. 47, 48.
20. Slater, Rosalie J. TEACHING AND LEARNING, pp. 170, 171.
21. Ibid., p. 172.

PILGRIMS AND PURITANS

22. Hall, Verna M. CHRISTIAN HISTORY, Vol. I, p. 182.
23. Ibid., p. 48.
24. Ibid., p. 246.
25. Ibid., p. 183.
26. Slater, Rosalie J. TEACHING AND LEARNING, p. 216.

LOCKE, MONTESQUIEU, BLACKSTONE

27. Hall, Verna M. CHRISTIAN HISTORY, Vol. I, p. 56.
28. Slater, Rosalie J. "Introducing Teachers to the Christian History Program." Foundation for American Christian Education, San Francisco. Unpublished.
29. Hall, Verna M. CHRISTIAN HISTORY, Vol. I, p. 139.
30. Slater, Rosalie J. TEACHING AND LEARNING, p. 176.
31. ENCYCLOPEDIA BRITANNICA, 11th Ed., 1910.
32. Slater, Rosalie J. TEACHING AND LEARNING, p. 176.
33. Hall, Verna M. CHRISTIAN HISTORY, Vol. I, p. 27.
34. Ibid., p. 131.
35. Ibid., p. 133.
36. Ibid., p. 132.
37. Ibid., p. 132.
38. Ibid., p. 133.
39. Slater, Rosalie J. TEACHING AND LEARNING, p. 176.
40. Hall, Verna M. CHRISTIAN HISTORY, Vol. I, p. 134.
41. Ibid., pp. 134, 135.

BEGINNING OF LOCAL SELF-GOVERNMENT IN AMERICA

42. Hall, Verna M. CHRISTIAN HISTORY, Vol. I, p. 150B.
43. Ibid., p. 150A.
44. Ibid., p. 271.
45. Ibid., p. 272.
46. Ibid., p. 275.
47. Ibid., p. 14.

PART II: OVERVIEW OF BACKGROUND OF CALIFORNIA

TO THE AMERICAN CHRISTIAN IN CALIFORNIA

1. Hall, Verna M. CHRISTIAN HISTORY, Vol. II, p. 8.

CALIFORNIA'S STEWARDSHIP

2. Hall, Verna M. CHRISTIAN HISTORY, Vol. I, p. 16.
3. Ibid., p. 6.

PART III: CHURCH AND STATE

1. Hall, Verna M. CHRISTIAN HISTORY, Vol. II, pp. 35-40.
2. Slater, Rosalie J. TEACHING AND LEARNING, p. 249.
3. Caughey, John and Laree. "Take Your Bible in One Hand," CALIFORNIA HERITAGE, p. 247.
4. Hall, Verna M. CHRISTIAN HISTORY, Vol. I, p. 388.

PART IV: SUGGESTIONS FOR STUDY: PRINCIPLES

1. Rose, James B. A GUIDE TO AMERICAN CHRISTIAN EDUCATION FOR THE HOME AND SCHOOL: THE PRINCIPLE APPROACH, p. 5.

SECOND LEADING IDEA

2. Hall, Verna M. CHRISTIAN HISTORY, Vol. I, p. 6A.

THIRD LEADING IDEA

AMERICA

3. Hall, Verna M. CHRISTIAN HISTORY, Vol. I, p. 28.

CONCLUSION TO INTRODUCTION

4. Hall, Verna M. CHRISTIAN HISTORY, Vol. I, p. 2.
5. Hall, Verna M. CONSIDER AND PONDER, p. XXIV.
6. Hall, Verna M. CHRISTIAN HISTORY, Vol. I, p. 248.
7. Hall, Verna M. and Rosalie J. Slater. THE BIBLE AND THE CONSTITUTION OF THE UNITED STATES OF AMERICA, p. 41.

CHAPTER I

THE PROVIDENTIAL DISCOVERY OF AMERICA AND CALIFORNIA

In CONSIDER AND PONDER, we read:

"GOD'S WISE AND BENEFICENT TIMING OF EVENTS:
Observe the hand of God in the wise and beneficent timing of events in the dawn of our history. The events of history are not accidents. There are no accidents in the lives of men or of nations. We may go back to the underlying cause of every event, and discover in each God's overruling and intervening wisdom...

No accidents in lives of men or nations

DISCOVERY AND PREPARATION OF AMERICA:
The discovery and preparation of this country to be the home of a great people, - the theatre of a new experiment in government, and the scene of an advancing Christian civilization, - is illustrative of this truth..."[1]

A. THE HAND OF GOD IN THE LIVES OF EXPLORERS LEADING TO THE DISCOVERY OF THE AMERICAN CONTINENT

MARCO POLO 1292

Marco Polo influenced Columbus

Marco Polo was one of the world's great explorers whose writings, THE TALES OF MARCO POLO, influenced Christopher Columbus, and were connected with the earliest Spanish explorations of the New World. Mr. Washington Irving states: "...the influence which the work of Marco Polo had over the mind of Columbus gives it particular interest and importance...He frequently quotes it, and on his voyages, supposing himself to be on the Asiatic coast, he is endeavoring to discover the islands and mainlands described in it, and to find the famous Cipango (Japan)."[2]

In THE TRAVELS OF MARCO POLO, edited by Manuel Komroff, we learn of the extent of Marco's travels:

"Marco Polo was the first traveller to cross the entire continent of Asia and name the countries and provinces in their proper consecutive order...

He was the first traveller to record the perilous deserts of Persia; to visit the jade-bearing streams of Khotan... to describe accurately the life of the people in China, Tibet, Burma, Siam, Ceylon, India...He gave us the very first hint of the existence of the dark land of Siberia, of Zanzibar...of Christian Abbyssinia and cannibal Sumatra... He described the dazzling court of Kublai Khan and the organization of the Mongol Army; ... he described

MARCO POLO
Greatest of All Travelers

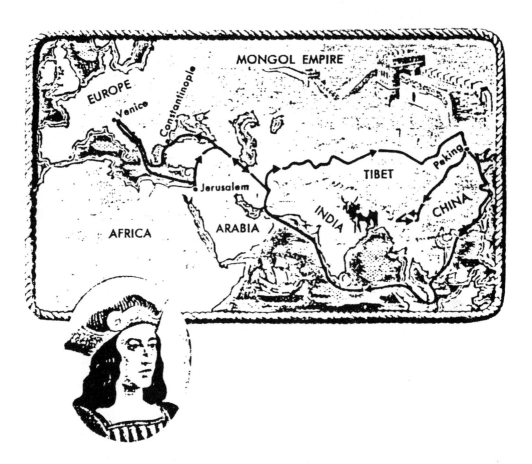

From a READER'S DIGEST ARTICLE
written for small children
by Donald Culross Peattie

the strange little birds and animals...temples with golden roofs...and many allegorical legends..."[3]

The Polos' First Journey to China

Marco's father and uncle were traders in precious gems in Venice. In 1255 they purchased a stock of jewelry in Constantinople to trade with the western Chinese, or Tartars, who had over-run many parts of Asia and Europe and who had settled near the Volga River in Russia. The brothers had an adventurous journey which eventually took them to northern China to the court of the Emperor, Kublai Khan[4], situated in what was formerly Peking, now called Beijing.

Marco on Second Journey

Kublai Khan interested in Christianity

On their second journey in 1271, Nicholas Polo took with him his son, Marco, born 1254. Furnished with doctrines of the Christian faith and holy oil from the lamp in the Sepulchre of our Saviour in Jerusalem, which the Khan had requested they bring back with them, the Polos set out for the remote parts of China. The Khan had also requested one hundred men well-instructed in the Christian religion. Only two friars accompanied the Polos but soon returned to Venice after experiencing great hardships from floods and snowstorms. The Christian missionaries never reached the Tartar Prince.

Mr. Fiske observed:

Opportunity lost

"It has been said that the failure of Kublai's mission to the Pope led him to the Grand Lama, at Thibet, who responded more efficiently and successfully than (Pope) Gregory X, so that Buddhism seized the chance which Catholicism failed to grasp."[5]

Land of Gog and Magog

On their incredible journey, the three Polos spent one year in the capital of a Chinese Province, Kauchan, where Marco learned much about the ways and customs of the Chinese people. They proceeded to Tenduc, which Marco speaks of as the land of Gog and Magog. From Tenduc, or Tendec, they journeyed along the frontier towns of Cathay, where cloths of silk and gold were manufactured, all of great interest to the European merchants.

Marco given great responsibility

When they were graciously received at the splendid palace of Kublai Khan, Marco made himself popular with the Khan. Marco learned the four principle languages of the country. The Khan realized Marco was trustworthy and had an eye for detail and observation, so the Khan gave him great responsibility in his kingdom by requesting that he journey over it and report his findings. For seventeen years, Marco gathered all kinds of information regarding the vast empire. The notes he made for the Khan are those from which he afterwards composed his TALES OF MARCO POLO.

Return to Italy

The Polos finally wished to return to Venice. Their opportunity arose when the Khan requested them to transport his granddaughter to Persia, where she was betrothed to a Mogul Tartar Prince. After they delivered the princess to Persia, they learned the Khan had died. They felt no obligation to return and continued home on the dangerous overland journey.

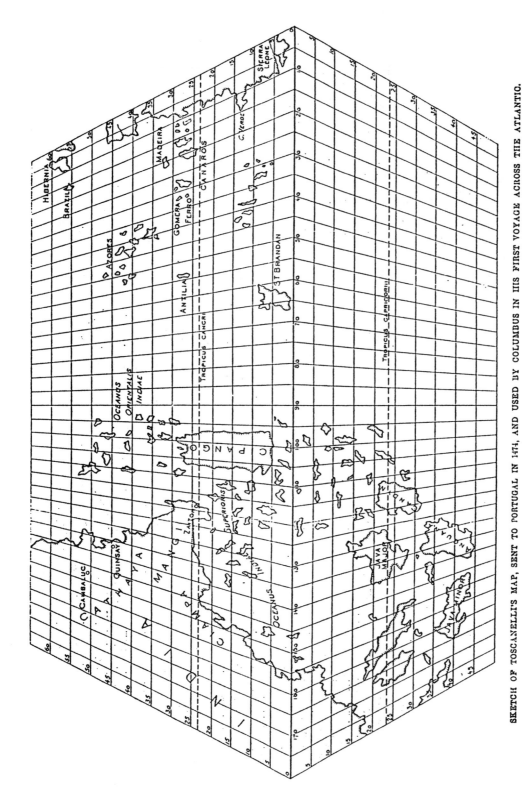

SKETCH OF TOSCANELLI'S MAP, SENT TO PORTUGAL IN 1474, AND USED BY COLUMBUS IN HIS FIRST VOYAGE ACROSS THE ATLANTIC.

Pozzo del Toscanelli was the great Florentine astronomer under King Alfonso V. of Portugal.

Map: From DISCOVERY OF AMERICA, Vol. I, by John Fiske

At that time, Genoa and Venice were rival city-states and owed their prosperity to the sea. Each desired the naval supremacy of Europe and control of the commerce of the East. Some months after his return, during one of the quarrels between Genoa and Venice, Marco commanded a Venetian galley at sea, was defeated in battle, and taken prisoner in Genoa.

TALES OF
MARCO POLO:
Providential

It was during his captivity that THE TALES OF MARCO POLO were written. It was <u>providential</u> that an Italian gentleman visited Marco, encouraging him to write of his adventures and that a scribe, apparently also a prisoner, was available to whom he dictated his experiences, which so captured the imagination of Columbus two centuries later. Mr. Irving states:

> "His splendid accounts of the extent, wealth, and population of the Tartar territories filled everyone with admiration. The possibility of bringing all of those regions under the Dominion of the Church, and rendering the Grand Khan an obedient vassal of the Holy Chair, was for a long time a favorite topic among the enthusiastic missionaries of Christendom, and there were many saints-errant who undertook to effect the conversion of this magnificent infidel."[6]

TALES inspire
adventurers and
discoverers

In the TALES, Marco wrote of Cathay (China) and Cipango (Japan). Cipango is clearly seen on the map made in 1474 by Pozzo del Toscanelli, the great Florentine astronomer and cosmographer. (See map, page 54.) A copy of this map was furnished to Columbus before he sailed on his first voyage. Because of Polo's writings, European monarchs and explorers long entertained the idea of a shorter route to trade with the wealthy countries of the Orient. Christopher Columbus was the mariner who opened the way.

"...There is nothing covered, that shall not be revealed; neither hid, that shall not be known." (Luke 12:2)

Nautical knowledge
gathered by
Henry of Portugal

Before Columbus sailed on his voyage of discovery in 1492, navigation had made some progress. Columbus had the nautical and geographical knowledge of his era which had been added to their maps and charts due to the endeavors of one man, Prince Henry, called The Navigator.

The Italian cities of Genoa, Pisa, and Venice kept great fleets upon the Mediterranean and produced very capable navigators who were willing to sail for any government which could furnish them with the means to sail. The Italians had long monopolized the trade with Asia for the rich produce of the Spice Islands and the silks, gums, perfumes, and precious stones of Egypt. Venice and Genoa became rich from this trade but the trade depended upon tedious overland caravans as well as internal navigation. To the price of every article was added the expense of transportation. A shorter trade route was desirable.

Henry, of
Portuguese and
English descent

However, it was Portugal which took the lead in finding an easier trade route. This was due to the scientific knowledge of navigation gathered by the genius and industriousness of Prince Henry of Portugal, born 1394. Prince Henry was the son of John the First of Portugal and Philippa of Lancaster, sister of Henry the Fourth of England. By birth, Prince Henry was Portuguese and English.

Goal: Overcome
sailing difficulties

Prince Henry's dream was to overcome sailing difficulties in order to sail around Africa to the south and sail to India, and to China, thus opening a direct route to the source of commerce.

Fear of the
unknown

Navigation of the Atlantic, called The Sea of Darkness, was very limited. Mariners distrusted the wide expanse of water which had no shore and where ships seemed to disappear over the horizon. They also believed that the earth, although round, was ringed by a torrid zone of impassable heat at the equator.

College of
nautical knowledge

To dispel these errors, Prince Henry established a naval college on a remote high point of land or rock projecting into the sea, at Sagres, the southwest extremity of Portugal. Here he constructed his observatory to which he invited the most eminent professors of nautical knowledge. He appointed James of Malorca as president, who was learned in navigation and skilled in making charts and instruments. All that was known to geography and navigation was gathered and made into a system. A great improvement took place in maps. The compass was brought into more general use, allowing the seamen to navigate on cloudy days and dark nights.

Fear slowly
overcome

Prince Henry had much opposition to overcome. Most of the people ridiculed his attempts to dispel ignorance. Doubt and prejudice were expressed

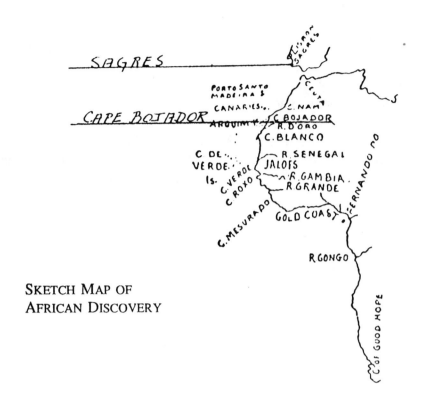

SKETCH MAP OF
AFRICAN DISCOVERY

Map: From CHRISTOPHER COLUMBUS, by Justin Winsor

MARINER'S ASTROLABE

*From García Palacio. The Altitude is
read from the upper pointer of the
Alidade*

"Columbus' Journal proves he was unable to use the astrolabe on his First Voyage....

Columbus took the course off his mariner's compass, which was the most reliable and the one indispensable instrument of navigation aboard."

ADMIRAL OF THE OCEAN SEA

Picture from: ADMIRAL OF THE OCEAN SEA,
by Samuel Eliot Morison

by the dull and the fearful. For twelve years Prince Henry sent out two or more sailing vessels with little results. No one had dared to sail beyond Cape Bojader (see map) until 1434 when Gil Eannes successfully did so. He found that the terrors of the ocean south of 28 degrees North Latitude did not exist. Consequently, more and more ocean explorers became eager to add to Prince Henry's store of knowledge.

Papal Bull, 1442

When Portuguese vessels brought back gold and a cargo of slaves from a point 400 miles beyond Cape Bojader in 1442, Henry obtained a Papal Bull from Pope Eugenius IV to protect the lands that Portugal might discover in the Atlantic.

When Prince Henry died in 1460, his caravels had sailed within a short distance of Sierra Leone on the coast of Africa. Numbers of sailors from Genoa were emigrating to Portugal, attracted by the explorations going on along the African coast.

Prince Henry enriched Portugal

By 1481, Portugal monopolized commerce with Africa through the efforts of Prince Henry and the maritime knowledge he accumulated. Portugal rose to be a rich and powerful nation through its knowledge of navigation. Also by 1481, a great impetus to navigation was received when King John II of Portugal, nephew of Prince Henry, commanded his astronomers, one of whom was Martin Behaim, to construct some instrument which would be a more certain guide to navigators. This resulted in a new kind of astrolabe. It enabled a navigator to learn his distance from the equator by the altitude of the sun; it provided a sure means of a return journey, destroying the worst fear connected with the sea. The discoveries of the Portuguese became the wonder and admiration of fifteenth century Europe.

Character of Prince Henry

Prince Henry was a man of self-discipline, a man not to be discouraged, one of the great men of his age. An expert in mathematics and astronomy, he had endless energy and industriousness. Often he worked all night, so devoted was he to his country and his dream for navigation. Devotion to an honest achievement often makes that achievement possible.

CHRISTOPHER COLUMBUS 1492

"They that go down to the sea in ships, that do business in great waters; These see the works of the Lord, and his wonders in the deep." (Ps. 107:23,24)

God's Timing

Christopher Columbus' voyages opened the idea that America was really a new world. In God's timetable, the time was right and the man was right. However, it had been "hidden away" until "God's hour had come for its occupancy."

Dr. D. S. Muzzey observed:

"Columbus was by no means the first European to visit the shores of the western continent. There are records of a dozen or so pre-Columbian voyages across the Atlantic by Arabians, Japanese, Welshmen, Irishmen and Frenchmen, besides the very detailed account in the Icelandic sagas, or stories of adventure, of the visit of the Norsemen to the shores of the western world in the year 1,000... But these voyages of the Norsemen to America five hundred years before Columbus were not of importance, because they were not followed up by exploration and settlement."[1]

Columbus' BOOK OF PROPHECIES

All of Columbus' sailing journals and most of his private letters give evidence of his biblical knowledge and his devout love for Jesus Christ. His little known and little quoted BOOK OF PROPHECIES, the only book he wrote, was a careful compilation of all the teachings of the Bible on the subject of the earth, distant lands, seas, population movements, undiscovered tribes, prophecies of the future spread of the Gospel throughout the whole world, prophecies of travel between distant places, prophecies of the end of the world and the establishment of the earthly kingdom of Jesus Christ.

Columbus read in Job of a place *"hid from the eyes of all living, and kept close from the fowls of the air,"* the way to which was known to God only (Job 28:21), and he prayed that he might be allowed to discover that place.

In Columbus' own words from THE BOOK OF PROPHECIES:

A student of many disciplines

"I prayed to the most merciful Lord about my heart's desire, and He gave me the spirit and intelligence for the task: seafaring, astronomy, geometry, arithmetic, skill in drafting spherical maps and placing correctly the cities, rivers, mountains and ports. I also studied cosmology, history, chronology and philosophy.

Inspiration from Holy Scriptures

It was the Lord who put into my mind (I could feel His hand upon me) the fact that it would be possible to sail from here to the Indies. All who heard of my project rejected it with laughter, ridiculing me. There is no question that the inspiration was from

59

the Holy Spirit, because he comforted me with rays of marvelous illumination from the Holy Scriptures...

No fear

No one should fear to undertake any task in the name of our Savior, if it is just and if the intention is purely for His holy service. The working out of all things has been assigned to each person by our Lord, but it all happens according to His sovereign will..."[2]

Christopher Columbus was born in Genoa, Italy, about the year 1435. We know from authentic documents that he arrived at Lisbon in the year 1470, and from this time his life becomes of historic importance.

The Toscanelli Map

Columbus corresponded with Pozzo (or Paulo) Toscanelli of Florence. According to a letter from Toscanelli to Columbus, Toscanelli's descriptions are taken from the book of Marco Polo. Toscanelli's map demonstrated that the earth was a sphere and that by sailing westward, one could reach China. Toscanelli had calculated the size of the earth almost exactly, but misled by the descriptions of the travelers to the Far East, he had made the continent of Asia extend eastward almost all the way across the Pacific Ocean. Columbus correctly calculated the length of the voyage necessary to reach land, although he always believed that the land he had reached was India and that its inhabitants were Indians. Columbus, actually in the West Indies, supposed that he was among the East Indies, or on the coast of Japan (Cipango), as described in Marco Polo's book.

Detailed plans

Columbus carefully laid his plans for his voyage of discovery to the minutest detail. He took his proposals to Genoa, then to Venice, but neither state could overcome the darkness of prejudice, pride and, of course, economy.

Isabella and Ferdinand victorious over Moors

In 1485, we find Columbus in Spain. The kingdoms of Arragon and Castile had been united by the marriage of Ferdinand and Isabella. As a result, Spain was united in its efforts of conquering the Moors, who once had spread over the whole country but were entrenched within the mountain boundaries of the kingdom of Granada. Ferdinand and Isabella were so occupied with their armies that they had no time to hear the pleas of Columbus. At length, their royal highnesses were victorious over the Moors at Granada. They rejoiced at having rid their kingdom of infidels, or non-believers, not only by banishing the Moors, but by an edict of March 30, 1492, driving 200,000 Jews from Spain.[3]

Spain financed Columbus

Columbus' friends persuaded the Queen to take on his enterprise, where the loss could be so little, while the gain might be so great. Her reply is legendary: "I undertake the enterprise for my own crown of Castile and will pledge my jewels to raise the necessary funds." The agreement was signed by Ferdinand and Isabella at the city of Santa Fe, in the plain of Granada, on the 17th of April, 1492.

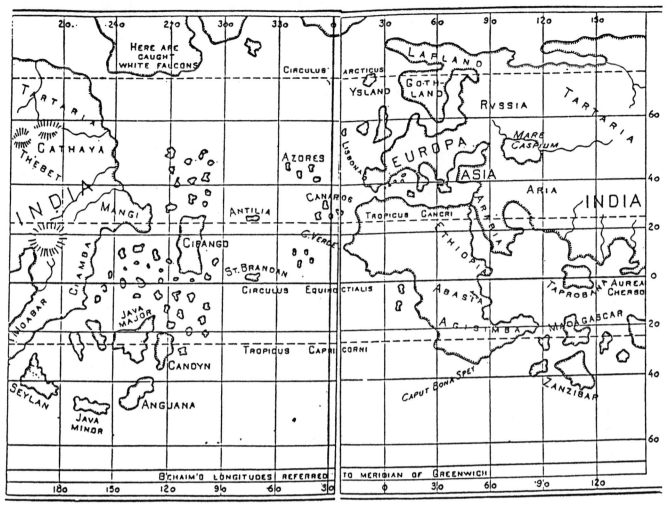

Martin Behaim's Globe, 1492, reduced to Mercator's projection.

Martin Behaim was an astronomer. He was author of the first almanac published in Europe, of priceless value to navigators. He was a friend of Columbus. Behaim finished this globe of the geographical views prevailing in maritime countries before Columbus' voyage of discovery.

Martin Behaim's Atlantic Ocean (with outline of American continent superimposed).

From: DISCOVERY OF AMERICA, Vol. I., by John Fiske

On August 3, 1492, Columbus sailed from Palos, Spain, in command of three caravels, the <u>Santa Maria</u>, the <u>Nina</u>, and the <u>Pinta</u>, with a total crew of ninety men. Columbus' son, Ferdinand, who was his biographer, states:

Exact journal

"During this voyage and indeed in all the <u>four</u> voyages which he made from Spain to the West Indies, the admiral was very careful to keep an exact journal of every occurrence which took place; always specifying what winds blew, how far he sailed with each particular wind, what currents were found, and everything that was seen by the way, whether birds, fishes, or any other thing."[4]

Magnetic Variation of the Compass

During his first voyage, Columbus was the first to notice the magnetic variation of the compass. A present-day physical scientist, Walter Dimmick, gives an explanation of this phenomena:

"Columbus made a great contribution to navigation when he discovered the <u>variation of the compass</u>. The north geographic pole of the earth is at the north end of the axis of rotation of the earth. On a clear night in the northern hemisphere, one can determine the direction of true north by sighting on the north star, Polaris, which is almost directly above the north geographic pole.

The magnetic compass points to the north magnetic pole. The north magnetic pole is in northern Canada somewhat south of the geographic pole. Therefore, the magnetic compass generally does not point directly to the north geographic pole, unless you are lined up with both poles. This magnetic compass error was known before Columbus made his voyages, but he sailed so far westward that he noted and recorded the change in the magnetic compass error. This has been called the <u>Variation of the Compass</u>."[5]

Danger of mutiny

Columbus' three ships experienced many adventures, all recorded by Columbus, the most frightening to the sailors being the times of the calm ocean, which could be disastrous to sailing vessels. Fear of perishing and never again seeing their loved ones made his crew mutinous. After three days of calm on Sunday, the 25th of September, there came a heavy rolling sea, which they had wished for. Washington Irving states:

God in control

"Columbus, who as usual considered himself under the immediate eye and guardianship of Heaven in the solemn enterprise, intimates in his journal that this swelling of the sea seemed <u>providentially</u> ordered to allay the rising clamors of his crew; comparing it to that which so miraculously aided Moses when conducting the children of Israel out of the captivity of Egypt."[6]

Columbus realized the mutinous attitude of his crew but he still maintained his patience. He soothed some with very gentle words, cajoled the

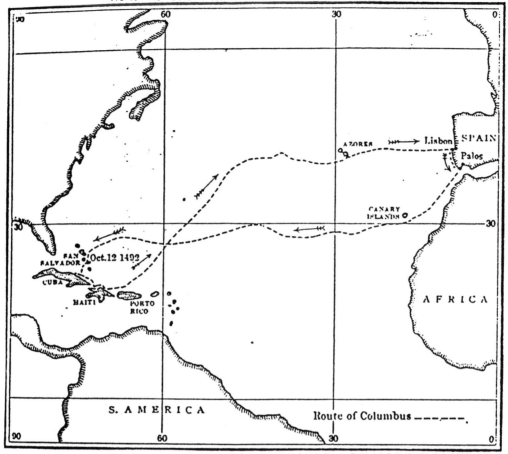

From: THE DISCOVERY AND COLONIZATION OF NORTH AMERICA,
by John Fiske

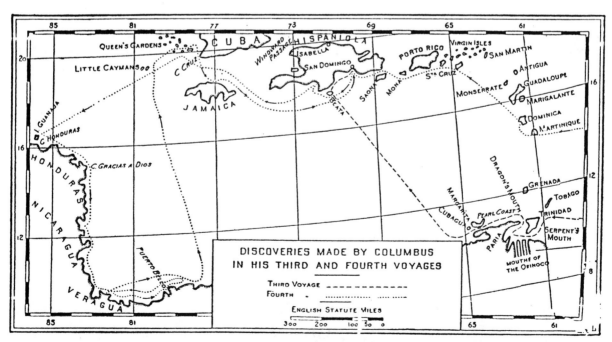

From: DISCOVERY OF AMERICA, Vol. I., by John Fiske

discontented, and finally threatened those who menaced him with punishment if they did anything to hamper the voyage.

The night before the discovery, after the evening prayers, Columbus made a speech to his crew, reminding them of the mercy of God in bringing them through such a long voyage of thirty-three days. On the morning of Friday, October 12, 1492, a sailor aboard the Pinta made the signal of seeing land! They thanked God for safe passage through waters which they believed had never before been traversed, and at their happy discovery of an unknown land.

The following is an interesting observation about Columbus by John Fiske in THE DISCOVERY OF AMERICA:

"Columbus, himself, after all his four eventful voyages across the Sea of Darkness, died in the belief that he had simply discovered the best and straightest route to the eastern shore of Asia. Yet from his first experiences in Cuba down to his latest voyage upon the coasts of Honduras and Veragua, he was more or less puzzled at finding things so different from what he had anticipated. If he had really known anything with accuracy about the eastern coast of Asia, he would doubtless soon have detected his fundamental error, but no European in his day had any such knowledge. In his four voyages, Columbus was finding what he supposed to be parts of Asia, what we now know to have been parts of America, but what were really to him and his contemporaries neither more nor less than Strange Coasts."[7]

Washington Irving's comments are more elaborate:

"Could he have known that he had indeed discovered a new continent, equal to the whole of the Old World in magnitude, and separated by two vast oceans from all the earth hitherto known by civilized man! How would his magnanimous spirit have been consoled, amidst the afflictions of age and cares of penury, the neglect of a fickle public, and the injustice of an ungrateful king, could he have anticipated the splendid empires which were to spread over the beautiful world he had discovered.[8]

Nor should we fail to notice how free he was from all feeling of revenge; how ready to forgive and forget on the least sign of repentance and atonement. He has been extolled for his skill in controlling others, but far greater praise is due to him for his firmness in governing himself."[9]

According to God's Providence, the events of history are not accidents. Columbus was used by God to discover the Carribean area, but he was not allowed to discover our own coast of Florida, although he was so close to it.

He represented a government where the state is more important than the individual. In mankind's endeavor to reconcile government with the God-given Liberty of the individual, our land was reserved for the Pilgrims and Puritans one hundred years after Columbus, in His Story.

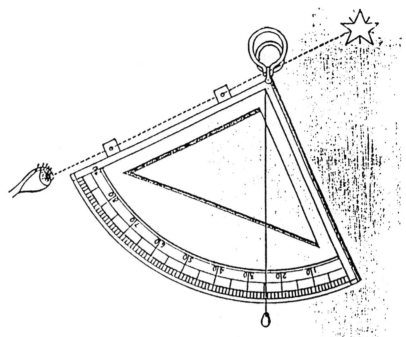

MARINE QUADRANT OF 1492

Altitude is read from the point where
thread cuts Arc

"The Common Quadrant...was the only instrument of celestial navigation that Columbus ever employed.

On a rolling and pitching ship it was very difficult to keep the plane of the quadrant perpendicular and at the same time catch your star through the pin holes."

ADMIRAL OF THE OPEN SEA
by Samuel Eliot Morison

"Conscience is the most sacred of all property."[1]

Spain's "right" to all infidel nations

After Columbus' first voyage, Europe generally accepted the idea that Cuba was the eastern end of the Asiatic continent and that the surrounding islands were in the Indian seas. The lands, therefore, which Columbus had discovered were called the West Indies. Although these territories were thought to be part of the empire of the Grand Khan, Spain believed it had a right to seize upon the territories of all infidel nations.

Pope, Supreme Ruler

Catholic countries regarded the Pope as having supreme authority over all spiritual and temporal things, so he was empowered to dispose of all heathen lands to those rulers who would bring them under the dominion of the church. Spain appealed to Pope Alexander VI for the protection of any lands they might discover. Accordingly, a Papal Bull, or edict, was issued May 2, 1493, giving to the Spanish sovereigns the same rights, privileges, and indulgences, regarding the newly-discovered regions, as had been given to the Portuguese with regard to their African discoveries.

World divided between Spain and Portugal

The Papal Bull of 1493 gave to Ferdinand and Isabella "and to their heirs forever, all those lands and islands, not then possessed by any other Christian prince, with their dominions, territories, cities, citadels, towns, places and villages, found or to be found, discovered or to be discovered, toward the West and South, of a north and south line drawn one hundred leagues* west and south of any of the islands called the Azores and Cape Verde Islands."[2] Thus, the Pope divided the undiscovered world between Spain and Portugal by a line of demarcation. All lands discovered west of this line were to belong to Spain; all east of it, to Portugal.

One year after Pope Alexander's Bull was issued, the demarcation line was moved 270 leagues farther west by the Treaty of Tordesillas. This imaginary line drawn from the north to the south pole, enabled Spain to lay claim to the Moluccas, while Portugal was able to claim Brazil.

The Pope believed it was his Divine Right to divide the known world between two Catholic countries, Spain and Portugal. But what of the rights of those countries not included in this partition? Let us read from CONSIDER AND PONDER, page 187:

Rights of Conscience, sacred and equal in all

"No action is a religious Action without Understanding and Choice in the Agent. Whence it follows, the Rights of Conscience are sacred and equal in all, and strictly speaking unalienable. This RIGHT OF JUDGING EVERY ONE FOR HIMSELF IN MATTERS OF RELIGION results from the Nature of Man, and is so inseparably connected therewith, that a Man can no more part with it than he can with his POWER OF THINKING: and it is equally reasonable, for him to attempt to strip himself of the POWER OF REASONING, as to attempt the vesting of another with this Right. And whoever invades this Right of another, be he POPE or CAESAR, may with equal Reason assume the other's Power of Thinking, and so level him with the Brutal Creation...."[3]

MAP OF THE DIVISION OF
THE WORLD MADE IN 1494

THE DISCOVERY AND COLONIZATION OF NORTH AMERICA,
by John Fiske

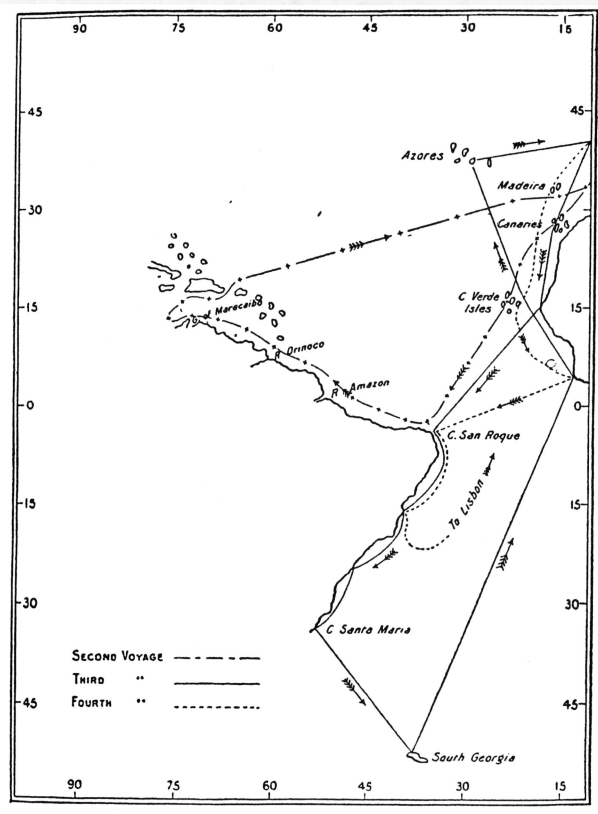

Second, Third, and Fourth Voyages of Vespucius.

From: DISCOVERY OF AMERICA, Vol. II, by John Fiske

68

VESPUCIUS   1501

"...Ye shall be witnesses unto me...unto the uttermost part of the earth."
(Acts 1:8)

There are many explorers in this period of discovery. We shall follow a few. Here, the continent of South America is discovered.

Americus Vespucius* was an Italian from Florence, born in 1451. He made four voyages of discovery, two for Spain and two for Portugal. The voyage which interests us is his third voyage, undertaken in 1501, for King Manuel of Portugal. Vespucius was the pilot on one of three ships which left Lisbon, Portugal, in May.

Vespucius sailed along coast of Brazil

It is important that we follow this fleet from place to place as they slowly discovered the entire coast of Brazil. (See map.) The ships passed by Madeira and the Canary Islands, and stopped at Cape Verde, off the coast of Africa. They set sail across the Atlantic Ocean in a south-westerly direction, and after a stormy crossing of 67 days, reached the coast of Brazil. They landed on Cape St. Roque. It was here that they encountered unfriendly natives who killed three of the sailors and to the horror of the rest of the crew, ate them. Realizing that these people were cannibals, the ships quickly left, sailing south to St. Augustine. As usual, the explorers gave names to the places they discovered.

An oriental paradise?

The progress of the ships was slow, as they coasted as close to the mainland as they dared. Frequently they went ashore to determine the degree of friendliness of the natives and to note their strange customs. They were amazed at the beauty of the colorful birds, the height of the trees, and the lush foliage. They wondered if this might be the outskirts of the famous oriental paradise. It was not until November 1, 1501 that they reached a bay, Latitude 13 degrees South, which they named Bahia de Todos Santos.

Pope's line of demarcation observed

In January, 1502, they arrived at a great bay. Believing this to be the mouth of a river, they named it Rio de Janeiro (River of January). By February 15, they had passed Cape Santa Maria. They were now in longitude more that 20 degrees west of the meridian of Cape San Roque and therefore out of Portuguese waters. They had sailed into Spain's area of the line of demarcation. Perhaps new lands toward the southeast might come within the Portuguese side of the line.

End of continent?

Vespucius was given command of the fleet and he made the decision to sail into the broad ocean, "trusting to Providence to land them somewhere in the region of gold."[1] It is speculated that his decision to change direction was based upon the belief that they may have "looked into the mouth of the river La Plata, which is a bay more than a hundred miles wide; and the sudden westward trend of the shore may have led him to suppose that he had reached the end of the continent."[2] Laying in fresh water and food for six months, they started on a southeast course of unknown realms.

Providential
decision at
Antarctica

On April 3, 1502, after having sailed 500 leagues, or 1,500 miles, southeast, a terrific storm arose. They had entered the Antarctic, unknowingly, and were experiencing intense cold, fog, long nights, and rough winds. On April 7 they sighted the island of South Georgia, 54 degrees S. latitude, and about 1200 miles east from Tierra del Fuego. The land was barren and uninviting. Vespucius realized the danger of their position: "If we had delayed that night we had all been lost."[3] Americus sailed nearer the Antarctic pole than any civilized man had ever been before, with the exception of Bartholomew Dias.

Excellent
navigating

Homeward bound, they sailed for the coast of Africa and on May 15 reached Sierra Leone, thence to Lisbon via the Azores, arriving home September 7, 1502. Vespucius was a mariner of the first magnitude. He sailed home with wonderful accuracy, a distance of more than 4,000 miles. In those days of limited navigational equipment, of wellworn sailing vessels and sails, it was a feat of navigation. They were sailing into the Sea of Darkness, across the world of the southern hemisphere. In this course from South Georgia to Lisbon, Vespucius sailed over an arc of 93 degrees, or more than one-fourth of the circumference of the globe.

Vespucius had sailed down the coast of a continent, which was unknown to the ancient geographers. In a letter to Lorenzo de' Medici from Lisbon, March or April, 1503, Americus Vespucius wrote:

South America,
called "a new
world"

"I have formerly written to you at sufficient length about my return from those new countries which in the ships and at the expense and command of the most gracious King of Portugal we have sought and found. It is proper to call them a new world."[4]

It is only the new countries visited on this third voyage, the countries from Cape San Roque southward, that Vespucius calls a "new world."

The Letter

Americus Vespucius was the first to extensively explore the coast of South America. He never dreamt that an whole continent should be named after him. A Latin translation of a letter written by Vespucius from Portugal in 1504 was published at St. Die in Lorraine, France, in April 1507. In his letter to Soderini, Vespucius gave a brief account of his four voyages.

From this letter, Martin Waldseemuller, a professor of cosmography at Die University, published a treatise about these voyages in his COSMOGRAPH-ICAL INTRODUCTIO. Dr. Fiske states:

> "The copy in the library of Harvard University, which I have now before me, was published August 29, 1507, - a little quarto of 52 leaves...In this rare book occurs the first suggestion of the name AMERICA. After having treated of the division of the earth's surface into three parts - Europe, Asia, and Africa - Waldsee-muller speaks of the discovery of a Fourth Part. Translated into English, it reads:

"America"

> 'But now these parts have been more extensively explored and another fourth part has been discovered by Americus Vespucius ...wherefore I do not see what is rightly to hinder us from calling it Amerige or America, i.e., the land of Americus, after its discoverer Americus, a man of sagacious mind, since both Europe and Asia have got their names from women. Its situation and the manners and customs of the people will be clearly understood from the twice two voyages of Americus...'"[5]

This was the first suggestion in print that the newly discovered fourth part of the world should be called "America."

Da Vinci Map

The reader will note the map on page 72, supposed to have been made by Leonardo da Vinci about 1514, which is the earliest known map with the name "America."

Mercator Map

The other map is by Gerard Mercator, an able geographer and mathemati-cian, whose important method of map projection is called the Mercator Projection. He is the first person who indicated upon a map the existence of a distinct and integral western hemisphere, the whole of which he called AMERICA.

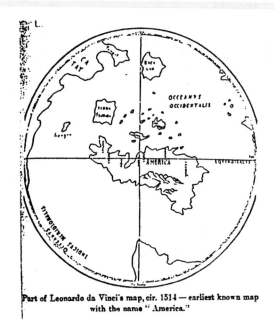

Part of Leonardo da Vinci's map, cir. 1514 — earliest known map
with the name " America."

Earliest map with name
"America"

Gerhardus Mercator (1512-1594), a
Flemish geographer, in 1568 produced the first map on a flat paper.

History records that he was arrested
for heresy. He escaped but forty-two
others seized with him were burnt
alive.

Sketch of Gerard Mercator's map, 1541.

Maps: DISCOVERY OF AMERICA, Vol. II.,
by John Fiske

72

"...the most High ruleth in the kingdom of men, and giveth it to whomsoever he will..." (Dan. 4:17)

Search for a strait

By the early 1500's it was believed that the land that was discovered to the west of Spain and Portugal might not really be China or India; that there may be a strait which connected the land north of the equator and the land south of the equator. Both Spain and Portugal sent out expeditions to try to discover this strait which may lead them to the Indian Ocean, and a shorter route to the Orient.

Balboa eluded creditors

Vasco Nunez Balboa, born 1475, was one of these adventurers sailing for Spain. He explored a part of the southwestern coast of the Caribbean Sea and became a planter in Haiti. He was not successful and incurred a great deal of debt. To escape his creditors, he placed himself in a barrel and was carried aboard one of Alonzo de Ojeda's sailing vessels which was bound for the mainland of South America to set up a new colony. Once on the mainland, they ran into trouble with the natives and every fighting man was needed. Balboa showed his talent for leadership, and suggested he be allowed to command a new and better settlement at Darien on the east side of what we now call the

Isthmus of Panama

Isthmus of Panama, having been there on a previous voyage. This colony was called Santa Maria del Darien.

Gold and greed

Balboa obtained a great deal of gold from the neighboring natives, with whom he had made friends. The son of an Indian cacique (chief) intelligently appraised these Spaniards as "a wandering kind of men, living only by shifts and spoil."[1] Wishing to impress the Spaniards, he gave Balboa and his men 4,000 ounces of gold and ornaments. It was the custom of Balboa to set aside one-fifth of the amount of gold for the crown and to evenly divide the rest among his men. A violent quarrel broke out among the men. The cacique's son said in dismay: "Why should you quarrel for such a trifle? If this gold is indeed so precious in your eyes that for it alone you abandon your homes, invade the peaceful land of others, and expose yourselves to such sufferings and perils, I will tell you of a region where you may gratify your wishes to the utmost. Behold those lofty mountains," he said, pointing to the south, "beyond these lies

News of a great sea

a mighty sea, which may be discerned from their summit... All the streams which flow down the southern side of those mountains into that sea abound in gold, and the kings who reign upon its borders eat and drink out of golden vessels..."[2] The young cacique told Balboa of many dangers of reaching this place, of the rugged territory, and of cannibals.

Balboa's good news was overshadowed by disturbing news from Spain. He was ordered to return to face criminal charges against him for "costs and damages." He was a man quick to make up his mind and decided to seek the southern sea, hoping this discovery would atone for his past with the King.

On September 1, 1513, Balboa left the little colony of Darien with 190 of his strongest men, a few blood-hounds which he had found helpful in Indian warfare, and a number of Indians knowledgeable of the wilderness. Thus, Balboa, a daring and desperate commander, started his journey in search of the great Pacific Ocean.

On September 6, he began the march into mountainous regions. It was very difficult. They were encumbered with heavy armor and weapons in a hot, tropical climate. They had to climb rocky precipices, and struggle through tangled forests. Deep and turbulent streams had to be crossed on rafts. At a village at the foot of the last mountain that remained to be climbed, the hungry and tired men had to fight a warlike cacique. Their muskets proved too much for the Indians. Only 67 of the original number of men remained to take part in this last encounter.

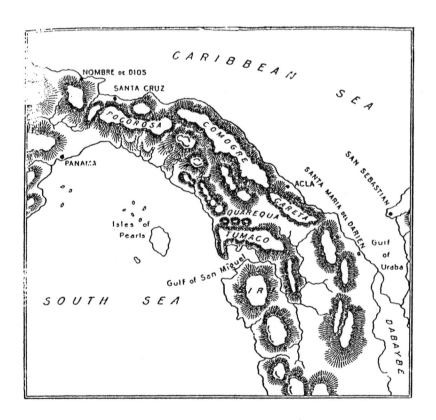

DISCOVERY OF AMERICA, Vol. II, by John Fiske

Discovery, 1513

On September 26, the weary men began to climb, and finally a bare summit alone remained to be ascended. Vasco Nunez Balboa commanded his men to halt and he walked alone to the mountain top. The long-sought Southern Sea lay before him in all its glorious majesty! He sank upon his knees and poured out thanks to God for being the first European allowed to make that great discovery.

As to the change in character which came upon Balboa after his discovery, let us read from Washington Irving:

Character change
in Balboa

"The character of Vasco Nunez had, in fact, risen with his circumstances, and now assumed a nobleness and grandeur from the discovery he had made, and the important charge it had devolved upon him. He no longer felt himself a mere soldier of fortune, at the head of a band of adventurers, but a great commander conducting an immortal enterprise. 'Behold,' says old Peter Martyr,* 'Vasco Nunez de Balboa, at once transformed from a rash royster to a politic and discreet captain' and thus it is that men are often made by their own fortunes...their latent qualities are brought out, and shaped and strengthened by events, and by the necessity of every exertion to cope with the greatness of their destiny."[3]

"...there is nothing covered, that shall not be revealed; and hid, that shall not be known." (Matt.10:26)

Balboa had discovered the magnificent body of water which they called the "South Sea." The extent of it was entirely unknown to Europeans; it was believed to be a part of Asia. No one, as yet, had found a strait, or water-way, connecting the Atlantic Ocean and this new body of water.

Search for a strait connecting two great Oceans

The "new world" of Columbus and Vespucius was supposed to be the eastern edge of Asia but there began to be doubt. To settle the question of the earth's rotundity, Ferdinand Magellan determined to embark on an expedition to circumnavigate the globe, a tremendous undertaking. There <u>must</u> be a strait connecting the two bodies of water, the Atlantic Ocean and this newly discovered Sea.

Young Magellan in Spice Islands, 1511

Ferdinand Magellan, born 1480, was of a noble Portuguese family. As a young sailor he had taken part in the Portuguese conquests of India. This took him to the Moluccas and Ceylon in the trade with the Orient for their rich spices. In 1511 he sailed to Java and the Spice Islands in the East Indies. It was while he was sailing the Indian Ocean that he had the idea that there should be another way to the Orient by a western passage, one which would save much time and money for the traders.

Expedition planned under Spain

Magellan's plan for an expedition was presented to his King, Manuel of Portugal, but it was rejected. Magellan renounced his ties to Portugal and presented his plan to the Spanish King Charles V. His proposal to reach the Spice Islands[1] by sailing west won the approval of Spain.

Pope divided world on opposite side of globe

In dividing the known world between Spain and Portugal, the Pope had not decreed any line of demarcation for the opposite side of the globe. So, before starting his enterprise, Magellan wrote a memorandum to Charles V for the Pope's approval, giving a proper drawing of a demarcation line between the spheres of Spain and Portugal in the East Indies, including the Moluccas or Spice Islands within the Spanish sphere.

Few returned

On August 10, 1519 Magellan left Seville, Spain, in command of five ships and about 248 men. Of the men, only thirty-one returned in the one ship that made the entire circumnavigation, the <u>Vittoria</u>. Four men finally showed up from one of the ships that had turned homeward early.

Character of Magellan

What kind of a man was Magellan? He was a "bold mariner," fearless, persistent in his purpose. At times he dealt with a mutinous crew in a most cruel manner, but he commanded adventurers and felt he had to maintain a firm hand over his subordinates.

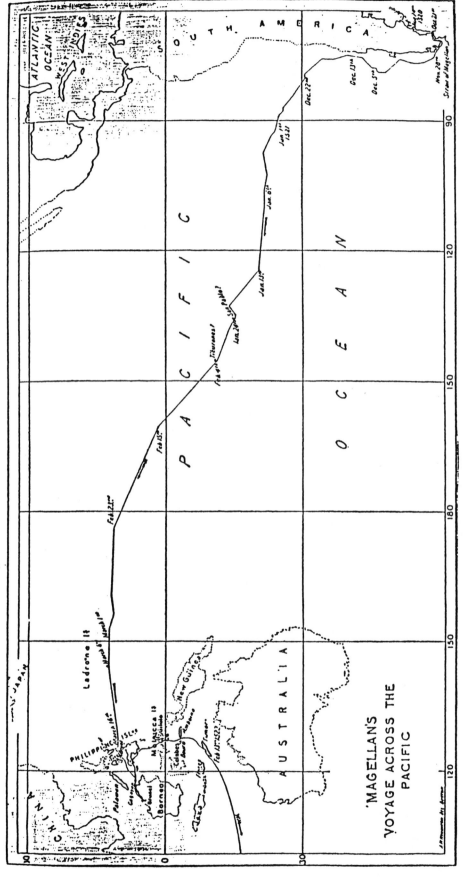

From: DISCOVERY OF AMERICA, Vol. II, by John Fiske

77

| Cold Coast of Argentina | From Seville, they sailed down the African coast, then to Rio de Janeiro in Brazil. On January 10, 1520 they reached the River La Plata, on the eastern coast of Argentina. By March, 1520, they had reached Port St. Julian, extreme southeastern coast of Argentina, where Magellan decided to stay for the rest of the winter. It was here that he crushed a frightening mutiny while they lay at anchor in a cold and dreary land. Most of the men wanted to return home but Magellan was determined to continue. |

The following is contributed by Walter Dimmick:

| The Magellanic Clouds | "One of Magellan's crewmen in 1520 discovered two objects in the night skies of the southern hemisphere visible to the naked eye. They are named the Large and Small Magellanic Clouds. The subject of much astronomical observation over the centuries since Magellan's ship discovered them, it has been determined that the Magellanic Clouds consist of a dense accumulation of stars, clusters, gaseous, and other nebulae. They are outside of our own galactic system with the distance from us currently calculated at about 170,000 light years. A light year is the distance light travels in one year, about six trillion miles. |

| A Supernova | In February, 1987, the Large Magellanic Cloud came into prominence again, when one of its stars (Sanduleak-69 degrees 202) exploded into a supernova, a dying star, briefly shining more brightly than 100 million suns and visible on earth to the naked eye."[2] |

| The Straits of Magellan | Magellan's ships turned south once more in August, battling strong winds and stormy seas. After having reached Cape St. Virgins at the end of October, they came upon a wide opening which Magellan believed was the passage they had sought for so long. With ships that had seen hard service, with provisions getting low and facing starvation, with fear in the hearts of his men, he gave orders to pass through the straits. It took them several weeks. |

They sighted a cold and rugged land, which they named Tierra del Fuego because at night they saw fires burning although the land was uninhabited. It was at this point that one of the ships, the San Antonio, weary of the long voyage, turned homeward. There were now three ships as one had been wrecked while exploring the straits.

| "Pacific" | In the strait which now bears his name, the Strait of Magellan, they steered through places "very large and in other places little more than half a league in breadth," between snow-covered mountains on one side and the land of the fires on the other. Emerging from these long-sought Straits on November 27, 1520, Magellan viewed the Great South Sea, which he named "Pacific" because the waves seemed so smooth and calm. |

"When the capitayne Magalianes (Magellan) was past the strayght and sawe the way open to the other mayne sea, he was so gladde thereof that for joy the teares fell from his eyes, and named the poynt of the lande from whense he fyrst sawe that sea <u>Cape Desiderato</u>. Supposing that the shyp which stole away had byn loste, they erected a crosse upon the top of a hyghe hyll to direct their course in the straight yf it were theyr chaunce to coome that way."[3]

Although a westward passage had been found connecting the Atlantic Ocean to the Pacific Ocean, Magellan and his men were to face extreme hardships. They sailed three months and twenty days on the vast Pacific Ocean before they saw any land. Many died. Providentially, the sea remained calm or those beaten ships with their feeble crews would have perished at sea.

March 6, 1521 they sighted land, The Ladrones (Isle of Thieves), but had to fight the natives. Their firearms were overpowering and the natives fled. They stocked up with fresh fruit, fish, and rested. On March 16 they arrived at the Philippine Islands.[4] Magellan had almost reached the Spice Islands and knew he had proved the earth to be round. However, here he met a tragic end. Zealous for the cause of Christianity, as the Spanish and Portuguese were for Catholicism, he foolishly tried to indoctrinate rebellious natives on the Island of Mactan, where the natives killed Magellan April 27, 1521.

The remainder of the men fled the Philippines, stopped at Borneo, lost another ship, and finally reached their goal, The Moluccas, the rich Spice Islands of the East, early in November. At Timor, a heavy cargo of cloves was taken in. The leaky <u>Trinidad</u> stayed behind with its crew. The <u>Vittoria</u> sailed for the Cape of Good Hope and home to Europe alone. It was a rough crossing and the crew was suffering from scurvy and starvation. In July, 1522, on its return voyage, the <u>Vittoria</u> was captured by the jealous Portuguese at the Cape Verde Islands. Thirteen men were imprisoned but the rest of the crew escaped. On the sixth of September, 1522, these "ghost-like" men arrived in Spain, having circumnavigated the world in three years.

This incredible voyage showed the true position of America with reference to the rest of the world. Ferdinand Magellan was the discoverer of the Strait to the new sea; he was the first to circumnavigate the globe; he proved that South America was a separate continent; he gave the name "Pacific" to the new body of water. Magellan linked western Europe with eastern Asia and found a direct route over the western ocean.

Magellan's victory was due largely to his persistence in his enterprise. He gave his life for a cause he felt was just and necessary. We might question his treatment of his men but we admire his bravery. God used Magellan to reveal to a waiting world His creation of continents and oceans.

"...His dominion shall be from sea even to sea..." (Zech. 9:10)

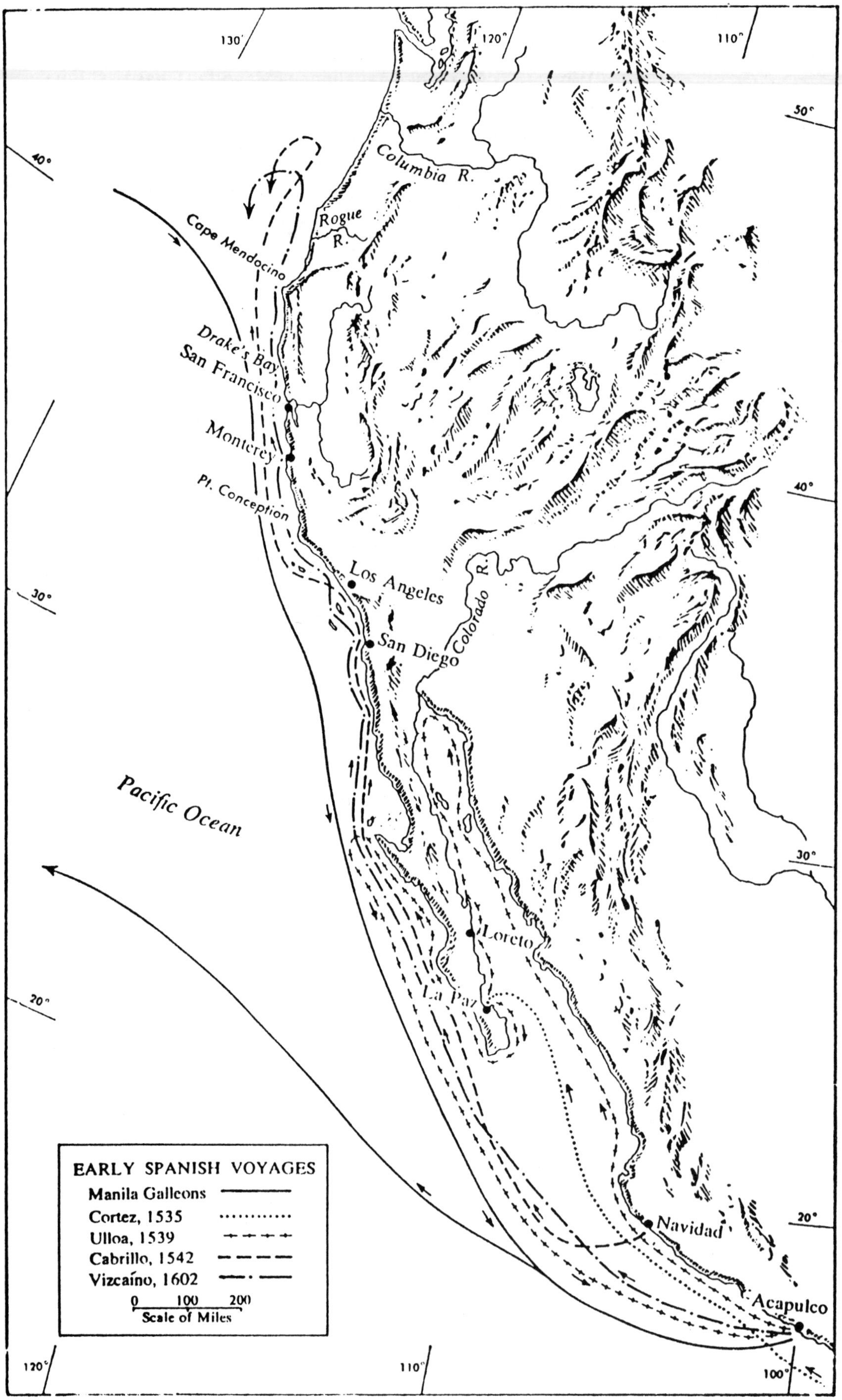
130°
120°
110°
50°
40°
40°
30°
30°
20°
20°
120°
110°
100°
Columbia R.
Rogue R.
Cape Mendocino
Drake's Bay
San Francisco
Monterey
Pt. Conception
Los Angeles
San Diego
Colorado R.
Pacific Ocean
Loreto
La Paz
Navidad
Acapulco
EARLY SPANISH VOYAGES
Manila Galleons
Cortez, 1535
Ulloa, 1539
Cabrillo, 1542
Vizcaíno, 1602
0 100 200
Scale of Miles

From: CALIFORNIA, A HISTORY, by Andrew F. Rolle

B. THE HAND OF GOD IN THE LIVES OF EXPLORERS LEADING TO THE DISCOVERY OF CALIFORNIA

CORTES: CONQUEST OF MEXICO, 1519-20
JIMENEZ: BAJA CALIFORNIA, 1533
ULLOA: GULF OF CALIFORNIA, 1540

"When the Lord thy God shall bring thee into the land whither thou goest to possess it, and hath cast out many nations before thee...

...thus shall ye deal with them; ye shall destroy their altars, and break down their images, and cut down their groves, and burn their graven images with fire.

Know therefore that the Lord thy God, he is God...and he will love thee..."
(Deut. 7:1,5,9,13)

HERNANDO CORTES

By 1518, the eastern borders of both of the great continents of North America and South America had been surveyed. The shores of the great Gulf of Mexico, however, and the rich interior of Mexico were yet to be explored. The conquest of Mexico fell to an adventurous young man, Hernando Cortes.

Cortes was born in Medellin, Spain, in 1485, in the reign of Ferdinand and Isabella. In 1516, the rule of Spain passed from Ferdinand and Isabella to their grandson, Charles V.

Route through new continent needed

When the little remnant of Magellan's expedition returned to Spain in 1522, after their three years' voyage, it began to be dimly realized in Europe that there was an immense ocean between the New World and Asia. It was clear that Magellan's route was too stormy for the small vessels of Europe of that period. A route was still needed to get past or through the barrier of land which we know as America, in order to get to Asia. Charles V of Spain encouraged his mariners to be the first to find such a route as he feared foreign colonial conquest, and there was always the quest for gold.

Charles V decided to fund a ship-building station at Zacatula on the west coast of Mexico.

Cortes at Zacatula

In 1519, we find Cortes in Cuba where his reputation for boldness and daring earned him the title of captain-general of a fleet of eleven ships sailing under the flag of Spain. Cortes established a ship-building station at the heavily timbered harbor of Zacatula. He sent carpenters and shipwrights to build four strong vessels. It was a laborious process. All of the iron work and rigging had to be brought by men and animals from the Atlantic port of Vera Cruz, where Cortes had established a village.

81

"The heart-breaking nature of carrying these heavy materials over six hundred miles (across Mexico) through the unbroken jungle, through boggy swamps and morasses infested with poisonous reptiles and torturing insects, through tropic heat and torrential rains, with the men under the necessity of going constantly armed against attacks of hostile natives, may well be imagined."[1]

THE CONQUEST OF MEXICO

Spaniards into Mexico, 1519

Cortes and his men entered Mexico City in 1519. The appearance of the large floating ships upon which the Spaniards had arrived, the horses on which they fought, and the noise of their artillery, all new to the native Indian population, made these natives astonished, fearful, and yet, full of admiration.

Advanced Aztec civilization

"The fortunes of Cortes had led him in the very beginning of his enterprises, to the one part of the newly discovered continent which was inhabited by a people farthest advanced toward civilization. While other adventurers, and even Columbus himself, had found only savages, dwelling without shelter under the open sky, he had found a wealthy people living in regularly built cities, whose kings dwelt in palaces, and who worshipped their gods in richly ornamented temples."[2]

Montezuma

The proud ruler of this civilization was the famous Montezuma, "the priest-commander." It is not necessary here to go into the details of how Cortes conquered the six thousand natives with only seven hundred Spaniards. Not all of Cortes' men relished the idea of fighting with such uneven odds. Some of them planned to seize a ship and return to Cuba. Their plot was discovered the night before they were to sail, and they were punished.

No retreat

Cortes realized there were soldiers upon whom he could not rely, who might try again to seize his vessels. He devised a plan to make it impossible for them to escape. He asked his pilots to make a survey as to the condition of the ships. They were found to be unseaworthy. He ordered all of them to be sunk, except one. Upon learning of this, his troops were astonished; they felt betrayed and abandoned in a strange and dangerous land. What did Cortes tell them?

Soft words

Prov. 15:1

Using tones of persuasion, not authority, he reasoned with them, convincing them that the fleet would not really be needed since they were all going to be so successful in the interior of Mexico; there were future riches and glory ahead of them. They shouted, "On to Mexico!"

"The destruction of his fleet by Cortes is perhaps, the most remarkable passage in the life of this remarkable man. History, indeed, affords examples of a similar expedient in emergencies somewhat similar; but none where the chances of success were so precarious, and defeat would be so disastrous."[3]

I would like to further quote Mr. Prescott, one of the most able authorities on the history of Mexico:

"It would be unjust to the Aztecs themselves, at least to their military prowess, to regard the Conquest as directly achieved by the Spaniards alone...The Indian empire was in a manner conquered by Indians. The first terrible encounter of the Spaniards with the Tlascalans, which had nearly proved their ruin, did in fact insure their success. It secured to them a strong native support, on which to retreat in the hour of trouble, and round which they could rally the kindred races of the land for one great overwhelming assault.

Indian empire conquered by Indians

The Aztec monarchy (under Montezuma) fell by the hands of its own subjects, under the direction of European sagacity and science. Had it been united, it might have bidden defiance to the invaders. As it was, the capital was dissevered from the rest of the country, and the bolt, which might have passed off comparatively harmless, had the empire been cemented by a common principle of loyalty and patriotism, now found its way into every crack and crevice of the ill-compacted fabric, and buried it in its own ruins.

Loyalty and Patriotism needed

Turmoil from within

Its fate may serve as striking proof, that a government, which does not rest on the sympathies of its subjects, cannot long abide; that human institutions, when not connected with human prosperity and progress, must fall, - if not before the increasing light of civilization, by the hand of violence; by violence from within, if not from without. And who shall lament their fall?"[4]

Analyzing the character of Cortes, Mr. Prescott writes:

Failing of the Age

"One trait more remains to be noticed in the character of this remarkable man; that is his bigotry (in another place, bigotry is called "policy"), the failing of the age, - for, surely, it should be termed only a failing. When we see the land, red with the blood of the wretched native, raised to invoke the blessing of Heaven on the cause which it maintains, we experience something like a sensation of disgust at the act, and a doubt of its sincerity. But this is unjust. We should throw ourselves back...into the age; the age of the Crusades. For every Spanish cavalier, however sordid and selfish might be his private motives, felt himself to be the soldier of the Cross. Many of them would have died in defence of it. Whoever has read the correspondence of Cortes, or, still more, has attended unto the circumstances of his career, will hardly doubt that he would have been among the first to lay down his life for the Faith. He more than once perilled life, and fortune, and the success of his whole enterprise, by the premature and impolitic manner in which he would have forced conversion on the natives.

Spirit of Christianity
lacking

To the more rational spirit of the present day, enlightened by a purer Christianity, it may seem difficult to reconcile gross deviations from morals with such devotion to the cause of religion. But the religion taught in that day was one of form and elaborate ceremony. In the punctilious attention to discipline, the spirit of Christianity was permitted to evaporate. The mind, occupied with forms, thinks little of substance. In a worship that is addressed too exclusively to the senses, it is often the case, that morality become divorced from religion, and the measure of righteousness is determined by the creed rather than by the conduct."[5]

AFTER THE CONQUEST OF MEXICO

Cortes, a
cunning man

"Whatever disregard Cortes may have shown to the political rights of the natives, he manifested a commendable solicitude for their spiritual welfare. He requested the emperor to send out holy men to the country... Twelve Franciscan friars embarked for New Spain, which they reached in 1524... All the inhabitants of the towns through which they passed came out to welcome them. They were met by a brilliant calvalcade, headed by Cortes. The general dismounted, and on bended knee kissed the robes of the principal friar. The natives, filled with amazement at the viceroy's humiliation before men with naked feet and tattered garments, gave them their utmost respect and regarded them as beings of a superior nature. One of the early historians 'does not conceal his admiration of this...condescension of Cortes,' which he pronounces 'one of the most heroical acts of his life!'"[6]

The business of the conversion of the Indians went on:

Ritual

"The Aztec worship was remarkable for its burdensome ceremonial and prepared its votaries (worshippers) for the pomp and splendors of the Romish rituals."[6]

How did the Spaniards convert the natives? Let us read of a quote by a Father Sahagun:

Method of
conversion

"We took the children of the caciques (chiefs) into our schools, where we taught them to read, write, and to chant. The children of the poorer natives were brought together in the court-yard, and instructed there in the Christian faith. After our teaching, one or two brethren took the pupils to some neighboring teocatti,* and, by working at it for a few days, they levelled it to the ground. In this way they demolished, in a short time, all the Aztec temples, great and small, so that not a vestige of them remained."[7]

Rebuilding

Cortes established a system of government for the different, yet antagonistic, races of Indian people. For the first time they were to be brought under a common form of government. He set about repairing the damages of war. He made efforts to find out the latent resources of the country, and to encourage production of those resources.

"The best wealth of the settlers was in the vegetable products of the soil...He had earnestly recommended the crown to require all vessels coming to the country to bring over a certain quantity of seeds and plants. He further stipulated that no one should get a clear title to his estate until he had occupied it eight years. He knew that permanent residence could alone create that interest in the soil, which would lead to its efficient culture."[8]

"New Spain"

"In the prosecution of his great enterprises, Cortes, within three short years after the conquest, had reduced under the dominian of Castile, an extent of country more than 400 leagues (about 1200 miles) in length, as he affirms on the Atlantic coast, and more than 500 leagues (about 1500 miles) on the Pacific coast, and with the exception of a few interior provinces of no great importance, had brought them to a condition of entire tranquility. In accomplishing this, he had freely expended the revenues of the Crown, drawn from tributes similar to those which had been anciently paid by the natives to their own sovereign; and he had, moreover, incurred a large debt on his own account, for which he demanded remuneration from the government. The celebrity of his name, and the dazzling reports of the conquered countries, drew crowds of adventurers to New Spain, who furnished the general with recruits for his various enterprises."[9]

While engrossed with the internal problems of the country, Cortes was still bent on his great plans of discovery.

Strait still needed

"...the letters of Cortes...touch frequently on this favorite topic. 'Your Majesty (Emperor Charles V) may be assured,' he writes, 'that, as I know how much you have at heart the discovery of this great secret strait (the mythical STRAIT OF ANIAN), I shall postpone all interests and projects of my own, some of them of the highest moment, for the fulfillment of this great object.'"[10]

BAJA CALIFORNIA

Always in back of Cortes' mind, there was the desire for riches. In orders to a lieutenant, he said:

"'I am informed that on the coast below which borders on this town (Colima) there are many provinces well populated with people, where it is believed there are many riches, and that in these parts there is one province which is inhabited by women without any men; and it is said of them that they produce their progeny in the same manner as is related in the ancient histories of the Amazons and in order to learn the truth of all this and of whatever there may be on that coast, you shall follow it down so that you may learn the secret of what is related above.'"[11]

Cortes may have been influenced by a novel popular in his day. See Text, under "The name CALIFORNIA."

FORTUN JIMENEZ 1533

After two failures, 1527 and 1532, Cortes set about to outfit two more ships for expeditions into the South Sea, one under command of Captain Diego Becerra with Fortun Jimenez as pilot. They were to learn the end of the coast (The Gulf of California). Also, to find the existence of the supposed "rich islands with pearls." Becerra was not popular with his men; mutiny ensued. Jimenez killed Becerra during the night while he slept, and seized the ship.

Either late in 1533 or early 1534, they reached the Bay of La Paz above the southern tip of the gulf shore of the Peninsula of California where it was said there were pearls. When the Spaniards went ashore they were attacked by savage Indians who killed Jimenez and all but two of his men, who made their way back to Cortes on the mainland. They had unknowingly succeeded in touching, for the first time, the Peninsula of Lower (Baja) California.

CORTES EXPLORES FARTHER (1535)

Cortes was restless in this land of Mexico, known as New Spain, and decided to take three ships himself to explore the South Sea. He marched from the City of Mexico to the Port of Santo Tomas and sailed for the country where Jimenez had been killed. In May of 1535, he entered the Bay La Paz, which he called Santa Cruz. He took the place in the name of Spain. Cortes sailed up the eastern side of the Gulf, afterwards called the Sea of Cortes, and returned to Santa Cruz, where he brought relief to the starving men in a little colony he had established there.

Cortes was disappointed that his arch rival, Antonio de Mendoza, had been appointed Viceroy of New Spain. Cortes decided to return to his wife and children in Spain. He left the colony of Santa Cruz in charge of Francisco de Ulloa. He charged Ulloa with further explorations of discovery of the South Sea and gave him three ships.

**Great military
captain**

"Whoever would form a just estimate of this remarkable man must not confine himself to the history of the Conquest. His military career, indeed, places him on a level with the greatest captains of his age. But the period subsequent to the Conquest affords different, and in some respects nobler, points of view for the study of his character. For we then see him devising a system of government for the motley and antagonistic races, so to speak, now first brought under a common dominion; repairing the mischiefs of war; and employing his efforts to detect the latent resources of the country, and to stimulate it to its highest power of production. The narrative seems tame, after the recital of exploits as bold and adventurous as those of a paladin (legendary hero) romance. But it is only perusal of this narrative, that one can form an adequate conception of the acute and comprehensive genius of Cortes."[12]

**Nobler abilities seen
after the Conquest**

FRANCISCO DE ULLOA 1539

At that time, Baja California was thought to be an island and was so pictured on all the maps. This error was corrected by Ulloa, under orders of Cortes.

**Ulloa obediently
explores Gulf of
California**

July 8, 1539, Ulloa and three small vessels left Acapulco, Mexico, towards the unexplored South Sea. At the beginning of their voyage they lost one ship and all aboard. They actually sailed the Gulf of California but were disappointed they found no outlet, which they could not find because it is a gulf. California was still considered an island.

They came to that part of the Gulf where the distance between the two coasts is narrowed by the Island Angel de la Guarda, but they could find no opening to the Sea. They began to wonder at this. Perhaps this is not an island after all. What we take for granted now, was puzzling to the seamen of the sixteenth century:

"Whereupon wee began to be of divers opinion, some thinking that this coast of Santa Cruz was a firme land, and that it joined with the continent of Nueva Espanna, others thought the contrary, and that they were nothing else but islands that were to the westward. And in this sort we proceeded forward, having the land on both sides of us, so farre that wee all began to wonder at it."[13]

They found where the Colorado River empties into the Gulf. It remained for Father Ugarte, a Jesuit Priest and explorer, to re-discover that Baja California was really a Peninsula. (See Text, page 124.)

Returning to Santa Cruz, Ulloa and his men rested and provisioned their ships. They left from Santa Cruz to cruise along the western coast. Attempting to round the southern point of the peninsula, they ran into heavy gales. They recorded: "...great rain and lightning and darkness every night, also the winds grew so raging tempestuous that they made us all to quake and pray continually to God to ayde us."[14] It took them eight days to round the point of the

peninsula and head north.

Landing on shore in December, they had to fight off an attack by Indians. During that month they encountered heavy northwest winds. January 5, 1540, they landed on Cedros Island, so-called because of the number of slender cedar trees. This Island they took in the name of Spain.

They wished to continue north along the coast of California but their ships had been battered by the storms, their provisions were low, so in April they decided to send one ship home. Ulloa was to continue in the command vessel. Ulloa turned northward. He continued to about 29 degrees north latitude but was compelled by strong winds to turn back to New Spain. He just missed Alta California.

Ulloa was the first to navigate the gulf, to which he gave the name "Sea of Cortes," now the Gulf of California. He explored both shores of the peninsula, determining it was not an island. The results of his discovery were published on a map in 1541 on which CALIFORNIA appears as the name of the lower part of the peninsula.

PRELUDE TO THE DISCOVERY OF UPPER CALIFORNIA

Cortes, a Spaniard, a Catholic, a soldier of fortune, a seeker of gold, was used by God to cleanse Mexico and the Indian population of barbaric idolatry. Cortes was also a soldier of the Cross. However misled were they as to the means they used to convert the infidel, they still were carrying out Christ's commands to *"Go ye into all the world and preach the gospel to every creature."* (Mark 16:15) It is the Hand of God that guides the paths of history. Mexico had to be Christianized before God allowed the discovery and possession of the land, California; first, Baja (Lower) California, then the Gulf of California, next Alta (Upper) California.

THE NAME "CALIFORNIA"

"The Lord reigneth; let the earth rejoice; let the multitude of isles be glad thereof." (Psalm 97:1)

Cortes had heard of a wonderful island of untold wealth to the north of Mexico. Cortes had sent out Jimenez to explore the north in 1533. Jimenez was killed, as we have just learned, but his men brought back to Mexico stories of riches. Cortes himself then went to investigate Baja California. Whether or not Cortes named this land "California" is hard to determine. Some say he did,

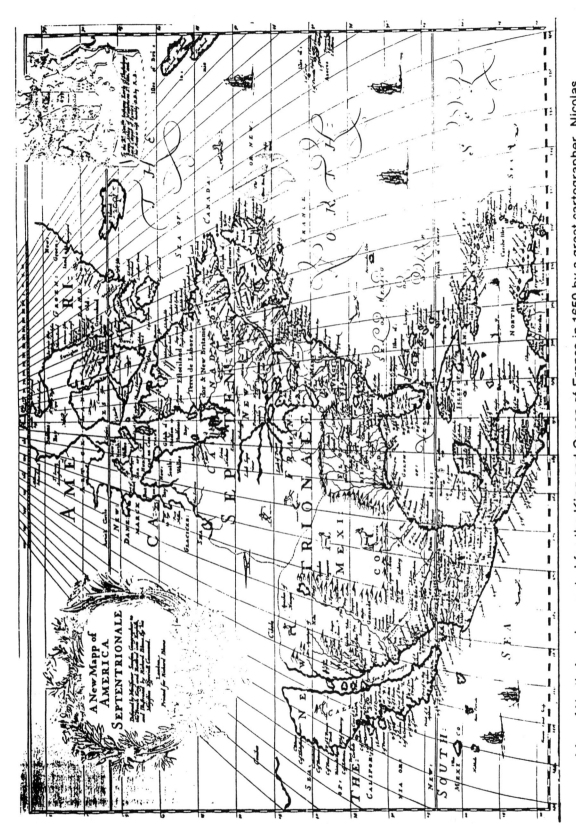

Map of North America created for the King and Queen of France in 1650 by a great cartographer, Nicolas Sanson. The map impressed the King of England and he had it translated and illustrated for use of his own royal court in 1670. This map shows California as an island completely separated from the North American Continent.

and others believe he could not possibly have given the name "California," a land of gold and pearls, to the barren shores they discovered. It was a mystery.

It remained for an American of stature to uncover why Cortes may possibly have given the name "California" to this western land. Reverend Edward Everett Hale, a Boston Unitarian minister, author of Man Without a Country, discovered an old Spanish novel in 1862, entitled Las Sergas de Esplandian (The Deeds of Esplandian). It had been written about 1510 by Garci Ordonez de Montalvo. It was a sequel to Montalvo's earlier novel Amadis of Gaul. Reverend Hale found in his research that just before California became the goal of foreign expeditions, especially those of a Spanish nature, there was reprinted in Spain this story of chivalry that had once been very popular in the time of the Crusades but which had come down from great antiquity as a story of traditional exploits.

Montalvo's romantic novel, The Deeds of Esplandian, was popular with educated Spaniards of Cortes' day. This novel describes a land in the western waters in the form of a great island, ruled by the beautiful heroine of the story known as Queen Calafia; the island over which she ruled was called "California." The description in the story stated that this wonderful island was on "the right hand of the Indies, very close to the side of the Terrestrial Paradise."

Queen Calafia's subjects "lived after the manner of Amazons." Calafia and her followers had trained griffins (large and ferocious birds) to capture and devour men, who were not allowed as subjects in their land. To gain fame for herself and her women subjects, the beautiful Calafia joined with the pagan Turks (Infidels) in their siege of Christian Constantinople. The griffins, unleashed to take part in the battle for the warrior women, were supposed to attack the Christian men; however, they indiscriminately devoured the Christians and the pagans. Queen Calafia lost face and so decided to enter the battle herself by offering to lead all the hosts of the pagans against all the hosts of the Christians, thereby proving the superiority of her women by capturing Constantinople for the pagans.

As the story unfolds, the Queen entered into battle against the Christian Crusader, Amadis of Gaul, King of England, and his handsome son, Esplandian; however, he loved and later wed the daughter of the King of Greece. Calafia and her forces lost the battle. She was personally conquered by Amadis and was taken prisoner by the Christians for a year. During this time she had an opportunity to learn of Christianity. She finally made a plea that if they would give her a Prince, a Christian for her husband, she would be subject unto him and would become a Christian. In her words, "For, as I have seen the ordered order of your religion, and the great disorder of all others, I have seen that it is clear that the law which you follow must be the truth, while that which we follow is lying and falsehood." So, Christianity was reportedly brought to California, an island "famous for its great abundance of gold and precious stones."[1]

"Thus saith the Lord...Call unto me, and I will answer thee, and shew thee great and mighty things, which thou knowest not." (Jer. 33:2,3)

Alta California   Now, at last, we enter Alta California with Cabrillo, who led the Spanish expedition along the Pacific Coast. To our knowledge, this was the first time men of the white race had ever set foot on the western coast of California.

Again, they were looking for the illusive Strait of Anian, (see Picture) which they thought would establish a shorter route from Spain to the East Indies.

The Strait of Anian may have been the Bering Strait, discovered in 1728 by Vitus Bering, a Danish navigator sent out by Peter the Great, Czar of Russia. In 1903, Captain Roald Amundsen sailed through winding channels of Arctic Sea from Christiana (now Oslo, Norway) and in 1906 steered through the Bering Strait to San Francisco.

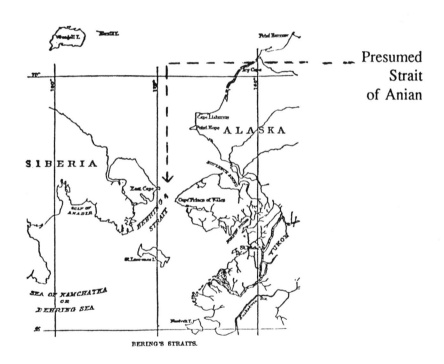

Presumed Strait of Anian

Map: From CHRISTOPHER COLUMBUS, by Justin Winsor

Coast of
Alta California   The Spaniards did not find the Strait of Anian, nor a waterway through America for the longed-for shorter route to the Orient. However, they did make a fabulous discovery when Cabrillo and his pilot, Ferrelo, extended knowledge of the Pacific Coast of California for at least 800 miles.

91

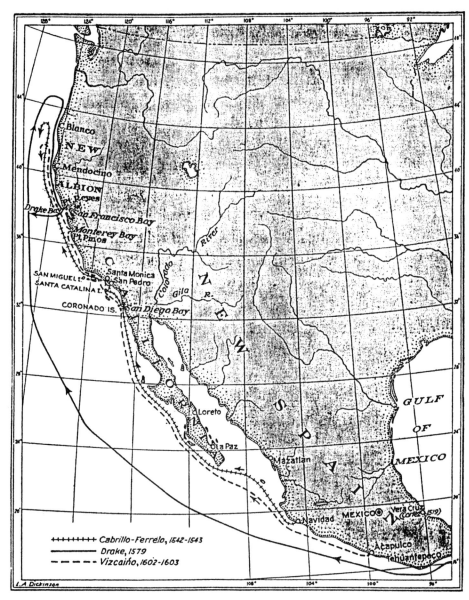

MAP SHOWING EXPLORATIONS ALONG THE COAST OF MEXICO
AND THE CALIFORNIAS

From: NEW CALIFORNIA THE GOLDEN,
by Rockwell D. Hunt

The story of Cabrillo and his pilot, Ferrelo, is told more in the manner of a ship's log. There are dates involved, and names given to this strange land by the Spaniards. It is interesting to us to learn the Spanish counterparts of the names and places we are so familiar with in California. For instance, we all readily recognize Fort Ross on our California coast, 75 miles northwest of the Golden Gate. The name they gave to the Northwest Cape opposite Fort Ross was El Cabo de Pinos because of the dense fir trees which grow down to the sea.

Dependence on God's Protection and Guidance

As we sail along with Cabrillo, let us see through his eyes the beautiful but barren coast, encounter the terrific storms, and feel the loneliness of the vast sea. His sailors suffered the cold and wet and hunger in frail ships far from home; they lost their commander but still continued their investigation of the California coast. It is a remarkable story of endurance, and one of faith. Constantly they depended upon God's protection and guidance. The result was knowledge for the European nations of the Pacific Coast, which was unknown until the Cabrillo expedition.

JUAN RODRIQUEZ-CABRILLO 1542

Cabrillo to explore unknown Coast

Juan Rodriquez-Cabrillo was a Portuguese mariner in the service of Spain. It is believed that he served in New Spain under Cortes in the conquest of Mexico. In 1542, the Vice-roy of New Spain, Mendoza, chose him to explore the unknown coast of Alta California.

June 27, 1542, Cabrillo sailed from Navidad on the coast of Mexico with two very poorly built, outfitted, and manned sailing vessels, the San Salvador, the flag-ship, and the Victoria, which had no deck.

Reached Ulloa's farthest limit

Cabrillo and his men started their expedition late in the season and ran into violent storms. It took them four days to cross the mouth of the Gulf of California. Finally they reached the Cedros Islands, discovered by Ulloa, and at length reached Cabo Bajo, 29 degrees 56 minutes latitude, believed to be Ulloa's farthest northern limit. From here on northward, they sailed in uncharted waters. Dr. Hunt remarked:

> "On and on sailed the two little ships, alone on the vast unknown sea, alone with their God in the wilderness of waters...Their brave captain did not read there the destiny that was in store for him - to make one of the most famous discoveries in the Spanish conquest of America, and to lay down his life in the doing of it."[1]

San Diego, 1542

September 28, 1542, three months after leaving Mexico, Cabrillo entered "a very good closed port, which they named San Miguel," known to us today as San Diego Harbor. They went ashore and for the first time met hostile Indians. Three of the Spaniards were hurt. As to the native Indians they encountered, here and elsewhere:

93

Christian kindness	"Cabrillo treated the Indians with kindness, making them gifts of beads and other trifles and endeavoring in every way to win their confidence. In this respect California is more fortunate in its early history than Mexico and South America, for its soil was never drenched with the blood of the unfortunate natives. The leaders of the various expeditions coming up this way, by sea and by land, were all men of superior character, and they came under strict orders from the home government to be just and forbearing in their dealings with the Indians."[2]
Catalina Island Santa Monica	October 7, 1542, they landed on Santa Catalina Island where they made friends with the natives. Their next stop was into the Bay of Santa Monica, which they called Bahia de los Fumos because of the many "smokes" they saw rising from the hills.
Ventura	October 10, they arrived in front of a beautiful large valley. The Indians of the village there came out to the harbor to greet them in many fine canoes, so the Spaniards called it El Pueblo de las Canoas. They were near today's Santa Buenaventura.
Santa Barbara Channel	October 13, they sailed through the Santa Barbara Channel, anchoring at Rincon, Carpinteria, above Point Goleta, at Canada del Refugio, and at Gaviota Pass.
Dos Pueblos	October 16, they dropped anchor at Los Dos Pueblos, the two towns which still bear the names given them by Cabrillo. These towns were built on either side of a small stream but the Indians of each differed considerably. They were of different race and language, and they could not communicate with each other. On one side they were short, thick, and dark; on the other side, they were tall, slender, and light.
Point Conception	October 18, they reached Point Conception, the western extremity of the Santa Barbara Channel. Here they found a large Indian population; the natives were superior to all the others they had seen during their voyage.
San Miguel and Santa Rosa Islands	At Point Conception they began encountering severe storms. They sighted the islands of San Miguel and Santa Rosa, which they named the Islas de San Lucas. They took refuge at an harbor at San Miguel Island, now known as Cuyler's Harbor.
	Here, tragedy struck the commander:
Cabrillo hurt	"While at this island Cabrillo met with an accident by which his arm was broken near the shoulder; and although he must have suffered severly and continuously as a result of it, during the little more than two months that he survived, it in no way relaxed his energies or lessened his determination to push his explorations to the farthest limit possible with the means he had."[3]

Gaviota Pass

After Cabrillo's unfortunate accident, they still continued northward in search of a great river they heard existed on the other side of Point Conception, which they had named Cape Galera. The winds were so great they were forced to anchor at Gaviota Pass, which they named El Pueblo de las Sardinas because the Indians kindly supplied them with sardines.

It was at Gaviota Pass that some of the native men were so friendly. The Indians went aboard the ships and while the Spaniards played bagpipes and a small drum, the natives danced and enjoyed themselves. It was a time of relief and release from the rigors of the sea.

Santa Lucia
Mountains

November 6, they headed out to sea but again ran into terrible storms. They spied the Santa Lucia Range of mountains which they named Las Sierras de San Martin. During this storm the two ships lost each other. It was a frightening time.

Near Fort Ross

November 14, the flagship San Salvador reached the Northwest Cape, which they named Cabo de Pinos, near our Fort Ross. They had passed by the Bay of Monterey, the Golden Gate, the Bay of San Francisco, and Drake's Bay, without knowing they were there.

Drake's Bay

November 15, they rejoiced and thanked God that they were again reunited with the little ship, Victoria. They did drop anchor at Drake's Bay but did not land. They called the land Bahia de los Pinos.

Farallones

November 18, they again missed the Golden Gate but noted the Gulf of the Farallones.

Cabrillo died,
San Miguel Island

November 23, because of storms, they were forced into their safe harbor on San Miguel Island to rest. Here, on January 3, 1543, Cabrillo died.

CHARACTER OF CABRILLO

We agree with Dr. Hunt that this was a man of courage, kindness, and faith:

A Man of Honor;
I Tim. 6: 12

"Herrara (historian) speaks of him as 'a man of courage and honor and a skilled navigator.' That he was beloved of his men is proved by the statement that 'they returned to Navidad sorrowful for having lost their commander.' His determined struggle to go on with the voyage despite the severe injury which he had suffered bespeaks his courage and endurance. His devotion to duty is shown in his dying charge to his men to carry on the voyage and explore all that coast as far as possible."[4]

Ferrelo headed
north; I Cor. 4:2

Bartolmi Ferrelo, the pilot of the flagship, San Salvador, obediently headed north.

February 25, 1543, he had again reached the Northwest Cape at Fort Ross, as far North as Cabrillo had gone.

Oregon

Ferrelo guided them as far as 41-1/2 degrees latitude, opposite the Rogue River in Oregon. However, they encountered furious storms. With the sea breaking in upon them, especially the Victoria with no deck, they decided to return home. These men were tired, frightened, and hungry.

March 3, 1543 they turned homeward.

Ship lost

Once more the two ships lost each other. Weeks passed and the San Salvador gave up the Victoria in deep sadness. The flagship sought shelter behind Santa Cruz Island.

March 5, they dropped anchor at Ventura, at Santa Catalina, and San Diego, looking for the Victoria.

Thanks for that
which was lost

March 25, they reached Cedros Island and two days later were overjoyed to spot the little lost Victoria. Prayers and thanksgiving were offered by all.

Better ships
needed

April 14, 1543 is the date when they arrived back in Navidad. Ferrelo wisely advised his government that such a voyage as they had made should only be undertaken with much stronger ships, better sails and rigging, and ample provisions.

Cabrillo,
"Columbus
of California"

The Cabrillo-Ferrelo expedition traversed the entire coast line of Alta California. Cabrillo has been called the "Columbus of California." This was a momentous happening in the Christian History of our land, for it gave to the world our beloved California.

Author's Personal
Note;
Ps. 119:27

(Here your author would like to insert a personal note: "The period of discovery, mostly by the Latin nations of the world, and the consequent discovery of California by the Spaniards, is a time of history that I had chosen to write about very briefly in the first edition of THE MAKING OF AMERI- CAN CALIFORNIA. I veered away from it, so anxious was I to write of the providential Protestant aspect of the formation of California as a State. But I have learned, God is no respecter of persons. He uses men and nations for His Purpose. He uses those courageous and faithful individuals who are ready to do His Will, to strive toward opening a new continent by sea, or brave the elements to create new paths for new nations.

"I have learned, through Christ, His Story, of the sacrifice that many discoverers, explorers, and settlers have had to make to keep alive the Chain of

Christianity. It is again the story of our dear Lord's Self-sacrifice, and I am in awe of it, and blest by it. I see it again and again throughout all His-Story.")

Settlement
came slowly

After the discovery of the coast of California by Cabrillo, it was more than 225 years before Alta California would be permanently settled.

In the meantime, knowledge of the California coast and harbors aided the Manila galleons in their trade with Europe.

Hispanic Museum, New York City

From: NEW CALIFORNIA THE GOLDEN,
by Rockwell D. Hunt

"...straightway he constrained his disciples to get into the ship, and go to the other side...

...when he had sent them away, he departed into a mountain to pray.

...when even was come, the ship was in the midst of the sea, and he alone on the land.

And he saw them toiling in rowing; for the wind was contrary unto them: and about the fourth watch of the night he cometh unto them, walking upon the sea, and would have passed by them.

But when they saw him walking upon the sea, they supposed it had been a spirit, and cried out:

For they all saw him, and were troubled. And immediately he talked with them, and saith unto them, Be of good cheer: it is I; be not afraid.

And he went up unto them into the ship..."

(Mark 6:45-51)

Ships important

Ships were an important element in Christianity. They were important, too, not only in the discovery of Alta California, but in creating a demand for further knowledge of the California coast. It was largely due to the shipping trade that safe harbors along the coast of California were sought by the mariners and merchants trading between the Philippine Islands and Spain.

Acapulco

Spain used Acapulco on the western coast of Mexico, "New Spain," as a port for her ships, called <u>Manila Galleons</u>.

1566

The galleons gradually had replaced the caravels that were used by Columbus and Vespucius, and the brigantines built by Balboa and Cortes. These galleons were larger and better ships, although clumsy. They were round-stemmed vessels with a few small cannon and catapults, somewhat like huge crossbows, on board. They were built for the merchant trade between Spain and the Philippine Islands. The first merchant galleon was sent to Manila in the Philippines from Acapulco, Mexico, in 1566. This trade continued for more than 200 years.

Philippine Islands

The Philippine Islands, discovered earlier by Magellan, was the place where Spain obtained rich cargo. Traders from China and Japan, the coasts of Siam (now Thailand), Borneo, the Moluccas, and other islands and countries brought their wares to the Philippine Islands to trade with Europe. Cargoes of silks, brocades, velvets, carpets, ivory, spices of all sorts, gems, gum, cotton cloth, thread, needlework, jewelry, cutlery, earthenware, plaited hats, and other goods not made in Europe were easily obtained.

Need for safe harbors on California coast

The voyage sometimes took six months. It was impossible to store fresh food on board for that length of time, so eventually the crew was limited to salt meat and hard biscuits until they could reach land again. Water was stored in jars in every part of the ship and they depended upon fresh rainwater to replenish their supply. An harbor on the California coast was needed to restore and refit the ships. Piracy was also a big factor in hastening their need for safe harbors.

Spain predominant

Spain claimed that no other nation was entitled to send its ships into the Pacific. On the Atlantic side, her colonial regulations forbid any trade with foreigners. Spain was stronger at sea than any other nation. England had just begun to build ships of war; France was poorly provided with ships; the Netherlanders seemed to be just beginning to learn to develop capable sailors.

Challenge by England

England was the first country to challenge the authority of the Pope to regulate the unexplored part of the world. Queen Elizabeth gradually encouraged her subjects to seek trade wherever they could find it. Englishmen were glad to plunder the rich cargoes of the Spanish galleons. The galleons' trade route was from the Philippines, along the coast of California to Acapulco, then overland by pack animals to Vera Cruz on the Atlantic coast of Mexico and on to Spain, or by sea through the Straits of Magellan and on to Spain. In either case, it was a long and dangerous journey.

Enter Drake

In 1577, Queen Elizabeth commissioned Francis Drake, a young and daring English seaman, to arrange an expedition into the Pacific. To England, and especially to Drake, the Spanish galleons became desirable "trophies."

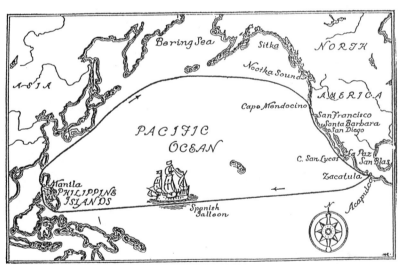

MAP SHOWING ROUTE OF MANILA GALLEONS

From: NEW CALIFORNIA THE GOLDEN,
by Rockwell D. Hunt

99

"...I will walk at liberty: for I seek thy precepts.

I will speak of thy testimonies also before kings, and will not be ashamed.

And I will delight myself in thy commandments, which I have loved."
(Psalms 119:45-47)

Catholicism versus Protestantism

Francis Drake represents a period in history in which there was a great struggle between the Catholic and Protestant forces, religiously, economically, and politically.

This affected America:

Spanish decline affected founding of America

"As regards America, it may be observed that from 1492 until about 1570 the exploring and colonizing activity of Spain was immense, insomuch that upon the southern half of the New World it has left its stamp forever...After 1570 this wonderful manifestation of Spanish energy practically ceased, and this is a fact of supreme importance in the history of North America. But for this abrupt cessation of Spanish energy the English settlements at Jamestown and Plymouth would have been in quite... dangerous a position.

Spain exhausted energies

In 1492 Spain was relieved of a task which had long absorbed all her vital energies, the work of freeing her soil from the dominion of the Moors.* In 1570 she was entering upon another task which not only absorbed but wellnigh exhausted her energies, the attempt to suppress Protestantism in Europe and to subdue the revolted Netherlands.** When she had once put her hand to this work, Spain had no surplus vitality left for extending her sway in America."[1]

Manila Galleons

Until challenged by the English, the Spanish galleons, with their rich cargoes, traveled between New Spain and Manila with no fear of enemy attack. Spain was the undisputed and most powerful nautical nation of the world. She felt protected by the Pope's edict which gave her the rights to the Pacific.

Spain's desire to convert England

However, Queen Elizabeth of England did not recognize the Papal Decree. Officially Spain and England were at peace, but unofficially there was a great contention between them. At the bottom of this contention was the "holy" desire upon Spain's part to Catholicize Protestant England. Toward this end, Spain planned many years to build a great Armada to conquer England. In fact, when the Armada was finally ready for its "holy crusade," King Philip was so sure of victory that he arranged for ecclesiastics to be on board for the purpose of converting the people after England was won.

England's challenge

Queen Elizabeth finally made the decision to challenge Spain's sea supremacy in the Pacific. Francis Drake had earned a reputation for being an outstanding navigator, and practically fearless. He became an excellent choice for the Queen's purpose of striking at the Spanish King Philip II.

SIR FRANCIS DRAKE 1579

Drake's heritage

Francis Drake's father was a Devonshire parson, whose counsel was dear to Francis' heart. Just as influential in the life of Philip of Spain was his mentor, the Holy Roman Emperor.

Drake, of
Puritan faith

Francis Drake was a Puritan. He was instilled by his preacher father in an unwavering faith in the Word of God. They also held the Roman Church to be outside of the kingdom of God. This motivated Francis in his zealous mission against the King of Spain. During the engagements of the Armada battles, Drake held unswerving confidence that God was on his side.

Seaman apprentice

Francis Drake was born in England about 1545. Early in life he was apprenticed to the master of a channel coasting vessel, and later sailed with Sir John Hawkins, who was to become Admiral of the English fleet which challenged the Spanish Armada. Drake was to be the Vice-Admiral.

Drake had been thoroughly prepared for Queen Elizabeth's confidence in him by his many voyages to various parts of the world, including the West Indies. He had a reputation for extraordinary courage and judgment.

"His Spanish prisoners speak of him as one of the greatest mariners and navigators in the world, and he did not hesitate to claim that distinction for himself."[2]

England pressed to
colonize new lands

England was pressed to challenge Spain because of past injuries Spain had dealt her; because England wished to extend her trade with the ports Spain had closed to her; because of England's quest for new lands to colonize; and because England, too, was searching for the Strait of Anian.

The Golden Hind

For this special expedition, the Queen and other private individuals equipped five vessels at Plymouth, England. The Pelican, Drake's flagship, was later rechristened the Golden Hind.

1577, secret
destination

The destination of these ships leaving Plymouth November 15, 1577 was purportedly Alexandria. But in reality they were headed for the Pacific, and Spanish territory. They wound their way through the Straits of Magellan, the first Englishmen to do so. Two of the ships had been destroyed, another disappeared in the darkness, and the fourth ship deserted and returned to England. On October 28, 1578, after fifty-one days of terrific storms, the lone Golden Hind landed on the extreme end of Tierra del Fuego. One of the sailors recorded:

Providential deliverance

"The violent storm without intermission; the impossibility to come to anchor; the want of opportunity to spread any sayle; the most mad seas; the lee shores; the dangerous rocks; the contrary and most intolerable winds; the impossible passage out; the desperate tarrying there; and inevitable perils on every side, did lay before us so small a liklihood to escape present destruction that if the special providence of God himselfe had not supported us, we could never have endured that wofull state...We escaped from these straits and miseries, as it were through the needles ey (that God might have the greater glory in our delivery) by the great and effectual care and travell of our general, the Lord's instrument there in."[3]

Trophies

Spanish booty was Drake's goal. He found a rich prize in the Valparaiso harbor. The surprised Spaniards hastily abandoned their ship and the town. The Englishmen gained gold, jewels, provisions, and merchandise. They also commandeered the Spanish ship's pilot, Nuno da Silva. Hereafter, the English "buccaneers" sacked ship after ship. Dr. Hunt remarked: "...during the whole of his operation on the West Coast, he (Drake) never killed a man."

As to his religion:

The Bible

"He professed to be very religious, and every day before sitting down to eat, at midday and when they supped, he had an uncovered table brought out. Upon this he placed a large Bible, and, kneeling down, bareheaded, he read from it. It was for taking part in these ceremonies that the Portuguese pilot, Nuno da Silva, was afterwards tried for heresy by the Spanish Inquisition."[4]

Nova Albion

Upon entering the Pacific, the expedition would explore the western shore of America from the Strait of Magellan to the presumed Strait of Anian. Beyond the limits of New Spain the northwest corner of North America, the expedition would make a "worthy attempt at discovery" of "very large Forreign Dominions" and search for the Strait of Anian. Although Drake abandoned his search, he did discover a "very large Forreign Dominion" on the Northwest coast of America which he named "Nova Albion" (New England).

"This country our General named Albion, or Nova Albion, and that for two causes, the one in respect of the white bancks and cliffes which lie toward the sea; the other that it might have some affinity, even in name also, with our country, which was sometime called."[5]

A year and an half after leaving Plymouth, Drake had navigated the Straits of Magellan off the tip of South America, endured raging storms, successfully captured Spanish treasure off the Spanish galleons, and unsuccessfully sought the Strait of Anian in "vile, thicke, and stinking fogges" off the coast of Oregon. After so many months at sea, Drake was in need of a safe harbor in which to careen his lone-surviving and leaking flagship, the <u>Golden Hind</u>.

California Harbor On June 17, 1579, Drake sailed his ship into "a faire and good Baye" near 38 degrees north latitude. He spent thirty-six days in this California harbor. He and his crew established a fortress, repaired the ship, traded with the friendly Mi-wok Indians who thought him a "fair God returned," made a short excursion to the interior, and observed the flora and fauna. In addition, he erected a brass plate commemorating the arrival of the <u>Golden Hind</u> in the harbor, and took possession of this discovery for Queen Elizabeth of England.

The Plaque The only physical evidence of Drake's presence in California is a Plaque, which was discovered overlooking Point San Quentin by a young man who climbed a hill looking for a place to relax after changing a flat tire in 1936. The brass plate reads:

> "Bee it knowne unto all men by these presents June, 17, 1579. By the Grace of God and in the name of Herr Majesty Queen Elizabeth of England and herr sucessors forever I take possession of this kin dome whose kind and people freely resigne their right and title in the whole land unto Herr Majesties keepeing now named by me to be knowne unto all men as Nova Albion. Francis Drake."***

Metallurgical and historical tests have proven the plate to be authentic, including the discovery of mineralized plant cells in the area of the "sixpence" hole.

Drake's Bay The actual site of his landing on the coast of California and the identity of the bay in which he moored have been disputed for more than three centuries. For decades the landing site was assumed to be Drake's Bay in Marin County, north of San Francisco. Some historians believe that Drake and the <u>Golden Hind</u> actually passed through the Golden Gate and anchored near Point San Quentin on the Marin shore of San Francisco Bay.***

Circumnavigation of the globe On July 21, 1579, Drake weighed anchor and departed the bay, landing the following day at the Farallon Islands before continuing across the Pacific on his voyage of circumnavigation of the globe. In September of 1580, Drake arrived home in England.

Early English interest in California In 1581, Queen Elizabeth knighted him and he is known to us as Sir Francis Drake. In the eyes of the Queen he had done a great service for England. He returned with an extremely rich booty from the Spanish ships; his was the second expedition to circumnavigate the globe and the first Englishman to do so; he marked the beginning of English supremacy at sea; and his landing on the coast of California foreshadowed English interest in obtaining California.

Different ideologies

Sir Francis Drake played a significant role in the defeat of Spain's "Invincible" Armada, which was destroyed in the English Channel in 1588. There was a strong belief in England that the forces of England and the forces of Spain represented the antagonistic religious views of Godliness and anti-Christ. Was this to be the battle of Armageddon?

Protestantism protected

With the defeat of the Spanish Armada, Spain's maritime supremacy had received a fatal blow. This allowed the English to proceed with colonization of America with little hindrance from Catholic Spain. This helped to keep alive the Chain of Christianity. The colonization of America, and subsequently the founding of California, was to become primarily a Protestant thrust.

Determination of Philip of Spain

We only have space for a portion of this fascinating and dramatic event. The Spanish Armada was a tremendous undertaking. Early in the 1580's Spain planned the "Enterprise of England." Philip II of Spain asked his admiral for an estimate of the naval forces needed for such an enterprise. The admiral's final estimate showed an appreciation of English naval strength.

Gigantic undertaking

The Marquis of Santa Cruz wanted 150 great ships and all the galleons available, all heavily armed merchant ships, 300 auxiliary craft – to be manned by 30,000 mariners to carry 64,000 soldiers. In addition, Philip would need 30,000 infantry and 4,000 calvary for land forces. These figures were probably correct to accomplish the mission, but were exhorbitant when considered financially. They also were counting on the English Catholics to help them.

Philip's personal war

Out of two plans, Philip made one of his own. The main function of the Armada was to convoy a landing force. It was a desperate gamble to conquer England or lose his whole army. Philip feared war with England but the execution of the Catholic Mary, Queen of Scots, beheaded by Elizabeth I of England, made Philip more eager to continue with his Enterprise.

Drake's personal war

Francis Drake also carried a personal vendetta against the Spanish for an earlier incident in the harbor of San Juan de Ulua with John Hawkins, where Spanish treachery forced them to return to Plymouth in a leaky little "bark" causing Drake to lose his entire investment.

Drake's circumnavigation of the world for England, his rich Spanish booty, his further raids upon Spanish galleons earned him a world-wide reputation. Because of him, no silver from Peru or Mexico had crossed the Atlantic in 1586; some great merchants of Seville were all but ruined; and there had been a minor panic among King Philip's bankers. In the eyes of the Spaniards, Francis Drake was a pirate. In the eyes of Drake, the Spanish Catholics represented Antichrist.

The Decisive Action off Gravelines
(Drake in the *Revenge* attacking Medina Sidonia in the *San Martin*)
By Oswald W. Brierly, R.W.S.

Spanish Commander Don Pedro de Valdez of the NUESTRA SENORA DEL ROSARIO surrendering to Sir Francis Drake, 1588.

To delay the Armada, in May of 1587, Drake made a very daring raid in Cadiz Harbor. Drake estimated he had sunk, or burned, or captured thirty-seven vessels there. He boasted he had "singed the king of Spain's beard." Drake knew beards grow again.

Drake warned the Queen that he knew Spain was preparing daily for an invasion of England; that the Spanish forces were alarmingly large; and that England should immediately reinforce her naval strength.

In June of 1587, Drake's foresight and brilliant strategy are seen in the following incident. At Cape St. Vincent, in the Azores off the coast of Portugal, Drake captured small boats which carried ordinary freight around the shores of Spain. He found them laden with cooper's stores. He knew their value. The navies of those days used casks as a prime necessity not only for storing water and wine but for salt meat, salt fish, biscuits, and all sorts of provisions. For light casks, well-seasoned barrel staves were essential. Drake burned the ones he found being transported to Spain. When the Armada finally sailed, its water barrels proved to be leaky and foul; much food spoiled because of green barrel staves and ill-made casks. One historian noted: "Burning those barrel staves was probably a graver blow to Spain than burning the ships in Cadiz Bay." It was a crafty act on Drake's part.

There were many providential happenings in this war of ideals which took place in the English Channel in 1588. It is an interesting study. And the outcome?

The results of the defeat of the Spanish Armada were far-reaching:

1. It demonstrated that the religion of one country should not be imposed upon the people of another country.

2. After 1588, the major states in Europe were starting to feel freer, to develop their own idea of nationality and religion.

3. The defeat of the Armada stood as an example of unwavering faith in the defence of liberty, of the triumph of right over wrong, of the strength of freedom against tyranny, even as David conquered Goliath.

Protestant England was free to colonize America.

"...Jesus...saw much people, and was moved with compassion toward them,
*   because they were as sheep not having a shepherd...*
...his disciples came unto him and said...
Send them away, that they may...buy themselves bread: for they have nothing
*   to eat.*
He saith unto them, How many loaves have ye?...they say, Five, and two fishes.
And when he had taken the five loaves and two fishes, he looked up to heaven,
*   and blessed, and brake the loaves, and gave them to his disciples to set*
*   before them; and the two fishes divided he among them all.*
And they did all eat, and were filled."
                    (Mark 6:34,35,36,38,41,42)

Sir Francis Drake had shocked the Spaniards into arming their Manila galleons; a foreign government establishing itself on the California coast was a frightening possibility.

Hazardous trip from Manila to Acapulco

Spain used Acapulco, on the coast of Mexico, as the starting point of her trade with the Philippine Islands. Luxury items such as silks and spices were a lucrative cargo for the Manila galleons. However, the heavily laden vessels returning from Manila back to Acapulco experienced an hazardous trip, often taking from seven to nine months. Supplies of food and water became a problem for such a long voyage. Also, storms were a problem to the unwieldy Manila galleons; not all the ships returned to Acapulco.

Safe harbor on California coast needed

Principally for these reasons, the Vice-roy of Mexico appointed Sebastian Rodriquez Cermenho, an able Portuguese navigator, "to explore and mark out all the parts of the entire course from the islands," in April of 1594. A safe harbor on the California coast was desperately needed. They needed a place where a galleon could be warned of the presence of pirates on the coast; a place where the crew could rest, replenish their provisions, and repair their ships.

1595

July 5, 1595 Cermenho sailed in the San Augustin from the port of Cavite in the Philippines bound for the coast of Alta California.

November 4, 1595 the coast of New Spain began to appear. They were a little north of Eureka, above 41 degrees. On the fifth, they sighted Cape Mendocino.

Drake's Bay

They finally anchored in Drake's Bay where Sir Francis Drake had been sixteen years before. There they encountered friendly California Indians. Cermenho took possession of the land for his King, and named the port San Francisco, confusing later historians.

A providential launch

Cermenho and his men made a short excursion into the interior. Then, providentially, they built a launch, in which they hoped to explore the coast closer to shore. Late in November, when the launch was nearly completed, a storm capsized the <u>San Augustin</u>. The ship and its entire cargo and provisions were lost. The little launch was all they had left to transport seventy men to Navidad, their home port, a distance of over 2,000 miles.

Their journey home is a sad story of suffering. Cermenho must have been a courageous and able leader. Mrs. Sanchez, historian, remarked:

Endurance and Courage

"The rather meagre accounts of this voyage shows it to have been one of the most remarkable for endurance and courage in the annals of the Pacific Ocean."[1]

Cermenho, faithful to assignment

They passed by the Farallones, not noticing San Francisco Bay as they passed by, and they called Monterey Bay <u>San Pedro</u>, which also confused later historians. The little launch with its weak and starving crew continued down the California coast. Cermenho never stopped making his careful survey, according to his instructions.

Near the Baja California coast, they experienced what they called a "miracle:"

Supply of fish

"We went on shore, where we found many wild onions and prickly pears, and likewise God willed that we should find a dead fish among the rocks, with two mortal wounds, and it was so large that the seventy of us sustained ourselves on it for more than a week, and if it had not been so large we would have perished there of hunger.[2]

...they still found themselves suffering from thirst, but that night another marvel occurred to remove this affliction."[3]

Supply of water

They were forced into a safe bay where they rejoiced to find a good stream of fresh water coming down from the mountains.

A "miracle"

They hurried on to Navidad, their home port north of Acapulco, arriving January 7, 1596. The officials of Navidad "regarded it as a miracle that so many people could have traveled so far in so small a craft."[4]

Lighter ships needed

Cermenho returned with an accurate description of the California coast. It was at this point that the Vice-roy of Mexico realized that trying to explore the coast in the heavy, unwieldy galleons was not practicable. Lighter, smaller ships were needed so they could sail closer to shore, and to sail directly from New Spain.

A new expedition was still needed to find a "way station" for the ships sailing from the Philippines down the coast of Alta California to Acapulco.

"I will say of the Lord, He is my refuge and my fortress:
my God; in him will I trust.
Thou shalt not be afraid for the terror by night;...
Nor for the pestilence that walketh in darkness;...
A thousand shall fall at thy side...but it shall not come nigh thee."
(Psalm 91:2,5,6,7)

The Conde de Monterey, Vice-roy of Mexico, was convinced by Cermenho's difficult voyage along the coasts of the Californias, and the wreck of his ship, San Augustin, that another way to explore the rugged California coastline was needed. Cermenho had recommended that exploration be made, not in the heavily laden Manila galleons, but by smaller and lighter ships leaving directly from New Spain.

Vizcaino to California Coast

In 1594, Sebastian Vizcaino, a successful merchant seaman knowledgeable of the route of the galleons, offered to furnish the government with information about the California country in exchange for a license to engage in pearl fishing in California. It wasn't until 1602 that Vizcaino was chosen to lead an exploratory expedition to California, under orders from the Conde de Monterey.

Orders from Conde de Monterey

March 18, 1602, Vizcaino received his formal orders from the Vice-roy and the Council of the Indies. He was to "make a thorough exploration of the coast from Cape San Lucas to Cape Mendocino, employing two ships of moderate size and a launch, which could get near the coast for close-up observations."[1] He was not to go inside the Gulf of California; he was to continue only beyond Cape Mendocino to Cape Blanco; he was not to stop for a thorough examination of any great bay but merely observe the entrance and shelter for shipping; he was to make no settlements; he was to avoid conflict with the Indians; and he was to maintain the names previously given to the discoveries.

Vizcaino's expedition was well provided for. The San Diego was his flagship; the Santa Tomas was the second ship; and the launch was named Tres Reyes. His entire crew consisted of two hundred men, a map maker, special counselors, three Carmelite friars, and Vizcaino's son.

May 5, 1602, the entire expedition left from Acapulco. On July 5, Vizcaino passed the line of what was to become Alta California. Then,

"Sunday, the 10th of the month (November)...we arrived at a port which must be the best to be found in all the South Sea (Pacific Ocean)...protected on all sides and having good anchorage."[2]

San Diego

They named this port San Diego.

110

On November 24, they sighted Catalina Island which they named <u>Santa Catalina</u> in honor of the day of Saint Catherine.

"It is to the Vizcaino expedition that we owe many of the coast place names most familiar to us - San Diego, Santa Catalina, Santa Barbara, Point Conception, Monterey, Carmel. The entrance into Monterey Bay and the act of taking possession was the principal event of Vizcaino's voyage."[3]

December 16, 1602, Vizcaino sailed into the Bay of Monterey, so named after the Conde de Monterey. Dr. Chapman quotes Vizcaino:

"'We found ourselves to be in the best port that could be desired, for besides being sheltered from all the winds, it has many pines for masts and yards, and live oaks and white oaks, and water in great quantity, all near the shore.

It is all that can be desired for commodiousness and as a station for ships making the voyage to the Philippines, sailing whence they make a landfall on this coast...if, after putting to sea, a storm be encountered, they (the Philippine ships) need not, as formerly, run for Japan, where so many have been cast away and so much property lost.'"

Dr. Chapman continued:

"...nearly all they had to say was true, save for the yarn about the excellence of Monterey as a sheltered port, but it was precisely this departure from strict accuracy that had the most effect; the legend of the port of Monterey became one of the moving factors for a century and a half in Spanish expansion to the northwest."[4]

This famous harbor had been glimpsed by Cermenho in 1595 and he had named it <u>San Pedro</u>. Here Vizcaino disobeyed his orders by re-naming it <u>Monterey Bay</u>, the name it enjoys today.

It was decided that the <u>Santa Tomas</u> should return to Acapulco with all the sick from scurvy,* the dreaded pestilence. Of the entire number of men aboard that ship, only nine survived.

From Monterey, the flagship and the launch headed north. January 5, 1603 they anchored outside of Drake's Bay. They passed Cape Mendocino but storm and sickness made them decide to return to Baja California. During the storm, the two ships parted and did not meet again until Acapulco port. Both ships missed the great San Francisco Bay. One of the reasons was perhaps the fog which enveloped it. After being separated from the flagship, the launch <u>Tres Reyes</u> sailed as far as Cape Blanco but only fourteen of the men were well enough to handle the launch, so they headed home.

The crew of the flagship <u>San Diego</u> was reduced to a few able men who were so weak from scurvy they were afraid to let go the anchor for fear of not being able to hoist it again. Vizcaino decided to sail directly to Mazatlan on the coast of Mexico to secure help. February 18, 1603 Vizcaino and five of his men who could walk, set out for assistance at Mazatlan. They walked through unfamiliar rough country, became lost, and providentially met a pack train which carried a message to Mazatlan to help his dying crew.

Here we come upon a remarkable circumstance, which helped the Spaniards realize the cause of the abominable scurvy,* and its cure.

> "One of the men happening to pick up and taste an acid fruit which grew wild there, was surprised to feel himself at once benefited. By means of this fruit and the fresh provisions sent them from Mazatlan, the entire crew recovered health, causing the utmost surprise when they landed at Acapulco on March 21, for they had been given up for dead."[5]

Vizcaino's expedition made a detailed account of the California coast as far as Monterey, and revealed to the viceroy the fine ports of San Diego and Monterey, although Vizcaino returned with only half of his crew.

Succeeding the Vice-roy Conde de Monterey was a new viceroy, Montesclaros, who opposed Monterey Bay as a way station for the Manila galleons. His argument was that the port might serve their enemies as well as themselves and that it was too far from Spain to defend. Colonization by Spain at Monterey was henceforth abandoned. For the next 167 years, California's coast lay dormant. The galleons continued to sail from the Philippines far from the shores of California. When they sighted the Santa Lucia Range, they continued to turn southward and then to limp home.

The lapse of 167 years between Vizcaino (1602) and Portola (1769), emphasized the utter isolation of Alta California and the low regard in which the Spaniards held it. California was a place that should have contained gold but apparently did not; a place where the Strait of Anian should have been and was not; a place with a barren and dangerous coast; a place that was a long and difficult journey by sea from Mexico northward; and a place whose land was impossible to travel on foot. After Spain lost its thrust toward the end of the sixteenth century, it moved slowly to expend money, with little chance of rich reward, to colonize the Spanish outpost in California.

Mrs. Sanchez observed:

> "In the deep recesses of the mountains (of California) the yellow gold lay hidden, waiting the picks and shovels of a more enterprising race."[6]

Crew depleted

Providential messengers

Healing fruit

Mission accomplished

Colonization abandoned for 167 years

Gold hidden *"...until he come whose right it is; and I will give it him."* (Ez. 21:27)

112

SPAIN'S DOMINATION, AND DECLINE

"...every good tree bringeth forth good fruit; but a corrupt tree bringeth forth
  evil fruit.
A good tree cannot bring forth evil fruit, neither can a corrupt tree bring forth
  good fruit.
Every tree that bringeth not forth good fruit is hewn down, and cast into the
  fire.
Wherefore by their fruits ye shall know them." (Matthew 7:17,18,19,20)

Spain's
"Day-in-the-sun"

The fifteenth and sixteenth centuries were Spain's "day-in-the-sun." The Spaniards were gold seekers. Their discovery of gold in Haiti of the West Indies and their conquest of the rich treasures of Mexico and Peru enticed thousands of adventurers, and likewise created thousands of black slaves in tropical America. There the Spaniards built up a huge empire, strictly controlled.

To understand the decline of Spain's power, we must go back a bit into its history.

1492, Spain
freed of "infidels"

In 1492, Spain finally won her long-sought freedom from the Moors. Up until that time the religious war had absorbed all her energies.

1492-1570,
Spain dominant

From 1492 until about 1570, Spain turned her energies toward exploring and colonizing.

After 1570,
attempt to suppress
Protestantism

After 1570, Spanish energy practically ceased. Her attempt to suppress Protestantism in Europe left her with little vitality to extend her sway in America. She had a tremendous empire to defend at home.

Here I am going to liberally quote Dr. John Fiske, who wrote THE DISCOVERY OF AMERICA in 1892.[1] His analysis of Spanish history appeals greatly to us as Protestant Christians. Dr. Fiske:

Decline due to
warfare for
religion

"...there was a clear causal connection between the task which Spain finished in 1492 and that upon which she entered a little before 1570. The transition from the crusade against the infidel to the crusade against the heretic was easy, and in her case almost inevitable. The effects of the long Moorish war upon Spanish character and Spanish policy have often been pointed out. The Spaniard of the sixteenth century was what eight hundred years of terrible warfare, for home and for religion, had made him.

This unceasing militancy trained the Spaniards for despotism."

The Sword and
the Cross

The church in Spain acquired more power than in all Europe. To the Spaniard, his religion was synonymous with his patriotism. This took the form of a terrific zeal to "Christianize" all infidels, wherever they were found.

have seen ample examples of this with the Spanish explorers, whose expeditions for their country were accompanied by this zeal to convert all to the Catholic faith. The sword and the cross traveled hand-in-hand.

Catholicism, chief antagonist of Reformation

"Unity in faith came to be regarded as an object to secure which no sacrifices whatever could be deemed too great. When, therefore, the Protestant Reformation came in the sixteenth century, its ideas and its methods were less intelligible to Spaniards than to any other European people. By nature this land of mediæval ideas was thus marked out as the chief antagonist of the Reformation."

1588, Spain crippled at sea

The crisis between the advocates of Protestantism and Catholicism culminated in the overthrow of Spain's "Invincible Armada" in 1588. Spain lost her power as a predominant maritime nation.

"A healthy nation quickly repairs the damage wrought by a military catastrophe, but Spain was not in a healthy condition. The overmastering desire to put down heresy, to expel the 'accursed thing,' possessed her."

Moriscoes

The Moors had developed a remarkable industrial civilization in Spain. As the Christian crusaders advanced, the Moslem population in Spain became converted to Christianity. These converts were known as Moriscoes but were despised by the Spaniards. This cast a "stigma" upon the laboring class as they were associated with the hated Moriscoes. It was the belief of the Catholic church that "it was impossible to tell whether they were Christians at heart or not..." No differences of opinion were allowed.

Spain in economic trouble

Spain expelled the Moriscoes. These were her best workers, in manufacture, cultivation and irrigation of the soil, and the wool trade. Whole villages were deserted. Most of them went to Morocco. This was the beginning of Spain's economic ruin.

The deadly Spanish Inquisition also contributed to Spain's downfall, for it suppressed free thought.

Spanish Inquisition stifled individualism

"It was a machine for winnowing out and destroying all such individuals as surpassed the average in quickness of wit, earnestness of purpose, and strength of character, in so far as to entertain opinions of their own and boldly declare them. The more closely people approached an elevated standard of intelligence and moral courage, the more likely was the machine to reach them... As the inevitable result, the average character of the Spanish people was lowered...Under this blighting rule of the Inquisition the general atmosphere of thought in Spain remained mediæval... The Spanish policy of crushing out individualism resulted in universal stagnation.

114

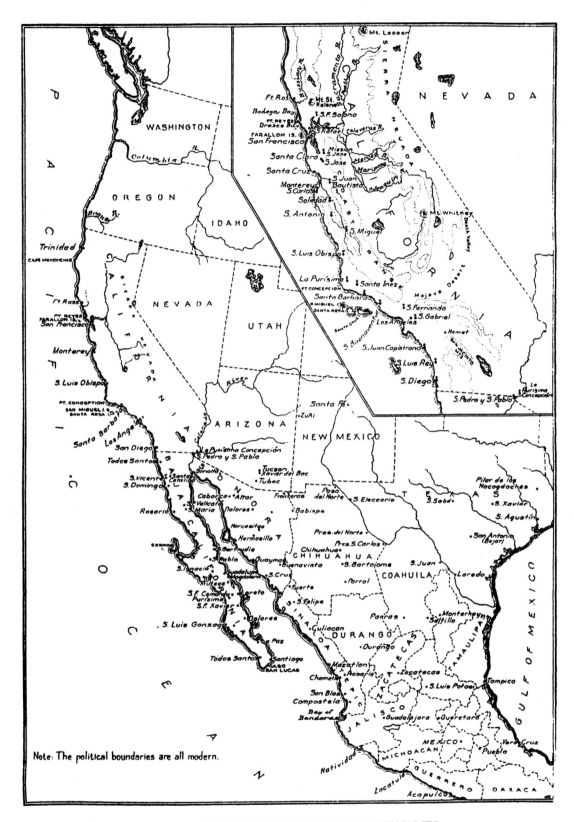

GENERAL MAP SHOWING SPANISH PLACE NAMES

From: A SHORT HISTORY OF CALIFORNIA,
by Rockwell Hunt and Nellie Sanchez

115

Under the rule of the Spanish Inquisition all the zeal and energy which we now devote to developing and stimulating popular intelligence was devoted to stunting and repressing it.

Lesson of Protestantism

...variety in religious beliefs is not an evil, but a positive benefit to a civilized community, whereas uniformity in belief should be dreaded...This is the true lesson of Protestantism, and it is through this lesson, however imperfectly learned, that Protestantism has done so much to save the world from torpor (mental or spiritual sluggishness) and paralysis."

Providential inheritance

In America, we have been protected against a state church, as existed in Spain. Providentially, our inheritance is from the English policy to "give full scope to individualism."

"That policy has been the chief cause of the success of English people in founding new nations..."

"Separation" of Church and State

What state can exist without God? In America, all churches support the State, the Constitution, the Civil Government of the land. The State, the Constitution, the Civil Government, in turn, protect the rights of the church. It is a beautiful balance. The separation of <u>one</u> religion from a state or nation is necessary, but religious freedom in a country is a privilege, and a right, which the State must recognize.

DISCOVERY OF AMERICA AND CALIFORNIA

We have just studied the interesting discovery period in which Spain played a most important part. From 1492 to 1570, Spain was the most powerful force in Europe. But Spain's power declined. Their huge empire under Charles V began to crumble when his despotic son, Philip II (1556-1598) waged an "holy" war against the Netherlands, and Queen Elizabeth of England stepped in to defeat his Spanish Armada (1588).

English Pilgrims colonize America

The Chain of Christianity was rapidly approaching America in 1620 with a tiny group of Christian Pilgrims who settled on its eastern border, there to set the stage for a magnificent country where religious freedom and the free and independent man were protected by a written constitution.

California neglected 167 years

While the Chain of Christianity was proceeding to America, California was neglected. Discovery, exploration, and settlement along the eastern seaboard of America by European nations continued because the Atlantic Ocean provided a natural approach from the continent of Europe. While in California in western America, there was the space of 167 years (1602-1769) where colonization and development were held up because the Pacific Ocean was so much more difficult to reach.

California colonized, 1769

Finally, we find out how the land of California was colonized.

REFERENCES TO CHAPTER I: PART A

MARCO POLO

1. Hall, Verna M. THE CHRISTIAN HISTORY OF THE AMERICAN REVOLUTION, pp. 46, 47.
2. Irving, Washington. LIFE AND WORKS OF WASHINGTON IRVING, Vol. II, Appendix, No. XXI, p. 267.
3. Komroff, Manuel. THE TRAVELS OF MARCO POLO, pp. xxv, xxvi.
4. Kublai Khan (born 1216); grandson of the famous conqueror Jenghiz or Ghengis Khan (born 1162).
5. Fiske, John. DISCOVERY OF AMERICA, Vol. I, p. 281.
6. Irving, Washington. LIFE AND WORKS OF WASHINGTON IRVING, Vol. II, Appendix, No. XX, p. 267.

COLUMBUS

1. Muzzey, David S. AN AMERICAN HISTORY, p. 8, Footnote 1.
2. THE PRESBYTERIAN LAYMAN, October 1971.
3. Fiske, John. THE DISCOVERY OF AMERICA, Vol. I, p. 445.
4. OLD SOUTH LEAFLET #29.
5. Contributed by Walter F. Dimmick, author of THE ELECTRO-MAGNETIC SYSTEM, published by Dimmick Research Labs, Gilroy, California, 1976.

   Also, see AMERICAN PRACTICAL NAVIGATOR, first published 1802, by Nathaniel Bowditch: Reprint U.S. Government Printing Office, Washington, D.C., 1939.

6. Irving, Washington. LIFE AND WORKS OF WASHINGTON IRVING, Vol. II, Book III, Ch. IV, p. 39.
7. Fiske, John. THE DISCOVERY OF AMERICA, Vol. I, p. 448.
8. Irving, Washington. LIFE AND WORKS OF WASHINGTON IRVING, Vol. II, Book XVIII, Ch. V, p. 231.
9. Ibid., p. 632.

PAPAL BULL OF PARTITION 1494

1. Slater, Rosalie J. TEACHING AND LEARNING AMERICA'S CHRISTIAN HISTORY, p. 139.
2. Eldredge, Zoeth Skinner. HISTORY OF CALIFORNIA, Vol. I, p. 12.
3. Williams, Elisha. THE ESSENTIAL RIGHTS AND LIBERTIES OF PROTESTANTS, 1744. (Article)

   * A Spanish league is about 3 miles.

VESPUCIUS

* The spelling of his name is from John Fiske, THE DISCOVERY OF AMERICA.

1. Wood, Eric. FAMOUS VOYAGES, p. 88.
2. Fiske, John. THE DISCOVERY OF AMERICA, Vol. II, p. 103.
3. Wood, Eric. FAMOUS VOYAGES, p. 89.
4. Fiske, John. THE DISCOVERY OF AMERICA, Vol. II, p. 108.

AMERICA

5. Fiske, John. THE DISCOVERY OF AMERICA, Vol. II, pp. 135, 136, 137.

BALBOA

1. Irving, Washington. LIFE AND WORKS OF WASHINGTON IRVING, Vol. II, Appendix, Ch. III, p. 562.
2. Ibid., p. 563.

   * Peter Martyr: An Italian living in Spain. "...he began in 1488 the writing of those letters of over eight hundred, (which) exist to attest his active interest in the events of his day. These events he continued to observe till 1525." (From CHRISTOPHER COLUMBUS, by Justin Winsor, p. 34.)

3. Irving, Washington. LIFE AND WORKS OF WASHINGTON IRVING, Vol. II, Appendix, Ch. XIV, p. 574.

MAGELLAN

1. Spice Islands or Moluccas: East Indies; three groups of islands in the Malayan or Indian Archipelago; traded spices such as cloves, nutmeg, mace, and sago (marrow of a palm tree used in medicine). "After Magellan's passage around Cape Horn to the Far East, the Spanish had laid claim to the Moluccas under the Treaty of Tordesilas (1494), but in 1528 they were bought out by the Portuguese, whose influence in the Moluccas was predominant until the arrival of the Dutch in the seventeenth century." (ENCYCLOPEDIA BRITTANICA, 14th Edition, page 682.)

2. Also, see ENCYCLOPEDIA BRITTANCIA, V. 173, No. 5, May, 1988, page 619.

3. Fiske, John. THE DISCOVERY OF AMERICA, Vol. II, p. 200.

4. "The Philippine Islands form part of the East Indian Archipelago. They were sometimes included in the Spice Islands. They were discovered by Magellan in 1521, coming by way of the Western Hemisphere, and were named for the King of Spain." (SHORT HISTORY OF CALIFORNIA by Hunt-Sanchez, page 17.)

REFERENCES TO CHAPTER I: PART B

CORTES, JIMENEZ, ULLOA

1. Hunt, Rockwell D. and Nellie Van De Grift Sanchez. A SHORT HISTORY OF CALIFORNIA, p. 41.
2. Eldredge, Zoe Skinner. HISTORY OF CALIFORNIA, V. I, p. 27.
3. Prescott, William. THE CONQUEST OF MEXICO, p. 203.
4. Ibid., p. 615.
5. Ibid., p. 685.
6. Ibid., pp. 636-7.
7. Ibid., p. 638.
8. Ibid., p. 639.
9. Ibid., p. 641.
10. Ibid., p. 640.
11. Hunt, Rockwell D. and Nellie Van de Grift Sanchez. CALIFORNIA AND CALIFORNIANS, Vol. I, p. 41.
12. Prescott, William. THE CONQUEST OF MEXICO, p. 641.
13. Hunt, Rockwell D. and Nellie Van De Grift Sanchez. SHORT HISTORY OF CALIFORNIA, p. 48.
14. Hunt, Rockwell D. and Nellie Van de Grift Sanchez. CALIFORNIA AND CALIFORNIANS, Vol. I, p. 49.

* Definition: "Teocottis are tall, truncated (having the end square or even) pyramids, on the summit of which men, women, and children were sacrificed to the gods." (Fiske, THE DISCOVERY OF AMERICA, Vol. I, page 119.)

THE NAME "CALIFORNIA"

1. Hale, Edward Everett. "The Queen of California," THE ATLANTIC MONTHLY, Vol. XIII, No. LXXVII, March 1864.

CABRILLO-FERRELO

1. Hunt, Rockwell D. and Nellie Van de Grift Sanchez. CALIFORNIA AND THE CALIFORNIANS, Vol. I, p. 71.
2. Hunt, Rockwell D. and Nellie Van de Grift Sanchez. A SHORT HISTORY OF CALIFORNIA, p. 25.
3. Eldredge, Zoeth Skinner. HISTORY OF CALIFORNIA, V.l, p. 61.
4. Hunt, Rockwell D. and Nellie Van de Grift Sanchez. CALIFORNIA AND THE CALIFORNIANS, Vol. I, p. 76.

DRAKE

1. Fiske, John. DISCOVERY OF AMERICA, Vol. II, pp. 554, 555.
2. Hunt, Rockwell D. and Nellie Van de Grift Sanchez. CALIFORNIA AND THE CALIFORNIANS, Vol. I, p. 83.
3. Ibid., p. 85.
4. Ibid., p. 87.
5. Ibid., p. 89.

DRAKE

*   Moors. The Moors (Mohammedans) entered Spain in 711. They conquered the whole peninsula. By the middle of the twelfth century the Moors had retreated to the kingdom of Granada. They were defeated in Granada during the reign of Queen Isabella and King Ferdinand in 1492, the same year Columbus discovered America. Hundreds of years of religious warfare had occupied the Spaniards.

**   Netherlands. Spain attempted to overthrow the "rebellious heretic," the Netherlands, with a crusade against that country such as the bloody Inquisition. Consequently, the rebellious Netherlands sided with the English against Spain in 1588 when they defeated the Spanish Armada.

***   See Robert H. Power, "Drake's Landing in California: A Case for San Francisco Bay," CALIFORNIA HISTORICAL QUARTERLY, Summer 1973, Vol. LII, No. 2.

****   See APPENDIX: Address by Verna Hall, THE HAND OF GOD IN AMERICAN HISTORY:ENGLISH PREPARATION, for further comments on roles in history by Portugal, Spain, and England with special emphasis on the Spanish Armada of 1588.

CERMENHO

1. Hunt, Rockwell D. and Nellie Van de Grift Sanchez. CALIFORNIA AND THE CALIFORNIANS, VOL. I, p. 105.
2. Ibid., p. 106.
3. Ibid., p. 106.
4. Ibid., p. 107.

REFERENCES TO CHAPTER I: PART B (Continued)

VIZCAINO

1. Chapman, Charles E. A HISTORY OF CALIFORNIA, THE SPANISH PERIOD, p. 131.
2. Ibid., p. 133.
3. Hunt, Rockwell D. and Nellie Van de Grift Sanchez. A SHORT HISTORY OF CALIFORNIA, p. 52.
4. Chapman, Charles E. A HISTORY OF CALIFORNIA, THE SPANISH PERIOD, pp. 134, 135.
5. Hunt, Rockwell D. and Nellie Van de Grift Sanchez. CALIFORNIA AND THE CALIFORNIANS, p. 117.
6. Ibid., p. 119.

  * "Scurvy: Med. A disease characterized by hemmorrhage, esp. into the skin and mucous membranes, by spongy gums, debility, etc. It results from lack of vitamin C." (WEBSTER'S COLLEGIATE DICTIONARY, Fifth Edition, 1938).

SPAIN'S DOMINATION, AND DECLINE

1. Fiske, John. DISCOVERY OF AMERICA, Vol. II, pp. 556-568.

CHAPTER II

EARLY HISTORY OF SPAIN IN CALIFORNIA

"Blessed is everyone that feareth the Lord; that walketh in his ways." (Ps. 128:1)

Dr. Chapman, an authority on the early history of California, wrote:

Providential
obscurity,
1602-1769

"Alta California was saved for over 150 years (1602-1769) in the blissful obscurity it needed if the English colonists who were just making their first successful settlements along the Atlantic coast (1607, 1620) were ever to have their opportunity to acquire the golden area on the Pacific."[1]

The age of the Conquistadors was over. Spain was interested in immediate economic gain but California was difficult and expensive to reach.

Isolation of
California

Geographically, California was very far from the centers of European civilization. By sea, the voyage around South America was dangerous. Ships were small and frail, and the rugged coasts of California were uncharted.

By land, there were immense distances to travel; little knowledge of the terrain; many mountain chains with long narrow valleys; the awesome Sierra Nevadas, and huge dusty deserts, all of which made communication difficult.

Slowly, at first, California yielded to entrance by the white man. Later, the abundant natural resources of California would be discovered; the port of San Francisco would be found to be one of the greatest in the world; California gold would show incredible wealth.

BAJA (LOWER) CALIFORNIA

1697 KINO, SALVATIERRA, AND UGARTE

Spanish Catholics,
used by God
to enter the
Californias

It was the desire of the Catholic church to convert the Indians to Christianity which led the Spaniards into Baja California. The Jesuit Order, Dominicans, and Franciscans all played a part entering the Californias.

By the close of the Seventeenth Century, the King of Spain opened up part of the Mexican District of Sinloa to the missionaries for christianizing Indians. This was Pimeria Alta, the name applied to southern Arizona, northern Sonora. To the northwest was Alta California.

First step to
occupy Californias

In 1687 Father Eusebio Kino of the Jesuit order crossed the Altar River and founded the mission Dolores in Pimeria Alta. This was the first step in the occupation of the Californias by Spain. Father Kino was the first to traverse in detail and accurately map the whole of Pimeria Alta. Father Kino began building missions in Pimeria Alta and ten years later put pressure on his superiors to extend the missions into Baja California.

Father Salvatierra, greatest of Baja priests

Kino and Father Juan Maria Salvatierra headed a movement for the occupation of Baja California. Spain's government reluctantly gave permission but consented only if the Jesuits provided their own funds. Father Juan de Ugarte, a member of the Jesuit College of Mexico City, suggested the establishment of a Pious Fund. With help of this fund, Salvatierra established the first permanent European settlement of Baja California at Loreto, and became priest, commander, and governor of this mother mission. A system of missions was begun which led to the establishment of twenty-three missions, fourteen of which survived. Building the missions in Baja California was a slow and laborious process.

Revival of Mother Mission at Loreto

When Father Kino died, Father Juan de Ugarte became his successor. When he arrived at Loreto in 1701, he found the mission deserted. Father Ugarte was a man of giant stature and strength. With great enthusiasm, he planted gardens, orchards; raised horses, cattle, sheep; cultivated fields and reaped harvests; made spinning wheels, looms, and a staff for holding flax, all the while trying to teach the Indians the basis for Christianity.

California not an island

Ugarte decided to explore by water. He found a grove of timber and hauled it for one hundred miles over the mountains to a mission on the coast. There he built a ship and in this made a voyage up the gulf. He proved Baja California was not an island, but a peninsula, and that the body of water was really a gulf.

1767 EXPULSION OF JESUITS

Franciscan Order predominated

It was a political decree of 1767 issued by the Spanish government which expelled the Jesuits and installed the Franciscans in California. Following the lead of Portugal and France, Spain had joined in a movement against the Jesuits then prevailing in Catholic countries. This resulted from fear that the Jesuits were planning a great revolution against the absolute monarchs of Europe. It actually had little to do with Jesuit activities in Baja California. Among the accusations against the Jesuits was misuse of the Pious Fund.

All members of the Jesuit Society were expelled from the King's dominions. In New Spain, their places were filled by Franciscan friars from the College of San Fernando in Mexico, headed by Padre Junipero Serra. Dominicans were assigned all missions south of San Diego in Baja California.

ALTA (Upper) CALIFORNIA

Spanish activity in California shifted to Alta or Upper California. There were three men mostly responsible for the colonization of Alta California by the Spanish.

Galvez,
the planner

Jose de Galvez, assumed the commission of Visitador-General of New Spain in 1765. His appointment marked the end of Spain's disinterest in her colonial possessions in California. Galvez was an energetic man with unlimited powers. He believed the northern possessions of Spain were threatened by the advance of the Russians across the Bering Strait, so he decided to occupy and settle San Diego and Monterey.

Serra, the
religious leader

Father Junipero Serra, accompanied by his biographer Father Francisco Palou, was eager to establish missions in Alta California. An ardent admirer of Serra, Palou wrote a glowing account of him. This historical record greatly helped create the legend of Father Junipero Serra. Here is clearly demonstrated the importance of the written word. In 1931, Serra, as founder of California's first missions, was honored for his unceasing toil for California by having his statue placed in National Statuary Hall in our Capitol at Washington, D. C.

Portola, the
military leader

Gaspar de Portola was sent out to New Spain in 1767 to be governor of the Californias. Along with Visitador-General Galvez and Father Serra, the decision was made to establish missions to spread the gospel of Catholicism and to christianize the Indians; to build presidios, or military strongholds to protect the missions; and create pueblos or religious towns to support the missions, in Alta California. Galvez placed Portola in command of the military troops which were to accompany Father Serra. This was the Spanish method of colonization, the cross accompanied by the sword. Their story on reaching San Diego, by ship and by land, is an impressive one of courage and determination. In 1769 the first Spanish mission in Alta California was founded.

THE EXPEDITION TO SAN DIEGO 1769

The expedition to San Diego was to be divided into two divisions to travel by sea, and two by land. They were all to meet in San Diego and then travel to Monterey.

To colonize
by sea

The sea division consisted of two small sailing vessels, the SAN CARLOS and the SAN ANTONIO. On Jan. 9, 1769, the little ship SAN CARLOS, under Lieutenant Pedro Fages who later became Governor of Alta California, headed for San Diego. The SAN ANTONIO was not ready until Feb. 15.

By land

By the end of March, the first land division under Captain Rivera y Moncada, accompanied by Serra's friend Fray Juan Crespi who left a diary of the entire march, started from Santa Maria on the northern border.

Portola
and Serra

The second land division under Governor Portola, accompanied by Serra, left on their march to San Diego May 15.

Suffering

The SAN ANTONIO arrived at the port of San Diego April 11. On April 29, the SAN CARLOS dropped anchor. The long voyage of 110 days from the cape had reduced the crew of the SAN ANTONIO, so ill from scurvy, that there was no man left with strength enough to lower a boat. Two-thirds of those aboard died and the rest were in poor condition.

On May 14, Captain Rivera and his first land division arrived. He moved the camp nearer the river and built a stockade for protection, California's first military fortification. The next six weeks were used in caring for the sick.

SAN ANTONIO
home for supplies

June 29, the last land division under Governor Portola arrived. He had less cattle with him and had had an easier trip. However, because of the loss of so many sailors, they decided to send the SAN ANTONIO back for supplies. Portola was to continue on to Monterey.

Portola wrote:

"Leaving the sick under a hut of poles which I had erected, I gathered the small portion of food which had not been spoiled in the ships and went on by land with that small company of persons, or rather say skeletons, who had been spared by scurvy, hunger, and thirst."[2]

Search for
Monterey

No Monterey?

Portola left San Diego for Monterey July 14, 1769. They passed by friendly Indians who provided them with food. It took six days to reach Monterey Bay but they could not recognize it according to the description Vizcaino had made of it in 1602. They decided they had not yet arrived at the Monterey Bay and continued north. They sighted "big trees" near Soquel and Portola gave them the name "Palo Colorado" or redwood. Near our present Stanford University, they named a giant tree "Palo Alto" or high tree.

San Francisco
Bay

Sergeant Ortega was sent ahead on a scouting expedition and came back with the exciting news of "a great arm of the sea, extending to the southeast farther than the eye could reach." They had discovered the Golden Gate of the San Francisco Bay.

Convinced that Monterey Bay had been left far behind them, Portola and his party retraced their steps, reaching Carmel Bay and crossing Cypress Point. Not finding Monterey Bay, although practically on its shores, they returned to San Diego, mystified.

Prayerful
petition

When Portola returned to the site of San Diego Mission and Father Serra, he found a sorry sight. Dangerously low on supplies, suffering from disease and scurvy, harassed by Indians, the little group prayed fervently that their ship, the SAN ANTONIO, would return with provisions to save them.

1769 SAN DIEGO MISSION

July 1769

Although the Serra, Portola expedition had indeed established the site of the Mission San Diego de Alcala July 16, 1769, there was doubt whether they could remain there. Sorrowfully, the decision was made to leave if the relief ship SAN ANTONIO had not returned by March 20. The whole camp was gloomy.

God honored
their prayers

On March 19, in the dim distance, a ship was seen sailing toward them. The SAN ANTONIO!

Dr. Rockwell Hunt wrote:

"The providential appearance of the SAN ANTONIO on March 23 with fresh supplies averted the withdrawal that seemed imminent. California was saved! The search for Monterey was to be renewed."[3]

1770 SECOND MISSION AT MONTEREY

Successful
march to
Monterey

Portola planned another land expedition to Monterey; this time, it was successful. Serra went by sea to join him and in 1770 they founded the Monterey Mission. Spain had finally made a successful effort to gain actual possession of California.

1769-1823 TWENTY-ONE MISSIONS

Spanish missions
in Alta California

Father Serra founded nine of the first chain of twelve missions. All twelve missions had easy access to the sea.

Father
Junipero Serra

In addition to Mission San Diego de Alcala (1769) and the Mission San Carlos Borromeo de Carmelo, established in Monterey in 1770 and moved by Father Serra to Carmel in 1771, Father Serra founded: San Antonio de Padua (1771, Monterey County); San Gabriel Arcangel (1771, Los Angeles County); San Luis Obispo (1772, San Luis Obispo County); Dolores, or San Francisco de Asis (1776, San Francisco County); San Juan Capistrano (1776, Orange County); Santa Clara (1777, Santa Clara County); San Buenaventura (1782, Ventura County).

Father Serra died in 1784 and his position as Father-President passed to Father Fermin Francisco de Lasuen (1785-1803), who completed the first chain of twelve missions with: Santa Barbara (1786, Santa Barbara County); La Purisima Concepcion (1787, Santa Barbara County); and Santa Cruz (1791, Santa Cruz County).

Father
Fermin Lasuen

Then a second chain of missions, or inner chain, was planned by Governor Neve and started by Father Lasuen: La Soledad (1791, Monterey County); San Jose (1797, Alameda County); San Juan Bautista (1797, San Benito County); San Miguel Arcangel (1797, San Luis Obispo County); San Fernando (1797, Los Angeles County); San Luis Rey (1798, San Diego County). Father Lasuen, as well as Father Serra, founded nine missions.

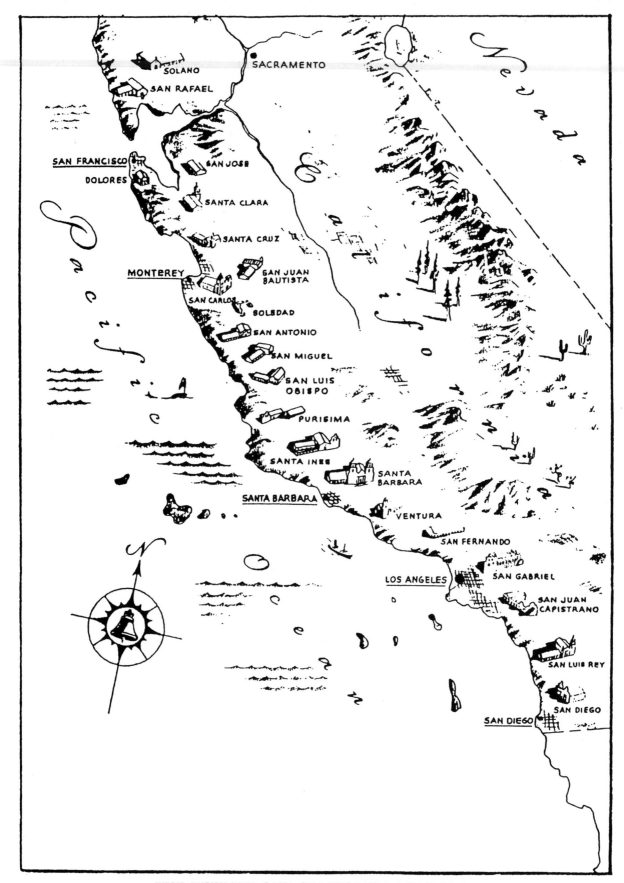

THE TWENTY-ONE CALIFORNIA MISSIONS

From: CALIFORNIA MISSIONS, by Ralph B. Wright, Editor; Herbert C. Hahn, Illustrator, California Mission Trails Association, Ltd., 1970

128

When Father Lasuen took over as Father-President of the Mission System in 1785, El Camino Real (The King's Highway) had become a well-traveled highway which linked the northern extremity at San Francisco with the southernmost mission at San Diego. The road, however, stretched great lengths through areas occupied by hostile Indians. This danger made it necessary to furnish military protection for all travelers. The Franciscans had long held hope of establishing a mission at the end of each day's journey along the road. That is why Lasuen established four missions from June to September of 1797, and erected a fifth in June of 1798. To do this, Father Lasuen had to traverse the whole length of the province, some 500 miles of difficult travel - this in his 77th year. But Lasuen had no Palou to write his biography, as had Father Serra.

Three missions were established after Lasuen's death: Santa Ynez (1804, Santa Barbara County); San Rafael Arcangel (1817, Marin County); and San Francisco Solano (1823, Sonoma County). The last three were founded more for military than religious reasons.

Concurrent with the establishment of the missions was the establishment of presidios: San Diego in 1769; Monterey in 1770; San Francisco in 1776; and Santa Barbara in 1782.

The founding of each mission in Alta California presents an interesting story. They were used as a means of bringing civilization to the land of California, hitherto occupied only by Indians.

The driving desire on the part of the Spanish missionaries to bring Christianity to these "heathens," was a noble idea but not entirely a successful one. The Indians of California had a culture so different from that of the Europeans. Their ways were not our ways, nor their God our God, by any means.

THE INDIANS OF CALIFORNIA

How long the Indians had occupied California before the white man came is unknown. Dr. A. L. Kroeber, the authority on the Indians of California, has this to say:

"It can...be suggested that by 2000 or 1500 B.C. the beginnings of native California culture as we know it had already been made.[4]

There has always existed a consensus of impression, among experienced as well as hasty observers, that a certain likeness runs through the culture of most of the tribes of California, northern, central, and southern. With scarcely an exception they were unwarlike; nearly all of them made excellent baskets, but were deficient in wood-working..."[5]

Dr. Chapman states:

California
Indians mild

"Hand-in-hand with...ethnological characteristics go the temperamental ones of an unwarlike nature and of a lack of the intensity and pride which are such strongly marked qualities of the American Indian as a whole."[6]

Temperament of
California Indians
providential
to Spaniards

Dr. Kroeber estimates there were probably 70,000 Indians between San Francisco and San Diego. He also believes that during the entire Spanish period, the Spanish population of California was never more than 3000. Dr. Chapman observes: "Against a determined and competent Indian people Spain would have found it impossible to prevail..."[7]

INDIAN CUSTOMS

The following discussion of Indian customs is compiled mainly from Dr. Charles E. Chapman's HISTORY OF CALIFORNIA: THE SPANISH PERIOD.

"Who told thee
that thou wast
naked?"
(Gen. 3:11)

Dress: Dress had little to do with style or morality... but depended more especially on climate. In summer the men wore a loin-cloth or nothing; there was no such thing as a sense of shame. The women wore an apron, or skirt, reaching from the waist to the knees, made usually of tule-grasses. Skins of animals gave additional warmth in winter. Ornaments of bone, shell, or wood were worn in the ears or hair or around their neck or wrists. The men often painted their bodies grotesquely...to frighten evil spirits and enemies away.

Santa Barbara
Indians most
advanced

Homes: Homes were simple in the extreme. The typical wigwam, made in conical shape of poles banked with earth, with an opening in the top for smoke to go out and air to come in, and with a slit in the side for an entrance, was most commonly used. However, the Indians of the Santa Barbara Channel, by far the most advanced, had well-fashioned huts of thatch.

ISLAND OF
THE BLUE
DOLPHINS

Author's note: When mentioning the subject of the Indians of the Santa Barbara Channel Islands, I pause to reflect upon a delightful story of a young Indian girl who was stranded alone on the desolate Island of San Nicholas, one of the islands in the Santa Barbara Channel. Her experience reminds us of the Indian heritage of this girl, Karana, or Won-a-pa-lei, "The Girl With The Long Black Hair."

This is a true tale set in the era of the late 1800's about Karana who spent eighteen years alone on the island, "around which the dolphins played." Her background of self-reliance in a natural setting, and acceptance of her fate, reminds us of her Indian heritage of resourcefulness and inner strength. She is known to history as The Lost Woman of San Nicolas, and your author has visited the plaque in her memory in the garden of the Santa Barbara Mission, where she lived after her rescue. Her story may be found in ISLAND OF THE BLUE DOLPHINS by Scott O'Dell: Boston, Houghton Miflin Co., 1960, a book for children.

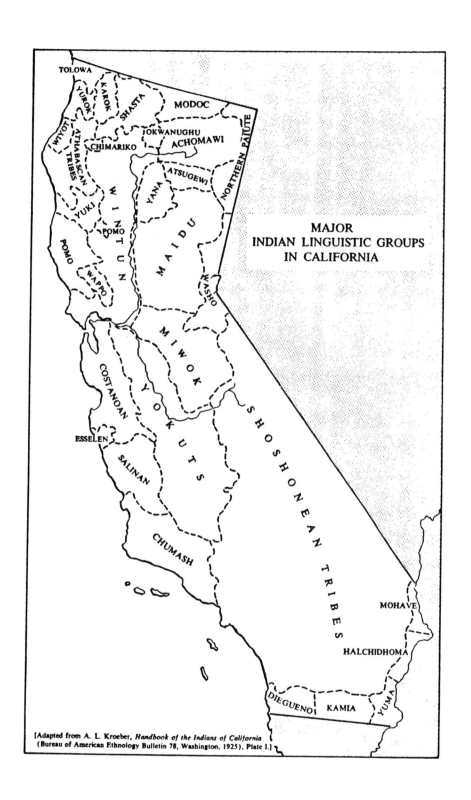

MAJOR
INDIAN LINGUISTIC GROUPS
IN CALIFORNIA

[Adapted from A. L. Kroeber, *Handbook of the Indians of California* (Bureau of American Ethnology Bulletin 78, Washington, 1925), Plate I.]

From: CALIFORNIA, A HISTORY, by Andrew F. Rolle, adapted from HANDBOOK OF THE INDIANS OF CALIFORNIA (1925) by A. L. Kroeber

The Temescal: For a cure, the sick sometimes resorted to a temescal. Often called a "sweat-house," a fire was built inside creating hot air. The native would work up a sweat, then rush outside and jump into cold water.

Property: Property and a kind of money existed. While shells were mostly used as money, obsidian and the skins of animals were also used as mediums of exchange.

Government: Government was mainly a matter for the individual family. There were tribal laws which were rigidly enforced. These dealt principally with murder and adultery. The tribal chiefs were usually hereditary, but in northern California the richest wielded the sceptre. The chiefs were leaders in war. They had no real power beyond that of their personal influence.

Marriage: Everywhere it was the usual practice for men to buy their wives. In the north it was purely an economic transaction, just as the purchase of a valuable skin would have been. The girl had no lawful right to refuse the man to whom her parents sold her. Divorce was at the will of the man.

Food: The diet of the California Indians left much to be desired. They ate very little meat, because they lacked domestic animals and were poor hunters. They ate nearly everything that teeth could bite which came their way. Coyotes, crows, lizards, rats, mice, frogs, skunks, snakes were eaten by many groups. Grasshoppers were a delicacy. Many Indians caught fish. Bear meat and the flesh of other large game were rarely eaten, not that the Indians objected to the taste, but because they believed that such dangerous creatures must be possessed of a demon, and to eat the meat would mean swallowing the demon. The Indians lived chiefly on foods that grew wild. Of these, acorns were easily the most important item. They were ground to a flour and cooked to make bread.

Author's note: Here I would like to insert the story of the discovery of Yosemite Valley. Part of the story has to do with the eating habits of the California Indian. I think you will find it interesting. You will find the story of Yosemite Valley in the Appendix.

Occupation: In time of peace the man "busied himself" in doing nothing, chiefly. Occasionally he would hunt or fish. The women did all the real work. They fashioned the waterproof baskets, stone-cooking vessels, and awls of bone. The northern and southern California Indians had canoes and rafts, but not those of the central regions. Nothing but tule rafts floated on San Francisco Bay.

War: It was in war that the men found their true occupation. They were far from cowardly; however, they had no idea of organization or discipline. Their weapons were nothing more elaborate than bows and arrows and clubs. They rarely resisted foreign invasion, yet weak as they were, they managed to give the missionaries and later the pioneers a great deal of trouble.

Personal Habits: The personal habits of the California Indians were, to say the least, filthy. Their houses and they themselves were covered with vermin, which they sometimes would catch and eat.

Author's note: If one could find the book entitled INCIDENTS ON LAND AND WATER, OR FOUR YEARS ON THE PACIFIC COAST by Mrs. D. B. Bates, Boston, 1860, it is a gem. It is an autobiography and real life experience of a gentlewoman who left her home in Boston in 1851 to sail for San Francisco, there to join her new husband.

While on this journey, she had three sailing vessels burned out from beneath her. Her descriptions of early San Francisco and Marysville are interesting. In her travels about California, she visited an Indian rancheria. She wrote:

"...We visited Yuba City, situated about half a mile from Marysville, on the opposite bank of Feather River. It may not be amiss to state, that Yuba City, with the exception of three or four houses, has been removed to Marysville. There is, however, an Indian rancheria existing there, which draws many visitors to the spot. We started, one bright morning, in a two-horse team, to visit the rancheria.

We saw them making their acorn bread (parn they call bread). To render it short and rich, they mashed up angle-worms, and put in it. After baking it, which they did by making an excavation in the earth, and building a fire therein; when the earth was sufficiently heated, they scraped out the ashes, put in the bread, and covered it over with hot ashes, - they generously insisted upon our eating a piece. The keeness of our appetites was considerably repressed, however, by witnessing the several employments of the tribe.

One old squaw was relieving her husband's head of a score of vermin, which she ate with an apparent relish. She practised, however, the principle of self-abnegation to perfection, by occasionally tossing some of the finest-looking ones down his throat, for which he smacked his thanks with apparent zest."

Religion: The keynote to a broad understanding of the Indian character lies chiefly in the study of his religion, as it does in the civilized world. There were gods, demons, and spirits, and omens and portents, everywhere and at all times. The profession of the sorcerer, soothsayer, and astrologer fared well among the Indians. Religion was quite apart from ideals of righteousness and good conduct. It was something to be guarded against rather than to embrace, for the gods were vengeful. Yet, certain of the California Indians had a hazy notion of a Supreme Being and of a future life. Once death came, it was necessary for the departed soul to race with the demons in order to get to heaven.

MEMOIRS
OF MY LIFE

Author's note: John Charles Fremont wrote a fascinating account of his three expeditions for the topographical division of the United States Engineers in MEMOIRS OF MY LIFE, (Chicago and New York: Belford, Clarke, & Co., 1887). His third expedition brought him into California in 1845-46, just at the time hostilities broke out between California and Mexico. In this one account of his contact with Indian ways, he wrote on pages 436-7:

"A day or two after, we saw mountain sheep for the first time in crossing the Basin. None were killed but that afternoon Carson (Kit Carson) killed an antelope...Well up, towards the top of the mountain, nearly two thousand feet above the plain, we came upon a spring where the little basin afforded enough for careful use. A bench of the mountain near by made a good camping-ground, for the November nights were cool and newly-fallen snow already marked out the higher ridges of the mountains. With grass abundant, and pine wood and cedars to keep up the night fires, we were well provided for.

Sagundai,* who had first found the spring saw fresh tracks made in the sand by a woman's naked foot, and the spring had been recently cleaned out. But he saw no other indications of human life. We had made our supper on the antelope and were lying around the fire, and the men taking their great comfort in smoking...Carson who was lying on his back with his pipe in his mouth, his hands under his head and his feet to the fire, suddenly exclaimed, half rising and pointing to the other side of the fire, 'Good God! look there!' In the blaze of the fire, peering over her skinny, crooked hands, which shaded her eyes from the glare, was standing an old woman apparently eighty years of age, nearly naked, her grizzly hair hanging down over her face and shoulders. She had thought it a camp of her people and had already begun to talk and gesticulate, when her open mouth was paralyzed with fright, as she saw the faces of the whites. She turned to escape but the men had gathered about her and brought her around to the fire. Hunger and cold soon dispelled fear and she made us understand that she had been left by her people at the spring to die, because she was very old and could gather no more seeds and was no longer good for anything. She told us she had nothing to eat and was very hungry.

We gave her immediately about a quarter of the antelope, thinking she would roast it by our fire, but no sooner did she get it in her hand than she darted off into the darkness. Some one ran after her with a brand of fire but calling after her brought no answer. In the morning, her fresh tracks at the spring showed that she had been there for water during the night. Starvation had driven her to us, but her natural fear drove her away as quickly, so soon as she had secured something to eat.

Before we started we left for her at the spring a little supply from what food we had. This, with what she could gather from the nut-pine trees on the mountain, together with our fire which she could easily keep up, would probably prolong her life even after the snows came. The nut-pines and cedars extend their branches out to the ground and in one of their thickets, as I have often proved, these make a comfortable shelter against the most violent snow-storms."

MISSION INDIANS

Indian culture would not have improved California

Although they had the advantage of numbers, knowledge of terrain, and distance from civilization, the California Indians could never have become a civilized people without the influence of Europeans.

Confusion of tongues

One of the difficulties with which the missionaries had to contend was their many different languages. Within the northern and southern boundaries there were 135 dialects. Interpreters were not to be had. They could not even understand each other's speech, as we have seen in the case of the tribes living across a stream from each other at Dos Pueblos.

In A SHORT HISTORY OF CALIFORNIA by Hunt-Sanchez, we read:

Solano

"The aboriginals of California stood lower in the scale of humanity - physically, morally, and mentally - than any of the other tribes of North America. One of the exceptions was Chief Solano of the Suisunes, for whom Solano County is named, and whom General Vallejo described as being a fine figure of a man, 6'7" tall and broad in proportion.[8]

Education of Indians

They had the surprising facility of acquiring the Spanish language, which they soon learned to speak clearly and correctly (under the tutelage of the mission priests). In the industrial schools of the missions, they became in a short time fairly skilled carpenters, weavers, farmers, etc., although they had never seen a house or a cow before the coming of the Spaniards.[9]

1776, an important year

It is an interesting coincidence that the work of these missions should have begun at nearly the same time as the American Revolution. The foundation ceremonies of San Francisco de Asis, October, 1776, were held in the same year as the proclamation of the Declaration of Independence, thus signalizing the year by a memorable event on each side of the continent, entirely independent of each other."[10]

Eleven years after the last mission at Sonoma had been established, the order was issued from Mexico (which had taken over California from Spain in 1821) that the missions be secularized, that is, turned over to local administrators.

Decline in
power of
missions

"Secularization" involved removing real properties from the hands of the missionaries and placing them under the management of civil administrators. The religious care of the new Indian citizens was to be left to secular priests, not the mission fathers.

For twenty years Mexico had had the desire to emancipate the Indians of California. By a sweeping decree of August 17, 1833, a general secularization plan was finally put into effect.

1834
Secularization

Governor Figueroa issued a proclamation August 9, 1834 defining the general terms of secularization. Ten missions were to be secularized in 1834; six in 1835; and five in 1836. The Indians were to get half of the mission lands.

Dr. Hunt remarked:

No abrupt character
change in Indians

"...what folly it was to expect that ten years would produce this radical change in the character and habits of an absolutely barbarous people like the aboriginals of California."[11]

Before the proposed plan had gone into effect, Governor Figueroa had asked the missionaries for their opinions. Their reply was:

"Although six times ten years had passed since the cross of Christ was first raised aloft at San Diego by Serra, the natives seemed no nearer the day of independence. They worked in the fields, in the mission shops, made brick and tiles, herded cattle, and did whatever else they were told to do...yet little progress had been made toward individual effort... In all but age and physical strength they were indeed still children."[12]

Secularization
little help
to Indians

What happened to the Indians attached to the missions? Although half of the mission property was to be theirs, they had no experience or training in handling property. None of them retained their allotments more than a few years. The cattle on the land was slaughtered by the missionaries to add the sale of the hides to their Pious Fund. Some of the Indians found employment on the ranchos; some as laborers in town; some succumbed to liquor and gambling; some left the coastal area to try to find homes with foreign tribes in the interior.

Dr. Hunt remarked in his CALIFORNIA IN THE MAKING:

"A recent tour of the twenty-one mission sites of Alta California from San Diego in the south to Sonoma in the north, has brought the writer fresh appreciation of the stupendous labors and deep devotion of the disciples of St. Francis of Assisi in their efforts to convert and civilize the rude aborigines... Still, it can never be forgotten that, cruelly secularized and destroyed in the years of the Mexican regime, they can never be restored to the status of original, active institutions. It is now almost as if they had never been...they live chiefly in memory."[13]

Providential aspect of secularization

Secularization of the missions indicated the end of control of the mission fathers. Providentially, it left a void, to be filled by the religious and governmental philosophy of another nation, as we shall see.

COLONIZATION OF CALIFORNIA

1773 DE ANZA

After the establishment of the first few missions, let us return to 1773 to find out how California was actually "peopled."

Land route needed to colonize California

To bring families into distant Alta California, it became necessary to establish a land route from Sonora in Mexico to Monterey and San Francisco Bay. It was extremely expensive to send supplies and animals from Loreto in Baja California. Furthermore, there would be increasing need of settlers in the northland. If a land route through Arizona could be found, it would greatly reduce the cost of grain and other supplies in Alta California and would make it possible to drive herds of live stock from Sonora. Thus the hold of Spain on the new country would be greatly strengthened.

Anza

Captain Juan Bautista de Anza submitted a proposal to Viceroy Bucareli for an expedition to open a mainland route from Northern Sonora to Monterey through Arizona. The impoverished Baja missions rendered the land route along the peninsula useless. His plan was accepted and he was also empowered to extend Spanish settlement to the strategic Bay of San Francisco. The opening of a trail from Sonora to Alta California had been the dream of Anza's family for three generations. Eventually, Anza led two expeditions to California, one to explore the trail and the other to bring settlers, including some for the new San Francisco site.

Route providentially abandoned

The goodwill of the Yuma Indians of Arizona was a vital factor in the success of Anza's expeditions and when that goodwill came to a tragic end a few years later in the Yuma massacre of 1781, the trail to California which Anza blazed was to be cut off for nearly half a century. Providentially, Spain's hold on California was greatly curtailed.

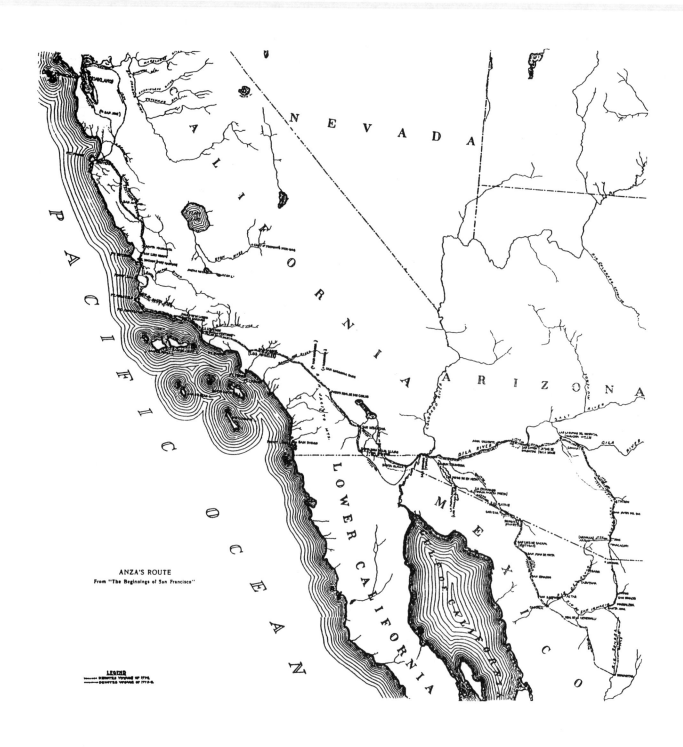

ANZA'S ROUTE
From "The Beginnings of San Francisco"

LEGEND
.... DENOTES VOYAGE OF 1774
———— DENOTES VOYAGE OF 1775-6

From: A HISTORY OF CALIFORNIA, Vol. I,
by Zoeth Skinner Edlredge

1774 FIRST EXPEDITION

1774 Trail blazed
through Arizona

Anza started from Tubac, near the southern boundary of Arizona in January 1774. He had with him, 34 men, 140 horses, 65 cattle for food, and 35 mules. Difficulty in crossing the Colorado River could never have been overcome if it had not been for the help of the Yuma Indians. It was a very hard journey but they found a pass in the Sierra Nevadas and even though they had rain and snow, they reached San Gabriel Mission on March 22, 1774, after a march of 700 miles from Tubac. Anza had found a way from Sonora to the sea. The party continued to Monterey and returned to Tubac May 26 over the same route. Anza made a full report of his expedition to the Viceroy in Mexico City.

SUMMER 1775 AYALA

Ayala:
San Francisco
Bay

In the summer of 1775 while Anza was organizing his party for a second crossing from Mexico into California, Lt. Juan Manuel de Ayala of the Spanish navy was ordered to explore the San Francisco Bay in his ship SAN CARLOS. He also was to prepare for the arrival of Anza's soldiers and colonists for the San Francisco presidio and mission. Ayala, in the SAN CARLOS made the first recorded voyage into San Francisco Bay. They anchored at Angel Island, or Island of Our Lady of the Angels, and explored the Bay and its branches for forty days. They marveled that inside the single entrance, which has since been called The Golden Gate, there were many anchorage ports. They recognized San Francisco Bay as one of Spain's finest possessions.

1775 SECOND ANZA EXPEDITION

1775
A remarkable
journey

Anza's second expedition started from Tubac, October 23, 1775. This expedition was responsible for the founding of the presidio and mission at San Francisco in 1776. They were a party of colonizers: Missionaries, married soldiers and their families, muleteers, domestic animals and beasts of burden, as well as servants - 240 people and 1000 head of livestock. The object was the founding of San Francisco. Anza brought that huge party safely across the Sierras without a single loss of life, in fact eight children were born enroute. Anza selected sites for the presidio and the mission of San Francisco, which

1776, San
Francisco under
Spanish monarchy

were established in 1776 under Moraga who had accompanied Anza. This was the culminating point in the Spanish conquest of California, and a strong link in Spain's chain of events forging her hold on California.

1776
Declaration
of American
Independence

Concurrently on the East coast of America, the golden Chain of Christianity was being strengthened by the thirteen little American colonies declaring their independence of Britain, July 4, 1776. This Chain proved to be stronger, as it was based upon the liberty of the individual as understood in the Scriptures.

Providential closing
of overland route

God moves in mysterious ways. The result of the Yuma tragedy proved to be a blessing as it closed the overland route leading from Mexico into California and perhaps averted greater tragedy had Spain been able to use it to strengthen her position in California.

Mistake of Croix

In 1776, the frontier provinces from Sinaloa, Sonora, and the Californias to New Mexico and Texas were detached from the control of the viceroy at Mexico City and placed under a commandante-general of the "Interior Provinces." The first Commandante-General of the Interior Provinces was Teodoro de Croix who was interested only in reducing expenses of the Californias. The Yuma Indians had helped Anza but Croix did not realize they were the most war-like tribe in California. The State of Arizona, as we know it today, was then part of the Californias. The Yuma Indians had become accustomed to presents from the Catholic priests to keep them happy and they became angry when the presents were necessarily curtailed because of lack of supplies. In 1780, two missions were founded on the California side of the Colorado River but were a mixture of presidio, mission, and pueblo - to conserve expenses, wholly inadequate in the eyes of the mission fathers in keeping the Indians in line.

Captain Rivera y Moncada had been appointed Lieutenant-Governor of the Californias and was stationed at Loreto to conduct the affairs of Baja California. He was given the task of recruiting colonists in Mexico for the proposed pueblo, Queen of the Angels, near the San Gabriel Mission. The first company of colonists traveled to San Gabriel Mission from Lower California along the coast, while Rivera led about forty soldiers and their families from south-western Arizona to the Colorado River where it joins the Gila River. Upon reaching Yuma, Arizona, Captain Rivera sent most of the company on to San Gabriel Mission. Rivera and about twelve of his soldiers camped opposite the settlement Concepcion to rest their horses and cattle.

Yuma massacre

The Yuma Indians were upset because they were afraid they were to lose their Colorado River homeland to these soldiers and colonists. Unfortunately, the soldiers antagonized the Indians, and their cattle ate the Indian's mesquite beans. The Yumas destroyed both missions, or settlements at Concepcion and Bicuner, and killed the priests, including Padre Garces, who had mapped so much of the Gila River. Captain Rivera and his men were killed in their camp. The women and children at Concepcion and Bicuner were held captive and later ransomed. This is not a pretty story, but its significance is that the Anza Trail remained cut off until 1820, out of fear of further reprisals from the Indians. As it was, there was no land communication between Mexico and California.

1781-1820:
No communication

END OF SPANISH RULE

For the next forty years from the Yuma Massacre in 1781 to the final collapse of Spanish rule over Mexico in 1821, Spain made little effort to strengthen its outposts in Alta California. There, as elsewhere, the over-extended Spanish colonial empire was on the defensive and crumbling.

Spain's glory was fading. The Napoleonic Wars led to the total destruction of its naval forces by Britain and in 1806 Napoleon invaded the Spanish peninsula, completely disrupting its government. Out of touch with Spain, nationalist feeling in Mexico began to be expressed in murmurs of revolt from the mother country.

1821 MEXICAN CALIFORNIA

1821 Mexican Independence from Spain

Beginning in 1808, a series of provincial revolutions dismembered the Spanish empire into independent republics. In 1821, Mexico won her independence from Spain and established a Mexican Empire, which included lands from Texas to California. The very name "New Spain" was dropped. In the Spring of 1822, Iturbide, General of the Mexican-Spanish revolution, proclaimed himself Emperor. Early in 1823, he was forced to abdicate and the Republic of Mexico, with its tri-colored flag, was created.

During the twenty-four years of Mexican reign in California, neglect continued. However, it was Mexico that secularized the missions, made most of the land grants, and opened import-export trade with California to other nations.

Forging the Chain

We leave California now in the hands of Mexico and center our attention on the Russian settlement on the northern coast of California. This is one of the most interesting and crucial times in forging the Chain of Christianity in California, and a pivotal point in California history.

1806-1841 RUSSIANS IN SPANISH AND MEXICAN CALIFORNIA

Russians claim Alaska

The history of the Russians in California goes back to Peter the Great of Russia. He had dreamed of conquest in America and wished to investigate the possibility of a land bridge connecting Asia with North America. The semi-circle of Aleutian Islands which stretch from Alaska in North America toward Siberia in Asia could lead one to this supposition. In 1725 a Danish navigator, Vitus Bering, carried out the Czar's orders by leading a party overland across the vast stretches of Siberia. In 1727, he reached the Pacific; in 1728, he sailed through the Bering Straits. It took thirteen years before Bering sighted the peak of Mt. St. Elias, thus establishing Russian claim to Alaska.

1799 Sitka

Russia established a colony at Sitka in Alaska in 1799 to trade in furs from the sea otter and other fur-bearing animals, and to trade with the Indians. Sitka was headquarters of the Russian-American Fur Company.

Rezánov, the Russian and Concepcion, the Spaniard

A few years later, Count Nikolai Petrovich Rezánov, Chamberlain of the Czar of Russia, visited their headquarters at Sitka and found them threatened with starvation. Believing he could trade with the Spaniards to the South, he sailed into San Francisco Bay in 1806. Knowing that Spain decreed it illegal

141

for California to trade with foreigners, he sought help of the Commandant Luis Arguello of the San Francisco Presidio anyway. Rezánov fell in love with Concepcion Arguello, the young and lovely daughter of the Commandant. Count Rezánov had little difficulty in getting the food and supplies for Sitka. He left the Arguellos, promising to return to marry Concepcion. Rezánov never returned, however, for he lost his life in Siberia on his return to Russia. Concepcion waited, finally became a Catholic nun, and learned the fate of Rezánov years later. She is buried in the Convent Cemetery, Benicia. This is a famous love story in California's history, and it has been enhanced by Bret Harte's beautiful and sympathetic poem:

REZÁNOV
1803

Count Nikolai Petrovich Rezánov

From: LOST EMPIRE, by Hector Chevigny

142

"Forty years on wall and bastion swept the hollow idle breeze,
Since the Russian eagle fluttered from the California seas;

Forty years on wall and bastion wrought its slow but sure decay,
And St. George's cross was lifted in the port of Monterey;

And the citadel was lighted, and the hall was gayly drest,
All to honor Sir George Simpson, famous traveler and guest.

Far and near the people gathered to the costly banquet set,
And exchanged congratulations with the English baronet;

Till, the formal speeches ended, and amidst the laugh and wine,
Some one spoke of Concha's lover, heedless of the warning sign.

Quickly then cried Sir George Simpson: 'Speak no ill of him, I pray!
He is dead. He died, poor fellow, forty years ago this day, —

Died while speeding home to Russia, falling from a fractious horse.
Left a sweetheart, too, they tell me. Married, I suppose, of course!

'Lives she yet?' A deathlike silence fell on banquet, guests, and hall,
And a trembling figure rising fixed the awestruck gaze of all.

Two black eyes in darkened orbits gleamed beneath the nun's white hood;
Black serge hid the wasted figure, bowed and stricken where it stood.

'Lives she yet?' Sir George repeated. All were hushed as Concha drew
Closer yet her nun's attire. 'Senor, pardon, she died, too!'"

1812
Fort Ross

Before he left for Siberia, Count Rezanov had advised the founding of a Russian colony in the territory of California. Accordingly, an exploring and trading expedition sailed into Bodega Bay in 1808 and in 1811, without Spain's consent, bought land from the Indians for a few trinkets, and raised the Russian flag, the Imperial flag of old Russia. The following year, 1812, the Russians built a fort twenty miles to the north of Bodega Bay at Fort Russ, or Fort Ross.

In a TRAVEL JOURNAL OF A RUSSIAN PRIEST, which he kept during his trip to Fort Ross in California and back to Russia from June 1 to October 13, 1836, we note that the Priest Veniaminov was struck most of all by California's physical environment. In his JOURNAL, he wrote:

"It must be confessed that the happy combination of California's
air, the clear, blue sky, the location, and the vegetation peculiar
to this latitude can at first strike and charm anyone who was born
(north of here) and had not been south of 52 degrees, especially
the inhabitants of Unalaska and Sitka."[14]

143

Veniaminov spent most of his time at Ross. He provided information on the number of Ross' settlers, their occupations, etc. In particular he noted:

"...that Fort Ross is not large, but it is a quite well built settlement or village consisting of 24 houses and several huts for the Aleuts and surrounded on all sides by plowland and forest; in the middle there is a small, square, wooden stockade with two blockhouses and several cannons and containing a chapel, the manager's house, the business office, a storehouse, barracks, and several dwellings for pious residents. Here there are 154 males and 106 females, a total of 260 souls, including 120 Russians, 51 creoles, 50 Kodiak Aleuts, and 39 converted Indians."

Their reasons for building the fort and establishing a colony were to supply the Russian-American Company at Sitka with agricultural provisions and for a convenient station to handle the pelts of the valuable little sea otter, found so plentifully along the coast.

1841 END OF RUSSIAN COLONIZATION

1823
Monroe Doctrine

Hearing of the extent of the Russian settlement on the California coast, the United States announced to the world in 1823 the contents of the Monroe Doctrine which clearly intended to prevent Russian advance. It stated that the American continents were no longer subjects for future colonization by an European power. This attitude of the United States was a chief factor in bringing to an end any policy of expansion in California that Russia might have held.

1841
Providentially,
Russians evacuate

Also, the fur supply became seriously depleted; their industries suffered serious decline. When Russia and Spain became allies in Europe, Russian ambition ceased to be directed toward North America. The Russians, therefore, decided to give up Fort Ross. It was purchased from them in 1841 by John A. Sutter, who had arrived in California in 1839 and planned to establish a strong colony on the present site of Sacramento. He purchased the movable property from the Russians for $30,000. The Russians departed from the California coast.

Now let us note an interesting conclusion to the church-state colonial ambitions of both the Russian and Spanish empires.

CLEARING THE WAY FOR PROTESTANTISM IN CALIFORNIA

Church-State

The church-state religion of Catholic Spain, represented by its last mission in Sonoma County, and the church-state religion of the Eastern Orthodox Church of Russia represented by its colony at Fort Ross in Sonoma County, were providentially no longer threats to the religious and governmental designs for California.*

Let me quote from a book by Leon L. Loofbourow, author of IN SEARCH OF GOD'S GOLD, a story of continued Christian pioneering in California. It was published under the auspices of The Historical Society of the California-Nevada Annual Conference of The Methodist Church, in cooperation with The College of the Pacific:

"Tides of empire and of Christianity, moving east and west, circled the globe and met – in California.

The Catholic Branch

'Beginning at Jerusalem' one branch of Christianity made its seat on the Tiber. From Rome it moved over western Europe. Checked for centuries by the Atlantic Ocean, it finally crossed that barrier. Spain's century in the sun had come. With irresistible onrush she claimed most of the Americas for the Spanish crown, and dedicated them to the Virgin Mary. Then the conquest collapsed from within. The last thrust of its expansion was the planting in Alta California of the series of presidios and missions from San Diego to Sonoma.

The Eastern Orthodox Branch

'Beginning at Jerusalem' also, the other branch of Christianity made its seat by the Bosphorus. From Constantinople it moved north over eastern Europe. It was checked for centuries by the Tartar barrier. Then came the empire of the tsars, which expanded eastward across Asia, establishing as it went the Russian Orthodox Church. But the driving power of tsardom failed. Its last thrust crossed Behring Strait and occupied Alaska and part of the western coast of North America. Its farthest outpost was named Rossiya (Russia, which we have shortened to Fort Ross) in Sonoma County. The Russian Orthodox Church at Fort Ross is only forty-five miles from the Roman Catholic Mission at Sonoma!

Sonoma County: Last mission secularized 1834; Fort Ross emptied 1841

Eastern Christianity represented by the Russian Orthodox Church and western Christianity represented by the Roman Catholic Church had circled the globe, to meet in this state. But neither Spanish church nor Russian church had had a strong reformation movement to purify its life from medieval incrustations. They faced each other in Sonoma County – exhausted. As Father Walsh, recent historian for the Church of Rome, expresses it, the curtain had been rung down. Most of the missions had been abandoned. The work of that church had a fresh start from the Atlantic seaboard. California's development, material and spiritual, required a new, vital force.

Luke 5:36,37,38, "New Wine"

This force came.

Door open for Protestant thrust

It came first in 1826 in the person of Jedediah Smith, Methodist 'Bible-toter,' first to cross Utah, Nevada, and the Sierra Nevadas,

145

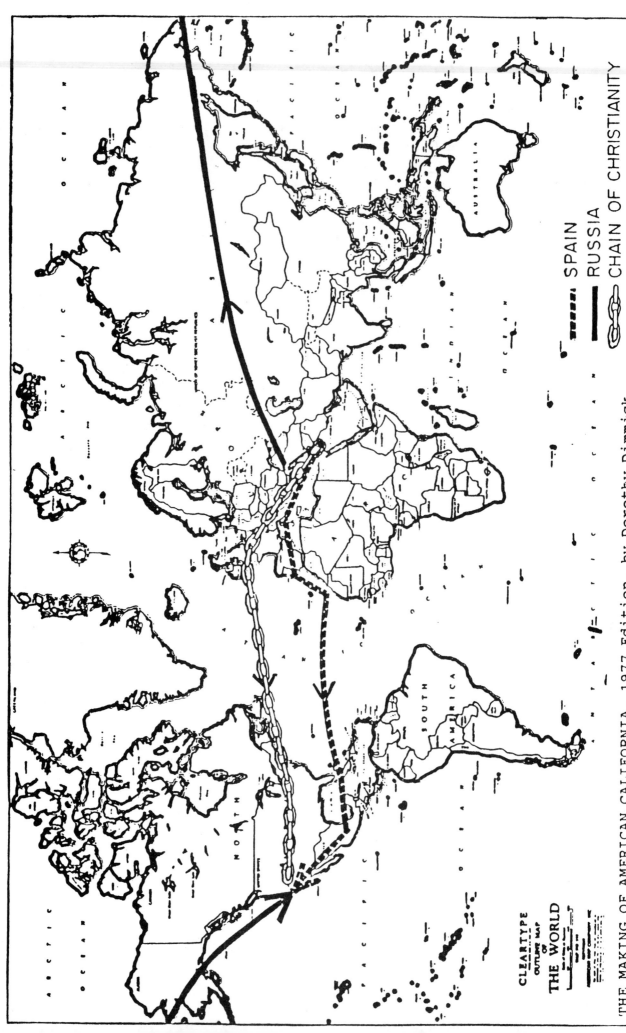

SPAIN

RUSSIA

CHAIN OF CHRISTIANITY

CLEARTYPE
OUTLINE MAP
of
THE WORLD

THE MAKING OF AMERICAN CALIFORNIA, 1977 Edition, by Dorothy Dimmick

pioneering the overland trail. He opened the door through which the United States and reformed religion entered California."[15]

The third branch of Christianity "beginning at Jerusalem," crossed Europe westward, was brought by the Pilgrims and Puritans to the east coast of America, and still traveling west with our pioneers over the Rockies and Sierras, entered California with "Bible-toter Jed." This was the entrance of the new and vital force of "reformed religion." This was the branch of Christianity upon whose principles the political structure of California was built.

1822-1846 MEXICAN CALIFORNIA

1845
Beginning war

We remember that in 1821 Mexico had won her independence from Spain, and established a Mexican Republic. By 1822, Mexico owned a great and huge state containing lands from Texas to California. Then in 1836, Texas won her independence from Mexico and declared herself an Independent Republic. Texas requested annexation to the United States which was delayed because Texas was a slave state, until she was formally admitted in 1845. The annexation of Texas to the United States was considered an act of war between Mexico and the United States, to be discussed later.

California
under Mexico

How did California fare under Mexican rule? Mexico failed to provide the relief so sorely needed in California. Throughout the Mexican era the potential resources of California remained not only undeveloped but largely unsuspected. The most substantial economic activity was cattle raising, and the chief commercial products were hides and tallow. There was virtually no manufacturing and an incredible lack of education.

American Christian
system of
measurement

As to the ranchos, there were about twenty private rancho land grants during the Spanish regime, and about five hundred during the Mexican period, most of them made after secularization. The maximum legal limit for a private rancho grant in California was 11 square leagues - about 50,000 acres, or 76 square miles. Minor discrepancies in boundary measurements were of no importance. The Spanish system of metes and bounds was used, creating years of legal complications in the United States courts. It was the Americans who brought with them the exact system of surveying, the Christian system, which brought order out of chaos.

MARIANO GUADALUPE VALLEJO

Vallejo

One of the outstanding contributors to California's three periods, the Spanish, the Mexican, and the American, was a native Californian, General Mariano Guadalupe Vallejo. A study of his interesting life is really a study of the governmental structure of the first two periods, giving us an appreciation of how the native Californians viewed the Americans in California.

Under the Mexican Governor Figueroa, who had made the plans for mission secularization, General Vallejo was made Administrator of the Sonoma

Mission, and grantee of the Petaluma Rancho (44,280 acres). Both the Sonoma Mission (1823) and the Petaluma Rancho or Adobe (1833) had been established by the Mexicans as hedges against the occupation by the Russians on the coast of California in Sonoma County. The Petaluma Adobe was a fort as well as a self-contained colony built by General Vallejo. Vallejo was made military commander of the whole northern frontier district under the Mexican regime. His personal estate contained over 150,000 acres, including the Soscol Rancho grant.

General Vallejo was of noble Spanish blood. His father had marched into California as a young soldier with Serra's party and had been assigned to the Monterey Presidio in 1770. In the old Spanish days of General Vallejo's father, there was a decided lack of women in California. It is interesting how this young soldier found his bride. He learned of a baby girl being born into a family of friends in San Luis Obispo. He immediately asked for her hand in marriage when she came of age, providing the young lady acquiesced. When the baby grew into a young lady and reached the marriageable age of fourteen, the young soldier and she were united in marriage. Mariano was born in 1808.

Mariano Vallejo was also a soldier, both during the Spanish and Mexican regimes. He rose in rank rapidly, was intelligent, self-educated, and ambitious. When Mariano was fourteen, an Englishman, Mr. E. P. Hartnell, arrived in Monterey. Hartnell was a talented linguist and tutored Vallejo so that he had a fair knowledge of Latin, French, and English. Mariano worked for Hartnell at his store in Monterey and learned the fundamentals of arithmetic and bookkeeping.

Mariano married the daughter of the well-known Carrillo family of Southern California and they had fourteen children. A literature class might appreciate how he named some of his children. Having imported the best library in California, Vallejo was an avid reader and the names of his children depended a lot upon what he was reading at the time: Andronica was named while Vallejo was reading Shakespeare's TITUS ANDRONICUS; Plutarco after PLUTARCH; Platon for Plato's REPUBLIC; Napoleon for THE LITTLE CORPORAL; and Luisa Eugenia was named after Empress Eugenia and her son, Luis.

1846 JUNTA

Vallejo loyal
to America

Mariano Vallejo was entirely devoted to California and wished only the very best for this land. He felt that California could best progress under the American nation. He was an astute student of history, more familiar with the American constitutional form of government than other Californios, and felt a kinship to the diligence and perseverance of the American foreigner.

Perhaps Vallejo's most important contribution came in April of 1846 at a "Junta" or meeting in Monterey. It was a military gathering of the Californios to discuss means of defense against foreign aggression. There were no records of that meeting but it is a tradition, widely believed in, that they discussed not

148

only a scheme of independence from Mexico but of possible annexation to a foreign power, either the United States, England, or France. These were all possibilities. These nations had all expressed an interest in California and we shall briefly go into the background of each before setting forth the opposing views of Californios at that Junta.

UNITED STATES INTEREST IN CALIFORNIA

1845 President
Polk's policy

The United States had long had her eye on California. Ever since the early trappers, traders, and settlers had entered this lovely land, the tales that they took East with them and the letters they wrote, aroused great interest. The explorers sent West by our government gave glowing reports, and a policy of acquisition set in. Recognizing Mexico's feeble hold on California, President Polk in 1845 determined that the United States should acquire California.

ENGLISH INTEREST IN CALIFORNIA

In 1843, the United States and England had a strained relationship. According to AN AMERICAN HISTORY by Dr. David Muzzey:

Mexico owed
Britain

"Mexico owed about $50,000,000 to British capitalists, for which her lands to the north and west of the Rio Grande were mortgaged. An independent state of Texas under British protection would have furnished Britain with cotton, and market for her manufactures unhampered by the tariff of the United States. Our minister to Paris wrote home in 1845, 'There is scarcely any sacrifice England would not make to prevent Texas from coming into our possession.'"[16]

In a speech in the United States Senate, General Dix, a member of the Military Committee of the Senate and a Senator from New York, gave clearly the attitude of England towards the United States at the time immediately preceding the declaration of war agaist Mexico. According to John Fremont's MEMOIRS:

Britain wanted
California

"He (Dix) made it clear that if the work on land had not been done on which Commodore Sloat based his raising of the American flag, Admiral Seymour (of the British navy) would have raised that of England, and California would have been lost to us; for with her vastly superior navy, the chances of war were largely against us."[17]

McNamara's
threat

As further evidence of Britain's interest in California, Father McNamara appeared on the scene. He was an apostolic missionary who had far-reaching plans to colonize California with Catholic emigrants from Ireland. He wished to revive the power of the Catholic Church as it had existed in the old missions. According to Fremont, Father McNamara wished to:

"1) advance the cause of Catholicism; 2) contribute to the happiness of his countrymen; 3) place an impediment to further usurpations on the part of an irreligious and anti-Catholic nation."[18]

He offered to the President of Mexico at least 10,000 colonists. The project was approved by Mexico and on July 4, 1846, McNamara and Mexico finally agreed on the colonization of Upper California by Irish families, three thousand in number, to whom each family would be given a square league of land, making in all thirteen and one-half million acres. McNamara traveled on British ships and during his stay in Mexico, lived either in the family of the English consul or the Mexican Charge d'Affaires. Again quoting Senator Dix from Fremont's MEMOIRS:

Britain behind
McNamara

"The grant to McNamara is so connected with the movements of the public vessels and public agents of Great Britain as to raise a strong presumption that he was secretly countenanced by the British Government...From all the circumstances connected with the transactions in California, we are constrained to believe that the British naval commander was fully appraised of McNamara's objects, as well as the design to place that country under the protection of Great Britain, and that he was there co-operating in the one, and ready to co-operate in the other."[19]

Fremont noted:

"It is in evidence that his (McNamara's) project secured the approbation of the Mexican Government; and that he went to California to perfect his plans under the auspices of the English Government. On the 20th of June he arrived at Santa Barbara, California, in the frigate JUNO which had brought him up from Mazatlan."[20]

Providentially,
McNamara
too late

But McNamara was too late. Here again we see the Hand of God in California's history. The Governor of California under Mexico, Pio Pico in Los Angeles, in a special session of the Assembly on July 7, 1846, approved the colonization project but on **that morning** the flag of the United States was hoisted at Monterey. Mexican authority ended in California.

FRENCH INTEREST IN CALIFORNIA

As far as one can discover, France posed a minor threat to overtaking California. California had been visited in 1786 by the Comte de la Perouse, who had made a world voyage of scientific exploration for the French government. Perouse observed California and believed its importance lay in the distant future.

France: Catholicism
attracted Californios

The greatest attraction of California to France was that it was a Latin nation and some of the Californios preferred to see California under Catholic

150

France than the Protestant nation of the United States.

There did appear such places as French Camp, south of Stockton, so-named because it was settled by the Hudson Bay Company's French-Canadian trappers.

BACK TO THE JUNTA OF 1846

Paul Revere's grandson, Joseph

All of these things, and more, must have been taken into consideration when the Mexican officials held their junta in 1846 to determine the future of California. Lt. Joseph Warren Revere, Paul Revere's grandson, arrived in Monterey while the junta was in session. In his book NAVAL DUTY IN CALIFORNIA, he published some interesting speeches of the Californios attending the junta, all from hearsay from "an intelligent member." Some of the leading Californios preferred a French protectorate; others preferred English protection. Castro and Pio Pico favored annexation to England or France, two powerful nations. It was the belief of these Californians that it was the right and duty of the weak to demand support of the strong. They believed it would be to their advantage to connect with one of these powerful nations.

Governor Pio Pico

Pio Pico was the last Mexican governor of Mexican California. Here is quoted his purported speech from Revere's book because it gives us an idea of California's plight under Mexico in 1846:

"'Excellent Sirs! to what a deplorable condition is our country reduced! Mexico, professing to be our mother and our protectress, has given us neither arms, nor money, nor the material of war for our defence. She is not likely to do anything in our behalf, although she is quite willing to afflict us with her extortionate minions, who come hither in the guise of soldiers and civil officers to harass and oppress our people. We possess a glorious country, capable of attaining a physical and moral greatness corresponding with the grandeur and beauty which an Almighty hand has stamped upon the face of our beloved California.

But although nature has been prodigal, it cannot be denied that we are not in a position to avail ourselves of her bounty. Our population is not large, and it is sparsely scattered over valley and mountain, covering an immense area of virgin soil, destitute of roads, and traversed with difficulty; hence it is hardly possible to collect an army of any considerable force. Our people are poor, as well as few, and cannot well govern themselves and maintain a decent show of sovereign power. Although we live in the midst of plenty, we lay up nothing; but, tilling the earth in an imperfect manner, all our time is required to provide proper subsistence for ourselves and our families.

Thus circumstances, we find ourselves suddenly threatened by hordes of Yankee emigrants, who have already begun to flock into our country, and whose progress we cannot arrest. Already have the wagons of that perfidious people scaled the almost inaccessible summits of the Sierra Nevada, crossed the entire continent, and penetrated the fruitful valley of the Sacramento. What that astonishing people will next undertake, I cannot say; but in whatever enterprise they embark they will be sure to prove successful. Already are these adventurous land-voyagers spreading themselves far and wide over a country which seems suited to their tastes. They are cultivating farms, establishing vineyards, erecting mills, sawing up lumber, building workshops, and doing a thousand other things which seem natural to them, but which Californians neglect or despise.

What then are we to do?... I pronounce for annexation to France or England... Have we not all lived under a monarchy far more despotic than that of France, or England, and were not our people happy under it?... Then may our people go quietly to their ranchos, and live there as of yore, leading a merry and thoughtless life, untroubled by politics or cares of State..."[21]

Revere

Revere remarked:

"Fortunately for California, and, as the sequel proved, for the views of the government of the United States, which already embraced the acquisition by treaty or purchase of that important territory, with its fine seaports, so essential to the interests of our growing commerce in the Pacific, a man was found at this crises whose opinions were more honest and enlightened than those of the military and civil rulers of his country. Like a true patriot, he could not endure to see the land of his birth traded away to any European monarchy, and he rightly judged, that although foreign protection might postpone, it could not ultimately avert the 'manifest destiny' of California...This man was Don Mariano Guadalupe Vallejo."[22]

Vallejo is purported to have opposed the views advanced by Pico, as reported by Revere:

Vallejo

"'...It is most true, that to rely any longer on Mexico to govern and defend us, would be idle and absurd... It is also true that we possess a noble country, every way calculated from position and resources, to become great and powerful. For that reason I would not have her a mere dependency upon a foreign monarchy, naturally alien, or at least indifferent to our interests and our welfare... Even could we tolerate the idea of dependence, ought

152

we to go to distant Europe for a master? What possible sympathy could exist between us and a nation separated from us by two vast oceans?

But waiving this insuperable objection, how could we endure to come under the dominion of a monarchy? -- for although others speak lightly of a form of government, as a freeman, I cannot do so. We are republicans -- badly governed and badly situated as we are -- still we are all in sentiment, republicans. So far as we are governed at all, we at least profess to be self-governed. Who, then, that possesses true patriotism will consent to subject himself and his children to the caprices of a foreign king and his official minions?...

We have indeed taken the first step, by electing our own governor, but another remains to be taken...it is annexation to the United States... Why should we shrink from incorporating ourselves with the happiest and freest nation in the world, destined soon to be the most wealthy and powerful? Why should we go abroad for protection when this great nation is our adjoining neighbor? When we join our fortunes to hers, we shall not become subjects, but fellow-citizens, possessing all the rights of the people of the United States, and choosing our own federal and local rulers. We shall have a stable government and just laws. California will grow strong and flourish, and her people will be prosperous, happy, and free. Look not, therefore, with jealousy upon the hardy pioneers who scale our mountains and cultivate our unoccupied plains; but rather welcome them as brothers, who come to share with us a common destiny.'"[23]

Providential exit from Junta

A vote was asked for at the junta but the meeting adjourned to reconvene in an hour. Vallejo thought that the partisans of monarchy had it all cut-and-dried, so he prevailed on the friends of the United States to leave Monterey. They did so and when the hour of voting came, there was no quorum and no definite conclusion to the weighty matter they had met to decide.

SPAIN AND MEXICO'S CONTRIBUTION TO CALIFORNIA

Little contribution to constitutional government of California

For romantic, commercial, and social reasons, California has promoted the Spanish period of her history. Actually, Spain's fifty-three years (1769-1822) of sovereignty in Alta California contributed little to the structure of our commonwealth, nor did the twenty-four years' occupancy of Mexico (1822-1846). We are grateful to Spain for the founding, and colonization of California; to the beautiful legacy of place names which are so abundant on the map of California; and the type of Spanish architecture we greatly admire. Mexico distributed many land grants; secularized the missions; and opened California ports to foreign ships.

153

From the time that the flag of the United States first flew over Monterey, the essential pattern of California's development was typically Anglo-Saxon. It is the pattern which Jamestown and Plymouth brought from England and occupied the Atlantic coast. That pattern moved westward across rivers, plains and mountains, and entered California in covered wagons. Homes, schools, churches, mining, intensive agriculture and industry came across the plains. All essential lines of civilization ran from the East coast of America to the West coast of California. We shall call this phenomenon, the extension of the Chain of Christianity into California.

Now let us see how those vital and energetic pioneers from America entered California.

REFERENCES TO CHAPTER II

EARLY HISTORY OF SPAIN IN CALIFORNIA

1. Chapman, Charles E. A HISTORY OF CALIFORNIA: THE SPANISH PERIOD, p. 142.

THE EXPEDITION TO SAN DIEGO 1769

2. Hunt-Sanchez. A SHORT HISTORY OF CALIFORNIA, p. 64.

1769 SAN DIEGO MISSION

3. Hunt, Rockwell D. CALIFORNIA'S STATELY HALL OF FAME, p. 42.

THE INDIANS OF CALIFORNIA

4. Kroeber, A. L. ANTHROPOLOGY, p. 319.
5. Ibid., p. 298.
6. Chapman, Charles E. A HISTORY OF CALIFORNIA: THE SPANISH PERIOD, p. 12.
7. Ibid., p. 12.

INDIAN CUSTOMS

* Sagundai was from the Delaware nation. Twelve men had been chosen to go with Fremont. These were known to be good hunters and brave men. Two of them were chiefs, Swanok and Sagundai.

MISSION INDIANS

8. Hunt-Sanchez. A SHORT HISTORY OF CALIFORNIA, p. 73.
9. Ibid., p. 74.
10. Ibid., p. 90.

SECULARIZATION OF THE MISSIONS 1834

11. Ibid., p. 252.
12. Ibid., p. 253.
13. Hunt, Rockwell D. CALIFORNIA IN THE MAKING, p. 119.

RUSSIANS IN SPANISH AND MEXICAN CALIFORNIA 1806–1841

14. TRAVEL JOURNAL OF THE PRIEST IOANN VENIAMINOV KEPT DURING HIS TRIP TO CALIFORNIA AND BACK FROM JUNE 1 TO OCT. 13, 1836.

CLEARING THE WAY FOR PROTESTANTISM IN CALIFORNIA

* The student is referred to THE CHRISTIAN HISTORY OF THE CONSTITUTION OF THE UNITED STATES OF AMERICA: SELF-GOVERNMENT WITH UNION, VOL. II:

> Page 129: "The Christian system, as it was hitherto taught, preserved its native and beautiful simplicity... The public teachers inculcated no other doctrines, than those that are contained in, what is commonly called, the Apostles Creed... This venerable simplicity was not, indeed, of a long duration;..."

> Page 130: "CORRUPTION INTRODUCES UNNECESSARY RITES AND CEREMONY: Primitive Simplicity Destroyed: Second Century."

> Page 134: "THE CHURCH-STATE IMPLEMENTED: Constantine and Other Emperors Use Power Of Civil Government To Forge A Policy of Forced Christianity: Fourth Century."

> Page 138: "CONSTANTINE the GREAT, by removing the seat of the empire to Byzantium, and building the city of Constantinople, raised up, in the bishop of this new metropolis, a formidable rival to the Roman pontif... This promotion...concluded, at length, in the entire separation of the Latin and Greek churches..."

15. Loofbourow, Leon L. IN SEARCH OF GOD'S GOLD, p. 9.
16. Muzzy, David S. AN AMERICAN HISTORY, p. 272.
17. Fremont, John C. MEMOIRS OF MY LIFE, p. 547.
18. Ibid., p. 551.
19. Ibid., p. 548.
20. Ibid., p. 552.
21. Revere, Joseph W. NAVAL DUTY IN CALIFORNIA, pp. 19, 20, 21.
22. Ibid., pp. 21, 22
23. Ibid., pp. 22, 23.

CHAPTER III

AMERICANS ENTER CALIFORNIA

"O bless our God, ye people, and make the voice of his praise to be heard:

For thou, O God, hast proved us: thou hast tried us, as silver is tried.

...We went through fire and through water: but thou broughtest us out into a wealthy place." (Ps. 66:8,10,12)

PIONEER ROUTES INTO CALIFORNIA

How did the pioneers from the eastern coast of America enter California in the Far West?

There were several routes to California, each offering certain advantages:

1) The overland route through the South Pass of the Rocky Mountains and over the Sierra Nevadas, or down the Old Santa Fe Trail.

2) The all-water route around Cape Horn.

3) The land and water route via Panama.

1) OVERLAND ROUTE

Over the Sierras in "prairie schooners"

From Independence, Missouri, most of the caravans took the central route. Over the Sierra Nevada Mountains in covered wagons was the most popular way of entering California. It was cheaper; families could travel together; they could take their personal possessions with them; and it offered adventure. This was a migration of mostly young men. However, grim determination and courage were demanded of those who attempted the overland trail. Most of the emigrants started in companies, pooling their funds and resources, each man pledged to shoulder his share of the work and danger. Few comprehended the dangers of the trail that lay ahead.

From the Missouri River to the heights of the Sierra Nevada, the exodus took place – wagons by day and camp fires by night. As long as they traveled in the Spring, it seemed like a holiday and a picnic and their spirits were high. There was rich pasturage for their cattle and oxen, plenty of water, and wild flowers.

Calif.-Oregon Trail

Dragoon: A soldier on horseback

The California-Oregon Trail was the same route until they split at Ft. Hall in Idaho, some trains going to California and some to Oregon. Dragoon Carleton of the United States Cavalry, assigned to Kearney's detachment to accompany some of the wagon trains to Oregon in 1845, remarked:

"Fifty large and well-built wagons covered with white canvas were drawn by three or four yoke of oxen. They moved in two columns opposite each other. Each man carried a rifle, a brace of pistols, and a large knife. The tramp of so many hoofs, the lowing of cattle, the neighing of the horses, the loud voices of the drivers, and the sharp and frequent cracking of their whips, the tinkling of the innumerable bells, the laughing and the shouting of the boys and girls as they frolicked between the two columns; the singing of the mothers to their little ones or their calling the children's attention: 'Those are the soldiers who are going with us,' and the singing of hymns or old familiar songs, all resounded on the hitherto silent prairie..."[1]

Overland route:
Four months

As the Dragoons passed many companies plodding along the old Oregon Trail, Dragoon Carleton, a seaman from Maine, further remarked:

"Judging from the way they go on, by the time the leading company reaches the valley of the Columbia, there will be a broad stream of the real Anglo-Saxon stock stretching from the Atlantic to the Pacific, a regular Life-river traveling at a steady three-knot current."

However, the pioneers often consumed their precious grain too soon. As the desert grew hot, the grass for their animals grew scant. The trail was littered with discarded baggage, broken wagons and skeletons of animals. A few turned back, but most of the emigrants tightened their belts and pushed forward. From the grassy lowlands, the trails rose to the tablelands, home of the mirage. They never could be sure whether they beheld reality or mirage on the horizon. Some Indians were friendly and some hostile, and attack by Indians was part of the journey most greatly feared by the emigrants.   Under the most favorable conditions, from Independence, Missouri, to California the trip could be made in 90 days; the average time overland was about 120 days.

THE OLD SANTA FE TRAIL

Old trade routes

Several thousand forty-niners going to California chose to go by way of the Santa Fe Trail. They might start from Missouri or Arkansas or Texas.

This, and the Old Spanish Trail, were trade routes established when the early trappers carried news from Upper California to Santa Fe that the Californians had fine horses and donkeys and that they sold them very cheap. Traders from Santa Fe began to cross the desert trails with loads of blankets and other useful things to trade for the Californian's horses and burros.

The traders used two trails: The Old Santa Fe Trail from Santa Fe, down the Gila River trail, across the Colorado Desert (name of a desert in Southern California), through the San Gorgonio Pass, through the San Bernardino Valley to the pueblo of Los Angeles. The other trail used by the traders was the Old

158

Spanish Trail, which went from Santa Fe across the Mohave Desert, through Cajon Pass, then through the San Bernardino Valley and into Los Angeles. In early Spanish days, California horses and donkeys were sent along El Camino Real to Los Angeles and there met the Santa Fe traders.

The emigrants who chose these trails, however, found themselves in the pueblo of Los Angeles, still 400 miles south of the gold fields.

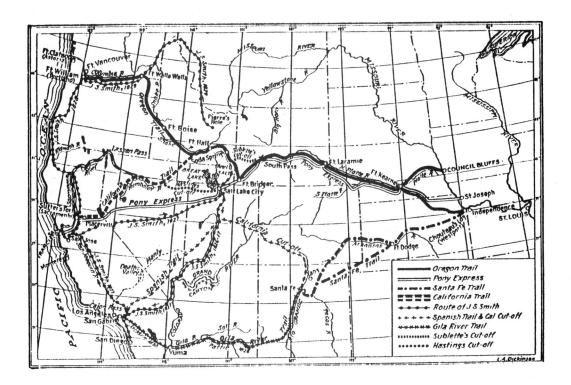

MAP SHOWING OVERLAND TRAILS

From: NEW CALIFORNIA THE GOLDEN, by Rockwell D. Hunt

THE LASSEN TRAIL

Some of the emigrants left the main trail to California on the Humboldt River on what was called Lassen's Cutoff. A signpost showed where it struck off west from the Humboldt. The sign did not say, however, that the Cutoff led across Black Rock Desert, followed by a hard climb to the Pit River, past dangerous Indians. Those that chose this path during the Gold Rush found themselves far north of the gold mines.

2) THE ALL-WATER ROUTE AROUND CAPE HORN

4th of July aboard ship

"Around the Horn," at the southern tip of South America, was a long and dangerous trip often chosen by emigrants from New England and the Middle Atlantic states. The ships carrying the argonauts were either sailing vessels, whalers, or cargo boats hastily fitted with bunks, often with three times as many bunks as their space justified. The sailing vessels making this voyage required six months or longer. If room permitted on board, the passengers entertained themselves with songs and dances or various games. American anniversaries, like the Fourth of July, were enthusiastically celebrated. The foreign ports were very interesting to the young Americans on board these vessels.

"Flying Cloud"

The graceful clipper ships constructed especially for California voyages won fame as the swiftest and most beautiful vessels afloat. They had long, sharp lines and a great spread of canvas, which gave them unusual speed. They made the trip from New York to San Francisco around Cape Horn in little more than one half the time required by the ordinary sailing vessels. The fastest time was made by the clipper ship FLYING CLOUD, anchor to anchor, New York to San Francisco in 89 days and 8 hours.

Stormy Straits
of Magellan

Navigating the Straits of Magellan was risky. Storms often forced the ships to stand by as many as six weeks before they could continue passage through the channel. On most ships during the rush for gold in California, there was very little room for exercise and the passengers suffered from cold, dampness, anxiety, and hunger. An equal danger were the weeks of calm the sailing ships encountered under the cloudless tropical skies. When this occurred, they had to run 1,000 miles off-course to catch the trade winds. After the hazardous voyage, the passengers were grateful for the sight of birds which indicated land, their Golden Land. Off the Pacific Coast, their first sighting was

"...a wealthy
place."

the outline of the foothills of California. The trip through the Golden Gate was an exciting experience, and finally, they spotted San Francisco, where every man hoped to find gold in abundance.

3) THE LAND AND WATER ROUTE BY PANAMA

No short-cut

The Panama route was considered a shorter way to reach California, which it was; it was also considered much quicker, which it was not.

This was the route selected by most of the men from the South Atlantic seaboard as well as some from the north. It was about 2500 miles from New York to Chagres, on the eastern coast of the Isthmus, sixty miles across the Isthmus to Panama, and about 3500 miles more to San Francisco.

Panama
and malaria

After arrival at the Gulf Port of Chagres, there was a two or three day journey across the Isthmus (60 miles) before the run up the Mexican coast to California. Up the river in dugout canoes made from a bay or mahogany tree, the passengers traveled across the tropics, heavy with fragrant blossoms, colorful with birds, and treacherous with cholera. Often the crossing lengthened into six days during heavy rains. The river brought them to Cruces, the head of navigation. Here again began the game of bargaining. The natives had to be hired to transport the passengers in their canoes; now mules were needed to transport the passengers and their cargo over the winding and narrow trail to Panama City and the Pacific Ocean. There was no wagon road, only a single trail cut through dense tropical undergrowth so narrow in places the rider had to draw his legs up before him in the saddle. The wait at Panama for another ship for San Francisco sometimes took several months, a dangerous and exasperating wait at the malaria and yellow fever city of Panama.

THE STEAMSHIPS

Mail: 1848-1849

The United States government contracted with the Atlantic Steamship Company to carry mail, and incidentally passengers, from New York to Chagres (2500 miles). The Pacific Mail Steamship Company, organized April 1848, was under contract to make connection at Panama with the Atlantic ships and to carry the mail twice a month from Panama to San Francisco (3500 miles). The CALIFORNIA, pride of the Pacific Mail, was a magnificent side-wheeler of 900 tons, fitted with accommodations for 120 passengers, but often carrying 500 to 1,000 passengers. The first Atlantic ship left New York for Chagres December 1, 1848. But the Pacific Mail steamer was 25 days late, forcing the passengers to wait in uncomfortable quarters at the disease-ridden port of Panama.

During the gold rush, few of the thousands who poured into Panama could be carried on steamers. The overland journey remained the most popular way of entering the golden land of California.

EARLY PIONEERS

The Mountain Men

The overland routes became well-traveled during California's Gold Rush but someone had to pioneer those routes. The earliest visitors were the "Mountain Men," so-called because they were the hunters, trappers and fur traders from the interior who pushed farther and farther west in search of game. The beaver was a fine fur, although not as fine as that of the sea otters, but there was a good market for their pelts and the Mountain Men were their hunters. These early Americans were great explorers. They knew the trails from the Missouri to the Pacific. When these men returned to the settlements in the East with the bundles of furs packed on their horses, they recounted fascinating stories and observations of the great western country. They were responsible for many an emigrant American family seeking a new home in the West.

1826 JEDEDIAH SMITH

Among the rugged, hardy, individualistic mountain men, Jedediah Smith was outstanding. He was the first American to blaze the overland trail to California and Oregon.

"Bible-Toter Jed"

This young man was known as "Bible-toter Jed." He combined the spiritual qualities of vision, good will, and faith along with the physical qualities of courage, daring, and endurance. Dale L. Morgan said of him:

"Jedediah Smith was an unlikely sort of hero for the brawling
West of his time, that West about which it has been said that

161

God took care to stay on his own side of the Missouri River. For Jedediah was a young man modest and unassuming, quiet and mild of manner, one who never smoked or chewed tobacco, never uttered a profane word, and partook of wine or brandy only sparingly on formal occasions. He took his religion with him into the wilderness and let nothing corrode it. That would have made him merely curious, except that he took with him also indifference to privation and personal suffering, endurance beyond the point where other men died, courage and coolness under fire, intelligence that impressed everyone, leadership of a high order, and energy and drive enough for three men."[2]

Support for
his family

The Smiths, and Jedediah's mother's family, the Strongs, were of old New England stock but his father chose to move westward. Jedediah was born in southern New York and grew up in Ohio and Illinois. Their Ohio farm, though worked by the sturdy Scotch-Irish Smiths, had seemed incapable of supporting and educating the growing family of eleven children. So Jedediah started for the West and the fur trade to ease the family responsibilities. Dale Morgan further wrote of Jedediah:

Successful
in business

"In many respects he exemplified the American genius. Jedediah Smith entered the West owning his rifle, his Bible, the clothes on his back and very little else. He returned to the States eight years later having sustained himself and a large business operation through all that time by his proficiency as a trapper and his adeptness as a trader."[3]

It is interesting to note that Jedediah Smith was an avid reader. His best friend in Ohio was a physician who undoubtedly was influential in the type of books Jedediah collected. He kept his books in St. Louis and evidently took different volumes on his successive trips. He had an unusual collection for a mountain man of the 1820's:

Matthew Henry's
Commentary

Clapperton's Second Expedition into Africa
Rollin's Ancient History
History of Ancient Greece
History of Mexico
Morris' Gazetteer
The Seaman's Daily Assistant
Natural Theology
Evidences of Christianity
Theological Dictionary
Henry's Exposition of the Scriptures (6 Volumes)
Josephus' Wars (4 Volumes)

Free traders

Smith adopted the method in his fur trade business of a rendezvous of the traders in place of the fort-trading posts and encouraged the free traders in place of the "engagees" or "voyageurs," thus putting to an end the Hudson Bay

Company's monopoly of the Pacific fur trade. As a result, the Americans continued to advance in Oregon, Washington, and Idaho, and the Hudson Bay Company lost interest.

1826, First overland party to California

In 1826, Smith led the first overland party into California. With fifteen men and fifty horses, his party left its headquarters on the Bear River near the area of Great Salt Lake. Following the Colorado River to where Needles now is, the company crossed the river into California. They left Bear Lake in August and he and his ragged, half-starved men reached San Bernardino the last of November. They reached the San Gabriel Mission in an exhausted condition. They had crossed the hot, barren southern desert, the first Americans to cross the continent to California. Lewis and Clarke had crossed the continent to Oregon. Now a second transcontinental door was opened.

Pathfinder

Jedediah wintered in the San Joaquin Valley in 1826. Twice in the Spring of 1827 he attempted to cross the heavy snows of the Sierras but failed. Then leaving the majority of his party with friendly Indians in the San Joaquin Valley, he and two men, seven horses and two mules went north to the American River and again attempted the crossing. It took eight days and cost two horses and one mule. It was quite a feat to cross the almost impassable Sierras in the deep Spring snows but he had accomplished the first recorded crossing of the mighty Sierra Nevada. His journey across the deserts of Nevada and Utah and return to the Great Salt Lake was remarkable for its courage and endurance. His accomplishment of blazing the overland Trail into California is greater, too, when we realize it was the belief of all that California could never be invaded. It was believed that the mountains could never be crossed, not even by hunters, and that the sandy desert was completely impassable. A student might want to trace his interesting life, learn of some of his wild adventures, and see God's Providence in his life.

Smith pioneered a third route. In December of 1827, he led a party to Oregon. He and his party made the first recorded journey by land up to the northwestern coast of California and Oregon.

Jedediah traveled tens of thousands of miles on foot and horseback. Through his untiring energy, his great courage, and his practice of the Christian religion, he opened the deserts and the mountains of the west to the thousands of emigrants who followed his trails.

"A Christian gentleman"

Dr. Robert Glass Cleland wrote of him:

"Smith's worth as an explorer, his resourcefulness as a leader, and his skill as a mountain man were only surpassed by his integrity and faith. Men spoke of him as a Christian gentleman. Those who knew him best said that he made religion 'an active principle from the duties of which nothing could seduce him.'...He was a man of good and honest and courageous heart."[4]

Let us again understand the real mission of Jedediah Smith, according to Dr. Loofbourow:

> "California's development, material and spiritual, required a new, vital force.
>
> This force came.

> It came first in 1826 in the person of Jedediah Smith, Methodist 'Bible-toter,' first to cross Utah, Nevada, and the Sierras, pioneering the overland trail. He opened the door through which the United States and reformed religion entered California."[5]

"PIONEER" VS. "ARGONAUT"

After the early trappers and hunters, a few pioneers entered California. Let us differentiate between the words "pioneer" and "argonaut."

From THE COURSE OF EMPIRE, we read:

> "Argonaut and pioneer are words used indiscriminately to describe the early comers to California, but basically the words are not similar but opposite, and much of the history of the state has been caused by the struggle between the two. To the pioneer, land and a home was the goal. The argonaut, as in the days of the Golden Fleece, was the gold seeker, rootless and irresponsible, with eyes turned back on some distant spot where, too often, he had left his conscience and his reputation while he journeyed afar in search of a stake."[6]

1832 THOMAS OLIVER LARKIN

One of the earliest American pioneers to establish himself in business on Mexico's coastal port of Monterey was Thomas Larkin who came from Massachusetts. At the suggestion of his half-brother, John Cooper, who was already engaged in trade there, Larkin made the long voyage around the Horn in 1832. One of the passengers on Larkin's ship was Mrs. Rachel Hobson Holmes who was on her way to join her husband at Hilo in the Sandwich or Hawaiian Islands. When she arrived at Hilo she discovered her husband had died, and a few months later Larkin proposed to her by correspondence. Their marriage ceremony was performed on board a ship off the Santa Barbara coast by the ship's owner and captain, John C. Jones, United States Consul at Honolulu. Mrs. Larkin was purported to be the first American woman to live in California.

Thomas Oliver Larkin was one of the few foreign residents who rose to a position of wealth and importance in California in spite of the fact that he refused to become a Mexican citizen, be converted to Roman Catholicism, or marry a local senorita.

The Larkin House in Monterey

Larkin became proprietor of a general store in Monterey and the middleman between the traders and the ranchers. Thus the ranchers and their families did not have to depend on the uncertain arrivals of trading ships. He also operated a successful business in redwood lumber, which he exported to the Sandwich or Hawaiian Islands and Mexico. In his designs for a home, for the custom house and other buildings, he established the Monterey style of architecture. His home, the Larkin House, is today registered in California as a California Historical Landmark (#106) and can be found at Jefferson and Calle Principal in Monterey.

Larkin eventually became a prime property owner. Reuben L. Underhill wrote of him:

Property owner

"With business prosperity came also the plans for landed wealth. To one like Larkin, born in New England while traditions handed down from the Puritans still existed, there was ever the urge to own land, be it a modest cottage home or a farm. This desire for property was a dominant trait of Larkin. It became a definite part of his ambitions soon after his arrival in California and he had even then determined to secure his share of the abundance of this new country. Following the completion of the wharf at Monterey he acquired a number of lots nearby."[7]

Underhill wrote of the character of the man Larkin in his personal life:

Family man

"Notwithstanding the demands of business and the growing complications of political affairs, Larkin never lost sight of the family welfare. Careful and solicitous of the happiness and comfort of his wife, who was none too robust, he showed much concern over their children as they came into being. Both parents, with their deep rooted New England traditions and a reverence for the Protestant faith in which they had been reared, found many complications in their desire to inculcate in their offspring those traditions and beliefs...Larkin was determined that his children should not be affected by the moral and spiritual environment in which they were born. The advantages of both education and traditional associations should be their lot; and as California could furnish neither, they were sent away, one by one, from the land of their birth, into a life of higher culture."[8]

Providentially, influential Larkin was made U.S. Consul to Mexico

On May 1, 1843, Larkin, the most influential American in Monterey, was appointed United States Consul at Monterey. Under United States President Polk and Secretary of State James Buchanan, America's only consul to Mexican California was to play an active part in relations between the Mexican government and the United States. He was one of the shrewdest and most far-sighted Americans in Mexico and in his new office, Larkin proved to be a capable moderator and an influence for America in its plans for obtaining California. It was Larkin's desire that California join his country in a peaceful way. This hope was crushed with the outbreak of the United States-Mexican War in 1846. Throughout this time, however, in spite of the fact that he was held captive by the Mexican government, he retained their esteem and friendship.

Another worker for the American acquisition of California was John Sutter, friend of Larkin. Through their mutual beliefs and hopes for California, they worked together.

1839 JOHN AUGUSTUS SUTTER

Sutter of Sutter's
Fort, Sacramento

Johann August Sutter, or John Augustus Sutter, was born in Baden of Swiss parents. He had been a young soldier in the Swiss army, then went into business. His business ventures in Europe were unsuccessful so he came to America to retrieve his fortunes. He arrived in San Francisco in July, 1839. Sutter was a forceful and very enterprising man. He applied for a grant of land from Governor Alvarado in Monterey. He was advised he must become a Mexican citizen, find a suitable tract of land, and return to the capital in a year and his naturalization papers and land grant would be ready for him. He selected the site for the famous Sutter's Fort at the juncture of the Sacramento and American Rivers, a grant of 11 square leagues.

From COURSE OF EMPIRE, we read:

"On his baronial leagues at New Helvetia, Sutter planted the choicest of trees and vineyards, he laid out roads and gardens; under his guiding hand hundreds of Indians sowed and reaped, his horses and cattle numbered thousands, his warehouses bulged with grain. Sutter's feudal barony was a beehive of industry, skilled workmen forged iron and carved leather, a flour mill ground his wheat, and the sawmill for his lumber was the site of Marshall's discovery of gold. He had tamed the Indians better than the padres, taught them the use of better food, the satisfaction of cleanliness, and the enjoyment of the products of effort. His lands stretched league after league, and his adopted country, Mexico, observing his fostering wisdom, granted him still further lands."[9]

When the Russians withdrew from California in 1841, Sutter bought their holdings. Both Sutter and the Californios were relieved when the encroachers upon the land decided to leave.

John Bidwell said of Sutter:

Pro-American

"The object of his admiration was the Republic of the United States. He was always an American at heart and longed for the

166

Sketched by J. W. Revere U.S.N.   Lith. of Wm. Endicott & Co. N.York.

SUTTER's FORT - NEW HELVETIA.

NAVAL DUTY IN CALIFORNIA by Joseph Warren Revere

day when Mexico and her revolutions would, as he believed, lose California to the United States."[10]

A decision
important
to America

Late in 1845, Sutter made a crucial decision which meant a great deal to the Americans who were his friends and associates. The Commissioner from Mexico arrived in California with authorization to make Sutter an offer. Since Mexico was not strong enough to acquire Sutter's empire by force of arms, they tried another way. The Mexican government offered Sutter one hundred thousand dollars, or the Mission lands of San Jose in their entirety in exchange for his grant. John Sutter's New Helvetia was the key to California. Although this was a magnificent offer, Sutter wanted the American flag to fly over California, so he refused the offer. We see The Hand of God in this decision. With Sutter's fort in the hands of the Mexicans, the Americans would have had a difficult time obtaining possession of California.

John Bidwell is generous in his praise of Sutter:

"He had come to the Pacific Coast without a great deal of money, but he had that which brought money – a magnificent address. He was of fine and commanding presence and courteous as a prince to all. I have never seen one more polished in his deportment. Always liberal and affable, no one could be more obliging than he, especially to needy or destitute strangers."[11]

A "good
Samaritan"

For years, John Sutter helped the many emigrants who entered California through the Sacramento Valley. Bidwell further said of him: "He was the most generous and hospitable of men. Everybody was welcome – one man or a hundred, it was all the same." He sent many rescue parties to aid those in distress while crossing the mountains. He gave them shelter until they regained their health, and gave employment to as many as he possibly could.

The discovery of gold on his property early in 1848 was a personal catastrophe to Sutter. The argonauts swarmed over his settlement, squatted his land, stole his wheat and cattle, and even occupied his house. Later, the land squatters defeated him in the United States' courts and established legal title to his lands.

1841 BARTLESON-BIDWELL PARTY

First organized party
into California

The Bartleson-Bidwell Party of 1841 was the first group of settlers to organize a party to cross the Rockies and Sierras into California.

During the autumn of 1840, as a result of trapper Antoine Robidoux's colorful stories about California and Dr. John Marsh's interesting letters about this western paradise, the town of Weston, Missouri, became excited about organizing a party to travel west. However, during the winter, California's Governor Alvarado arrested Isaac Graham and other Americans which discouraged the newly formed "Western Emigration Society." John Bidwell, a young school teacher, was the only one of the original company who decided to go on

168

and in the spring of 1841, a new company of 47 persons, including 15 women and children, started from Independence, Missouri. John Bartleson was elected captain. No one in the group had ever been West and their only maps were inaccurate. They fell in with a party of trappers and missionaries going out to found a mission in Idaho, headed by the famous guide of the Rocky Mountain region, Thomas Fitzpatrick.

Joined "Broken Hand" Fitzpatrick

Desertion and forgiveness

Upon leaving the Oregon Trail and starting out across the Great Basin for California, about half of the emigrants decided to go to Oregon with Fitzpatrick; several decided to return to Missouri. Those that were left managed to find the Humboldt River but had to abandon their wagons. Bartleson and eight other men took the best horses and deserted the party near the Humboldt Sink and rode ahead. They failed to find a pass and returned to the party full of remorse for their rashness. Without chastising them, Bidwell accepted them into the party again, but this time, Bidwell was the captain.

Bidwell's DIARY

Bidwell had promised his friends he would keep a journal of his journey to California, noting the incidents of his trip and giving his observations of the country after his arrival. He called his diary, "A Journey to California," a day-to-day record of the journey from May 18, 1841 to November 6, 1841. One writer said of this journey: "Bidwell's record of this journey is fascinating - full of pathos for the inexperienced travellers; delight in the descriptions of the land as they crossed it; heartache at their lack of food, fear of hostile Indians, knowledge of the terrain, or even the distance to California."

The guiding Hand

Having miraculously found their way over the Sierras, the first organized emigrant train to California reached John Marsh's ranch on November 4, 1841. Bidwell soon arrived at Sutter's, about seventy-five miles north of Marsh's. Bidwell joined Sutter's employ and became his trusted secretary and friend.

"Prince of Pioneers"

Bidwell had an active part in the movements in California during the eventful years of the American conquest as well as during the gold rush and the building of the state of California. He is called the "Father of Chico," and "The Prince of Pioneers" by Dr. Rockwell Hunt.

ANNIE BIDWELL

A Christian union

Here we must mention Annie Ellicott Kennedy Bidwell. John Bidwell, a bachelor, and a Congressman, was a very welcome visitor in the Kennedy home in Washington in 1865. Annie was a devout Presbyterian and insisted John become a Christian before she would consider marriage.

Their wedding on May 16, 1868 was quite a social event in the nation's capital. Present were President Johnson, General Grant, and General Sherman.

Bidwell Mansion in Chico

Mrs. Bidwell showed a great interest in the Mechoopda Indians who lived on their beautiful 25,000 acre Rancho Chico. She was a tireless worker for Christian activities and a faithful, positive support for the General.

John Bidwell became a leading agriculturalist in California, candidate for Governor, and unsuccessful candidate of the Prohibition Party for the presidency of the United States. He truly emulated the Christian qualities of honesty, morality, and integrity in every phase of his life. Annie was his inspiration.

1842 JOHN CHARLES FREMONT

To find a path
to the Pacific

John Fremont is regarded as the central figure in the actual conquest of California. Fremont was a young officer of the United States Topographical Engineers when he was assigned to an expedition for the United States into the Rocky Mountains in 1842 for the purpose of examining the South Pass and finding the best route for overland travel to the Pacific Coast. His guide and friend was the famous scout, Kit Carson.

Pathmarker

While Jedediah Smith was known as the Pathfinder, John Fremont is known as the Pathmarker. His careful recordings and observations were an important factor in the opening of the West. To acquaint the reader with his five exploring expeditions, and a bare outline of his interesting life, let us quote from THE OLD SOUTH LEAFLET, NO. 45:

1842,
Expedition No. 1

"Save Lewis and Clarke alone, there is no name in the annals of the exploration of the Rocky Mountains so brilliant or noteworthy as that of John C. Fremont. In 1842, when not yet thirty years old, Fremont, then a lieutenant in the corps of topographical engineers, projected a geographical survey of the entire territory of the United States, from the Missouri River to the Pacific Ocean. He left Washington May 2, 1842 (his first expedition), under the direction of the War Department, to explore the Rocky Mountains, and particularly to examine the South Pass. He accomplished his task in four months, exploring the Wind River Mountains and ascending their highest point, since known as Fremont's Peak. His report attracted great attention both in this country and in Europe.

1843-44,
Expedition No. 2

In May, 1843, he set out with thirty-nine men on a much more comprehensive expedition (his second expedition). In September, after travelling more than 1,700 miles, he came in sight of the Great Salt Lake, of which very inaccurate notions had obtained until his time. His accounts had an important influence in promoting the settlement of Utah and the Pacific States. He proceeded north to the Columbia River, which he followed to its mouth. He returned to the upper Colorado and thence pushed his way over the mountains, through the snows, enduring terrible hardships, to the Sacramento Valley in California. In March, 1844, he turned southward, then crossed the Sierras, and returned by way of Salt Lake to Kansas, which he reached after an absence of fourteen months.

From: MEMOIRS OF MY LIFE,
by John Charles Fremont

1845-46,
Expedition No. 3

In 1845 he set out on a third expedition, to explore California and Oregon. (It was at this time that he became involved in the U.S.-Mexican War in California. Fremont's MEMOIRS tell his story well...)

On July 4, 1846, he was elected governor of California by the American settlers, and became involved in troubles which led to his leaving the army.

1848,
Expedition No. 4

In 1848 he started on a fourth expedition, at his own expense, this time to find a southern route to California. He now settled in California, and in 1849 was elected one of the two senators to represent the new State in the United States Senate.

1853,
Expedition No. 5

In 1853, after a year in Europe, he fitted out a fifth exploring expedition for California, in which his party suffered terrible privations for fifty days living on horse flesh, and for forty-eight hours at a time being without food of any kind. His name had now become prominent in politics, on account of his opposition to the extension of slavery; and in 1856 he became the first Republican candidate for the Presidency."[12]

Larkin's
character sketch

Among the Larkin Papers is what Mr. Underhill called "Larkin's masterpiece, his richest contribution to the field of historical data - a pen-sketch, a character delineation, of the aloof, inscrutable John Fremont."[13] It was written by Mr. Larkin August 2, 1856 at the time Fremont was the first Republican nominee for President of the United States, and is recorded in part here:

"'I have yours of May 31, enquiring respecting Col. Fremont. From '45 and '46 to '50 I was officially and socially acquainted with Col. Fremont who resided in my house at Monterey, months or weeks at a time from 1850 to'54. I was with him on several occasions in Calif. New York & Washington.

He was of reserved and distant manners, active & industrious in his official duties, anxious to finish the business on hand & before him & to be on the march to accomplish more, generally remaining in tent if no house. Rather adverse to company & to extending the circle of his acquaintances, but polite kind and courteous to every one. Not communicative unless drawn into conversation by others, who then found him so & intelligent in his remarks. Without any coarseness or profanity although 10 or 12 years in the mountains & in exploring expeditions.

Neither Mr. or Mrs. Fremont visited the Catholic Priest or Church in Monterey unless as a visit of curiosity. At a later period they attended the Episcopal Church in San Francisco. I have heard

MEMOIRS OF MY LIFE,

BY

JOHN CHARLES FRÉMONT.

INCLUDING IN THE NARRATIVE FIVE JOURNEYS OF WESTERN EXPLORATION,

DURING THE YEARS

1842, 1843–4, 1845–6–7, 1848–9, 1853–4.

TOGETHER WITH A SKETCH OF THE LIFE OF

SENATOR BENTON,

IN CONNECTION WITH WESTERN EXPANSION.

BY

JESSIE BENTON FRÉMONT.

A RETROSPECT OF FIFTY YEARS,

COVERING THE MOST EVENTFUL PERIODS OF MODERN AMERICAN HISTORY.

SUPERBLY ILLUSTRATED BY ORIGINAL PORTRAITS, DESCRIPTIVE PLATES,
AND, FROM THE MISSOURI RIVER TO THE PACIFIC, BY A SERIES
OF SKETCHES AND DAGUERREOTYPES MADE
DURING THE JOURNEYS.

THE ILLUSTRATIONS ARE MASTERPIECES OF

DARLEY, HAMILTON, SCHUSSELE, DALLAS, KERN, WALLIN AND OTHERS.

ENGRAVED UNDER THE SUPERVISION OF

J. M. BUTLER,

WITH MAPS AND COLORED PLATES.

VOL. I.

CHICAGO AND NEW YORK:
BELFORD, CLARKE & COMPANY.
1887.

Interesting Face Plate from John C. Fremont's MEMOIRS.
Volume II was never written.

173

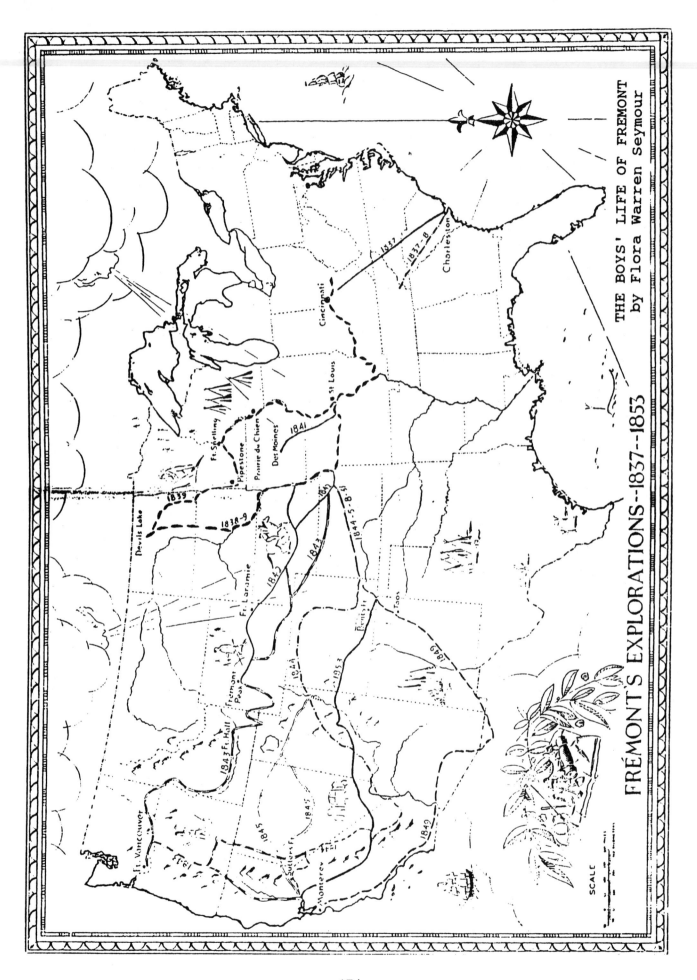

FRÉMONT'S EXPLORATIONS--1837--1853

THE BOYS' LIFE OF FREMONT
by Flora Warren Seymour

174

(by public rumor) that they were married by a Catholic priest. I can imagine that a traveller of 8 or 10 years companionship with men of every grade & profession who for so long a time had been removed from the influences of conventional rules of society would accept the professional services of a clergyman of almost any denomination.

I consider Mr. Fremont a just, correct and moral man, abstemious, bold and persevering...

During the campaign of '46 & '47 the Native Californians saw much of Fremont & in general speak favorably of him to this day...'"

John Fremont was an explorer, sometimes traveling with rough mountain men, men who learned to trust him. One of his closest friends and companions was the great Indian scout, Kit Carson, who could neither read nor write, but nevertheless the two men viewed each other with admiration. Fremont was educated, had a keen mind, but appreciated the talents and skills of others. To illustrate his early education, please turn to the Appendix for a sketch of JOHN CHARLES FREMONT.

It would be a mistake not to mention Fremont's wife, Jessie Benton Fremont. Theirs was a true love story, a story of marital devotion which withstood many trials.

JESSIE BENTON FREMONT

Jessie Benton, daughter of Senator Thomas H. Benton of Missouri, met Charles Fremont when she was sixteen and he, twenty-seven.

In the Prologue to MEMOIRS OF MY LIFE by John Charles Fremont, Jessie merely stated of Mr. Fremont: "Coming home from school in an Easter holiday, I found Mr. Fremont part of my father's 'Oregon work.' It was the spring of '41; in October we were married, and in '42 the first expedition was sent out under Mr. Fremont."[15]

On page 66 of MEMOIRS, Colonel Fremont wrote in 1856:

A love story

"In the family of Mr. Benton were four sisters and but one son... Jessie was the second daughter.

I went with the eldest of the sisters to a school concert in Georgetown, where I saw her. She was then just in the bloom of her girlish beauty, and perfect health effervesced in bright talk which the pleasure of seeing her sister drew out. Naturally I was attracted...

Her qualities were all womanly, and education had curiously preserved the down of a modesty which was innate... She had inherited from her father his grasp of mind, comprehending with a tenacious memory; but with it a quickness of perception and instant realization of subjects and scenes in their completed extent which did not belong to his; and with these, warm sympathies - a generous pity for human suffering, and a tenderness and sensibility that made feeling take the place of mind; so compelled was every impulse to pass through these before it could reach the surface to find expression. There was a rare union of intelligence to feel the injury of events, and submission to them with silence and discretion; and withal a sweet, and happy, and forbearing temper which has remained proof against the wearing of time."

Loyalty

Her life was intricately interwoven with the history of California in that period. The Fremonts spent their lives in the public eye. He was an explorer of the West; she was the homemaker raising two children alone much of the time. He was a soldier fighting for California, and she was a soldier's wife. He was in California, and she was the first American woman to cross through Panama to meet him in California, almost losing her life to the dreaded yellow fever. He was court-martialed, and she was so emotionally involved that she lost a child during the trial. He was a Senator from California, and a candidate for President of the United States; she was a politician's wife. He was the land-owner of gold fields in Mariposa, and she was the brave soul who lived in a rough cabin.

The Fremonts experienced times of wealth and times of poverty. To supplement their income when he was ill, Jessie turned to writing. She was talented. She wrote many magazine articles, and published books such as: SOUVENIRS OF MY TIME, FAR WEST SKETCHES, A YEAR OF AMERICAN TRAVEL, THE STORY OF THE GUARD, THE WILL AND THE WAY STORIES.

Irving Stone has written a wonderful biographical novel of Jessie Benton Fremont. You would enjoy it.[16]

1843 LANSFORD W. HASTINGS

In LIFE BEFORE GOLD, John Bidwell tells us of Lansford Hastings:

An ambitious man

"In 1841 there was likewise no lawyer in California. In 1843 a lawyer named Hastings arrived via Oregon. He was an ambitious man, and desired to wrest the country from Mexico and make it a republic. He disclosed his plan to a man who revealed it to me. His scheme was to go down to Mexico and make friends of the Mexican authorities, if possible get a grant of land, and then go into Texas, consult President Houston, and go East and write a book, praising the country to the skies, which he did, with little regard to accuracy. His object was to start a large immigration, and in this he succeeded. The book was published in 1845, and undoubtedly largely induced what was called the 'great immigration' of 1846 across the plains, consisting of about six hundred.

Providential interference

Hastings returned to California in the autumn of 1845, preparatory to taking steps to declare the country independent and to establish a republic and make himself president. In 1846 he went back to meet the immigration and to perfect his plans so that the emigrants would know exactly where to go and what to do. But in 1846 the Mexican war intervened, and while Hastings was gone to meet the immigration, California was taken possession of by the United States."[17]

EMIGRANT'S GUIDE

Hastings' EMIGRANT'S GUIDE was quite misleading and did cause many delays for the pioneers. It was used by the Donner party and was one of the factors which caused the worst disaster in the history of the California Trail.

Again, we see The Hand of God in California history when Hastings' personally ambitious plans were thwarted.

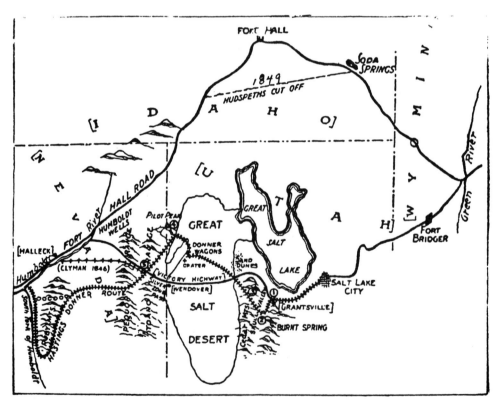

CALIFORNIA TRAILS VIA SALT LAKE CITY, SHOWING THE HASTINGS-DONNER ROUTE OF 1846

Based on map in Charles Kelly's ("Salt Desert Trails.")

From: FORTY-NINERS, by Archer B. Hulbert

1843,
Small parties

After 1843, immigration into California continued in small parties. They were usually just strong enough to protect themselves against hostile Indians.

1844,
First wagons
over Sierras

In 1844, the Stevens-Murphy party from Missouri was the first to succeed in getting wagons over the Sierras, and also the first to make use of what would later be the main route over Donner Pass, although that name was not used until after the tragedy which was to follow two years later.

In SUTTER'S OWN STORY, John Sutter wrote:

A haven of refuge

"'All immigrants were hospitably received by me. I took into my service as many as I could, and others could stay under my roof as long as they liked. When they left me I provided them with passports which were respected everywhere. All the buildings and houses of my settlement were filled every winter with wet, poor, and hungry immigrants - men, women, and children. Sometimes the houses were so full of people that I could hardly find a place to sleep. Most immigrants arrived in a destitute condition. Very few had saved their teams and some had lost everything on their journey across the continent. Often I had to go with my men to pull them out of the snow, and I was able to save many lives in this way.'"[18]

1845, most
to Oregon

In 1845, 250 more Americans came to California, 150 of them men. The largest emigrant party of 1845 was the John Grigsby-William B. Ide company with more than 100 members.

In 1845, however, the majority of emigrants headed for Oregon. In the winter of 1844-1845, great numbers of them assembled on the Missouri frontier to prepare for their long journey to Oregon in the spring. In 1845, about 3000 emigrants entered Oregon. Colonel Stephen Watts Kearny of the First Regiment of Dragoons was under orders of the government of the United States to escort the emigrants. Colonel Kearny had been instructed to ascertain the military resources of the country and obtain all of the information he could about the Indian tribes along the route. Kearny followed the general direction of the now well-known Oregon Trail.

1846, needed
settlers

While Oregon was the goal of the emigrants from America in 1843, 1844, 1845, due to the challenge of the "Fifty-four Forty or Fight," which was the slogan of the settlers against the encroachment of Britain in Oregon, the year 1846 brought a second wave of emigrants to California. "The Great Immigration of 1846" was largely a result of the wide publicity and effective promotion work of Lansford Hastings. More than twice as many, about 600, came in 1846 as had arrived in 1845. Perhaps God had a Hand in this, too, because the American settlers were in California almost at the very moment of the American conquest and were needed to defend their homes against Mexican hostility. No doubt their presence in California prepared the way for the inevitable outcome.

Donner tragedy
discouraged
immigration

The last wagon train of 1846 was the Donner party. Their harrowing experiences on the California Trail discouraged the tide of emigrants until the intoxicating discovery of gold in 1848 started the tremendous influx of '49ers.

While we are reviewing immigration in California, let us take a look at the over-all picture of what happened to California between the years of 1846-1850. The CALIFORNIA MEMORIAL, an official California document which has been reprinted for you in the Appendix, recorded that the population in 1846 in California was 10,000. According to their incomplete census of 1850, the population had increased to 100,000. Walter Colton, who spent from 1846 to 1850 as the Alcalde or Mayor of Monterey, claimed there were 200,000 persons in California in 1850, "with a resistless tide of immigration rolling in." Dr. Rockwell Hunt, an authority on California history, said there were about 115,000 in California in 1850, more nearly correct. But it still stands that in 1850, 80,000 Americans and 20,000 foreigners entered California. Most of that number came by the overland route across the Sierra Nevadas.

1846 DONNER PARTY

Ignorance of
the terrain

Almost every account of the history of California tells the story of the Donner Party, the worst single disaster of the westward migration. It is the story of thirty-one emigrants who started out with great hopes and happy hearts from Springfield, Illinois, for California in 1846. They were joined by other wagon trains, totaling 87 persons. On May 11, they reached Independence, Missouri, in excellent condition. They had good equipment, plenty of supplies, livestock, and money but ignorance of the terrain they were to cross lulled them into delays which cost many their lives. It was necessary that an overland party cross the Sierra Nevada before the snow fell. In the Fall of 1846, there was an exceptionally early snow fall and the Donner party was caught just three miles before reaching the summit.

Early snow

Wrong turn

They made their first mistake at Fort Bridger, Wyoming, where the decision was made to take the Hastings Cutoff south of Great Salt Lake instead of taking the California Trail northwest of the Lake. They had a difficult time because there was no road and Hastings' advice was so misleading. It took them thirty days to reach the Lake when it should have taken them twelve days.

Fateful decision
to camp

Beyond the Great Salt Lake they had to abandon thirty-six of their oxen on the desert and the party all had to walk to lighten the load of the surviving weak oxen. On September 24 they rejoined the main route, and on October 22 made their forty-ninth crossing of the Truckee River in 80 miles. An exhausted party made another mistake in their decision to camp for four days before crossing the mountains. By this time, tempers were growing short and harmony in the wagon trains was lacking. Each party decided to cross by itself. October brought the first snow and one by one the wagons had to be abandoned.

Most of the party reached the shores of Truckee Lake, now called Donner Lake, by the first of November. Here they stopped to camp three miles short of the Sierra summit and were snowed in by a blinding snowstorm. So they then decided to build a few log huts to wait until Spring.

Quarrel

As they had previously ascended the mountains, there had been a terrible quarrel between James F. Reed and John Snyder. Reed struck Snyder a lethal blow and the party banished Reed from the camp with no food. Mr. Reed left behind him his wife and four children but eventually saved many lives by returning with a rescue party.

Prayer for deliverance

Most of the party was snowed in until February of 1847. It is a story of cold, misery, and starvation. But it is also a story of heroism, compassion, and selflessness. Regardless of creed, many heads were bowed together in prayer for deliverance.

Relief parties

The first relief party under Captain R. P. Tucker endured tremendous difficulties in reaching the party. They had sent ahead their food supplies. Upon reaching the Donner camp, they were astonished to find their food had been eaten by wild animals. James Reed returned with the second relief party to find his wife and four children still alive. There were four relief parties. The cost was great as many of them gave their lives endeavoring to bring the Donner party members down from the Sierra.

The Donner Monument

Today we may visit the Donner Monument overlooking the shores of Donner Lake. Looking around at the awesome grandeur of the mountains, it is hard to believe that the early emigrants walked over the Sierra Nevada Mountains into California.

While the pioneer Donner party was struggling over the Sierras in 1846, California was undergoing a dramatic change. Mexico's weak hold on California was finally overcome by American forces. By the time the last members of the Donner party arrived in the Sacramento Valley, California was safely in the hands of the United States.

MONUMENT TO THE DONNER PARTY

The inscription on the base of the monument reads: "Virile to risk and find, kindly withal and a ready help, facing the brunt of fate—indomitable, unafraid."

This is a magnificent bronze and stone statue at the entrance to Donner Lake Park. It depicts the hopeful, and sometimes tragic, pioneer family as they search for the California Trail. The woman is holding a baby in her arms, while she is standing close to the man who is peering into the distance. At his side is a little boy clutching his father's leg.

From: NEW CALIFORNIA THE GOLDEN, page 192,
by Rockwell D. Hunt

REFERENCES TO CHAPTER III

AMERICANS ENTER CALIFORNIA

OVERLAND ROUTE

1. Hunt, Aurora. MAJOR GENERAL JAMES HENRY CARLETON, 1814-1873, WESTERN FRONTIER DRAGOON, pp. 90-91.

JEDEDIAH SMITH

2. Morgan, Dale L. JEDEDIAH SMITH, AND THE OPENING OF THE WEST, p. 8.
3. Ibid., p. 8.
4. Cleland, Robert Glass. THIS RECKLESS BREED OF MEN, p. 120.
5. Loofbourow, Leon L. IN SEARCH OF GOD'S GOLD, p. 10.

PIONEER VS. ARGONAUT

6. Bari, Valeska, Ed. THE COURSE OF EMPIRE, FIRST HAND ACCOUNTS OF CALIFORNIA IN THE DAYS OF THE GOLD RUSH OF '49, p. 8.

OLIVER LARKIN

7. Underhill, Reuben L. FROM COWHIDES TO GOLDEN FLEECE, p. 56.
8. Ibid., p. 65.

JOHN AUGUSTUS SUTTER

9. Bari, Valeska. Op. Cit., p. 8.
10. Dana, Julian. SUTTER OF CALIFORNIA: A BIOGRAPHY, p. 114.
11. Ibid., p. 114.

JOHN CHARLES FREMONT

12. "First Ascent of Fremont's Peak," OLD SOUTH LEAFLET #45, p. 16.
13. Underhill, Reuben L. Op. Cit., p. 251.
14. Ibid., pp. 251-252.

JESSIE BENTON FREMONT

15. Fremont, John Charles. MEMOIRS OF MY LIFE, p. 15.
16. Stone, Irving. IMMORTAL WIFE.

LANSFORD W. HASTINGS

17. Bidwell, John. "Life in California Before the Gold Discovery," THE CENTURY MAGAZINE, Dec. 1890 and Feb. 1891.

IMMIGRATION

18. Gudde, Erwin G. SUTTER'S OWN STORY, p. 16.

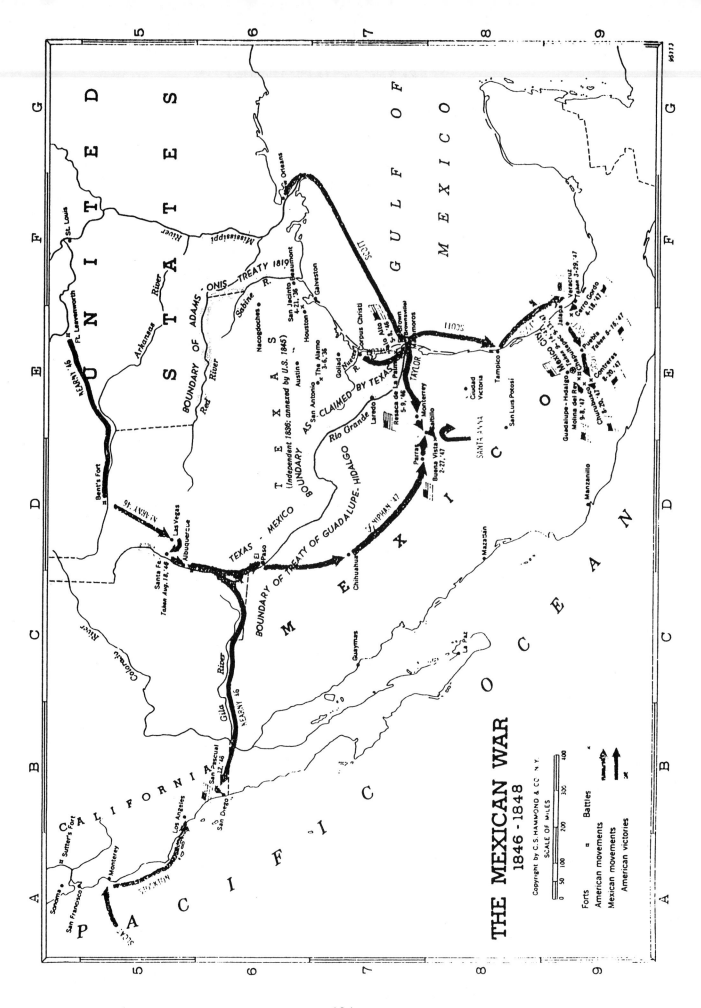

THE MEXICAN WAR
1846-1848

Copyright by C.S. HAMMOND & CO. N.Y.

SCALE OF MILES

50 100   200   300   400

Forts
Battles
American movements
Mexican movements
American victories

CHAPTER IV

GOD'S PROVIDENCE IN AMERICAN CONQUEST OF CALIFORNIA

"...though we walk in the flesh, we do not war after the flesh: (For the weapons of our warfare are not carnal, but mighty through God to the pulling down of strong holds;)" (II Cor. 10:3,4)

According to Dr. Rockwell Hunt, there were three stages in the American acquisition of California:

Three stages of Conquest

"First, the peaceful entrance into California of trapper, trader, and settler; second, the desire of the United States government to possess this land so favorably reported upon by explorers, which finally amounted to a definite policy of acquisition; and third, the actual military and naval operations in connection with the Mexican War that completed the conquest."[1]

COMMODORE JONES AT MONTEREY: OCTOBER 20, 1842

Early mistake

In 1842 the feeling of American leaders toward California was reflected in the action of Commodore Thomas ap Catesby Jones, commander of the American Pacific Squadron, who had been cruising along the coast of South America. He received a false report from Callao, Peru, that the United States and Mexico were at war. He believed the English fleet was on its way to take over Monterey, so he quickly sailed into Monterey Bay and raised the American flag on October 20. The surprised Mexicans gave no resistance. The "American occupation" lasted one day. Jones was finally convinced by Thomas Larkin that no such war existed and that he had been completely misinformed. So he hauled down the American flag, apologized to the Mexican government, and sailed away. This action illustrated the anxiousness on the part of Americans toward acquiring California, and their distrust of British designs on California.

PRESIDENT POLK'S ATTITUDE TOWARD CALIFORNIA: 1845

America's acquisition policy

President James K. Polk brought with him to his administration (1845-49), an intense desire to acquire California. The Mexican Governor Micheltorena had been deported from California, which ended Mexico City's last attempt to govern California. No one trusted Great Britain and in 1845, American eastern newspapers were advocating the acquisition of California. American immigration to California was greatly increasing. In fact, 1846 was to become the year of the "Great Immigration."

UNITED STATES CONSUL APPOINTED CONFIDENTIAL AGENT

Peaceful annexation sought

President Polk would like to have purchased California so he sent John Slidell on a special mission to Mexico with an offer of as much as forty million dollars for Upper California and New Mexico. Slidell's mission failed so Polk appointed United States Consul Thomas O. Larkin as "confidential agent in California" on October 17, 1845 to try to graciously persuade the Californians to secede from Mexico and seek American protection.

Larkin, the successful business man in Monterey, was overwhelmingly in favor of American acquisition. He was a contender for peaceful annexation of California to the United States. He now was instructed by James Buchanan, Secretary of State, to warn the Californians against any attempt to bring them under the jurisdiction of foreign governments. He was also to "'arouse in their bosoms that love of liberty and independence so natural to the American continent.'" In the disputes between Mexico and California, Buchanan wrote to Larkin, "'we can take no part,'" unless Mexico "'should commence hostilities against the United States; but should California assert and maintain her independence, we shall render her all the kind offices in our power as a Sister Republic.'"[2]

FREMONT'S SECOND EXPEDITION 1843-1844

Early expedition into California

To bring John C. Fremont into focus in California, we return to his 1843-1844 second United States' expedition under the Topographical Engineers to Oregon and California. As THE OLD SOUTH LEAFLETS stated, his exploring party was away from home for fourteen long months. Crossing the Sierra Nevada Mountains in the middle of winter, his party suffered great hardships.

Discovery, Pyramid Lake, Nevada

One of the interesting events of this expedition was his discovery of Pyramid Lake in Nevada. He wrote in his MEMOIRS on January 13, 1844:

"The next morning the snow was rapidly melting under a warm sun. Part of the morning was occupied in bringing up the gun;

and, making only nine miles, we encamped on the shore, opposite a very remarkable rock in the lake, which had attracted our attention for many miles. It rose, according to our estimate, 600 feet above the water; and, from the point we viewed it, presented a pretty exact outline of the great pyramid of Cheops. The accompanying view presents it as we saw it. Like other rocks along the shore, it seemed to be encrusted with calcareous cement. This striking feature suggested a name for the lake; and I called it Pyramid Lake..."[3]

Fremont continued southward through the San Joaquin Valley to Tehachapi Pass returning to Utah via the Santa Fe Trail. The expedition seemed to increase Fremont's popularity at home, and general interest in California.

FREMONT'S THIRD EXPEDITION 1845

In May of 1845, Fremont was appointed to lead a third government expedition to the Pacific Coast and was appointed a Lieutenant Colonel.

Enroute to California on January 24, 1846, he wrote home to his wife, Jessie Benton Fremont in Missouri, what he had discovered of the Big Basin:

Knowledge of Big Basin, a help to later emigrants

"You know that on every extant map, manuscript or printed, the whole of the Great Basin is represented as a sandy plain, barren, without water, and without grass. Tell your father that, with a volunteer party of fifteen men, I crossed it between the parallels of 38 degrees and 39 degrees. Instead of a plain, I found it, throughout its whole extent, traversed by parallel ranges of lofty mountains, their summits white with snow (October); while below, the valleys had none. Instead of a barren country, the mountains were covered with grasses of the best quality, wooded with several varieties of trees, and containing more deer and mountain sheep than we had seen in any previous part of our voyage...

I have just returned with my party of sixteen from an exploring journey in the Sierra Nevada, from the neighborhood of Sutter's to the heads of the Lake Fork. We got among heavy snows on the mountain summits; they were more rugged than I had elsewhere met them; suffered again as in our first passage; got among 'Horse-thieves' (Indians who lay waste the California frontier), fought several, and fought our way down into the plain again and back to Sutter's...

I am now going on business to see some gentlemen on the coast, and will then join my people, and complete our survey in this part of the world as rapidly as possible. The season is just now

187

arriving when vegetation is coming out in all the beauty I have
often described to you...

All our people are well, and we have had no sickness of any kind
among us; so that I hope to be able to bring back with me all that
I carried out.   Many months of hardships, close trials, and
anxieties have tried me severely, and my hair is turning gray
before its time..."[4]

FREMONT AT GAVILAN PEAK

Fremont's encounter
with Mexican
General Castro

The "gentlemen on the coast" were the Mexican officials, including
General Jose Castro, commander of the Mexican army, whose permission
Fremont needed to bring his party into the Mexican settlements to refit and
obtain supplies that were necessary.   He and his sixty men appeared to the
Mexican officials as somewhat military but he explained his object was to
explore the direct routes to the Pacific Coast and to do topographical survey
work. Permission was granted.   However, while he was in the San Jose Valley,
Castro got orders from Mexico to oust him, by force if necessary, and Fremont
was angry at this change of mind.   So, considering this an insult to himself and
his country, he determined to take a stand against Castro.

When Fremont left for the West, there was no war between the United
States and Mexico, but it was anticipated.   He was given instructions, verbally,
what to do in the event of war.   Communication was difficult and he was given
discretion to act as he saw fit.

Fremont went up to the Gomez Rancho on Gavilan Peak, northeast of
Monterey, and there built a small log fort and raised the American flag (March
1846).   He had fifty men with him.   He kept in touch with Confidential Agent
Larkin as to what was going on below his camp.   He wrote in his MEMOIRS:

"From the fort by aid of the glass we could see below, at the
Mission of San Juan (Bautista), Castro's troops gathering, and by
the vaqueros we were informed that Indians (Mansos) were being
brought into their camp and kept excited by drink."

On the third day, he wrote:

"Thinking I had remained as long as the occasion required...I
gave the order to prepare to move.

The protecting favor which the usage of all civilized governments
and peoples accords to scientific expeditions imposed on me,
even here, a corresponding obligation; and I now felt myself
bound to go on my way, having given General Castro sufficient
time to execute his threat.   Besides I kept always in mind the
object of the Government to obtain possession of California and

188

would not let a proceeding which was mostly personal put obstacles in the way."[5]

In the meantime, Castro had posted a notice that a band of bandaleros (robbers), under Captain Fremont of the U.S. Army had threatened to exterminate the Californians but Castro with two hundred patriots of Mexico had driven them away!

Larkin was so worried by all of this that he asked the Navy to send a Man-Of-War to the coast for the protection of the Americans.

FREMONT OVERTAKEN BY GILLESPIE

Unofficial
Government orders
carried to Fremont

On Fremont's return in southern Oregon, he was overtaken one night by a messenger from the United States Government, Lt. Archibald Gillespie of the Marine Corps. He and the rancher-guide Neal had narrowly escaped the Tlamath Indians. Fremont said: "A quick eye and a good horse mean life to a man in an Indian country. Neal had both. He was a lover of horses and knew a good one; and those he had with him were the best on his rancho."[6] Fremont's party were all delighted to see Gillespie as they had had no word from home for eleven months. Fremont continued:

"Mr. Gillespie informed me that he had left Washington under orders from the President and the Secretary of the Navy (Bancroft) and was directed to reach California by the shortest route through Mexico to Mazatlan...

"...designs of
the President"

The mission on which I had been originally sent to the West was a peaceful one, and Mr. Bancroft had sent Mr. Gillespie to give me warning of the new state of affairs and the designs of the President."[7]

Fremont now became, not an explorer, but an officer of the American Army with knowledge that the government of the United States intended to take California. He had no official written instructions but a letter from Senator Benton and verbal instructions from Gillespie.

He wrote in his MEMOIRS:

"This officer informed me that he had been directed by the Secretary of State to acquaint me with his instructions, which had for their principal objects to ascertain the disposition of the California people, to conciliate their feelings in favor of the United States; and to find out, with a view to counteracting, the designs of the British Government upon that country...

Neal had much to talk over with his old companions and pleasurable excitement kept us up late; but before eleven o'clock all were wrapped in their blankets and soundly asleep except myself. I sat by the fire in fancied security, going over again the home letters. These threw their own light upon the communication from Mr. Gillespie, and made the expected signal. In substance, their effect was: The time has come. England must not get a foothold. We must be first. Act; discreetly, but positively."[8]

Fremont returned to California and the surprised settlers, and the adventurers, flocked to his camp near the Marysville Buttes, eager to follow wherever he might lead.

UNREST

Mexicans deterred in annexation plans

In the meantime, the Californians were meeting in Monterey trying to determine the future of their territory. Here it was that Mariano Guadalupe Vallejo, favoring annexation to the United States, walked out of the Mexican Junta, providentially preventing the vote for annexation to England. (See page 148, Chapter II, under "1846 JUNTA.")

Americans chafe under Mexican law

In various parts of California, a restlessness was felt. Fremont received information from the settlers that the Indians were leaving their rancherias and taking to the mountains, indicating hostility. Sutter warned Fremont that General Castro sent messengers amongst the Indians to raise them against the settlers. A ship captain and an American, Nathan Spear, had been assaulted on the streets of Yerba Buena (San Francisco) and nothing had been done about it. In Monterey on April 30, 1846, a notice was issued by the Californians that any foreigner who had not become a Mexican citizen could not own land and would have to leave the country.

The first hostile act after Fremont returned was the seizure by American Ezekiel Merritt and others, of Mexican horses being driven from Sonoma to Santa Clara Valley. The seizure of the horses was quickly followed by the colorful Bear Flag episode.

THE BEAR FLAG REPUBLIC   JUNE 1846

Settler's desire for an American Republic

On June 14, 1846, at dawn a party of thirty-three Americans under William Ide surrounded the home of Vallejo, Commandante of Northern California, in Sonoma. Although Vallejo was one of the most distinguished men in California and pro-American, he was captured, made a prisoner of war and sent to Fremont's camp, then to Sutter's Fort. Several weeks later he was released. It was not known in California at that time if there was war between the United States and Mexico. The group of settlers had no right to raise the American flag over Mexican territory, so the famous Bear Flag Republic was born.

The famous Bear Flag

The flag was made in the front room of the barracks and sewn by Benjamin Dewell. The base of this flag was white cotton cloth. Across the

190

bottom was sewn a red strip four inches wide which was taken from a red flannel petticoat that had been worn by a pioneer woman across the plains. The star and bear were outlined in ink and filled in with linseed oil and Venetian red. The bear represented the strongest animal in California and the star was a reminder of Texas, the Lone Star State, whose formal admission to the United States had taken place December 29, 1845. Under the bear the words CALIFORNIA REPUBLIC were written. The Californians watched the procedure with much more curiosity than anger, and scoffed at the crudeness of the flag.

THE BEAR FLAG

The Bear men divided themselves into three companies. However, before operations could begin, Commodore Sloat had raised the American flag over Monterey and the Bear Flaggers were only too happy to substitute the American Flag for the Bear Flag to join Sloat and Fremont for the completion of the conquest.

The Revere name   God guides all generations in their activity in keeping alive the Chain of Christianity and carrying out His purpose. He used Paul Revere of the early colonial generation to further the American Cause during the American Revolutionary times of 1776. Then, He used Lt. Joseph Warren Revere, grandson of Paul Revere, in the times of the United States-Mexican War of 1846 which brought California into the American nation. Lt. Joseph Revere, stationed aboard the PORTSMOUTH which was anchored at Yerba Buena, was ordered by Captain Montgomery on July 9, 1846 to take down the Bear Flag in Sonoma and raise the stars and stripes of the flag of the United States. The patriotic kin of Paul Revere, by the grace of God, was on hand in the Far West to attend a significant task for his country. All of the ideas of the American Revolution had traveled west to California, as symbolized by this act.

UNITED STATES-MEXICAN WAR: OVER THE BOUNDARY OF TEXAS

Texas, a
State, 1845

Ever since Mexico had rebelled against Spain and become independent in 1822, it had a most disorderly government. Mexican generals of the army were in the habit of seizing supreme power and forcing the people to obey them, while the American settlers were not in the habit of obeying anyone whom they had not helped elect, or obeying laws they had not instigated through their representatives. In 1835, they openly rebelled in Texas and drove the Mexican troops out. The next year Santa Ana, the Mexican ruler, invaded Texas in a most cruel manner, murdering prisoners, sick, and wounded. However, the Texans, under General Sam Houston, met him with far fewer men at San Jacinto, near Houston, and beat his army thoroughly. Mexico made no further attempt to conquer Texas, which remained an independent republic until it was admitted to the Union as a slave state in 1845.

Mexico still claimed Texas as part of her territory and was displeased when the United States annexed Texas. Mexico did not intend war but steps taken made it inevitable.

Disputed Area
by Mexico and
the United States.

Map from AN
AMERICAN
HISTORY,
by David Muzzey

192

The western boundary of Texas was unsettled. Mexico claimed it was the Nueces River; Texas, that it was the Rio Grande. Between the Nueces and Rio Grande was a strip of territory which was claimed by both. In this dispute was the origin of the Mexican war. Early in 1846 General Taylor, United States Commander in Texas, was ordered by President Polk to take possession of the disputed territory. Taylor crossed the Nueces at Corpus Christi, marched to the Rio Grande, and camped at Brownsville.

Taylor found that Mexican troops were crossing the Rio Grande and he sent a scouting party of dragoons, under Captain Thornton, up the river from Brownsville. Thornton's party was surprised and captured by a superior force of Mexicans. Several men were killed and wounded; this was the first bloodshed of the war.

As soon as the news of the capture of Thornton's scouting party reached Washington, the President sent word of the situation to Congress for consideration. Congress declared that war "existed by the act of the Republic of Mexico," May 12, 1846. It was the intention of the United States to acquire California in the event of such war.

JOHN D. SLOAT

In June of 1846, Commodore John Sloat had sailed from Mazatlan in Mexico aboard the flagship SAVANNAH for Monterey to protect American interests. He had knowledge of hostilities on the Rio Grande but did not know of the formal declaration of war. General Stephen Kearny participated as one of the commanders of the American forces in Mexico. He and his army moved across New Mexico and Arizona into California.

Sloat was fearful of making the same mistake Commodore Jones had made in 1842. The last of June, 1846, Commodore Sloat arrived at Monterey. All expected him to raise the flag, but he did not. Lack of communication with Washington made it difficult for him.

Fremont had asked aid of the PORTSMOUTH's Captain Montgomery at Yerba Buena for supplies and munitions, with the message that American settlers in the Sacramento and San Joaquin Valleys were alarmed by the Californians threatening movements. Fremont needed supplies to protect their own lives and those of the Americans but Sloat instructed Montgomery to give him no aid whatsoever.

The story of the night preceding the raising of the United States flag in Monterey was told by Ex-governor Rodman Price of New Jersey who at that time was an officer aboard the CYANE in the Pacific Squadron under Commodore Sloat's command.

Mr. Price believed the moment so critical that he said "as if by inspiration"[9] he obtained the captain's gig late at night and visited Commodore

Sloat. The Commodore received Price who urged him to reconsider Fremont's request, and to raise the flag immediately on shore and declare a military occupation. Sloat relented and the flag of the United States was ordered raised at Monterey the next morning, July 7, 1846.

The Proclamation of Occupation was written the night of July 6 before Mr. Price departed for the CYANE.

The military Proclamation of Occupation was just and considerate, recognizing the fact that Sloat had no strong military opposition to placate. On July 7, 1846, with definite but unofficial information, Sloat proclaimed:

Sloat's
Proclamation

"To the inhabitants of California: The central government of Mexico having commenced hostilities against the United States of America by invading its territory and attacking its troops and these nations being actually at war by this transaction, I shall hoist the standard of the United States at Monterey immediately, and shall carry it throughout California. I declare to the inhabitants that, although I come in arms with a powerful force, I do not come among them as an enemy; on the contrary, I come as their best friend, as henceforth California will be a portion of the United States and its peaceful inhabitants will enjoy the same rights and privileges as the citizens of any other portion of that territory, together with the privilege of choosing their own magistrates and officers for the administration of justice among themselves and the same protection will be extended to them as to any other state in the Union. They will also enjoy a permanent government, under which life, property and the constitutional right and lawful security to worship the Creator in the way most congenial to each one's sense of duty will be secured...Under the flag of the United States, the country will rapidly advance and improve, both in agriculture and commerce, as, of course the revenue laws will be the same in California as in all other parts of the United States, affording them all manufactures and produce of the United States free of any duty... All persons holding titles to real estate or in quiet possession of lands under a color of right, shall have those titles and rights guaranteed to them...All provisions and supplies of every kind furnished by the inhabitants for the use of the United States ships and soldiers will be paid for at fair rates; and no private property will be taken for public use without just compensation at the moment. Signed, J. D. Sloat, Commander-in-Chief of the United States Naval Force in the Pacific."[10]

The English admiral, Seymour, arrived a few days afterward in the war ship COLLINGWOOD, and the first thing he said on receiving Sloat was, "Sloat, if your flag was not flying on shore I should have hoisted mine there."[11]

THE CALIFORNIA BATTALION

Governor Rodman Price, then Purser Price of the CYANE, later recorded:

The California
Battalion

"Fremont organized a military battalion, and afforded protection to Americans at Sutter's Fort, and marched south to punish General Castro for the warfare they had waged against him. This military organization of Fremont's is historically known as the renowned California Battalion, and became the active power of subduing California. And in a revolt of the Californians to our authority after their submission, Fremont's command again brought them to submission. About two weeks after the flag was raised, Fremont came with his command to Monterey and volunteered their services to Commodore Stockton, who had succeeded Sloat, and was anxious to carry an active war against the Californians in arms against us.

The English admiral was still at Monterey when Fremont came, and looked on with his officers with much interest. It was, indeed, a novel and interesting sight - the command, numbering two or three hundred men, marching in a square, within which was the cattle which they were driving for their subsistence. They were mostly clothed in buckskin, and armed with Hawkins rifles. The individuality of each man was very remarkable. When they dismounted, their first care was their rifle. Fremont, by his explorations and the geographical and scientific knowledge he had given to the world, was the conspicuous figure. The hunters and guides of his exploring party were the next objects sought for. Kit Carson and the Indians accompanying him were the objects of much attention."[12]

SUBMISSION OF THE MEXICANS

Commodore
Robert Stockton

Commodore Robert F. Stockton accepted the command from Commodore Sloat who had been in ill health for some time. Robert Stockton came from generations of American patriots, as his grandfather, Richard Stockton, had been a signer of the Declaration of Independence, and his father had been a United States Senator. Commodore Stockton commissioned Fremont a major and Gillespie a captain. The California Battalion was actually a United States Navy Battalion of mounted riflemen under Stockton.

Military movements:
First phase

The first phase of the conquest of California began when Fremont and his party boarded the CYANE and sailed to San Diego. Stockton reached San Pedro and on August 13, 1846, their combined forces entered Los Angeles without resistance. Four days later, the Commodore proclaimed California free of Mexican domination.

Now that southern California was under control of the Americans, Commodore Stockton issued a new Proclamation on August 17, 1846 in Los Angeles.

Stockton stated that the California Battalion of Mounted Riflemen were in control of the Mexican province; that the territory of California now belonged to the United States; that military law would prevail; that Stockton, as Commander-in-Chief, would be Governor of California. Upon his leaving California, Stockton had planned to turn over the governorship to Fremont. Later, this plan was challenged by General Stephen Kearny.

Stockton decreed September 17, 1846 as the date that towns and districts in California would elect civil officers. The local alcaldes came under military control; some local officers were elected.

It is here that Stockton appointed Walter Colton, a United States Navy Chaplain, as Alcalde of Monterey. He succeeded Purser Rodney M. Price and Dr. Edward Gilchrist, both of whom had been appointed by Commodore Sloat.

The first phase of the conquest of California was over.

REVOLT OF THE MEXICANS

The second phase began.

Second phase

Commodore Stockton had left Captain Gillespie with fifty men in charge of Los Angeles. Stockton and Fremont left for the north. However, Gillespie was unnecessarily harsh with the Angelinos and they revolted with most of southern California following suit. An outbreak of overwhelming forces of Californians forced Gillespie to surrender. He was allowed to retreat to San Pedro harbor.

Mexicans superior in southern California

Captain Mervine was sent south with about 250 men to meet with Gillespie at San Pedro. And the battle of the Dominguez Rancho followed. The Mexicans were armed with eight foot lances and the Americans were forced to retreat with four dead and six wounded. It looked as if the whole country from Santa Barbara to San Diego had turned to the Californians.

In the meantime, Fremont marched south.

General Stephen W. Kearny, Dec. 6, 1846

General Stephen W. Kearny had been ordered across New Mexico to help Stockton. He believed California had already been conquered and only had one hundred men with him. On December 6, 1846, the Californians intercepted Kearny with as many men. The battle of San Pasqual followed. The Californians were mounted on fast, well-trained horses and led by Andres Pico. The Americans found their short sabers a poor match for the long deadly lances. Eighteen Americans were killed and the same number were wounded. It is here that Kit Carson and Lt. Edward F. Beale secured help from Stockton.

196

KIT CARSON

The American
Scout

A few words should be said about Kit Carson, the famous American scout. He could neither read nor write but he told his "story" to a doctor who recorded it and in that book are many fascinating stories of the frontier life. The book is KIT CARSON'S OWN STORY by Col. D. C. Peters.[13]

Kit, born Christopher, was of Scottish blood and came from Kentucky. His family was carried by the Western Movement to Missouri. In 1826, his father died and Kit was apprenticed to an harsh Missouri saddler. Kit ran away to join an expedition to Santa Fe, and soon joined Ewing Young's trapping party in the Southwest. With the depletion of the beaver colonies, Carson quit hunting and in 1842 joined Fremont's first expedition. He was also a member of Fremont's second expedition to Oregon and California in 1843-44. Kit volunteered as one of the California Battalion in the United States- Mexican War and distinguished himself at San Pasqual. Then he married an Indian woman, settled in Taos, New Mexico. In 1853 the government appointed him Indian Agent at Taos in charge of two Ute tribes.

Kit Carson was a mountain man, hard, practical, always dealing with the unknown. He was cool-headed, a deadly shot, modest, Christian with a great faith in the power of the Almighty. He was the Indian's greatest friend; yet, he could be their mortal enemy.

THE BATTLE OF SAN PASQUAL

Desperate situation
for Americans

When General Kearny and his men were helplessly surrounded by the Mexicans at San Pasqual, Kit was among them. With their horses gone, men wounded, without food or water, Carson, and an Indian, and Lt. Beale offered to go on a dangerous mission for help from Stockton in San Diego.

Providential
deliverance

They started out, each with a revolver, a sharp knife, and no food. When darkness fell, they made their way down the hill, avoiding Andres Pico's mounted lancers. The Mexicans had doubled the guard as they knew Carson was in camp. The three volunteers crawled, pulling off their shoes leaving their naked feet exposed to the prickly pears. At one time, Beale thought it was all over but Carson said: "I have been in worse places before, and Providence saved me."[14] They crawled for two miles in open valley over rocks, stones, and rubble. They lost their shoes and traveled all night barefoot through the woods. They laid low in daylight and continued again at night. They had thirty-five miles to travel. The Indian, who was familiar with the territory, arrived at Stockton's camp first; Beale was carried by Stockton's guard, suffering injuries to his feet. In San Diego, they found Stockton's relief party ready to set out.

Los Angeles
reoccupied
by Americans

After being rescued and refreshed, Kearny joined his forces to Commodore Stockton's and with about six hundred men reoccupied Los Angeles on January 10, 1847.

God's Purpose
for California

You will read in our history books that this was a "comic opera" war, much to do about nothing, that each side chased the other around California without engaging in a major, full-scale war. After having read the accounts of these skirmishes, and why they traveled the length of California to meet on the battleground but briefly, your author concludes that it was no comic opera to those involved at the time, to those who were wounded, suffered, and gave their lives. Providentially, it was not a major war. Their activities were **all** that were necessary to the winning of California for the Americans. God's purpose for California was being carried out.

Americans desire
individual liberty

There were Americans in California by the thousands, chafing and straining under old Mexican law, and they were crying to be taken into the Union so they could get on with the business of establishing the great state which California has become. They needed law and order and justice but most of all, they needed the individual liberty which had become an integral part of their daily lives under the American form of government. Remember, Mexico had neglected California. It was ripe for the taking by some nation, and the Americans believed it belonged to its nearest neighbor, the United States.

TREATY OF CAHUENGA PASS IN CALIFORNIA

Mexican
capitulation,
Jan. 13, 1847

On January 13, 1847, Andres Pico, brother of California's last Mexican Governor Pio Pico, surrendered to Fremont at Cahuenga Pass. Fremont was on his way south. He had captured Don Jesus Pico who was head of the insurrection around San Luis Obispo. Fremont spared the life of Don Jesus, who was a cousin of Andres Pico, commander at San Pasqual. Don Jesus accompanied Fremont on his march and they reached the camp of Don Andres at the Mission of San Fernando. Here Don Jesus set up a meeting between Fremont and Don Andres and the terms of the capitulation by the Mexicans in California were agreed upon. California was left peacefully in the possession of the United States.

TREATY OF GUADALUPE HIDALGO BETWEEN MEXICO AND THE U.S.

Peace Treaty,
Feb. 2, 1848

It was not until February 2, 1848 that war was officially ended with the Treaty of Guadalupe Hidalgo. Guadalupe Hidalgo was a village in Mexico where the treaty was drawn up. On September 14, 1847, General Winfield Scott had entered Mexico City and raised the flag of the United States. By the terms of Guadalupe Hidalgo the United States agreed to pay the Mexican Republic the sum of fifteen million dollars, and Alta California became a part of the territory of the United States. Nearly two fifths of Mexico's total area, more than one-half million square miles, was ceded to the United States.

America gains a
huge, wealthy
territory

The Mexican territory at the opening of the war included what are now the States of California, Nevada, Utah, Arizona, New Mexico, and parts of Colorado and Wyoming. Mexico had done little to settle this territory which was not more than a wilderness. No one suspected that it contained a wealth of gold, silver, and other minerals. It was known to be fertile and contained the

198

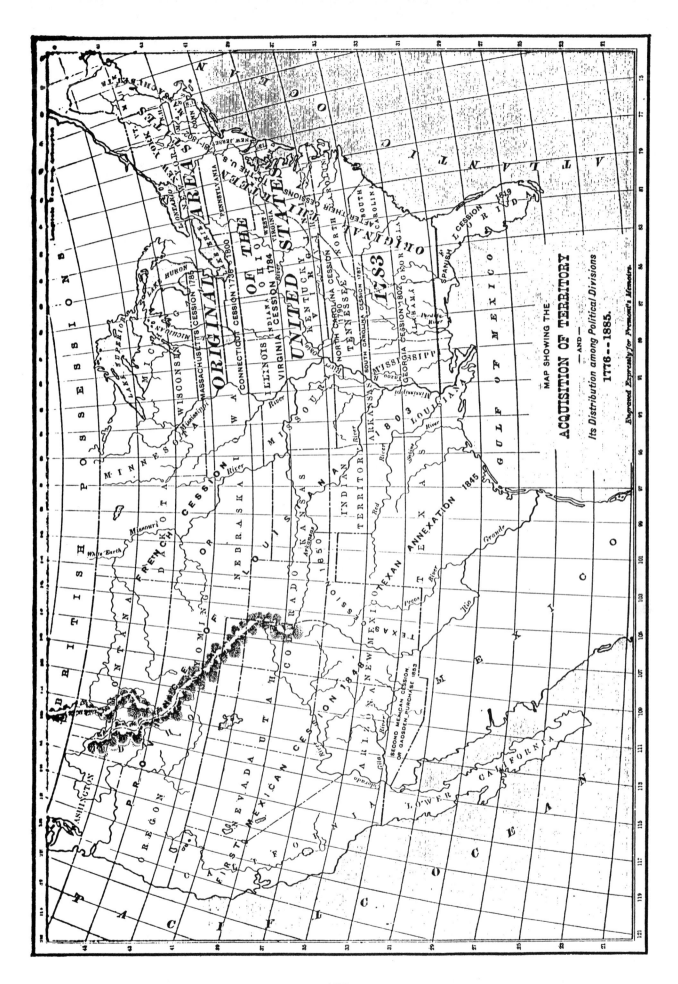

finest harbor on the Pacific Coast, the San Francisco Bay, the entrance to which had been named by Fremont, the Golden Gate.

TERRITORIAL ADDITIONS

Divine Plan for
United States of
America

Putting history in a larger perspective, let us look at the territorial additions which comprise the United States. The annexation of Texas, the cession of California by Mexico, and Gadsden Purchase, which took place south of the Gila River in 1853, added 967,451 square miles to the United States. This was more than the area of the United States in 1783, and almost as much as the Louisiana Purchase. The additions gave the United States the form and boundaries which are still retained with the exception of the purchase of Alaska in 1867 and the annexation of Hawaii in 1898. This was God's Plan for America. When we realize that the forms of government established in this entire area were seeded by the Christian Pilgrims of 1620, we say, Thank Thee, Father!

The territorial growth of the United States may be divided into five great divisions:

1. The United States as left by the Revolution, altogether east of the Mississippi, with Florida added in 1819;

2. Louisiana, west of the Mississippi, with Oregon added in 1846;

3. Texas in 1845, and the Mexican cessions including California in 1848;

4. Alaska in 1867;

5. Hawaii in 1898.

THE GOVERNMENT OF CALIFORNIA UNDER THE UNITED STATES

Now that California had been conquered by the United States, how was she governed? California remained under military law from early in 1847 until the acting military governor called a Constitutional Convention for September, 1849. In the meantime, gold was discovered in California on January 24, 1848.

CHRONOLOGY: UNITED STATES - MEXICAN WAR 1846-1847

"Though an host shall encamp against me, my heart shall not fear:
though war should rise against me, in this will I be confident.

One thing have I desired of the Lord, that will I seek after;
that I may dwell in the house of the Lord all the days of my life,
to behold the beauty of the Lord, and to enquire in his temple.

For in the time of trouble he shall hide me in his pavilion:
in the secret of his tabernacle shall he hide me;
he shall set me up upon a rock.

And now shall mine head be lifted up above mine enemies round
about me: therefore will I offer in his tabernacle sacrifices of joy;
I will sing, yea, I will sing praises unto the Lord."
(Psalm 27:3,4,5,6)

For those students interested in a more detailed summary of the United States-Mexican War of 1846-47, I have added a CHRONOLOGY of the events revolving around John C. Fremont as the central figure. These extracts are taken from Allan Nevins, FREMONT: PATH-MARKER OF THE WEST, Vol. I. (Copyrighted by Allan Nevins, 1939, 1955; republished in the American Classics Series, Frederick Ungar Publishing Company, New York, 1961. It contains map of Fremont's Explorations, 1838-53.)

SECOND EXPEDITION:

May, 1843	In Kansas City (with canon).
June 1- Nov.5, 1843	Between Missouri and the Dalles of the Columbia.
November 25, 1843	Left Columbia.
December 13, 1843	Pulled howitzer through snow.
December 25, 1843	Reached lower Oregon.
January 10, 1844	Reached Pyramid Lake.
January 18, 1844	Reached Carson River. Decided to cross Sierras into California.
January 19, 1844	Camped near present Virginia City.
January 29, 1844	Abandoned howitzer.
February 6, 1844	Sighted Valley of the Sacramento.
February 20, 1844	Had crossed Summit of Carson Pass.
March 6, 1844	Reached Sacramento Valley and Sutter's Fort.
March 8, 1844	Pitched camp at juncture of American and Sacramento Rivers.
March 22, 1844	Broke camp. Moved near Sinclair's ranch.
March 24, 1844	(Neal left behind in California as he requested.) Had supplies from Sutter who was paid in drafts upon Topographical Bureau, which he cashed at 20% discount.
Homeward Journey: August 6, 1844	Returned home to Missouri. Returning, he skirted western base of of Sierras to a pass (Walker's Pass); thence southeast toward Santa Fe by Spanish Trail; halted before reaching New Mexico and turned into Colorado, thence to headwaters of the Arkansas.

THIRD EXPEDITION:

February, 1845	Mexican Governor Micheltorena ousted from California capital at Monterey; California now an independent Republic; Pio Pico now Governor at new capital, Los Angeles; Jose Castro, military Commandante at Monterey.
August (late), 1845	Fremont left St. Louis for Bent's Fort, thence to Colorado. Traveled west of Salt Lake over flat, arid desert - 60 miles across, called Hasting's Cut-off.
August, 1845	Zachary Taylor ordered to go to the Nueces River to the strip of land claimed by United States and Mexico.
Sept. 12, 1845	Mexican orders to halt passports to foreigners; had to become Mexican citizens to hold land.
Nov. (early), 1845	Continued westward across Nevada. Reached Ogden River which Fremont re-named Humboldt. Also, early in November, Archibald Gillespie left Washington.
Nov. (late), 1845	At Humboldt, Fremont split his party. Kern to lead one - to follow Humboldt to its termination in Carson Sink, to go to eastern foot of Sierras and to follow mountains south to Walker's Lake; Joseph Walker was guide.
	Fremont took ten men from Humboldt across bed of Great Basin, westward; with Carson.
	Fremont went through Central Nevada, thence to Walker's Lake which lies near western boundary of Nevada, its southern tip opposite Sacramento. Fremont proved Great Basin safe to traverse.
November 24, 1845	Reached Walker's Lake. Other party then joined Fremont. Started to snow. Again split party. Kern sent south along Sierras until opposite southern California.
	Fremont went directly over Mountains. Both to meet at Tulare Lake.
December, 1845	Reached Salmon Trout River flowing into Pyramid Lake. Four days later the party was on east side of Truckee or Donner Pass.
December 4, 1845	Began descent into California.
December 9, 1845	Reached Sutter's Fort on American River. He had really pioneered a feasible trail between Salt Lake and northern California. Surveyed as he went.
December 10, 1845	Rode from camp site into Sutter's Fort. Needed supplies.
December 14, 1845	Fremont marched south to find Kern. Rode south along San Joaquin Valley. Did not find his party; returned to Sutter's Fort, arriving there January 14, 1846.
January 13, 1846	Slidell mission failed so President Polk ordered Zachary Taylor to advance to the Rio Grande to take possession of strip of land claimed by both Mexico and U.S. Action led directly to war.
Meanwhile	Archibald H. Gillespie was on his way through Mexico to California with official messages for Sloat, Larkin, and Fremont.*

----

* For Gillespie's reports, letters to the Sec. of Navy, see CALIFORNIA HISTORICAL SOCIETY QUARTERLY, XVII (1938), pp. 123, 271: G. W. Ames, Jr., "Gillespie and the Conquest of California."

	Fremont, waiting for Kern party, decided to visit principal California settlements.
January 19, 1846	Fremont took Sutter's launch down the Sacramento River to Yerba Buena to see American Vice-Consul William A. Leidesdorff. Thence on horseback to Monterey, where he saw U.S. Consul Larkin who took him to "gentlemen on business," Castro, Alvarado, etc. Fremont said he was on scientific expedition; that he may return home via Colorado.
Feb. (middle), 1846	Whole expedition united at a ranch thirteen miles southeast of San Jose, a few miles from present Lick Observatory.
Feb. (end), 1846	Set out for southwest (Monterey).
March 3, 1846	Camped at Hartnell's ranch near Salinas.
	Ordered out of California by Castro. Fremont believed this an insult to a scientific expedition of U.S.
March 6-9, 1846	Marched men to Hawk's Peak in Gavilan Mts. Raised U.S. flag; built fort; remained three days.
	Larkin concerned; requested Washington send a warship from Mazatlan (Mexico) to Monterey.
March 8, 1846	Taylor's troops crossed Nueces River into disputed territory; Slidell sent home by Mexico; Gillespie almost to Honolulu on way to California.
March 24, 1846	Fremont left Sutter's Fort; crossed Oregon line.
March (end), 1846	At Lassen's Ranch in northern California, 200 miles from Sutter's Fort. Stayed six days. Started to leave but weather inclement.
April 11, 1846	Returned to Lassen's Ranch for two weeks.
April 17, 1846	Gillespie reached Monterey by way of Vera Cruz, Mexico City, Mazatlan, Honolulu.
April 17, 1846	Castro ordered all non-citizens of California to leave.
April 24, 1846	Fremont left Lassen's. First day of clash between Mexico and U.S. on Rio Grande.
May 6, 1846	Reached Klamath Lake. Explored Cascade Range.
May 8, 1846	Neal rode into camp with a companion. Had ridden hard. Said Gillespie on way with letters for Fremont.
	Fremont took ten men back thirty or forty miles to meet Gillespie at southern end of Klamath Lake. Gillespie brought Fremont a copy of an official despatch from Secretary of State Buchanan, some American newspapers, notes from Jessie and Benton, and verbal explanations. There is a question as to secret instructions Gillespie had for Fremont. The official despatch was dated October 17, 1845 and was addressed to Larkin with a copy for Fremont. Larkin was told Washington had reason to fear England or French aggression in California and to use friendly appeal to Californians for U.S.*
May 12, 1846	Congress declared war against Mexico.
May 24, 1846	Fremont's expedition arrived back at Lassen's Ranch.
May & June, 1846	Castro was assembling an army from Monterey to Sonoma to meet any invasion. Created alarm amongst American settlers.

----

* For English intent upon California, see Nevins, PATHMARKER, p. 283.

	Intrigue between Pio Pico in south and Jose Castro in north. Civil strife of Mexicans would result in either a republic or annexation of California by a foreign power.
May 25, 1846	From Lassen's Ranch, Fremont requested supplies of Captain Montgomery on PORTSMOUTH.
May 29, 1846	Gillespie left for Yerba Buena. Fremont left for Sutter's Fort. Learned Castro was engaging the Indians to burn settlers' crops, plotting to shoot Sutter, and planning to stop all immigration.
May (end), 1846	To intimidate Indians, Fremont sacked their villages.**
May 30, 1846	Fremont arrived at Marysville Buttes. Attracted settlers.
June (early), 1846	Mexicans collected horses. Ezekiel Merritt led American settlers who took away horses from Mexicans.
June 14, 1846	Bear Flag Episode. Vallejo, as prisoner, taken to Sutter's Fort. Fremont put Kern in charge there.
(June 15, 1846)	(Secretary Buchanan and the British Minister at Washington signed the treaty partitioning Oregon at the 49th parallel, adding the states of Oregon, Washington, Idaho to U.S.)
June 23, 1846	Castro sent troops to Sonoma. Brief encounter near San Rafael. Mexicans routed. Fremont chased retreating Mexicans who escaped. Two American immigrants, Cowan and Fowler, tortured and killed by Mexicans.
July 2, 1846	Fremont crossed San Francisco Bay to Fort Point and seized little fort there. Here he named San Francisco Bay the "Golden Gate."
July 4, 1846	Fremont in Sonoma celebrating the Fourth. Organized California Battalion of 234 men. (U.S. Government later paid for local cattle butchered for army; reimbursed Sutter for use of his Fort. See Nevins, p. 279.) Fremont received news U.S., Mexico at war.
July 7, 1846	Sloat, with no official notice of U.S.-Mexican War, demanded Monterey to surrender. He had learned May 31 of battles of Palo Alto and Resaca de la Palma in Mexico.
July 10, 1846	Fremont made a Lt. Colonel in U.S. Army.
July 19, 1846	Fremont marched California Battalion into Monterey. Taylor had driven Mexicans across the Rio Grande. Mormon Battalion of 16,000 crossed Missouri; at Council Bluffs on way to California. Emigrants pouring in. Thousands of volunteers rushed in; U.S. Grant and Robert E. Lee were young officers. General Kearny was assembling an army at Bent's Fort

---

** Indian threat seemed real: There were reportedly 20,000 Indians between Lassen's Ranch and San Diego. According to Nevins, p. 261: "Both physically and mentally this lazy treacherous and thievish race were greatly inferior to the best plains Indians, like the Sioux or Cheyenne, but when aroused or collected in numbers, they were a real menace. Fremont shared the almost universal frontier dislike of the savages, whom he regarded as untrustworthy, vindictive and cruel." Fremont had never forgotten a cruel sight he had seen after Indians finished off a party of immigrants.

	to invade New Mexico and California.
	Donner party on way to California, only to get caught in blizzard of 1846.
	In New England, war with Mexico unpopular; in West, received with enthusiasm.
July 23, 1846	Commodore Sloat turned over his command of Pacific Fleet to Commodore Stockton.
July 29, 1846	Stockton and Fremont planned land campaign. Fremont's Battalion taken into naval service; Fremont a major; Gillespie a captain. California Battalion of 220 fighters went by sea in CYANE to San Diego. Received cordially by native Californians, unexpectedly.
	Beyond San Pedro, Fremont joined Commodore Stockton to attack Castro. Marched north.
August 13, 1846	American army entered Los Angeles unopposed.
(August 15, 1846)	(The CALIFORNIAN, first California newspaper appeared.)
August, 1846	Kearny with 2,000 men took Santa Fe, N.M.
September, 1846	Colton appointed Alcalde of Monterey.
	Fremont sent north to Sacramento Valley to muster stronger force; Stockton promised him California governorship.
	Now three military districts in California: Fremont in north; Stockton in the middle; Gillespie left in charge of Los Angeles in south with fifty volunteers.
September 22, 1846	Four hundred Californians overthrew Gillespie.
September 25, 1846	Expeditionary force of 300 dragoons under General Kearny headed for California. On the way, met Kit Carson with official dispatches for Washington. Carson said California in American hands. Kearny kept only 100 dragoons and ordered Carson to guide him to Los Angeles.
September 29, 1846	Gillespie surrendered Los Angeles. Put upon merchant ship at San Pedro.
Oct.1 - Dec.15, 1846	Guerilla fighting in the south; much marching and countermarching of small forces.
October, 1846	Fremont went south to Santa Barbara with 170 men. Returned to Monterey learning of Mervine's defeat. Recruited 428 men, including Kern's garrison at Sutter's Fort and enlisted Indians and Grigsby's Sonoma men.
Nov. (end), 1846	Fremont moved toward San Luis Obispo. Here captured Don Jesus Pico. Pardoned him.
Dec. (early), 1846	Kearny reached California. Commodore Stockton had sent Gillespie from San Diego with small force to meet Kearny.
December 6, 1846	Kearny with Gillespie's men (about 160) met enemy at San Pasqual and lost 21 men fatally wounded. At nine or ten miles farther at Rancho San Bernardo, Kearny held at bay on a hill by Californians. Carson, Beale and Indian boy volunteered for dangerous mission to evade captors and obtain help from Stockton in San Diego.
December 10, 1846	Stockton's 180 soldiers and marines under Lt. Gray reached Kearny; Californians dispersed.
	At San Diego, Kearny with 50 men, with 60 of Gillespie's sharpshooters, and 430 of Stockton's men plus Indians and others (about 600

	men), re-grouped to march northward to route out Castro.
December 25, 1846	Fremont's army endured bitter cold and wind atop ridge behind Santa Barbara.
January 5, 1847	Warmer weather; reached San Buenaventura.
January 8, 9, 1847	Final decisive engagements between Californians and Stockton's army. Enemy retreated to Pasadena.
January 10, 1847	Americans under Stockton and Kearny took Los Angeles; Gillespie raised U.S. flag.
January 11, 1847	Two riders informed Fremont that Kearny and Stockton had defeated Californians and on January 10 had re-taken Los Angeles.
January 12, 1847	Fremont camped near Mission San Fernando. Negotiated terms of surrender of Californians under their Commander, Don Andres Pico. Fremont completed capitulation with Treaty of Cahuenga. War was over in California.*

----

* For defense of Fremont's actions in California during War, see Nevins, PATHMARKER, pp. 281, 284.

REFERENCES TO CHAPTER IV

GOD'S PROVIDENCE IN AMERICAN CONQUEST OF CALIFORNIA

1. Hunt, Rockwell D. NEW CALIFORNIA THE GOLDEN, p. 169.

U.S. CONSUL APPOINTED CONFIDENTIAL AGENT

2. Bean, Walton. CALIFORNIA, AN INTERPRETIVE HISTORY, p. 94.

FREMONT'S SECOND EXPEDITION 1843-1844

3. Fremont, John C. MEMOIRS OF MY LIFE, p. 314.

FREMONT'S THIRD EXPEDITION 1845

4. Ibid., pp. 452-453.

FREMONT AT GAVILAN PEAK

5. Ibid., p. 460.

FREMONT OVERTAKEN BY GILLESPIE

6. Ibid., p. 487.
7. Ibid., p. 488.
8. Ibid., p. 489.

JOHN D. SLOAT

9. Ibid., p. 541.
10. Bancroft, Hubert H. THE WORKS OF HUBERT HOWE BANCROFT. History of California, Vol. V., pp. 234-237.
11. Fremont, John C. MEMOIRS OF MY LIFE, p. 542.

THE CALIFORNIA BATTALION

12. Ibid., p. 542.

KIT CARSON

13. Grant, Blanche C., Ed. KIT CARSON'S OWN STORY OF HIS LIFE AS DICTATED TO COLONEL AND MRS. D. C. PETERS.

THE BATTLE OF SAN PASQUAL

14. Fremont, John C. MEMOIRS OF MY LIFE, p. 589.

CHAPTER V

THE PROVIDENTIAL DISCOVERY OF GOLD

"For no other foundation can no man lay than that is laid, which is Jesus Christ. Now if any man build upon this foundation gold, silver, precious stones, wood, hay, stubble; every man's work shall be made manifest..."
(I Corinthians 3:11,12,13)

GOLD

Providential aspect
of California's gold

GOD, GOLD, AND GOVERNMENT is the title of a book but those three words truly express the Gold Rush phase of California's history. For if it had not been for the Hand of God, gold would have been discovered long before the Spaniards or Mexicans had lost control of California. The acquisition of California by the United States would have been a very difficult problem, if indeed we could have obtained her at all. If it had not been for The Hand of God, California's government would have reflected the Roman civil law, instead of the Anglo-Saxon common law so dear to the hearts of liberty-loving Americans. God brought forth the Gold at the right time enabling California's Government to be American.

EARLY GOLD DISCOVERIES

Waiting for
God's Timetable

Gold discoveries had been made before 1848. Mission Indians used to bring small deposits of the metal to the padres. In fact, in 1841, John Bidwell told of an early discovery of gold in Los Angeles County:

"The yield was not rich; indeed it was so small that it made no stir. The discoverer was an old Canadian Frenchman by the name of Baptiste Ruelle..."[1]

As the mines Ruelle discovered were too poor to be worked, he went to work for Sutter in the Sacramento Valley. He claimed that in 1843 he had discovered gold also on the American River and told Sutter about it. He wanted a "stake" from Sutter to prospect for gold but Sutter thought he really wanted provisions to leave on a trek for Oregon and refused him. Nothing came of this.

Bidwell also told of another "discovery" on the Bear River in the Sierras early in the Spring of 1844 by a Mexican working for Sutter named Pablo Gutierrez.[2] Bidwell arranged to go up into the mountains with Gutierrez in March of 1844. He showed Bidwell the place but said he could not get out the gold without a "batea." Bidwell, misunderstanding his Spanish, thought a batea was a complicated machine. Actually it was nothing more than a wooden bowl which the Mexicans used for washing gold. Bidwell asked him where he could get one and Gutierrez said "Mexico." Bidwell was afraid Pablo would never return if he once got to Mexico so they agreed to save their money and buy one in Boston, but Boston was six month's voyage by ship. They could have waited for one of the four or five vessels which arrived each year in California from the Eastern seaboard of the United States, bringing goods needed by the Mexican people and returning to Boston with hides from California. However, in 1844 a revolt took place in California and the plans of Bidwell and Guttierez were interrupted. They never did look for the gold.

"...the time was right..."

In 1848, the time was right and gold was discovered on John Sutter's property.

JUST BEFORE THE DISCOVERY OF GOLD

Prosperity for Sutter

Let us look at John Sutter's property in California just before gold was discovered:

"The year following the American conquest (1847) was the most prosperous and promising in the history of New Helvetia. Within the short space of eight years, the activities of the enterprising Swiss had changed the wilderness into bustling communities. In December of 1847, Sutter, since April United States sub-Indian agent for his district, could report that the population of the Sacramento Valley numbered 289 white people and 479 tame Indians, besides over 21,000 wild Indians. Sixty houses had been erected in the territory of which Fort Sutter formed the nucleus. A tannery, six mills, and a number of industries were operated by Sutter and his neighbors. Over 14,000 fanegas (bushels) of wheat were harvested during the season, and the live stock was counted by the thousands. Three miles below the Fort the town of Sutterville was laid out and gave promise of a healthy development. A few good harvests would have sufficed to rid New Helvetia of its debts, and Sutter could hope to become in due time the richest man of the Pacific Coast.

Sutter said: 'After the war things prospered for me. I found a good market for my products among the newcomers and the people of the Bay district. My manufactures increased and there was no lack of skilled mechanics. I had a number of looms and the natives came to buy leather, shoes, saddles, hats, spurs, bridles, and other articles which were turned out by my shops. Agriculture increased until I had several hundred men working in the harvest fields, and to feed them I had to kill four or sometimes five oxen daily. I could raise 40,000 bushels of wheat without trouble, reap the crop with sickles, thrash it with hones, and winnow it in the wind. There were thirty plows running with fresh oxen every morning... The Russians were the chief customers for my agricultural products. I had at the time twelve thousand head of cattle, two thousand horses and mules, between ten and fifteen thousand sheep, and a thousand hogs. My best days were just before the discovery of gold.'"[3]

Steps to gold
discovery: Marshall
employed by Sutter

James Marshall had purchased two leagues of land (about 8,878 acres) in the Sacramento Valley and had started stocking it with cattle. When the war broke out, he joined the California Battalion. After American control was established, the Battalion was disbanded but the soldiers were unpaid for their services. Penniless, Marshall returned to the Sacramento Valley to find his ranch overrun and his livestock scattered or stolen. Unable to continue farming without animals or the means to purchase them, Marshall made his way to Sutter and eventually suggested a partnership in the lumber business.

Sutter hired the two millwrights, Marshall and Gingery, on May 28, 1847 to erect a large grist mill at Brighton on the American River as Sutter's mill at the Fort had been inadequate for a long time to supply their flour.

Sutter told his own story of James Marshall:

"A more difficult problem was the erection of a sawmill. There was no timber in the valley and it was necessary to go into the intermediary mountains to find a suitable place for this mill.

Character
of Marshall

Now there was in my employ the above-mentioned John (sic James) Marshall, a man of Scotch extraction and a native of New Jersey. He had been with me since the war and I esteemed him highly as a good mechanic. He made plows, looms, spinning wheels, and similar things. He was a spiritualist and a very queer person... He used to dress in buckskin and wear a serape.

"...a sawmill in
the mountains."

With this man I discussed the possibility of building a sawmill in the mountains. He believed that he could do it, and I was sure that I could not find a more dependable man for the job. I agreed to pay all expenses and to give him an interest in the mill. In view of its remoteness and the large number of men necessary for its construction, the sawmill meant a heavy financial burden from the very beginning.

On the 21st of July Marshall left for the mountains with an Indian Chief, Nerio, in search of a site for the mill. We decided to build it at Cul-luma or Coloma, on the southfork of the American River. Since all the provisions and machinery had to be brought up from the Fort, I had the Indians build a wagon road to Coloma. On August 28th (1847), Marshall and John Wimmer left for the mill site, followed soon by the Wimmer family, 17 Mormons, and five other men. Mrs. Wimmer was the only woman in the party and was to cook for the workers."[4]

DISCOVERY OF GOLD

El Dorado County,
California

Sutter's Mill, Coloma
El Dorado County, California

Picture: Painting by Charles Nahl
Map: Recreation and Tour Guide
El Dorado County, California

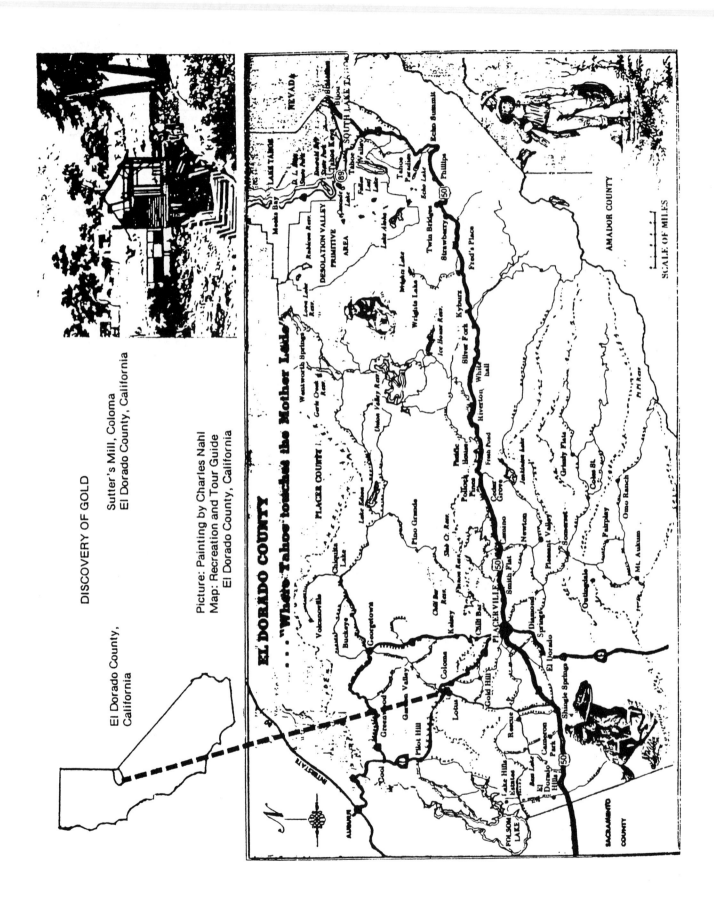

EL DORADO COUNTY
... "Where Tahoe touches the Mother Lode"

1848, gold in
the tail race

The first particles of gold were picked up in the tail race by Marshall five months later on January 24, 1848. The diary of one of the Mormons, Henry Bigler, recorded the date. James Marshall told his own account of what then happened:

"In about a week's time after the discovery I had to take another trip to the fort; and, to gain what information I could respecting the real value of the metal, took all that we had collected with me and showed it to Mr. Sutter, who at once declared it was gold, but thought with me that it was greatly mixed with some other metal. It puzzled us a good deal to hit upon the means of telling the exact quantity of gold contained in the alloy; however, we at last stumbled on an old American cyclopedia, where we saw the specific gravity of all the metals, and rules given to find the quantity of each in a given bulk. After hunting over the whole fort and borrowing from some of the men, we got three dollars and a half in silver, and with a pair of scales we soon ciphered it out that there was no silver nor copper in the gold, but that it was entirely pure.

News spread
like wildfire

This fact being ascertained, we thought it our best policy to keep it as quiet as possible till we should have finished our mill. But there was a great number of disbanded Mormon soldiers in and about the fort, and when they came to hear of it, why it just spread like wildfire, and soon the whole country was in a bustle. I had scarcely arrived at the mill again till several persons appeared with pans, shovels, and hoes, and those that had not iron picks had wooden ones, all anxious to fall to work and dig up our mill; but this we would not permit. As fast as one party disappeared another would arrive, and sometimes I had the greatest kind of trouble to get rid of them. I sent them all off in different directions, telling them about such and such places, where I was certain there was plenty of gold if they would only take the trouble of looking for it. At that time I never imagined that the gold was so abundant."[5]

The secret was out and the word spread rapidly. When Sam Brannan, a Mormon and businessman from Sacramento, walked the streets of San Francisco with a bottle of gold dust in his hand, shouting "Gold! Gold! Gold from the American River!" he stirred up a tempest. As the news traveled, it became more and more exaggerated.

No gain for
Marshall

What did the discovery of gold do for Marshall? In the COURSE OF EMPIRE, we read:

"Of the disasters which fell upon him from the discovery of gold, Marshall might have spoken almost endlessly. The magnitude of his discovery was his ruin. Through '48 the gold seekers harrassed and annoyed him. Everytime he opened his cabin door it was to find miners eagerly demanding the secret of locations... Mobs swarmed to the mill.

Returning after weeks to the mill, Marshall found all his land in the possession of squatters. Wherever he went, he was followed... (The great rush of '49 became to him a positive danger and several times his life was saved by friends.)

In his meagre little cabin Marshall lived to see the miracle wrought by his discovery of gold. All about him were evidences of the fabulous riches in which he had no share."[6]

Sutter shamefully
treated

As to Sutter's fate, let him tell it:

"I was the victim of every swindler who came along. I understood little about business and was foolish enough to have faith in men who cheated me on every side. Before the discovery of gold I had honest men around me like Bidwell, Hensley, Reading, etc. These had inspired me with confidence in human nature and caused me to trust many a sharper who was swept into California on the wave of gold excitement.

My grist mill was never finished. Everything was stolen, even the stones... The miners would not buy anything that they could more easily steal. They stole the cattle and the horses, they stole the bells from the Fort and the weights from the gates, they stole the hides, and they stole the barrels... My property was entirely exposed and at the mercy of the rabble. I could not shut the gates of my Fort in order to keep them out; they would have broken them down. The country swarmed with lawless men... I was alone and there was no law..."[7]

BY LAND AND BY SEA

The gold-seekers of 1848 and the gold-seekers of 1849 differed. In SUTTER OF CALIFORNIA, we learn:

1848:
Conscientious
neighbors

"Those of the first year (1848) were acquainted with their neighbors, had trafficked with them, were original settlers or trappers or hunters. They were a rough-and-ready sort with the wilderness code still strong in a majority of buck-skin covered breasts, just in the matter of personal property rights. Again, they were only a handful compared to the later arrivals. It remained for the men of '49 to really usher in the astounding phenomena of 'The Great Madness.'"

They came by sea:

"The CALIFORNIA carrying 400 gold seekers, entered the Golden Gate on February 28, 1849. She was the first vessel to bring treasure hunters from the eastern seaboard. Over the side went everyone – passengers, captain and crew. She was an abandoned ship thirty minutes after she made harbor. Some of her complement left San Francisco on their way to the mines before nightfall. From then on the sea lanes brought them ceaselessly."

They came by land:

"White-covered caravans were hastening overland to Sutter's Fort, as imposing as the sea migration. From all the states they came to Independence, or its vicinity, to organize and start in May, 1848. From that month on, one long line of wagons and pack trains were strung out as far as Fort Laramie. Cholera, fever, scurvy, hunger, exhaustion – all took their toll. A nation was on the march for John Sutter's gold. Forty-two thousand of them came to New Helvetia in 1849."[8]

WALTER COLTON'S DIARY

Walter Colton, a chaplain in the United States Navy given the assignment of Alcalde of Monterey during the American occupation, wrote a very interesting diary, THREE YEARS IN CALIFORNIA (1846-47-48):

"June 20, 1848. My messenger sent to the mines, has returned with specimens of the gold; he dismantled in a sea of upturned faces. As he drew forth the yellow lumps from his pockets, and passed them around among the eager crowd, the doubts, which had lingered till now, fled... The excitement produced was intense; and many were soon busy in their hasty preparations for a departure to the mines. The family who had kept house for me caught the moving infection. Husband and wife were both packing up; the blacksmith dropped his hammer, the carpenter his plane, the mason his trowel, the farmer his sickle, the baker his loaf, and the tapster his bottle. All were off for the mines, some on horses, some on carts, and some on crutches, and one went in a litter... I have only a community of women left, and a gang of prisoners, with here and there a soldier, who will give his captain the slip at the first chance. I don't blame the fellow a whit; seven dollars a month, while others are making two or three hundred a day! that is too much for human nature to stand.

Tuesday, July 18. Another bag of gold from the mines and another spasm in the community. It was brought down by a sailor from Yuba River, and contains a hundred and thirty-six ounces. It is the most beautiful gold that has appeared in the market... My carpenters, at work on the school-house, on seeing it, threw down their saws and planes, shouldered their picks, and are off for the Yuba...

Saturday, September 16. The gold mines are producing one good result; every creditor who has gone there is paying his debts. Claims not deemed worth a farthing are now cashed on presentation at natures great bank. This has rendered the credit of every man here good for almost any amount. Orders for merchandise are honored which six months ago would have been thrown into the fire. There is none so poor, who has two stout arms and a pickaxe left, but he can empty any store in Monterey. Nor has the first instance yet occurred, in which the creditor has suffered. All distinctions of means have vanished; the only capital required is muscle and an honest purpose."[9]

AT THE MINES

Americans trained in self-government

Most of the gold-seekers were from America and fortunately the experience of the Anglo-Saxon had trained him in self-government. It was tested here as the desire for law and order superseded the crazy desire for gold. In a modern textbook, Walton Bean observed:

Pilgrim influence

"In devising their own mining codes the Argonauts were acting in a tradition of American frontier self-government that went all the way back to the Mayflower Compact."[10]

In his GOLD DAYS, Owen C. Coy tells the story of what happened at the mines:

"He (the prospector) had traveled far, perhaps quite alone, perhaps as a member of some little company; he had carried on his own back tools and food and rifle across country still impassable for a pack animal; he had spent days in barren, heart-breaking toil, and nights at the mercy of murderous Indians, and at last he had 'struck it rich!' But before his dream of fortune might be realized there came others who had spied on his movements, followed his trail, and overtaken him in time to divide the fruits of his suffering, his patience, and his skill. Such an incident was described by E. G. Buffum, who found a rich ravine and hoped to make a fortune from the location. Within twenty-four hours he was traced, and the gulch was overrun with other miners. About $10,000 was taken in a few days, of which the discoverer realized only about $1,000. This was the danger

216

point in California life — excited men in a remote mountain gorge, with gold uncovered at their feet and loaded weapons in their hands. And this was the salvation of that life; they put their guns aside, sat down and talked things over, estimated the richness of the placer, and apportioned it fairly between them.

Miner's protection

Since the lure of abundant wealth had brought men of all kinds and races together it would appear natural that human cupidity should here have a chance to express itself without restraint and that spoils would go to the man with the strong arm and finger quick on the trigger.

Mining laws defined and enforced

It was under these circumstances that the adventurers of the Gold Days, of their own initiative, instituted neighborhood and district laws for the purpose of defining for a brief time their rights as temporary owners of the mining claims, thus to avoid the collisions that would inevitably arise through conflicting rights and demands. On every bar, gulch or ford where gold was found such laws were adopted as the majority of the miners saw fit to enact. These were not always set down in written documents, for frequently in the early days they were formed through mere verbal understanding.

Generations of Americans' aptitude for self-government

One of the first things done in the founding of a new camp was to enact a set of rules regarding the holding of mining claims. To draw up such a set of laws was not a new idea to most of the men. In many cases groups of men had associated themselves together in companies before leaving the eastern states, whether to sail around the Horn or to make the great trip across the plains. Although very few, if any, of these associations had been able to weather the unforeseen conditions that later arose, yet in the gold fields existence of those rules and the ease with which their members were able to abolish or modify them indicates an aptitude for government characteristic of a people which had for generations been accustomed to self-government."[11]

Socialism at mines did not work

One of the rules of these companies generally read: "That we work together in the mines, and use our tools in common." This did not work out when the miners reached the mines and saw the conditions under which they had to work and live. They were eager to own their own tools, work independently at the diggings, and keep "the fruit of their own labor." The socialistic aspects of the companies, share-and-share alike, fell apart as some found the labor too hard, some fell ill, and some were freeloaders. The working miner was willing to pool his resources en route to California, but his fiercely independent nature longed to build his estate upon his own labor and industriousness, which was part-and-parcel of the American way. Most of the companies disbanded at the mines.

"...The principle which formed the basis for all the regulations of the mining camps was, that all men are equal and that each should have an equal opportunity so long as he did not encroach upon the rights of others."[11]

COMPASSION AT THE MINES

...encouraged
individuality...

"The early miners of the Far West showed large and noble capacities for bringing order out of chaos, strength out of weakness, because they were a picked body of men, and also because the life they led fostered friendship, encouraged individuality, and compelled the closest social union."[12]

There is a little story in MINING CAMPS which well illustrates the miners' compassion:

Practical charity

"To a little camp of 1848...a lad of sixteen came one day, footsore, weary, hungry, and penniless. There were thirty robust and cheerful miners at work in the ravine; and the lad sat on the bank, watching them a while in silence, his face telling the sad story of his fortunes. At last one stalwart miner spoke to his fellows, saying: 'Boys, I'll work an hour for that chap if you will.'

At the end of the hour a hundred dollars worth of gold-dust was laid in the youth's handkerchief. The miners made out a list of tools and necessaries. 'You go,' they said, 'and buy these and come back. We'll have a good claim staked out for you. Then you've got to paddle for yourself.' Thus genuine and unconventional was the hospitality of the mining camp."[13]

MINING LAW

THE AMERICAN
SYSTEM OF
MINING LAW
adopted world-wide

One author calls the "AMERICAN SYSTEM OF MINING LAW, a system that is honored throughout the civilized world..."[14] It has been recognized by the California State Legislature, by Congress, and by the United States Supreme Court.

American
Common Law

"In the days of early mining in California and elsewhere, from the very necessity of the circumstances in which the miners found themselves, customs grew up which soon became a guide for all, or in mass meetings regulations were adopted concerning mining rights, and rules as to working them, which had the force of law in the locations where adopted, and constitute the American common law on mining for precious metals.

American instinct
for public meetings

These meetings were held at a known place in the district, upon previous notice that the meeting would take place for the purpose intended, either to establish the laws for the first time, or to alter

218

or repeal those formerly established. One of the miners present acts as the presiding officer, another as Secretary, who keeps a record of the proceedings of the meeting, and afterwards hands the laws adopted to the Recorder elected, who records them, as directed, in a book kept for that purpose. The laws are adopted in the usual way of conducting public meetings...but with the business tact of American instinct for public meetings.[15]

...just and fair...

The rules and regulations originally established in California have, in their general features, been adopted throughout all the mining regions of the United States. They were so wisely framed and were so just and fair in their operation that they have not to any great extent been interfered with by legislation, either State or National, and they are subject to the same rules of construction as statutes. But the rule, regulation, or custom to be valid must not only have been established but it must be in <u>force</u> in the district at the time the location is made. It does not, like a statute, acquire validity by the mere enactment, but from the customary obedience and acquiescence of the miners following its enactment. It is void whenever it falls into disuse and is generally disregarded."[16]

In reviewing the impact of the gold rush, the writer goes on to say:

Energy of the
gold rush

"The exodus to California in the time of the gold fever...pushed forward the onward march of events with an intensity and a rapacity never before known. It disclosed possibilities, developed energies, and promoted activities fraught with influences still affecting the destinies of the race.

It strengthened
individual character

...We can now only briefly indicate...some of the more manifest outgrowths of the California gold excitement. It widened the scope of vision, and broadened and strengthened individual character.

It strengthened
One Nation
Under God

The production of gold and silver gave staying power to the Government while engaged in a struggle for national life... It reacted upon the sleepy provincialism of older communities, and taught them a broader sense of the immensity of our domain and the indissoluble links of a common destiny. It has demonstrated the possibility, under a free government, of the people by their own industry creating for themselves a safe means of commercial exchange, and thus enhancing the possibilities of industrial pursuits.

It fostered a
security based upon
reason and morality

The purpose of the foregoing references has not been so much to point out the glories of material advancement, as to delineate in perspective that which is the crowning glory of all; that from which results law, order, liberty, protection to person and prop-

Sketched by J. W. Revere U.S.N.   QUICKSILVER MINE - NEAR SANTA CLARA.   Lith. of Wm Endicott & Co. N. York.

220

erty, a sacred regard for the rights of others, joined with an absolute independence of individual effort in security, a security based upon reason and a sense of moral obligation. The aptitude of the American people for such achievement the American mining law amply proves, and the course of its advancement, the history of its growth, should be interesting as well to the student of law as to the miner whose welfare is dependent upon its due administration."[17]

THE NEW ALMADEN MINE[18]

God's Hand: California independent of Europe

With so much gold being mined from the gold fields of California in those early days of 1848 to about 1853, it was providential that California developed her own quicksilver mine, not having to depend on Europe. Quicksilver is used in processing gold, and cinnabar is the rock that contains quicksilver.

THE PROVIDENTIAL DISCOVERY OF CINNABAR

Cinnabar in the Santa Clara Valley

In 1845, Andres Castillero, a captain in the Mexican army, arrived at the Mission Santa Clara to visit Upper California. He had been trained at the College of Mines in Mexico City in geology, chemistry, and metallurgy.

Castillero noticed that the local Indians used a red rock in various ways for its brilliant color. He believed the red rock might be cinnabar, the ore of mercury, and asked the Indians to lead him to the secret place where they found the rock. They led him to the hills deep in the Santa Clara Valley. Castillero had observed similar rock in his native Spain at the quicksilver mines of La Mancha. He believed he had made a great discovery, and indeed he had. He planned to make a legal claim to the property. The land was a Mexican grant owned by Berryessa.

Mining law in Mexican California stated that a mine must show development. Castillero began experimenting, pulverizing and heating the rock which condensed into liquid metal or quicksilver. By December 3, 1845, he managed to obtain a certificate of possession. However, by August of 1846, he had run out of funds and needed new equipment and supplies, so he decided to sell.

Barron-Forbes

Castillero found a buyer, Barron-Forbes Company, in Mexico. In 1846, Alexander Forbes and Eustace Barron acquired two-thirds of the mine shares and began the operation of the first organized mining company in California.

NEW ALMADEN

Alexander Forbes' mining operation was named "New Almaden" after the great Almaden mine in Spain which had been successfully operating for centuries. During the 1849 gold rush, the Cinnabar Hills Mine in New Almaden became one of the greatest quicksilver mines in the world.

The boundary agreement of the mine was contested by Berryessa and Larios. Their land extended into the property of the mining company. Although they had obtained an injunction by the Board of Land Commissioners against operation of the mine, it still continued to operate into the year 1861. The case was taken to the Supreme Court and became an explosive issue. President Lincoln finally relieved the situation; litigation ceased in 1864.

SPANISHTOWN

Contribution of
Mexican laborers

In 1847, the first settlement near the mine was called "Spanishtown," which was predominately occupied by imported Mexican workers and their families. The Mexican laborers were particularly skilled in locating the veins of cinnabar. They eventually built a Catholic Church on the hill, and operated schools from grades 1-3 to teach English.

ENGLISHTOWN

Contribution of
Cornish miners

At the time of the California gold rush, mining in Cornwall, England, was on the decline. The miners readily accepted work at New Almaden, bringing their families. They had been bred in their native land to work at the Cornwall mines and were hearty and vigorous workers.

The Cornish miners established their own village at New Almaden called "Englishtown." They built a Methodist Episcopal Church and stayed pretty much to themselves. A school was established from grades 1-8, which was built in 1871.

NEW METHODS

Henry W. Halleck

Barron-Forbes Company hired Captain Henry Halleck, a graduate of West Point, who had legal training in land grants, as director of mining operations. He improved the operations, replacing the hard labor of the men with better methods. He installed a mechanical steam hoist; constructed a tunnel into Mine Hill; a machine shop to repair the equipment; a 22′ diameter water wheel; all of which accelerated the ore production. The orders for quicksilver poured in from all parts of the world.

Eventually, the Quicksilver Mining Company of New York, Pennsylvania, bought out Barron-Forbes for $1,750,000. The pioneers in mining in California, Barron and Forbes, returned to Mexico having produced $15,000,000 in quicksilver. The Quicksilver Mining Company ended operation in 1912.

GOLDEN SAN FRANCISCO

Since a permanent commonwealth was built in California in the middle of the gold rush frenzy, we wonder how order could have come forth from such chaos as existed in the city of San Francisco. In the book, IN SEARCH OF

GOD'S GOLD, we read of the early name of the city when it was little more than a Mexican pueblo:

"Yerba Buena"

"As the skippers entered the Golden Gate there was no good anchorage near the Presidio or Mission. But three miles inside the Gate, sheltered by Telegraph Hill, was a cove. And back of the cove, surrounded by scrub-covered sand dunes, was an open area. In the center was a spring, with fields of fragrant herb about it, which the Spanish called <u>yerba buena</u> -- the good herb. Here was what seamen wanted -- safe anchorage, fresh water, open ground, adjacent wood. <u>El Paraje de Yerba Buena</u>, the Place of the Good Herb, was predestined to greatness."[19]

"San Francisco"

In 1847, the name <u>Yerba Buena</u> was changed to <u>San Francisco</u>.

By 1849, the gold rush had brought thousands of gold hunters into the city. The busyness and confusion in the streets reflected the eagerness of the argonauts to quickly attend to the business of buying mining supplies and be off for the diggings.

In the ANNALS OF SAN FRANCISCO, we read:

Population

"Population of San Francisco at the close of 1849 was about 20,000 to 25,000 people, mostly adult males...

Housing

There was no such thing as a home to be found. Scarcely even a proper house would be seen. Both dwellings and places of business were either common canvas tents, or small rough board shanties, or frame buildings of one story. Only the great gambling saloons, the hotels, restaurants, and a few public buildings and stores had any pretensions to size, comfort, or elegance. The site on which the town is built was then still covered with numberless sand hills...

Hulls of
ships rotted

We have occasionally alluded to the desertion of seamen. At the time of which we write (1849) there were between three hundred and four hundred large and square-rigged vessels lying in the bay, unable to leave on account of want of hands. Many of these vessels never got away, but, in a few years afterwards, rotted and tumbled to pieces where they were moored. As stores and dwelling-houses were much needed, a considerable number of the deserted ships were drawn high on the beach, and fast embedded in deep mud, where they were converted into warehouses and lodgings for the wants of the crowded population. When subsequently the town was extended over the mud flat of the bay, these ships were forever closed in by numberless streets and regularly built houses both of brick and frame...

The circulation of money – partly coin, partly gold dust, – was very great. Men had a sublime indifference to the smaller pieces of coin, and talked as familiarly of dollars as people elsewhere would of dimes. A copper coin was a strange sight. There was nothing less received for any service, however slight, than half a dollar."[20]

1848 prices

When one considers that the wages that a soldier made in June, 1848, in Monterey was only $7.00 a month, according to the diary of Walter Colton, prices in San Francisco rose to an exorbitant amount: A meal was expensive in a restaurant in San Francisco, 1849. Bean soup was $1.50; 18K Hash was $2.50; and coffee, $1.00.

"Rents were correspondingly enormous. Three thousand dollars a month, in advance, was charged for a single store of limited dimensions, and rudely constructed of rough boards. A certain two-storey frame building, known as the "Parker House," and situated on Kearny Street, facing the plaza, paid its owners one hundred and twenty thousand dollars a year in rents...

Rapid building

The year 1850 saw a wonderful improvement in the aspect of San Francisco... The buildings in the business quarter were now remarkable for their size, beauty and solidity. The tents and shanties of last year had totally disappeared from the centre of town, while many of the old frame buildings that had not been destroyed by fire were replaced by others of a larger and stronger kind, if not by extensive fireproof brick structures."[21]

The Phoenix

From 1849 to 1851, San Francisco experienced six great fires. They were largely due to the wooden framework of the buildings. San Francisco kept rebuilding itself after each fire, until finally buildings were constructed of imported granite from China and brick from the Atlantic seaboard, England, and Australia. Citizens became active in their support of effective fire departments. The emblem of the City of San Francisco is a Phoenix, which was a miraculous bird in the Egyptian religion supposed to have lived for five hundred years. It was consumed in fire by its own act and rose again in youthful freshness from its own ashes. We might like to think of fire as a purifying influence, elevating the city of San Francisco.

Americans desire order

Out of chaos, finally came order in San Francisco:

"Instead of the old scenes of terrible confusion...as existing at the close of 1849, the city, only one twelvemonth later, presented an orderly, decent and busy aspect, with moderately clean and regular streets, houses of fair proportions, prices of provisions and goods reasonable, markets supplied with every luxury for the table, convenient wharves for shipping, 'expresses' by sea and land, a dozen churches, half-a-dozen banking establishments, several theatres, seven daily newspapers, magnificent hotels and restaurants, handsome public carriages... Numerous associations were organized for municipal, defensive, literary, charitable, musical, social and similar purposes just as we find in the old established communities..."[22]

One of the early residents of San Francisco, Mr. William F. White, wrote PIONEER TIMES IN CALIFORNIA. Mr. White arrived in California from New York on board the SOUTH CAROLINA on June 30, 1849, having paid $350.00 for his passage. He emphasized the positive aspect of pioneer life and paid a glowing tribute to the pioneer women of San Francisco:

The Women
of '49

"There never was in the annals of the world a nobler class of women than the women of '49. They were patient, they were enduring. They accepted terrible privations, and faced dangers and trials without a murmur... When I speak of the 'women of '49,' of course I do not speak of the poor, abandoned creatures who so filled the imaginations of the authors of the 'Annals.' No, I do not speak of them, or think of them...they were as nothing in numbers when compared to the whole female population of San Francisco... I speak of the women whose devotion, unobtrusive piety, good example, and constant whisperings of encouragement to the worldly-minded men of their households, were the chief cause of churches, schools, orphan asylums, and many other useful and benevolent associations, springing like magic into existence in every part of the city."[23]

Mr. White viewed the miner of '49:

The Miners
of '49

"To look at the returned miners in those days in San Francisco the first impression you would get was that they were all of a roughcast of men, uneducated and savage. Their uncut hair, their long beards, their red flannel shirts, with flashy red Chinese scarfs around their waists, the black leather belt beneath the scarf, fastened with a silver buckle, to which hung the handsome six-shooter and bowie knife, the slouched wide-brimmed hat, the manly, bold, independent look and gait of the man as he walked along, made each one look the chief of a tribe of men you had no knowledge of before. Get into conversation with this man, and you will find, to your surprise, in nine cases out of ten, a refined, intelligent, educated American, despising the excesses of the idle and the dissipated. You will find his whole heart on his old home and those he has left there. Look up as he speaks to you of wife and children and draws from beneath his red shirt a photograph of those loved ones, and you will find him brushing away tears that have fallen on his great shaggy beard. Stand behind such a looking man in the long line from the Postoffice window, waiting for his turn to get letters. See; he takes his

225

letters from the clerk at the window, and his whole frame shakes with emotion, and, as he looks at the well known handwriting, his handkerchief is again on his face."[24]

Of the churches of 1849 and 1850, Mr. White wrote:

The Churches of '49

"On Sundays, in '49 and '50, I often took pleasure in visiting the churches of the various denominations, just to see what progress we were making in the all-important point of obtaining a worthy female population; and I used to find myself perfectly astonished at the fast increase of both women and children. Their universal attendance at church was, too, a striking feature of the women of '49... Of course I do not allude to the abandoned class when I say this. A pleasing picture, too, of religious progress in San Francisco at that time was the total absence of sectarian bitterness... The clergymen, of all denominations, in San Francisco – Protestant, Catholic and Jewish – worked, each in his own way, like a band of brothers, ever ready to praise and commend each other on all proper occasions. Shoulder to shoulder, they worked, warring only on vice and immorality... This good-will between religious people and the untiring activity and zeal of the women, accounts for the wonderful prosperity of the churches of the various denominations in San Francisco."[25]

EARLY PROTESTANT CHURCHES IN CALIFORNIA

Notes on early Protestant missionary work

The first Protestant ministers who arrived in San Francisco in the mid-1800's had a lot of pioneering to do. I have recorded here a few "bits and pieces" of information regarding the first missionaries to California from different denominations. It is suggested that students research some references to early missionary work in California in their own churches. I am sure your minister can help you.

Presbyterian

In 1846, "...Captain John B. Montgomery, a Presbyterian ruling elder, is reported to have conducted a service at Yerba Buena, the first public Protestant service held in what became San Francisco."[26]

Methodist

In 1846, "Adna A. Hecox, a local preacher of the Methodist Church settled in Santa Clara and began services there."[27]

There were two Methodist preachers, Reverend William Roberts and J. H. Wilbur, who arrived in San Francisco on April 24, 1847 via the bark WHITON.

226

"In 1846 the Rev. William Roberts was appointed missionary superintendent for Oregon, and he was instructed by his Board to survey California as a missionary field en route. He reached San Francisco on April 24, 1847, on the barque WHITON, accompanied by his assistant, the Rev. James H. Wilbur. The following day Roberts preached in the dining room of an old adobe hotel, with a billiard room and a saloon on one side, and two card rooms on the other, all doing business. John H. Brown, the proprietor of the hotel wrote: 'The congregation was not fashionable but deeply attentive and well pleased with the sermon. I can say that many who were at that meeting had not been to any place of worship for ten or fifteen years previous to that occasion.'

Wilbur was troubled about holding a service amid such surroundings, and said that Roberts had preached 'where Satan had his seat.' It is interesting to note that William Taylor wrote concerning Roberts that he carried 'a Bible in one hand and a good Colt's revolver in the other.'

During several weeks in the Bay area a Methodist class of six members was organized, and on May 16 Wilbur organized a Sunday school, the first Protestant organization in the state."[28]

The experience of William Taylor, famous Methodist street preacher of those early California days, is recounted in IN SEARCH OF GOD'S GOLD:

"Portsmouth Square may be prosy enough now, with a few loiterers sitting near the Robert Louis Stevenson monument. But on Sunday, December 3, 1849, there was probably more hell let loose on its four sides than on any comparable frontage in the world. William Taylor took a carpenter's bench from the front of a gambling joint, seated his wife and another woman, and mounting the bench sang in his magnificent voice strong enough to be heard in half the tents and shacks of what was then San Francisco...

That morning when he had announced to his congregation that there would be service at 3:00 on the Plaza, consternation reigned. It was absolutely unsafe!... Gambling was the big industry of the city. Its gentry tolerated no nonsense. And Sunday was their big day.

But there stood William Taylor! Before the first stanza was finished (he sang seven) a crowd surrounded him. He said that for variety Peter's congregation at Pentecost could not begin to equal his.

'In your tedious voyage around the Horn, or your wearisome journey over the plains, or your hurried passage across the Isthmus, losses and gains have constituted the theme of your thoughts and calculations. Now I want you to employ all your mathematical skill on a mighty problem – What shall it profit a man if he gain the whole world and lose his own soul?'

There was neither murder nor disorder that Sunday afternoon on Portsmouth Square. That was the first of six hundred sermons William Taylor preached on plaza, street corners, docks of young San Francisco. During a hundred of these he used a whisky barrel as a platform. Crude, effervescent individuals often interrupted with horseplay. But Taylor never lost a congregation, even when some wag rang the fire bell to divert the crowd. A quick bit of wit regained attention, after which he used the interruption to drive home his fervent appeal."[29]

In 1855, the ANNALS OF SAN FRANCISCO paid tribute to Mr. Taylor:

"Probably no man in modern times has followed up the practice of out-door preaching so successfully and to so great advantage, as Mr. Taylor, whose unremitting zeal and religious deportment have gained for him the esteem and admiration of the entire San Francisco community."[30]

Episcopal

"The Rev. T. M. Leavenworth, an Episcopal clergyman, arrived in San Francisco on April 18, 1847 as chaplain of Company F of Colonel J. D. Stevenson's regiment; May 2, he preached in Brown's Hotel."[31]

Mormon

"In December of 1847 a new school house was completed in San Francisco by Samuel Brannan, a Mormon elder, and services were held in it on December 26, the preacher probably being Elihu Anthony, a Methodist."[32]

Baptist

The pioneer preacher of early Baptist history in California was Osgood Church Wheeler, the first Baptist missionary to California.

"On Friday, December 1, 1848, Dr. Wheeler and his wife sailed out of New York harbor on the steamer FALCON. Wheeler organized the First Baptist Church in San Francisco and served as its pastor. Much of his time was devoted to counseling new arrivals as many of the young gold seekers had letters of introduction to him.[33]

He was generous in opening his pulpit to ministers of other denominations. The Rev. William Taylor, a Methodist, preached in the Baptist Church on two Sundays after his arrival. Wheeler's name occurs repeatedly in reports of dedications, special gatherings,... There was nothing small or narrow about him. He was a Baptist but he was not sectarian. He saw the kingdom of God as something larger than the Baptist fellowship.[34]

Discouraging factors in Wheeler's situation were numerous, as illustrated in his statement that he had 'never seen a harder task than to get a man to look through a lump of gold into eternity.' But in spite of all the difficulties and disappointments he kept on with his work, serving his fellows in every way possible.[35]

The year 1850, which brought statehood to California, was an important one in the early history of California Baptists. In that year the first advance was made under the leadership of Wheeler, for churches were established at San Jose and Sacramento, and a Baptist Association was organized. In addition, Baptist Churches were reported organized at Shaw's Flat and at Mud Springs, and the California Baptist Ministers' Conference at San Francisco came into being."[36]

The Chaplaincy

"...although services such as these (in 1848) were held from time to time as opportunity offered and as preachers were available, there were no regular Protestant services. It was not until the establishment of the City Chaplaincy (in San Francisco) that regular weekly worship became possible.[37]

The first regularly organized Protestant work in San Francisco began in November, 1848, under the leadership of the Rev. Timothy Dwight Hunt.

Hunt, a New School Presbyterian, arrived in San Francisco from Honolulu on October 29. A growing need for regular church services and for the work of a minister had manifested itself, and funds had been raised for this purpose. On November 1, 1848, a meeting of citizens was held in the Public Institute to consider the matter, and five trustees were elected. Hunt was invited to accept the position of 'City Chaplain,' to preach each Sunday in the Public Institute on Portsmouth Square. He accepted, and the next day entered upon his duties...

This chaplaincy met a deep need in the life of San Francisco in those early days. Congregationalists, Baptists, Methodists, Presbyterians, Episcopalians, and others united in the interdenominational services and work.

Thirty years later he (Hunt) wrote concerning this early project: 'In the judgment of the best people on the ground, a union movement under a chaplaincy was deemed the best. Religious people were few. They were of all persuasions. No three people were the same. The demand was for the Sabbath and the Gospel, not for name and sect... The chaplaincy worked admirably. The minister was preacher and pastor to all... Ignoring differences, we were Christ's - combined for Christian fellowship and work."[38]

Congregational

The Congregationalist, Dr. William C. Pond, is called "One of the Pilgrim Fathers of the Pacific." Dr. Pond, from the year of his arrival in 1853 into California, devoted his life to missionary work, and he lived to be ninety-one.

"...Though not one of the earliest, (he) was one of the youngest and most alert and the one who has had the longest term of active service..."[39]

He is credited with saving from ruin the Pacific Theological Seminary, and of ministering to the Chinese in San Francisco at a time when "they were friendless, homeless and ill-treated."[40]

The book GOSPEL PIONEERING: REMINISCENCES OF EARLY CONGREGATIONALISM IN CALIFORNIA is Dr. Pond's autobiography; his early experiences are interesting.

In 1852, William Pond decided to accept a call for missionary work in California, as he desired "foreign" missionary work. He expected hardship and physical difficulties far away from his old home in New England. The redeeming feature of his call to California was that, unlike a call to Africa, he could preach in his mother tongue. In 1852, New England generally viewed California as a dry, "barren country, with nothing but its gold to reward adventure and toil."[41]

In his own words, Dr. Pond later wrote:

"All this will be sufficiently amusing in these days in which the world is coming to see in California its very paradise."[42]

Although Thomas Starr King, a Protestant, is the patriot and preacher of Civil War fame, his name is inserted here because his statue resides along with that of Father Serra, a Catholic, in the National Statuary Hall, Washington, D.C. They were selected as the most distinguished representatives of California.

"He (Starr King) was educated in the excellent public schools of Charlestown, whose residents in that day were chiefly of American stock, and whose proximity to Boston and Cambridge imparted an unusual degree of culture to its society, while the traditions clustering around Bunker Hill and the early struggle for national independence made it one of the shrines and nurseries of American patriotism.[43]

Starr King had already a national reputation when he came to California in the spring of 1860 as a minister-elect of the Unitarian Society in San Francisco.[44]

At the outbreak of the Civil War he wholeheartedly took up the cause of the Union, never hesitating to use his pulpit to point the way of true political and moral principles.[43] The brilliant labors of King in his campaigning for the United States Sanitary Commission, which he deemed the world's grandest scheme of charity, will never be forgotten. This work called him not only to various parts of California but also to Washington, and even Vancouver, B.C.[45]

'Tonight,' he writes humorously from the mining town of Yreka, 'I am to speak in a village with the sweet name of Dead Wood, and tomorrow at the very important and cultivated settlement of Rough and Ready. Scott's Bar wants me; Horsetown is after me; Mugginsville bids high; Oro Fino applies with a long petition of names. Mad Mule has not yet sent in a request; nor Piety Hill, nor Modesty Gulch; but doubtless they will be heard from in due time. The Union sentiment is strong; but the secessionists are watchful and not in despair'... He was effective with rough miners and cowboys as with cultivated city audiences. Mr. King declared that he never knew the exhilaration of public speaking until he faced a front row of revolvers and bowie knives...[46]

To Thomas Starr King...is due the credit for bringing California into the chief place among the states for her princely contributions to the treasury of the commission... Thus did California gold nobly assist in preserving the great American Union."[47]

A natural question arises: We study so much of the activity in northern California during the gold rush days, but what was happening in southern California?

In her book on WILLIAM WOLFSKILL, pioneer of the Old Spanish Trail from Santa Fe to Los Angeles in 1831, the authoress, Iris H. Wilson, gives us a picture of the South:

Population growth enough to admit California to the Union

"As a result of the Gold Rush of 1849, California had a population large enough to allow its admission to the union in September 1850. This phenomenal growth...caused a number of changes in the southern portion of the state as well as the northern center of activity. A new city was now coming into existence in Los Angeles — an American growth grafted upon a Spanish stock. However, because of the inaccessibility of the area, the change from the old order to the new was not as rapid as in other regions. Between Los Angeles and the eastern states was a great gulf of distance and danger, which only the hardiest ventured to cross.

Los Angeles remote

Raising stock more prosperous

The discovery of gold which brought some 80,000 people to the northern part of the state in one year, affected the southern part in a reflexive way. In the decade from 1850-1860 several thousand of the gold seekers drifted down from San Francisco, some of them with a little capital acquired in the diggings, but more of them penniless; and some of both kinds located permanently in Los Angeles. Also there were those who left the eastern states in the expectation of mining for gold but were dissuaded by the stories of failure and turned their course to the south, where they were told 'men grow rich quickly in raising stock.'

But the total number who made their way into this (the southern) part of the territory was not large, and of those who came many soon returned to the east, their dreams of sudden wealth failing to materialize.

The Pueblo of Los Angeles

Some commerce was carried on between Los Angeles and Arizona and during the fifties there was trade with the mining camps of the north. The pueblo (of Los Angeles) was a station on the route from Texas and the southern states to the gold fields of northern California, and many of the gold seekers passed through. Except for these sources of revenue, however, the people of Los Angeles enjoyed whatever means that came out of the territory immediately surrounding them.

232

The first American census, taken in 1850, showed the population of the city (of Los Angeles) to be 1,610 and of the county 3,530. It has been estimated that prior to the gold rush the population in the city had reached almost 3,000 (depleted by gold rush to about one half). The census of 1860 showed an increase in the city to 4,399 and in the county to 11,333.

During the thirty years from 1850 to 1880, the growth of Los Angeles was slow. It remained throughout most of that period a Spanish-American rather than an American city. The failure to advance was due to the apparent inability of the country (mostly desert) to support a larger population. The old Spanish California tradition of a carefree life, with its interest in music, dancing, fiestas and rodeos, continued through the mid-1870's."[48]

AN AMERICAN COMMONWEALTH

On page 61 of IN SEARCH OF GOD'S GOLD, we read:

"The mining rush did not begin the western trek. Before gold was discovered there had been an increasing number of wagon trains moving westward. The majority of Argonauts were normal Americans, though living under very abnormal conditions. The gold rush was more spectacular, both in its coarseness and its strength, than any other phase of the western migration. But it was part and parcel of that movement. It was typically American in its pattern. That familiar pattern made California an American commonwealth. Our civic and cultural foundations are of the Protestant type, not Russian or Roman..."[49]

Gold was discovered near Sutter's Fort in California on January 24, 1848. Providentially, this did not happen until California was safe in the hands of the Americans. As a result of the Gold Rush of 1849, California had enough population to allow it to become the thirty-first state of the Union.

While the contest between the United States and Mexico was taking place in California, and while the gold rush was at its height in California, how was California governed?

REFERENCES TO CHAPTER V

THE PROVIDENTIAL DISCOVERY OF GOLD

EARLY GOLD DISCOVERIES

1. Bidwell, John. "Life in California Before the Gold Discovery," THE CENTURY MAGAZINE, Dec. 1890 and Feb. 1891, p. 40.
2. Ibid., p. 42.

JUST BEFORE THE DISCOVERY OF GOLD

3. Gudde, Erwin G. SUTTER'S OWN STORY, pp. 184-186.

JAMES WILSON MARSHALL

4. Ibid., pp. 187-188.

GOLD DISCOVERED JANUARY 24, 1848

5. Gillespie, Charles B. "Marshall's Own Account of the Gold Discovery," THE CENTURY MAGAZINE, Feb. 1891, Vol. XLI.
6. Bari, Valeska, Ed. THE COURSE OF EMPIRE, FIRST HAND ACCOUNTS OF CALIFORNIA IN THE DAYS OF THE GOLD RUSH OF '49, pp. 65-66.
7. Gudde, Op. Cit, pp. 223-224.

BY LAND AND BY SEA

8. Dana, Julian. SUTTER OF CALIFORNIA: A BIOGRAPHY, p. 335.

WALTER COLTON'S DIARY

9. Colton, Walter. THREE YEARS IN CALIFORNIA, pp. 246, 248.

AT THE MINES

10. Bean, Walton. CALIFORNIA, AN INTERPRETIVE HISTORY, p. 121.
11. Coy, Owen Cochrane. GOLD DAYS, pp. 170-172.

COMPASSION AT THE MINES

12. Shinn, Charles H. MINING CAMPS, pp. 5, 6.
13. Ibid., pp. 104-105.

REFERENCES TO CHAPTER V (continued)

MINING LAW

14. Ibid., p. 6.
15. Rickets, A. H. "A Dissertation Upon The Origin, Development, and Establishment of American Mining Law," ELEVENTH REPORT OF THE STATE MINERALOGIST, p. 523.
16. Ibid., p. 524.
17. Ibid., p. 522.

THE NEW ALMADEN MINE

18. Source: Lanyon, Milton and Laurence Bulmore. CINNABAR HILLS: THE QUICKSILVER DAYS OF NEW ALMADEN, 1967.

GOLDEN SAN FRANCISCO

19. Loofbourow, Leon L. IN SEARCH OF GOD'S GOLD, pp. 43, 44.
20. Gihon, John, James Nisbet, Frank Soule. THE ANNALS OF SAN FRANCISCO.
21. Ibid., p. 253.
22. Ibid., p. 304.
23. White, William F. A PICTURE: PIONEER TIMES IN CALIFORNIA, p. 64.
24. Ibid., p. 99.
25. Ibid., pp. 104-105.

EARLY PROTESTANT CHURCHES IN CALIFORNIA

Presbyterian

26. Fleming, Sandford. GOD'S GOLD: THE STORY OF BAPTIST BEGINNINGS IN CALIFORNIA, 1849-1860, p. 64.

Methodist

27. Ibid., p. 64.
28. Ibid., pp. 64, 65.
29. Loofborow, Op. Cit., pp. 45, 46.
30. Gihon, Nibet, Soule, Op. Cit., p. 695.

Episcopal

31. Fleming, Op. Cit., p. 65.

Mormon

32. Ibid., p. 66.

Baptist

33. Ibid., p. 55.
34. Ibid., p. 60.
35. Ibid., p. 61.
36. Ibid., p. 77.

The Chaplaincy

37. Ibid., p. 66.
38. Ibid., p. 67.

Congregational

39. Pond, William C. GOSPEL PIONEERING: REMINISCENCES OF EARLY CONGREGATIONALISM IN CALIFORNIA, p. iii.
40. Ibid., p. iv.
41. Ibid., p. 16.
42. Ibid., p. 15.

Thomas Starr King

43. Wendte, Charles W. THOMAS STARR-KING:PATRIOT AND PREACHER, p. 6.
44. Ibid., p. 5.
45. Hunt, Rockwell D. CALIFORNIA'S STATELY HALL OF FAME, p.329.
46. Wendt, Op. Cit., p. 195.
47. Hunt, Op. Cit., 329.

SOUTHERN CALIFORNIA

48. Wilson, Iris H. WILLIAM WOLFSKILL, 1798-1866, pp. 185-187.

AN AMERICAN COMMONWEALTH

49. Loofbourow, Op. Cit., p. 61.

CHAPTER VI

"For unto us a child is born, unto us a son is given; and the government shall be upon his shoulder..." (Isa. 9:6)

CALIFORNIA'S FIRST CONSTITUTIONAL CONVENTION

AMERICANS DEMAND GOVERNMENT

End of war 1848   At the end of the Mexican-American War, the treaty, signed at Guadalupe Hidalgo, was ratified in May 1848 by Congress, and the official news reached California on August 6, 1848. California was now conquered territory.

California was to see a great change in its government. New principles of government were to be installed in California for the first time.

MILITARY GOVERNMENT: LAW OF OCCUPIED TERRITORY IN EFFECT

U.S. Military occupation   From the outbreak of the war in 1846 until the ratification of the treaty of peace, California followed the general practice for an occupying force (U.S.) to continue the law system of the occupied territory (Mexican law) if it did not conflict with accepted ideas of justice held by the invaders (U.S.). Theoretically, Mexican law was in force. The American commanders were also ex-officio governors. So, the "governorship" passed from Commodore Sloat, to Commodore Stockton, to Colonel Fremont, to General Kearny, to Colonel Mason: five governors in the first ten months.

GOVERNORS

Commodore John D. Sloat, on July 15, 1846, after raising the United States flag at Monterey, willingly relinquished his command and the "governorship" to Commodore Stockton.

Commodore Robert F. Stockton, as governor, had prepared a plan for a civil government for California and even drafted a constitution, but this was interrupted by a series of revolts by native Californians, and further by the entrance into California of General Kearny in November 1846. Kearny's claim that he had the right to govern the conquered territory had been weakened by his defeat at San Pasquel, and Stockton was generally recognized by the people as military commander and territorial governor until his departure. On January 14, 1847, Stockton tendered Colonel Fremont his commission as governor.

For fifty days, Colonel John Charles Fremont, although acting in direct disobedience to Kearny's order to relinquish the governorship to him, was generally accepted by the people as governor. In February 1847, orders came from Washington that the senior officer of the land forces, General Kearny, should be governor. Then followed the Kearny-Fremont controversy which ended in the Fremont court-martial, conviction, and remission of punishment.

237

On March 1, 1847, General Stephen W. Kearny assumed the governorship and designated Monterey as the capital. But the situation in California was chaotic still when Kearny left Monterey on May 31, 1847, being succeeded in military and civil command by Colonel Mason.

During Colonel Richard B. Mason's governorship, ending with the treaty of peace with Mexico August 6, 1848, California was under strict military rule. Under this rule, the energetic American settlers grew quite restless; their dissatisfaction finally became bitter complaint. The absence of a fixed well-defined, and understood law brought forth the loudest complaints. As the months passed, and immigration increased, as the country gradually developed, all without a uniform system of law, and with a government which no one understood, the situation was critical.

Governor Riley

When Mason ended his governorshp and General Bennett Riley took over, the Treaty of Guadalupe Hidalgo had been signed (February 2, 1848) and ratified (at Queretaro on May 30). By its terms the territory of California had been ceded to the United States, of which it became completely a part. The news reached California August 6, 1848 and Governor Mason announced it in a Proclamation. He fully expected the Congress of the United States to confer upon the people of California "the constitutional rights of citizens of the United States." But, California was destined to continue through many trying months practically without any organized form of government.

DIFFICULTY OF INTERNATIONAL LAW

California subjected to international law

The observance of this practice of international law was most difficult in California. 1) The laws were in a foreign language; 2) They were not widely known; 3) And the procedures, as well as the laws themselves, seemed arbitrary to Americans. In his A SELF-GOVERNING DOMINION, page 12, Wiiliam Henry Ellison remarked:

> "Partly because the California (Mexican) system of law and judicial procedure was at variance with American practices, in some measure because the old order was unsuited to what was developing, and even more because it is a trait of Americans to want to run things according to their own pattern, the growth of American law in California was rather rapid."

Unable to find rules which governed the conduct of their everyday business, the feelings of those common-sense pioneers were reflected in an article in the CALIFORNIA STAR of March 27, 1847, entitled "The Laws in Force":

Confusion

> "Some contend that there are really no laws in force here, but the divine law and the law of nature, while others are of the opinion that there are laws in force here if they could only be found...Both sides, however, seem to agree that the 'former usages' have been

in force...We have not been able to discover any traces of written law particularly applicable to this territory except the Bandos of the Alcaldes which could not have been intended to apply to any except those within their jurisdiction. We have frequently heard it stated that there are general written laws of the people of the whole territory, but we have not as yet been able to discover their 'whereabouts'... It seems to us that the continuance of the former laws in force, when it is impossible to produce them in any court in the country, or for the people to ascertain what they are, will be productive of confusion and difficulty."

POWER OF ALCALDE

Absolute Power

The prevailing system of government in Mexican California, which the military governors necessarily adopted, was based on the powers of the alcalde and so contrary to American principles of government. The alcalde was supposed to be elected by the town citizens subject to confirmation by the governor; however, the Mexican governor simply appointed the alcalde when he considered it necessary or preferable. The alcalde was mayor, sheriff, and judge, often arresting a person, presiding over his trial, passing sentence, and enforcing the sentence. In his person he combined judicial and executive powers and often legislative powers. His jurisdiction sometimes extended for hundreds of miles into the country.

Americans, whose background was widely different, were shocked at the lack of separation of the legislative, executive, and judicial powers. Walter Colton wrote of the alcalde powers in THREE YEARS IN CALIFORNIA, page 55:

"Such an absolute disposal of questions affecting property and personal liberty never ought to be confided to one man. There is not a judge on the bench in England or the United States whose power is so absolute as that of the alcalde of Monterey."

Americans dissatisfied

A system which apparently satisfied the pastoral scene of Mexican California did not satisfy Americans and they demanded a better governmental system than the Mexican law gave them. We are here reminded of Daniel Webster's statement of 1851 from THE CHRISTIAN HISTORY OF THE CONSTITUTION, Vol. II, page 7:

"I have said, Gentlemen, that our inheritance is an inheritance of American liberty. That liberty is characteristic, peculiar, and altogether our own. Nothing like it existed in former times, nor was it known in the most enlightened states of antiquity; while with us its principles have become interwoven into the minds of individual men, connected with our daily opinion, and our daily habits, until it is, if I may so say, an element of social as well as of political life; and the consequence is, that to whatever region an American citizen carries himself, he takes with him, fully developed in his own understanding and experience, our American principles and opinions and becomes ready at once, in cooperation with others, to apply them to the formation of new governments..."

TRIAL BY JURY

Lacking common law principles

The growth of American law in California was rapid because Americans began to succeed Mexicans, or Spaniards, as alcaldes, almost immediately following the conquest. While theoretically the Mexican civil law continued in force, in fact, the Americans, especially the newly appointed alcaldes, had brought their own notions of common law principles and forms. Trial by jury was introduced by the first American alcalde of Monterey, Walter Colton. In A SELF-GOVERNING DOMINION, pages 12-13, we read:

Anglo-Saxon justice

"In the application of common-law procedure, Walter Colton, about a month after he became American alcalde of Monterey, empaneled the first jury ever summoned in California. The case was that of Charles Rousaillon whom Isaac Graham had accused of stealing a quantity of lumber. A jury was called for September 4 and the trial held. A third of the jury were Mexicans, another third Californians, and the rest Americans. The prosecuter used the English language, the defendant French, and the jury, except the Americans, Spanish. W. E. P. Hartnell, an Englishman, acted as interpreter. The jury deliberated for an hour and returned a verdict acquitting the accused, with certain recommendations in regard to the cost of the trial. This was the beginning of the administration of Anglo-Saxon justice in California. Very soon this method became a common practice of the country, although there was no law providing for it until California became a state. It was not long before American settlers claimed jury trial as a right, and the Mexican Californians themselves were forced to adopt it. As early as December 29, 1847, Governor Mason issued a general order for trials by jury in all cases...more than one hundred dollars."

GOLD HINDERED LAW ENFORCEMENT

Lack of law and order during Gold Rush

The difficulties of the governmental situation in California were further complicated by the discovery of gold on January 24, 1848. When the citizens of a town left for the gold fields, the machinery of government in that community suffered a serious setback, and law enforcement was a problem. In March of 1847, Colonel J. B. Stevenson's regiment of New York Volunteers arrived in California. They had been recruited with the understanding that they would be disbanded at the end of the war and would thus provide not merely a garrison but a body of permanent American settlers. But with the war over, they were discharged and so reduced the military force in California to two companies of Regulars, and desertions to the mines were rapidly thinning their ranks. The great migration to the land of gold had begun. California had become the "focus of the world's attention." The discovery of gold greatly hastened the movement among the settlers toward popular organization of government.

A CONSTITUTION FOR CALIFORNIA IN THE WIND

Governor Mason was aware of the public dissatisfaction and of the difficulties brought about by the lack of an adequate law system. He was working on a solution when he was replaced by Governor Riley on April 12, 1849. When Mason turned over the office of the governor to Riley, he advised him to call a constitutional convention to provide a state government for California.

CONGRESS DISAGREEMENT

For three sessions Congress had failed to agree on any system of civil government for California from 1846-1849. They were bogged down over the political struggle which had raged since the introduction of Representative David Wilmot's proposal that slavery be forbidden in any territory acquired from Mexico.

THE WILMOT PROVISO

From Johnston's HISTORY OF THE UNITED STATES, 1892, p. 260:

The slavery issue

"In 1846, when it was first suggested to make Mexico give up territory, David Wilmot, a member of Congress from Pennsylvania, introduced that which was called from him the Wilmot Proviso. It appropriated money to buy the territory, *provided* that slavery should not be allowed in it. The South proved to be opposed to it; it never became law; and the new territory was acquired without it. Thus, when this administration ended, the United States owned a vast amount of new territory, without being able to decide whether slavery was to be allowed or forbidden in it."

STEPS TOWARD A CONSTITUTIONAL CONVENTION

The first step toward provisional government was an enthusiastic meeting of the citizens of the Pueblo of San Jose. The San Jose meeting recommended a convention be held in 1849 to elect a candidate for governor.

Congress had provided for a territorial government in Oregon in the Spring of 1848 and Peter Burnett had been a leader in the formation of such a government and a member of Oregon's Supreme Court. He had come to California in the gold rush along with "at least two thirds of the population of Oregon capable of bearing arms," according to his RECOLLECTIONS AND OPINIONS, page 152. In January 1849, Peter Burnett presided over two meetings in Sacramento which dicussed "the necessity and propriety of organizing a Provisional Government for the Territory of California."

A similar meeting was held in San Francisco at Portsmouth Square on February 12, 1849, where they created their own Legislative Assembly for the District of San Francisco. Meetings were also held in Sonoma and Monterey.

LAW AND ORDER LACKING

In April of 1849 General Riley succeeded Mason. Late in May he received the news that Congress had again adjourned without agreement on a territorial organization for California, and on June 3 he issued his own call for a constitutional convention. Governor Riley had intelligently studied questions of law and government in California. He intended to follow Mason's practices.

Governor Riley had been projected into a difficult situation. Elisha Crosby in MEMOIRS, p.42, wrote:

"Every man carried his code of laws on his hip and administered it according to his own pleasure. There was no safety of life or property so far as the intervention of law was concerned; there was no police. Spanish law was in operation here then and the only way it could be enforced was through the Military Governor and the Prefects and Alcaldes holding office under him. It was an unknown system to our people and we were absolutely in a state of chaos; society was entirely unorganized..."

PROCLAMATION

Governor Riley took the initiative to issue a Proclamation on June 3, 1849. (The lengthy Proclamation may be found in J. Ross Browne's REPORT OF THE DEBATES IN THE CONVENTION OF CALIFORNIA ON THE FORMATION OF THE STATE CONSTITUTION, in September and October, 1849, pages 3-5.) Governor Riley described the institutions and laws as they then existed, and pointed out the necessity of completing the organization of the civil government, and need for a convention to provide a state or a territorial government in California subject to the approval of Congress. In explanation of what was proposed, he listed the various officials and outlined their functions. His scheme of government recognized Spanish forms fully, but gave an American character to the administration by making the officers of the law elective instead of appointive. In the document, Riley ordered an election to be held on August 1, 1849 for the purpose of: 1) Choosing officials to serve until January 1, 1850; 2) Electing delegates to a convention for the purpose of drawing up a state constitution, or organizing a territorial government. He specified that thirty-seven delegates should be elected from the several districts, to meet at Monterey on September 1, 1849.

ARGUMENT OVER WHICH PLAN TO FOLLOW

After the Proclamation was issued, San Francisco held a meeting on June 12 in Portsmouth Square to consider the proposed convention. At first they defied the proclamation, insisting they had a right to organize their own government for their protection. However, public opinion turned toward obtaining a government regardless of the "Settlers Plan" or the "Administration Plan."

The Settlers believed the moment the Treaty of Guadalupe Hidalgo took effect, the Constitution of the United States and American principles were extended over the territory of California. Since Congress had failed to provide a territorial government, they believed it was no usurpation on the part of the people to legislate for themselves in self-defence. Senator Benton advocated this theory.

The Administration Plan, adhered to by Buchanan in Washington, advocated that under a general principle of the law of nations, the laws of California, which were proclaimed to be in force after the American conquest, must continue in full force until changed by Congress.

The San Francisco District Legislature dissolved when the people decided to turn unreservedly toward Riley's plan. Speeches were made in other districts by Riley, William Gwin, Peter Burnett, and Thomas King to interest the people in the organization of a government for California.

THOMAS B. KING

"All things work together..." (Rom. 8:28)

With the arrival of Thomas Butler King in California in the early Spring of 1849, we come to what one may call a happy coincidence, or the Hand of God operating in California's history. Thomas King had been sent as secret agent of the United States to California to acquire the fullest possible information and to urge the people to give themselves a state constitution that they might petition Congress for admission into the Union. King arrived in California at the time when General Riley's Proclamation (June 3, 1849) was being issued. As a consequence, the leading settlers of the territory agreed to Riley's plans for calling a constitutional convention. Just one month earlier (April 3, 1849), President Zachary Taylor had instructed King to encourage California to create its own state constitution. Riley had decided to call a constitutional convention *before* the arrival of King. All had the same idea in mind and it manifested itself as progress toward civil government in California in a very agreeable way.

Before the middle of July 1849, it was decided that:

"...He doeth according to his will...and none can stay his hand..."
(Dan. 4:35)

1) There should be a constitutional convention as proposed in Governor Riley's Proclamation of June 3;

2) That the election of delegates should take place on August 1;

3) That the convention should meet at Monterey on September 1;

4) That until a constitution could be drawn up and adopted the *de facto* government should continue to operate.

Riley, in his Proclamation, had stated that there should be thirty-seven delegates, but because the districts of San Jose, San Francisco, Sacramento, and the San Joaquin had grown rapidly in population since the date of the Proclamation, the convention membership was increased to forty-eight.

In the meantime, an adequate hall had been constructed in Monterey for the distinguished lawmakers.

THE CONSTITUTIONAL CONVENTION

"And to the angel of the church in Philadelphia write; These things saith he that is holy, he that is true, he that hath the key of David, he that openeth, and no man shutteth; and shutteth, and no man openeth; I know thy works; behold, I have set before thee an open door, and no man can shut it...."

(Revelation 3:7,8)

COLTON HALL

From THREE YEARS IN CALIFORNIA, American Alcalde Walter Colton entered in his diary:

Colton Hall, Monterey

"Thursday, March 8. The town-hall on which I have been at work for more than a year, is at last finished. It is built of a white stone, quarried from a neighboring hill, and which easily takes the shape you desire. The lower apartments are for schools; the hall over them, seventy by thirty, is for public assemblies. The front is ornamented with a portico, which you enter from the hall. It is not an edifice that would attract any attention among public buildings in the United States; but in California it is without a rival. It has been erected out of the slender proceeds of town lots, the labor of the convicts, taxes on liquor shops, and fines on gamblers. The scheme was regarded with incredulity by many; but the building is finished, and the citizens have assembled in it, and christened it after my name, which will now go down to posterity with the odor of gamblers, convicts, and tipplers. I leave it as a humble evidence of what may be accomplished by rigidly adhering to one purpose, and shrinking from no personal efforts necessary to its achievement."[1]

Convention assembled

On Monday, September 3, 1849, in Colton Hall in Monterey, forty-eight delegates met to draw up California's first constitution. Kimball H. Dimmick was elected Temporary Chairman, Henry G. Tefft, Secretary Pro Tem. The permanent officers were Dr. Robert Semple of Benicia, President; William G. Marcy, Secretary; and J. Ross Browne, Reporter. Organization was completed by naming the chaplains: Samuel H. Willey, Protestant, who was to alternate with two Catholic Fathers for prayer.

Purpose

Here was a unique Constitutional Convention. Of different nationalities, those of American birth were in the majority. It was to frame an American constitution that the delegates had come together. Their task was difficult: To form a constitution for a recently conquered, almost wholly unorganized territory; with Congress in a state of violent debates about California, and with repeated failures to legislate concerning them; with a province of vague boundary in a highly upset condition due to the gold rush, increased population, and fast-growing economy. Theirs was an extremely delicate situation demanding the utmost skill.

237h

However, the delegation was up to the task. There were seven Spanish-Californian delegates, who were treated with great respect. General Vallejo was better acquainted with American institutions and laws than his Spanish peers.

Of the four foreign-born delegates, Captain Sutter, a Swiss, stood prominent.

Of the Americans, twenty-two represented a substantially larger number from the Northern states rather than the fifteen from the Southern slave states. The fourteen lawyers formed the largest single occupational group. One delegate, B. F. Moore, gave his occupation as "elegant leisure." About one-half of the members were less than 35 years old.

The Districts represented were: From the South: San Diego (2); Los Angeles (5); Santa Barbara (2); San Luis Obispo (2). From the North: Monterey (5); San Jose (7); San Francisco (8); Sonoma (3); Sacramento (8); San Joaquin (6).

THE PREAMBLE TO THE CONSTITUTION

Walter Colton made an appeal to the Christian community of California:

"The moulding hand of religion"

The Bible, necessary

"With the Christian community California has higher claims than those which glitter in her mines. The moral elements which now drift over her streams and treasured rocks will ere long settle down into abiding forms. The impalpable will become the real, and the unsubstantial assume a local habitation and a name. Shall these permanent shapes, into which society is to be cast, take their plastic features from the impress of blind accident and skepticle apathy, or the moulding hand of religion? These primal forms must remain and wear for ages the traces of their deformity or beauty, their guilty insignificance or moral grandeur. Through them circulates your own lifeblood; in them is bound up the hopes of an empire. Not only the destiny of California is suspended on the issue, but the fate of all the republics which cheer the shores of the Pacific. The same treason to religion which wrecks the institutions of this country, will sap the foundations of a thousand other glorified shrines. It is for you, Christian brethren, to prevent such a disaster; it is for you to pour into California an unremitted tide of holy light. The Bible must throw its sacred radiance around every hearth, over every stream, through every mountain glen. The voice of the heralds of heavenly love must be echoed from every cliff and chasm and forest sanctuary. On you devolves this mission of Christian fidelity. It is for your faith and philanthropy to say what

238

California shall be when her swelling population shall burst the bounds of her domain. You can write her hopes in ashes, or stars that shall never set. Every school-book and Bible you throw among her hills will be a source of penetrating and pervading light, when the torch of the caverned miner has gone out."[2]

In an article which prefaces a 1965 edition of THE ORIGINAL CONSTITUTION OF THE STATE OF CALIFORNIA, 1849, is written:

"Liberty traced
to dependency
on God"

"Walter Colton sensed the commonness of the faith in which all believed even if it was a faith represented by different churches. This faith they proudly declared in the PREAMBLE to the Constitution. For here is a declaration representing the confluence of two cultures of Western Civilization. The PREAMBLE incorporated the philosophy that individual liberties are traced to a dependency upon God and as such could be suspended in proportion to the degree that Faith subsides."[3]

The PREAMBLE reads:

"We, the people of the State of California, grateful to Almighty God for our freedom, in order to secure and perpetuate its blessings, do establish this Constitution."

"TO CREATE A STATE"

Books lacking

There was a great absence of books of reference in Monterey. There may not have been more than fifty books of law or history in the whole town. Copies of the Iowa and New York State Constitutions were on hand, thoughtfully brought to the Convention by Mr. William Gwinn. That is probably why California's first constitution so closely resembles that of Iowa. Iowa had become a "free" State in 1846.

Prayer

The first regular session was "opened with prayer to Almighty God for His blessing on the body, in their work, and on the country." Provision was made whereby the convention should be opened each day with prayer.

They first determined to create a constitution for a state government, not a territorial government.

DECLARATION OF RIGHTS

In A SELF-GOVERNING DOMINION, we read:

"Although it was not finally passed until October 10, it is worthy of note that these delegates of the new frontier made a bill of rights the first burden of their thoughts and actions.

239

In the discussions of the several fundamental questions, carried on while the bill of rights was under consideration, the young constitution makers of California demonstrated their versatility, ability, and unexpectedly good mental equipment. Men of twenty-five to thirty years of age argued like seasoned political scientists. This is particularly true with respect to the arguments and the action of the convention in the following stated principles that a bill of rights, when appended to a constitution, should be only declaratory of general fundamental principles, that the objective of the constitution was to organize the government and prescribe the nature and extent of the powers of its several departments, and that legislative enactments could not properly be included in such a document."[4]

Article I, Section 1 of the Declaration of Rights:

Life, Liberty, and Property

"All men are by nature free and independent, and have certain inalienable rights, among which are those of enjoying and defending life and liberty: acquiring, possessing and protecting property: and pursuing and obtaining safety and happiness."

SLAVERY

An additional section was inserted into the Bill of Rights stating: "Neither slavery nor involuntary servitude, unless for punishment of crimes, shall ever be tolerated in this State." This section, almost without debate, was unanimously adopted, although fifteen of the delegates were from slave states. At this time in history, the country was divided into fifteen free states and fifteen slave states. Dr. Rockwell Hunt observed:

California, a free State

"The institution of American slavery had passed the zenith of its power, and henceforth was destined steadily to decline. The great Commonwealth of California, entering the Union as the sixteenth free State, forever destroyed the equilibrium between North and South."[5]

Although the question whether slavery should be allowed in California had been settled, the question whether free negroes should be permitted to live in California was still to be considered. Much discussion followed. Although many definitely were in favor of keeping free negroes out of California, a general fear existed that an article excluding them might imperil the approval of the constitution by Congress. A strong group, therefore, adhered to the principle that exclusion should be accomplished by law through the Legislature, and not through the constitution. In 1849-50, black people were referred to as "negroes," which means "black" in Spanish.

RIGHT TO VOTE

There were sharp differences of opinion as to what constituted a "citizen" when it came to the right to vote. The Indian was not considered a citizen. They finally determined:

Every white
male citizen...

"Every white male citizen of the United States, and every white male citizen of Mexico, who shall have elected to become a citizen of the United States, under the treaty of peace exchanged and ratified at Queretaro, on the 30th of May, 1848, at the age of twenty-one years, who shall have been a resident of the State six months next preceding the election, and the county or district in which he claims his vote thirty days, shall be entitled to vote at all elections which are now or hereafter may be authorized by law: Provided, that nothing herein contained, shall be construed to prevent the Legislature, by a two-thirds concurrent vote, from admitting to the right of suffrage, Indians or the descendants of Indians, in such special cases as such a proportion of the legislative body may deem just and proper."[6]

DUELING

Risking rights
of citizenship

One of the interesting provisions was the inclusion of a provision forbidding dueling. The lengthy arguments brought out clearly the difference in feeling as persons from one area of California tried to place the standards in the constitution which prevailed in their sections, particularly those from the frontier areas of California. Some argued that to forbid dueling would discourage street fights and destroy the belief that dueling and honor were synonymous. Others claimed that a man who was willing to risk his life when his honor was assailed, would risk all his rights of citizenship on the same ground.

CORPORATIONS

Corporation,
a legal person

"The term 'corporations' as used in the constitution was to be 'construed to include all associations and joint-stock companies, having any of the powers or privileges of corporations not possessed by individuals or partnerships.' It was provided that 'all corporations shall have the right to sue and shall be subject to be sued, in all courts, in like cases as natural persons' - a significant recognition at this early date that a corporation is a legal person."[7]

DEBT

Limits of State
indebtedness

The matter of state debts was discussed. There was general distrust of banks and fear of "wildcat currency." Written into the constitution were the articles restricting the power of the Legislature to create corporations by special act, or to charter banks. It is interesting that they withheld the power to issue paper money for circulation, depending entirely upon their acceptance as a State and the issuance of their currency by the United States. They restricted the Legislature from creating a state debt over $300,000 except by the people at a general election, and other restrictions.

COMMUNITY PROPERTY LAW

Separate property rights for married women brought forth much discussion. It finally passed as:

Exception to the
Common Law

"All property, both real and personal, of the wife, owned or claimed by her before marriage, and that acquired afterwards by gift, devise, or descent, shall be her separate property; and laws shall be passed more clearly defining the rights of the wife, in relation as well to her separate property, as to that held in common with her husband. Laws shall also be passed providing for the registration of the wife's separate property."[8]

Here is one of the few instances that the Roman Civil Law superseded the English Common Law in the constitution. The arguments for civil law are interesting. According to A SELF-GOVERNING DOMINION, Mr. Ellison stated:

Civil Law

"In support of this section it was argued that, since in California the civil law is the law of the land and under it the rights of the wives are protected, failure to secure and guarantee the rights of the wife to her separate property would be 'a very decided invasion upon the people of California.' Henry W. Halleck in his defense of the section said that, although he was 'not wedded either to the common law or the civil law, nor as yet to a woman,' he did have hopes of being wedded sometime, and would, therefore, advocate including this section in the constitution as an 'inducement for women of fortune to come to California' and 'the very best provision for getting wives that we can introduce into the constitution.' He called upon all bachelors in the convention to vote for it. Others argued for the section because it had been the law of the country; because, in this advancing age, state after state had adopted the principle; because the marriage contract is a civil contract, with the law prescribing the rights of the contracting parties, and therefore one party should not be put into the position of having to relinquish rights and property in contracting marriage...."[9]

The arguments against separate property rights for married women are so interesting that they are included here from the record of Mr. J. Ross Browne made in DEBATES OF CALIFORNIA CONVENTION. Mr. Charles T. Botts, originally from Virginia, a resident of Monterey at the time of the Convention, argued:

Common Law

"That you may know how it is, Mr. Chairman, that the common law views this contract, I will read you the words of one of the oldest commentators upon it: 'By marriage' says Blackstone, 'the husband and wife are one person in law.' This is but another mode of repeating the declaration of the Holy Book, that they are flesh of one flesh, and bone of bone. That is the principle of the common law and it is the principle of the Bible. It is a principle, Mr. Chairman, not only of poetry, but of wisdom, of truth, and of justice. Sir, it is supposed by the common law that the woman says to the man in the beautiful language of Ruth: *'Whither thou goest I will go; and where thou lodgest, I will lodge; thy people shall be my people, and thy God my God.'* (Ruth 1:16) This sir, is the character of that holy ceremony which gentlemen have considered as a mere money copartnership. Sir, it is this view of that contract that has produced that peculiar and lovely English word <u>home</u>, which it has been said no other people on the face of the earth know. It arises from the very peculiar light in which the English law looks upon this social relation. Bear that in mind, you who love your homes. I tell you, Mr. Chairman, that if you introduce this clause, you must take care to carry along with it a speedy and easy and effectual way of procuring divorces, for they will come as sure as you live, as a necessary consequence. That very moment that you set up two heads in one family, you sow dissentions which lead to applications for divorces, and your courts and Senate chambers will be filled with them."[10]

As a matter of further interest, Mr. Botts entered into a small discourse in defense of common law versus civil law:

In defense of Common Law

"The gentleman from San Joaquin (Mr. J. Jones) would make you believe that the common law is inexplicable and incomprehensible, that it is so musty from its long existence, that no man can tell what it is. I believe, sir, that there are gentlemen on this floor who are somewhat conversant with the common law; who have explored the musty volumes of the common law, and dug out of them great and glorious principles; principles upon which the Constitution of the United States is founded; principles which are now the fundamental law of twenty-nine of the thirty States of this Union. For gentlemen to say here that we have no right to adopt the common law – that it is unintelligible, that it is written in dog latin or some other dead language, and that no man knows what it is – I trust, sir, that under the writings of Blackstone, Kent, and of all common law writers, through all the reports of the various States of the Union – the large field of learning – that we have such a common law, that he who runs may read. It is entirely useless here to go against the common law. Nine-tenths of all the population of this country are its warmest advocates. They have been born and brought up under its glorious protection; they have learned it from their boyhood; they understand its provisions, and have been protected under its influence. And, Mr. Chairman, these are not the men to throw away the early predilections of their youth, to discard what they know to be good, and embrace something that they know not of; and are these men to be told that, because the civil law may have heretofore existed in this country, that it shall forever exist? No, sir...."[10a]

EDUCATION

In A SELF-GOVERNING DOMINION, we read the education provided for in California's first constitution:

Four provisions

"Of the four sections on this subject, the first provided for the election, every three years, of a superintendent of public instruction. The second significantly asserted in its opening statement: 'The Legislature shall encourage, by all suitable means, promotion of intellectual, scientific, moral, & agricultural improvement.' The section provided for receiving the proceeds of lands given by the United States for the support of schools, as well as all estates of persons who died without leaving a will or heir, and it declared that such other means as the legislature might provide should be 'inviolably appropriated to the support of common schools throughout the State.' The third section required the maintenance of a school in each school district for at least three months of the year. Section four provided that 'The Legislature shall take measures for the protection, improvement, or other disposition of such lands as have been, or may hereafter be reserved or granted by the United States, or any person or persons to the State for the use of a University.' It also provided that 'funds accruing from the rents or sale of such lands, or from any other source,' for the purpose stated, should make a permanent fund, the interest of which should be applied to the support of the university 'with such branches as the public convenience may demand, for the promotion of literature, the arts and sciences, as may be authorized by the terms of such grant.'"[11]

After the constitution was approved, Reverend Samuel Hopkins Willey, Chaplain of the Convention, immediately started to organize an institution of higher learning for California. From Rockwell Hunt's HALL OF FAME, we read:

College of
California,
a Christian
institution

"Scarcely had the Monterey convention of 1849 completed its task of constitution making before he (Reverend Willey) began actively to plan for a California college or university. It is recorded that on October 22, 1849, in the stirring young city of Sacramento, 'three pioneers started the organized movement for this early-day educational enterprise and began immediately to enlist the interest of others.' These pioneer missionaries were Samuel H. Willey, a graduate of Dartmouth, J. A. Benton, a Yale graduate, and S. V. Blakeslee, a graduate of Western Reserve. Adverse conditions militated against the success of this first movement to organize a college. With Dr. Willey's encouragement, however, Henry Durant, a Yale alumnus who had recently arrived in California, opened a preparatory school in Oakland in 1853; and on April 13, 1855 the charter of the College of California was granted. Three years later Berkeley was formally chosen to be the future site of the College of California, founded as a Christian institution."[12]

GAMBLING

A decision based
upon morality

There was a provision made in the constitution preventing gambling or revenue from gambling ever being part of California. "No lottery shall be authorized by this State, nor shall the sale of lottery tickets be allowed." Efforts that were made to strike out this section sound very much like the arguments for gambling which are used today: That it would deprive the State of much revenue; restrict future legislatures; misrepresent the people who had sent delegates to the convention because it would limit the amusements in which the people may or may not indulge; and that the constitution should only lay down broad and general principles of religious freedom. In support of the section, it was argued that something was wrong if a state could not raise revenue without entering into a system of legalized gambling; that the well-being of society was involved; that the state should be prohibited from a practice condemned in individuals; that the convention should limit the powers of the Legislature, and that this was the place to begin. The convention voted that lotteries should be prohibited.

EASTERN BOUNDARY

The vast land called
"California"

The most lengthy and lively discussion in the convention concerned the eastern boundary. California, as a Mexican province ceded to the United States, was of vast but not strictly defined territorial extent, which included the great desert east of the Sierra Nevada and the fertile district inhabited by the Mormons. It consisted of all of the present territory of California, Nevada, Utah, and Arizona, and parts of Wyoming, Colorado, and New Mexico, almost 450,000 square miles.

Established
boundaries

The northern boundary at the parallel (latitude) of 42 degrees was formed by a treaty with Spain in 1819. The western boundary was formed naturally by

245

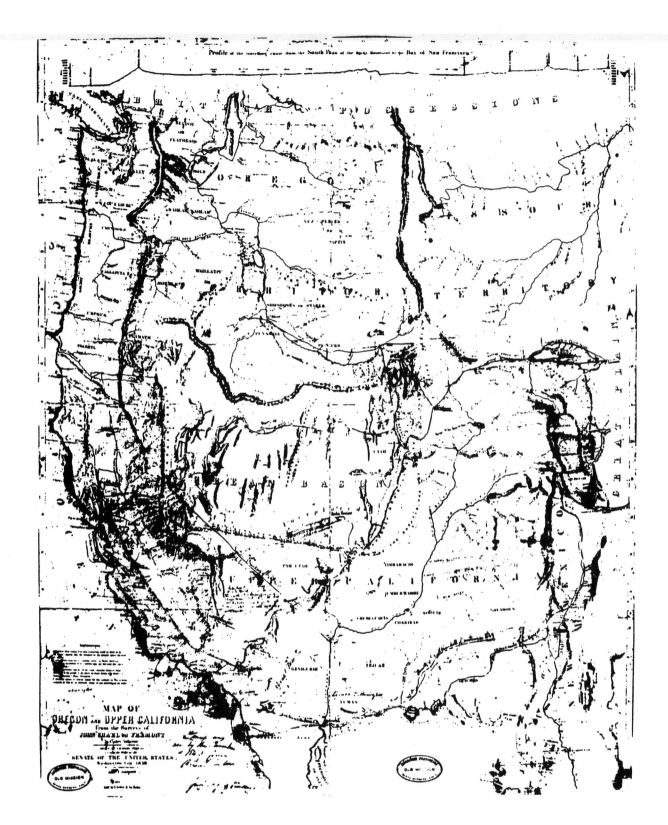

Map of Oregon and Upper California by John Charles Fremont, 1848, which the Constitutional Convention worked with to determine the eastern boundary of California. The original map is in Colton Hall, Monterey. This small copy was made by the Santa Barbara Mission and obtained from The Wells Fargo Museum in San Francisco.

the Pacific Ocean. The southern boundary formed a line between Upper and Lower California set by the Treaty of Guadalupe Hidalgo with Mexico. The great question was the eastern boundary.

The big question
                    The main argument was whether to use to the fullest extent the territory, or prescribe California within narrow limits. One idea was to include all of California and not dismember the State. This would give protection to the thousands of Mormons, including great wealth in the vast territory. The other idea was that the 20,000 Mormons were unrepresented in the convention, and they had already applied for a territorial government. Also, such a vast territory would invite subdivisions that would be awkward. They argued that a large territory would be unwieldy and would require legislators months of travel to reach the capital, and besides, the Southern States in Congress would not permit a free state as large as all the Northern States in the Union.

Finally, the plan for a smaller state proposing a boundary as we now know it, running south on 120 degrees west longitude to Lake Tahoe (then Lake Bigler), then southeast along the Sierra Nevada to the Colorado River, was adopted by a large majority.

SEAL

The convention voted to pay $1,000 to Caleb Lyon to superintend the engraving of "The Great Seal of the State of California." Major Robert S. Garnett had drawn the design, to which Mr. Lyon had made additions. Mr. Lyon described it:

> "Around the bend of the ring are represented thirty-one stars, being the number of States of which the Union will consist upon the admission of California. The foreground figure represents the goddess Minerva having sprung full grown from the brain of Jupiter. She is introduced as a type of the political birth of the State of California, without having gone through the probation of a territory. At her feet crouches a grizzly bear feeding upon the clusters from a grapevine, emblematic of the peculiar characteristics of the country. A miner is engaged with his rocker and bowl at his side, illustrating the golden wealth of the Sacramento, upon whose waters are seen shipping, typical of commercial greatness; and the snow-clad peaks of the Sierra Nevada make up the background, while above is the Greek motto 'Eureka,' (I have found,) applying either to the principle involved in the admission of the State, or the success of the miner at work."[13] (See page 250.)

In CALIFORNIA, AN INTERPRETIVE HISTORY, Walton Bean wrote:

> "One point of dissension was raised: General Vallejo objected to the bear. It reminded him of the indignities he had suffered in

the Bear Flag Revolt, and he proposed that it be removed from the seal unless it were shown as secured by a lasso in the hands of a vaquero. In the end he accepted the assurances of Anglo-American delegates that this particular bear signified no offense to the native Californians."[14]

CONCLUSION

There were, of course, many other measures included in the Constitution that have not been mentioned here.

Six weeks in
session, 1849

The Constitutional Convention completed its work on October 13, 1849, having been in session since September 3, 1849. While the members signed the Constitution, the loud booming of cannon resounded through the hall. The flags on board the ships in port were run up and the firing of thirty-one guns proceeded at the Fort.

Thanks to Riley

The entire body of members went to General Riley's house and Captain Sutter, on behalf of the Convention, expressed gratitude for the aid and cooperation given by the Executive. The General's reply was a simple, warm, yet eloquent desire for the good of California. He concluded his remarks with a tribute to his secretary, Captain Halleck.

Celebration Ball

Colton Hall was then prepared for a celebration ball. Through the contribution of $25.00 each, the members raised $1,000 for the entertainment. The cleared hall was decorated with young pines from the forest. Three improvised chandeliers gave light. In addition to the convention members, sixty or seventy ladies and gentlemen were present among whom was Bayard Taylor. In his ELDORADO, he said:

> "The dark-eyed daughters of Monterey, Los Angeles and Santa Barbara mingled in pleasing contrast with the fairer bloom of the trans-Nevadian belles. The variety of feature and complexion was fully equalled by the variety of dress. In the whirl of the waltz, a plain, dark, nun-like robe would be followed by one of pink satin and gauze; next, perhaps a bodice of scarlet velvet with gold buttons, and then a rich figured brocade... Scarcely a single dress that was seen that night belonged entirely to its wearer..."[15]

American
capacity for
self-government

The achievement of the Constitutional Convention illustrates the capacity of the American people for self-government. The document received the highest commendation from all sources as the "embodiment of the American mind, throwing its convictions, impulses, and aspirations into a tangible, permanent shape."[16]

"Section 6 of Article XII: This Constitution shall be submitted to the people, for their ratification or rejection, at the general election to be held on Tuesday, the thirteenth day of November next (1849)..."[17]

Constitution
in Spanish
and English

Copies of the Constitution, printed in English and in Spanish, were quickly carried to each town and camp and rancho, accompanied by the following:

From the Members of the Constitutional Convention
To the People of California:

"The undersigned, Delegates to a convention authorized to form a Constitution for the State of California, having to the best of their ability, discharged the high trust committed to them, respectfully submit the accompanying plan of Government for your approval..."[18]

The rather lengthy letter from the Delegates to the People summarized well the American philosophy behind the deliberations of the Convention. Only excerpts can be stated here:

Laws based upon
principles of
equity and justice

"...it is confidently believed, when the government as now proposed, shall have gone into successful operation, where each department thereof shall move on harmoniously, in its appropriate and respective sphere; when laws based on the eternal principles of equity and Justice, shall be established; when every citizen of California, shall find himself secure in life, liberty and property – all will unite in the cordial support of institutions, which are not only the pride and boast of every true hearted citizen of the Union, but have gone forth, a guiding light to every people...

Citizens duty
to vote

...the undersigned...earnestly recommend it to your calm and deliberate consideration and especially do they most respectfully urge on every voter to attend the Polls. The putting into operation of a Government, which shall establish justice, ensure domestic tranquility, promote the general welfare and secure the blessings of civil, religious and political liberty, should be an object of the deepest solicitude to every true hearted citizen, and the consummation of his dearest wishes. The price of liberty is eternal vigilance, and thus it is not only the privilege but the duty of every voter, to vote his sentiments. No freeman of this land who values his birth-right and would transmit unimpaired to his children, an inheritance so rich in glory and in honor, will refuse to give one day to the service of his country.

Let every qualified voter go early to the polls and give his free vote at the election appointed to be held on Tuesday the 13th of November next, not only that a full and fair expression of the public voice may be had for or against a Constitution intended to secure the peace, happiness and prosperity of the whole people, but that their numerical and political strength may be made manifest, and the world see, by what majority of freemen, California the bright Star of the West, claims a place in the diadem of that glorious Republic, formed by the Union of thirty-one Sovereign states.

(Signed) R. SEMPLE, President, Convention."[19]

On November 13, 1849, the Constitution of the State of California was ratified by an almost unanimous vote. Peter H. Burnett was elected Governor. John McDougal was elected Lieutenant-Governor. Edward Gilbert and George W. Wright were elected Representatives to Congress.

Since Congress still had not accepted California as a State by December 15, 1849, California held its first Legislature.

THE GREAT SEAL OF THE STATE OF CALIFORNIA

From PICTORIAL HISTORY OF CALIFORNIA

I do solemnly swear, that I will support the Constitution of the United States, and the Constitution of the State of California; and that I will faithfully discharge the duties of the office of Governor of the State of California, according to the best of my ability.

Peter H. Burnett

Sworn to, and subscribed before me, this twentieth day of December A.D. 1849—

K.H. Dimmick
Judge Supr Tribunal

Oath of Office
of the Governor

December 20. 1849—

1.

No-One

251

FIRST CALIFORNIA LEGISLATURE

The first California Legislature was generally composed of men of honesty and integrity. Their objective was to make California eligible as a State within the United States. However, the Legislature adjourned four and one-half months before California was admitted into the Union.

Organization

From Rockwell Hunt's BIDWELL, PRINCE OF PIONEERS, we read of the organization of that first California Legislature, composed of thirty-six members of the Assembly and sixteen Senators:

"On Thursday (December 20, 1849), Peter H. Burnett took the oath of office as governor (administered by Judge Kimball H. Dimmick). Accordingly, General Bennet Riley, who had served as de facto military governor, issued a proclamation resigning his powers to the elected civilian officials. At the same time he relieved his secretary of state, H. W. Halleck, from further duty.

How U.S. Senators elected in 1849

After the inauguration of Governor Burnett, Senator Bidwell moved, in accordance with a joint resolution, that the **senate** proceed to the election of two United States senators, which motion was adopted. However, the nonconcurrence of the assembly resulted in the appointment of a committee of conference... In the election which followed, John C. Fremont was chosen on the first ballot, and William M. Gwin was successful on the third ballot. By the election of December 22, state officers were selected and a provisional government organized 'for the administration of California until such time as Congress should see fit to extend the laws of the United States over this territory.'"[20]

STEPHEN J. FIELD

Eminent members

That first legislature was composed of some members who were to exert great influence on their state and their country. One such member was Stephen J. Field.

Dr. Rockwell D. Hunt included Stephen Field in CALIFORNIA'S STATELY HALL OF FAME, giving us a brief sketch of his life and contribution to California.[21]

Stephen J. Field was born in Connecticut, a brother of David Dudley Field, the eminent jurist, and Cyrus W. Field, founder of the Atlantic Cable. His family had a tradition of distinguished public service. According to the standards of his day, he was an old man of thirty-three when he headed for California. Travel was nothing new to him, however, as he had accompanied a missionary brother-in-law to Smyrna when he was thirteen; there, he studied Greek and Turkish. Before entering California, he had graduated from Williams

College and entered the law office of his older brother in New York, obtaining the training and experience which he used in California.

Elected to the first legislature in California, Field unaided wrote the Code of Civil Procedure, establishing a judicial system for the state, which the Legislature adopted with practically no changes. In the final hours of the session, Field presented a measure embodying an entire criminal code. The Legislature accepted Field's code. Field's next vote of confidence was his selection as Associate Chief Justice of the California Supreme Court. President Lincoln elevated him from this position to the Supreme Court of the United States, where he served for thirty-four distinguished years, the longest term which any justice had served on the Federal Supreme Bench.

CREATION OF COURTS

In A SELF-GOVERNING DOMINION, Mr. Ellison summed up the Judiciary system adopted in California:

Acts to establish
jurisdiction of courts

"The first of a series of laws creating the courts was the act passed on February 14, 1850, which provided for the organization of a supreme court, with a chief justice and two associate justices, determined the method of their selection, and described the court's jurisdiction and procedure. A second law, with the date of February 28, 1850, was an act to abolish courts of the second instance and third instance which had been organized upon occupation of the territory by American troops, and to provide for the supersession of courts of the first instance, together with the offices of alcaldes, prefects, subprefects, and other minor semijudicial officials, as soon as the new courts and new county offices were organized. A third act, passed on March 16, provided for the organization of district courts; it divided the state into nine judicial districts, each with a resident judge. On April 11, the legislature passed an act to organize a court of sessions in each county, which should be composed of the county judge and two justices of the peace, and on April 13, an act making provision for county clerks became law; these acts established the jurisdiction of the court and clearly defined certain procedure. The old judicial system and the old judicial offices were swept away and for all time abrogated by this series of legislative acts."[22]

COMMON LAW VERSUS CIVIL LAW

The "Report of Mr. Elisha O. Crosby on Civil and Common Law" dated February 27, 1850, found in JOURNAL OF THE SENATE OF THE STATE OF CALIFORNIA; AT THEIR FIRST SESSION, is a very interesting study. One of the most important duties of this first legislature was to choose the system of law which should serve as the basis of jurisprudence of their courts. Was the common law or the civil law the most desirable for use in California? Mr. Crosby was chairman of the committee assigned to this investigation.

In A SELF-GOVERNING DOMINION, we read:

"The report included a classic statement of the origins, history, and character of both the civil and the common law, indicating the Latin origin of the civil law and the Anglo-Saxon origin of the common law. It pointed out that English colonies all over the world clung to the common law, and that in the United States, of the three states of non-English background – Louisiana, Florida, and Texas – which formerly had been under civil-law countries, only Louisiana retained the civil law. The committee maintained that the civil law looked to quiet and repose, with somewhat strict control, rather than to the promotion of activity and progress, and that it looked to the spirit of the past, filled with memories of an antiquated order of things; whereas the common law made an independent being of a man when he became twenty-one, fostered his independence, recognized him as capable of making a contract for himself, treated him as a freeman, and gave him responsibility. The common law was thus a system through which energetic and vigorous life could express itself in progress for the future."[23]

The Report from the SENATE JOURNAL stated the basis of the Common Law:

Basis of
Common Law

"The Common Law is that system of jurisprudence which, deducing its origin from the traditionary customs and simple laws of the Saxons, becoming blended with many of the customs and laws of the Normans, enriched with the most valuable portions of the Civil Law, modified and enlarged by the numerous Acts of the English Parliament, smoothed in its asperities and moulded into shape by a succession of as learned and wise and sagacious intellects as the world ever saw, has grown up, during the lapse of centuries, under the **reformed religion** and enlightened

"Reformed
religion"

philosophy and literature of England, and has come down to us, amended and improved by the American Legislature, and adapted to the republican principles and energetic character of the American people. To that system the world is indebted for whatever it enjoys of free government, of political and religious liberty, of untrammelled legislation, and unbought administration of justice. To that system do we now owe the institution of trial by jury, and the privileges of the writ of Habeas Corpus, both equally unknown in the Civil Law. Under that system all the great branches of human industry – agriculture, commerce, and manufactures – enjoy equal protection and equal favor; and under that, less than under any scheme ever devised by the wisdom of

254

man, has personal liberty been subject to the restrictions and assaults or prerogative and arbitrary power.

Basis of Civil Law

The Civil Law, on the other hand, is that system which, based upon the crude laws of a rough, fierce people, whose passion was war, and whose lust, conquest – received, in its progress through the various stages of civilization from barbarism to luxurious and effeminate refinement, a variety of additions and alterations, from the Plebiscita of the Roman Plebeians, from the Senatus-consulta of the Roman Senate, from the decrees of Consuls and Tribunes, from the adjudications of praetors, from the responses of men learned in the laws, and from the edicts and rescripts of the profligate tyrants of Rome, until, in the early ages of Christianity, the whole chaotic mass was, by the order and under the patronage of the Emperor Justinian, systematized, reduced into form, and promulgated for observance by the Roman people, in the shape of four books called the Institutes, fifty books known as the Pandects, and certain additional edicts designated as the Novels of Justinian. Thereafter, and until the final downfall of the Eastern Empire of Rome, the Justinian code furnished the guide for the legal tribunals throughout the provinces subject to the Imperial sway, in all cases political, civil, and criminal, except so far as particular decisions were commanded, annulled, or modified by the arbitrary will of despotic power. But, as century after century, wave upon wave of Northern barbarism poured down on the effeminacy of Southern Europe, sparing in its course neither the intellectual nor the material monuments of civilization, the administration of Roman law was, city after city, and province after province, gradually obliterated at the same time, and to the same extent, that Roman power was crushed, and Roman institutions demolished. The whole system of Justinian was at length swept from the face of the earth, or buried in the recesses of cloisters, alike forgotten and unknown. In the twelfth century, however, a copy of it was accidentally discovered at Amalfi, in Italy; and owing to the arbitrary nature of some of its provisions, as well as to the wisdom and excellence of its general features, it was seized upon with avidity by the clergy, as favorable to their spiritual authority, and by the monarchs, as conducive to the support of their despotic power. It was at once taught in the schools, studied in the convents, sanctioned by the kings, and commanded by the Holy Father himself, who held the keys of heaven. In a few years it became the prevailing system of laws throughout most of that portion of Europe, in which the founder of Christianity was respected, and the saints and martyrs adored. Thus, as in earlier times, the fine arts, literature, philosophy, and graceful superstitions of Greece, had captivated the rude minds and softened the stern natures of the Roman people; so centuries afterwards, the refined system of Roman

255

jurisprudence overthrew the uncouth customs and ill-digested laws of its conquerors, and led captive kings and nobles, clergy and laity, in the progress of its triumphal procession.

"With the exception of England..."

With the exception of England alone, the code of Justinian became engrafted upon the local institutions of each separate principality and kingdom, and constituted a general system of European law; but neither the favor of kings, the denunciations of priests, nor even the fulminations from the Papal See itself, could ever induce the English barons, the English courts, or the English people, to receive it as a substitute for their own favorite and immemorial customs. At this early period, then, when the dawn of a new civilization was just beginning to burst upon the world, the kingdoms of Europe, though united in religious superstitions, were divided in reverence for laws. That division has continued to the present day; and has also extended over the islands and continents, not then known, but since discovered and occupied.

English colonists cling to Common Law

Wherever the English flag has been unfurled upon a savage or hostile shore, possession has been taken at the same time in the name of its sovereign, and in behalf of its laws; and upon whatever bleak and rockbound coast an English colony has been planted, there also have the colonists established the Common Law, and ever afterwards clung to it as the inalienable birthright of themselves and their children, with a tenacity that no power, no suffering, no fear of danger, no hope of reward, could induce them to relax. In the same way has the Roman or Civil Law gone hand in hand with the extended dominion of the continental nations of Europe. Thus it happens that at the present time the whole Christianized world is ruled by one system or the other."[24]

Americans apply Common Law principles

Of the practical considerations, the committee called attention to: 1) The Americans, finding in California little enforcement of laws and much confusion, had effected order and organization by applying the common law, the only system with which they were acquainted. The committee contended: "The first settlers of the United States brought with them from the mother country the Common Law, and established it in an uninhabited region. The emigrants to California have brought with them the same system, and have established it in a country almost equally unoccupied."[25] 2) They had made their bargains pursuant to it; employing its usual formalities, they had executed their contracts, deeds, and wills, solemnized their marriages, and followed its rules in distributing property. 3) The large majority of lawyers and judges of California were familiar with the common law and could easily obtain reference books concerning it whereas civil law was written in works in a foreign language which were costly and rare.

Further arguing against the civil law system, they stated:

Civil Law,
radical change
to Americans

"A system of laws always becomes inseparably interwoven and intimately blended with the character of the community, reared under and habitual to them. A substitution so great as would be that of the Civil for the Common Law, of a whole system, so radical and entire, and over a community so extensive and homogenous as the American population of California, though often attempted, has never yet once met with success. You might as well undertake to eradicate the American character and plant the Mexican in its stead – to substitute the Catholic for the Protestant religion, by statute – to abolish the English language and sanction none but the Spanish, by legislative enactment; for the laws, not less than the character, religion, and language, constitute part and parcel of the American mind."[26]

The AMERICAN
Common Law

The Committee recommended: "The courts shall be governed in their adjudications by the English Common Law, as received and modified in the United States; in other words, by the **American Common Law**."[27] The Senate accepted the report and the common law was adopted on April 13, 1850.

INTERNAL AND EXTERNAL LAW

Ponder...

The Christian day-school student might think on these things:

Common Law:	Internal; Bible-based.
Civil Law:	External; statute law.

Common Law:	Becoming extinct.
Civil Law:	Means deterioration of our country.

Common Law:	Moses' Ten Commandments added to, to become ecclesiastical law.
Civil Law:	Built up from the time of Justinian, 4th Century A.D. Rewritten by Napoleon, 1804.

Internal Law:	Highest sense of advent of birth of Jesus.
External Law:	Scribe and Pharisee. *"For I say unto you, That except your righteousness shall exceed the righteousness of the scribes and Pharisees, ye shall in no case enter into the kingdom of heaven."* (Matt. 5:20)

CREATION OF COUNTIES

Twenty-seven
counties

An important duty of this first California Legislature was that of dividing the newly created state into counties. Under the Mexican regime Alta California had consisted of five districts: San Diego, Los Angeles, Santa Barbara, Monterey, and San Francisco. For the purpose of selecting delegates to the constitu-

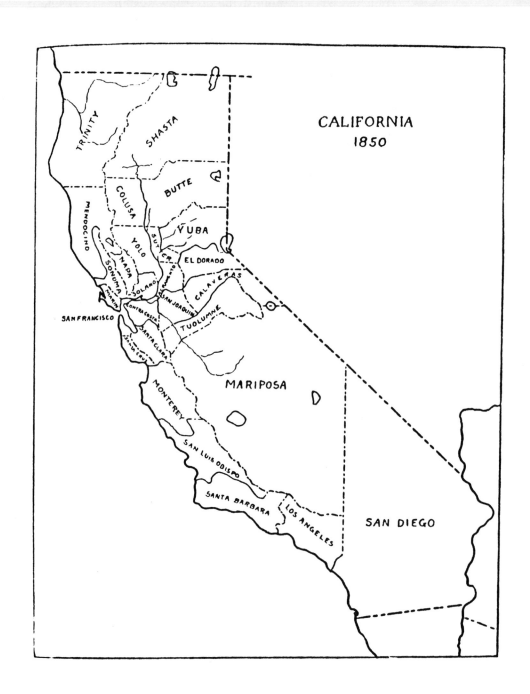

TWENTY-SEVEN ORIGINAL COUNTIES OF CALIFORNIA

From: Owen C. Coy. CALIFORNIA COUNTY BOUNDARIES.
Publication of the California Historical Survey Commission.
Sacramento: California State Printing Office, 1923.

tional convention in Monterey in 1849, there were added San Luis Obispo, San Jose, Sonoma, San Joaquin, and Sacramento. The task of devising a complete system of counties was assigned to a special committee of the Legislature. The "Report of Mr. Pablo de La Guerra on COUNTIES AND COUNTY BOUND-ARIES," dated January 4, 1850 stated:

"The time, occupied by your Committee in this work, has been unavoidably protracted until now, on account of the circum-stances and difficulties by which they were surrounded; such as the total absence of maps sufficiently correct to enable your Committee to determine, with requisite accuracy, the courses of rivers, mountains, and other natural landmarks, which they have been compelled to adopt, in most cases, as the limits of the different Counties...

Your Committee would further state, that they have not deemed it practicable to form any Counties entirely of Mining Districts, on account of the transitory character of the majority of the Mining Population; and that they have, in all instances, placed the Mining Districts within those Counties most convenient of access, and with which their trade and communication are chiefly confined."[28]

See Appendix

One of the most interesting reports presented to the Legislature was that of General Mariano G. Vallejo on THE DERIVATION AND DEFINITION OF THE NAMES OF THE SEVERAL COUNTIES OF CALIFORNIA, dated April 16, 1850. (See Appendix.) Twenty-seven counties had been created.

In preparing his Report, General Vallejo stated that the Committee labored under great disadvantages due to the absence of certain works on the early history of California. He said: "...your Committee have been compelled to depend almost entirely upon recollection and upon oral information in the preparation of the following Report." General Vallejo added:

"Your Committee would also ask the indulgence of the Senate for having introduced under the name of some of the Counties anecdotes and incidents of a personal character not properly belonging to 'the derivation and definition' of the names of those Counties. But the circumstances mentioned have become so well known in those Counties, and some of them are so intimately connected with the family history of the compiler of this Report, that they have been permitted to find a place therein."[29]

FINANCING THE STATE

In his JOHN BIDWELL, PRINCE OF CALIFORNIA PIONEERS, Dr. Hunt gave us further information about this first Legislature, of which John Bidwell was an active and useful member:

"Financing the new state government, which had no money, presented another problem. By virtue of legislative enactments the state incurred its first indebtedness. By an act of February 1, 1850, a temporary loan was authorized on the basis of state bonds amounting to $300,000 payable in six months with interest at 3 per cent per month. Another act was passed February 27 authorizing a loan of $1,000,000 for a period of twenty years, bonds for which were to bear interest at not to exceed 10 per cent per annum, payable semi-annually."[30]

NAVIGATION OF STREAMS

Dr. Hunt continued:

"A question that was later to become highly important to California was the navigation of streams. Bidwell's report on the subject was adopted, resulting in provision for the incorporation of steam-navigation companies...

His services and those of his colleagues laid strong and enduring foundations for the powerful new state even before its admission into the Union."[31]

UNPRECEDENTED ACTION OF CALIFORNIA

There was no precedent for the conditions under which the First California Convention was held. No part of the country had gained admission as a state without some years of territorial existence and governmental sanction. Texas might claim exemption to this but she had a full-fledged independent government before she was asked to become part of the Union.

De Facto military government inadequate

Congress devised many plans for the disposition of California, one of them being to admit the whole province of California as one huge territory and split it up into states as necessity demanded. None of the plans were wholly acceptable to Congress, however. The procrastination of Congress had provided no government for California and left her to herself. The de facto government set up by the military was inadequate and the population influx due to the gold discovery made it clear that if she was to remain a part of the United States, she would have to take matters into her own hands. Hence, she formed herself into a State and held her First State Legislature. Still, Congress took no action.

Why did Congress hesitate to admit California as a full-fledged state?

DEBATES IN UNITED STATES CONGRESS

Jan., 1850, President recommended

After the work of the first California Legislature, news of California's action was received at Washington by President Fillmore. (Fillmore was elected Vice President in 1848 and succeeded to the Presidency when President Taylor

260

died in 1850.) President Fillmore informed Congress in his Message of January 24, 1850 that the people of California had formed a plan of a state constitution and would ask for admission as a State. He recommended they be accepted as a State if their Constitution was found to be in compliance with the Constitution of the United States, and he also recommended that the people in the balance of the territory be given the privilege of governing themselves.

Congress' dilemma

The Congressmen at Washington found no flaw in the Constitution of California, nor any particular fault with it. It was a question of the North-South balance of free state and slave state. At that time, there were fifteen free states and fifteen slave states in the Union. California would enter the Union as the sixteenth free state, thus destroying the balance that had so long been maintained between North and South. California had written into her Constitution: "Neither slavery nor involuntary servitude unless for punishment of crime, shall ever be tolerated in this state."

THE 31ST CONGRESS

A select body of statesmen

The 31st Congress went to work with bills, resolutions, amendments to bills and substitute bills. About 170 speeches were made by the country's greatest statesmen: Webster, Calhoun, Clay, Benton, Seward, Douglas, Cass, Jeff Davis, Houston, the then-unknown Lincoln, and many other extremely capable men. Their ideas, their understanding, their handling of the English language, and no doubt their delivery, reminds one of the Founding Fathers' generation.

One of the more flowery speeches was made by William H. Seward of New York on March 11, 1850:

Seward:
California
is welcome...

"California, that comes from the clime where the West dies away into the rising East; California, which bounds at once the empire and the continent; California, the youthful queen of the Pacific, in robes of freedom, gorgeously inlaid with gold – is doubly welcome."[32]

Seward referred to a "Higher law" which brought him praise:

"The Constitution regulates our stewardship; the Constitution devotes the domain to union, to justice, to defense, to welfare, and to liberty. But there is a higher law than the Constitution, which regulates our authority over the domain, and devotes it to the same noble purposes. The territory is a part – no inconsiderable part – of the common heritage of mankind, bestowed upon them by the Creator of the Universe."[33]

He then proceeded to answer the various objections to the admission of California that had been voiced in the Senate such as: California comes unceremoniously without a preliminary consent of Congress; she has assigned her own boundaries without the previous authority of Congress; she is too large; no census had been taken; and she comes under Executive influence.

Mr. Seward continued:

"California is already a State, a complete and fully appointed State. She can never again be less than that. She can never be a province or a colony; nor can she be made to shrink and shrivel into the proportions of a federal dependent territory... We shall never agree to admit California, unless we agree now. Nor will California abide delay. I do not say that she contemplates independence; but if she does not, it is because she does not anticipate rejection... I shall vote for the admission of California, without conditions, without qualifications, and without compromise."

Disagreement in Congress
And still Congress could not agree upon California. Because California had set herself as a "free" state, many southern members were determined to resist the admission of the new state. There were other difficulties. Texas claimed a part of New Mexico and was preparing to send armed men to enforce her claim. However, most of the national difficulties were mixed up with the matter of slavery. The North complained that the selling of slaves in the national capital was a national disgrace. The South complained that the laws for returning runaway slaves were disobeyed or resisted in the North.

THE MEMORIAL

See Appendix: The Memorial
On March 12, 1850, the day after Seward's speech, Senators Gwin and Fremont and Representatives Wright and Gilbert, delegates from California, presented to the Senate and the House of Representatives of the United States, a Memorial, setting forth the circumstances leading to the formation and adoption of California's Constitution. (See Appendix.)

California expressed dismay
The California delegation endeavored to answer the charges and arguments of the powerful force opposed to California's admission. They showed that the de facto government was insufficient in their country. They stated that it was not a constitution by order of the Executive but one in which the people of California took the initiative. They expressed dismay that the Congress had not opened its doors to their state as they believed they had acted with the "approving voice of the American people."

The delegates said:

"The people of California are neither rebels, usurpers, nor anarchists. They have not sought to sow the seeds of revolution, that they might reap in the harvest of discord. They believe that the principles that guided them are true – they know that the motives which actuated them are pure and just – and they had hoped that their action would be acceptable to every portion of

262

their common country. They did not expect that their admission as a State would be made the test question upon which would hang the preservation of the American Union, nor did they desire such a result; but urged by the imperative and extraordinary necessities of their country, they united in such action as they believed would secure them a government under and in conformity to the Constitution of their country....

In thus presenting the certified copies of their State Constitution and their credentials, and asking the admission of the State, and that they may be permitted to take their seats in your respective bodies, the undersigned feel that they would neglect an important duty if they failed to assure you of the anxious desire for the perpetuity of this Union which animates all classes of their constituents. Born and reared under its protecting influences, as most of them were, their patriotism is as broad as the Republic – it extends from the Atlantic to the Pacific – it is as deep as the current of their mighty rivers – as pure as the never-melting snows which crown their mountains, and as indestructible as the virgin gold extracted from their soil. Coming as they nearly all do from the different States composing the Union, deeply impressed, as most of them have been by passing through foreign lands, with the immeasurable superiority of American institutions and American character, it would be strange, indeed, if they did not turn with reverence and affection toward their country, its institutions and its people. Possessed, too, in a remarkable degree, of intelligence, enterprise, and ability, rich in high moral qualities, industrious, energetic and honest, firm in their devotion to order and justice, they compose a community which has no superiors in the elements which constitute a citizen's glory, and a nation's greatness.

Loyal to American institutions and character

This people request admission into the American Union as a State. They understand and estimate the advantages which will accrue to them from such a connection, while they trust they do not too highly compute those which will be conferred upon their brethren. They do not present themselves as suppliants, nor do they bear themselves with arrogance or presumption. They come as free American citizens – citizens by treaty, by adoption, and by birth – and ask that they may be permitted to reap the common benefits, share the common ills, and promote the common welfare, as one of the United States of America!"[34]

Request admission

Memorial should be read by Californians today!

William Ellison remarked: "Whether the memorial of the California delegation markedly influenced the vote for the admission of California it is not possible to say, but in it the facts concerning California's action were stated fairly and in words that can profitably be read by Californians today."[35]

263

THE OMNIBUS BILL

Alexander Johnston gave us a summary of the Compromise reached by Congress:

Divine intervention
at crucial time

"(Henry) Clay was a great settler of the difficulties of the kind. He had contrived the Missouri Compromise of 1820, and the compromise tariff in 1833. He was in the Senate at this time, and he contrived a third compromise, or settlement of difficulties. In May, 1850, all the matters above stated...were referred to a committee of which he was chairman. This committee proposed a general plan of settlement, covering so many different measures that it was commonly called the Omnibus Bill. All its parts were passed and became laws in September; and they are called, together, the Compromise of 1850.

The Compromise
of 1850

The Compromise of 1850 included five parts. 1) California was admitted without slavery; 2) Texas was to receive $10,000,000 for giving up her claims to New Mexico; 3) The rest of the Mexican cession, outside of California, was to be divided into two territories, Utah (including Nevada) and New Mexico (including Arizona); and slavery was neither forbidden nor permitted in them; 4) Slavery was still to be permitted in the District of Columbia, but there was to be no buying or selling of negroes; 5) A new fugitive-slave law was passed.

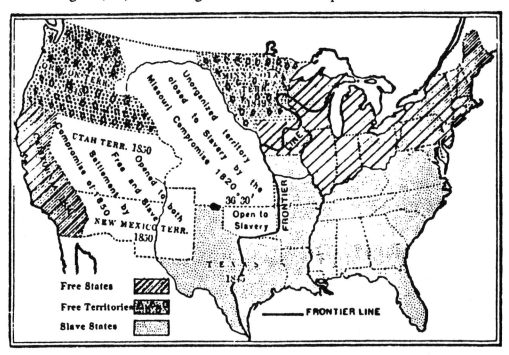

STATUS OF SLAVERY, COMPROMISE, 1850

From AN AMERICAN HISTORY, by David Muzzey

264

The Fugitive Slave Law was provided for the arrest of runaway slaves in the Northern States by United States officers. If a person was arrested as a runaway, his testimony was not to be taken; and for this reason there were cases of great cruelty, arrests and convictions of persons who probably never had been slaves. As soon as the law began to be enforced, it excited the only strong opposition that met any part of the Compromise of 1850."[36]

STATEHOOD

September 9, 1850

On August 13, the Senate voted on the Omnibus Bill and accepted it; it passed the House on September 7. The Bill was signed by President Fillmore on September 9, 1850. California became the thirty-first State of the United States of America.

News of the admission reached San Francisco on the morning of October 18 via steamer. Business was suspended for the day and the people celebrated.

Governor Burnett was in San Francisco the day that the news of California's admission into the Union arrived. He described the excitement of the times:

Wildly exuberant

"It so happened that I arrived in San Francisco on my return from Sacramento, the same day of the arrival of the steamer from Panama bringing the welcome intelligence of this event. We had a large and enthusiastic meeting in Portsmouth Square that evening. Next morning I left for San Jose on one of the Crandall's stages....

After passing over the sandy road to the Mission there was some of the most rapid driving I ever witnessed. The distance was some fifty miles, most of the route being over smooth, dry, hard prairie, and the drivers put their mustang teams to the utmost of their speed. As we flew past on our rapid course, the people flocked to the road to see what caused our fast driving and loud shouting, and without slackening our speed in the slightest degree we took off our hats, waved them around our heads, and shouted at the tops of our voices: 'California is admitted to the Union!' Upon this announcement the people along the road cheered as loudly and heartily as possible. I never witnessed a scene more exciting, and never felt more enthusiastic..."[37]

THE CALIFORNIA STATE CAPITAL

The capital of old Spanish and Mexican California had been Monterey. It was there that the First Constitutional Convention was called because it remained the capital during the military occupation of California.

265

Sketched by J. W. Revere U.S.N.

MONTEREY - CAPITOL OF CALIFORNIA.

Lith. of Wm. Endicott & Co. N. York.

San Jose:
December 1849

The First Constitutional Convention designated San Jose as the location of the First California Legislature, held in December of 1849. The First Legislature left the permanent location of the state capital open to bids from rival towns, and the contest began.

The most advantageous offer seemed to be that of M. G. Vallejo, who proposed to lay out a town on the Carquinez Straits, in or near which he would give the state 156 acres of ground and $370,000 toward the cost of public buildings. This amount was to be paid over a period of two years. Vallejo suggested the city be called "Eureka" but he was overruled and the city was named "Vallejo."

San Jose:
January 1851

Vallejo: 1852;
to Sacramento

The second Legislature met in San Jose again in 1851. On January 5, 1852, the third session convened in Vallejo but the new building was not yet finished and the legislators were not comfortable, so the legislators moved to Sacramento.

Sacramento
(flood): 1852

Back to Vallejo:
1853

Sacramento suffered a flood in 1852, dampening the spirits and persons of the Legislature, and so the fourth Legislature again opened in Vallejo in 1853. There were less than twenty houses in Vallejo at that time and the accommodations of the new town continued to be unsatisfactory to legislators. Because of later financial difficulties, Vallejo asked to be released from his pledge to California for the state buildings.

Benicia:
Remainder of 1853

Benicia now stepped into the competition. General Vallejo had given the land for the city from his extensive Spanish land grant. Thomas O. Larkin, the only American consul to Mexico before the war and a wealthy merchant in Monterey, had financed the town of Benicia. Dr. Robert E. Semple, tallest man in the territory (6'8") and President of the First Constitutional Convention, had laid out the plans for Benicia in 1847. The city of Benicia had been named after Vallejo's wife, Dona Francesca Benicia Carrillo Vallejo. Benicia was in the path of the emigrants coming down the Sacramento Valley to San Francisco, and later in the path of commerce between Sacramento and San Francisco. Benicia had promised the Legislature the "gratuitous use of the City Hall at Benicia as the State House, in case the Legislature should deem it expedient to remove from Vallejo." The remainder of the Fourth Session (1853) was held in the new capital. On February 9, 1853, a grand complimentary ball was held in the Assembly Hall (Second Floor) of the State House and a band from the nearby Benicia military barracks played far into the night.

Benicia:
January 1854

Sacramento:
February 1854

When the fifth Legislature met at Benicia, in January, 1854, a strong political movement was already underway to have the capital transferred to Sacramento. Sacramento offered the State the free use of the courthouses there and fireproof vaults for the public moneys and records, which Benicia did not have, plus a lot for the capitol building. Governor Bigler's second term inaugural ceremonies and ball were held in Benicia on January 7, 1854. After the inauguration ceremonies died away, the proposed change was hotly debated and Sacramento won out. The Legislature moved en masse on February 26, 1854 to their new permanent location in Sacramento.

Within five years, the seat of government of California moved from San Jose to Vallejo; to Sacramento; back to Vallejo; to Benicia; and at last in 1854, permanently to Sacramento.

1st	San Jose	December 1849
2nd	San Jose	1851
3rd	Vallejo	January 5, 1852
4th	Sacramento	1852
5th	Benicia	February 9, 1853 – January 2, 1854
6th	Sacramento	February 26, 1854, permanently.

Benicia Capitol 1853–1854

REFERENCES TO CHAPTER VI

STATEHOOD

THE CONSTITUTIONAL CONVENTION

1. Colton, Walter. THREE YEARS IN CALIFORNIA, p. 356.

THE PREAMBLE TO THE CONSTITUTION

2. Ibid., p. 399.
3. Klotz, Edwin F. "The Confluence of Cultures," THE ORIGINAL CONSTITUTION OF THE STATE OF CALIFORNIA, 1849, p. 9.

DECLARATION OF RIGHTS

4. Ellison, William H. A SELF-GOVERNING DOMINION, CALIFORNIA, 1849-1860, p. 28.

SLAVERY

5. Hunt, Rockwell D. THE GENESIS OF CALIFORNIA'S FIRST CONSTITUTION (1846-1849), p. 42.

RIGHT TO VOTE

6. Ellison, Op. Cit., p. 29. (For discussion of Suffrage, see J. Ross Browne, REPORT OF THE DEBATES IN THE CONVENTION OF CALIFORNIA ON THE FORMATION OF THE STATE CONSTITUTION, IN SEPTEMBER AND OCTOBER, 1849, pp. 61-76, 305-307, 323, 340, 341.)

CORPORATIONS

7. Ellison, Op. Cit., p. 33.

COMMUNITY PROPERTY LAW

8. Ibid., p. 38. (For discussion of Separate Property Rights for Married Women, see J. Ross Browne, Op. Cit., pp. 257-269.)
9. Ellison, Op. Cit., p. 39.
10. Browne, Op. Cit., p. 267.
10a. Ibid., p. 266.

EDUCATION

11. Ellison, Op. Cit., p. 39. (See J. Ross Browne, Op. Cit., pp. 202-211.)
12. Hunt, Rockwell D. CALIFORNIA'S STATELY HALL OF FAME, p. 222.

SEAL

13. Browne, Op. Cit., p. 304.
14. Beane, Walton. CALIFORNIA, AN INTERPRETIVE HISTORY, p.132-3.

CONCLUSION

15. Taylor, Bayard. ELDORADO, p. 160.
16. Hunt, THE GENESIS OF..., Op. Cit., p. 57.

...SUBMITTED TO THE PEOPLE...

17. THE ORIGINAL CONSTITUTION OF THE STATE OF CALIFORNIA, 1849, published by Telefact Foundation, p. 98.
18. Ibid., p. 103.
19. Ibid., pp. 106-107.

FIRST CALIFORNIA LEGISLATURE

20. Hunt, Rockwell D. JOHN BIDWELL, PRINCE OF PIONEERS, pp. 164, 165.

(Note: In 1913, the method of choosing California senators was changed. Our representatives to Congress are still elected by the people by popular vote, but, since 1913, our senators are also elected by popular vote, instead of being chosen by their peers in the Senate as being the most capable statesmen to represent California.)

STEPHEN J. FIELD

21. Hunt, CALIFORNIA'S STATELY HALL...Op. Cit., p. 333.

CREATION OF COURTS

22. Ellison, Op. Cit., p. 68.

COMMON LAW VERSUS CIVIL LAW

23. Ibid., p. 69.
24. JOURNAL OF THE SENATE OF THE STATE OF CALIFORNIA AT THEIR FIRST SESSION, pp. 464, 465. (A copy may be obtained from the California State Library, Law Department, Sacramento.)
25. Ibid., p. 475.
26. Ibid., p. 479.
27. Ibid., p. 480.

CREATION OF COUNTIES

28. Ibid., p. 411.
29. Ibid., p. 522.

FINANCING THE STATE

30. Hunt, JOHN BIDWELL, PRINCE...Op. Cit., p. 168.
31. Ibid., pp. 168, 169.

THE 31st CONGRESS

32. Hunt, Rockwell D. "1850, Year of Destiny."
33. Ellison, Op. Cit., p. 91.

THE MEMORIAL

34. Browne, Op. Cit., Appendix, pp. XXIII
35. Ellison, Op. Cit., p. 95.

THE OMNIBUS BILL

36. Johnston, Alexander. HISTORY OF THE UNITED STATES, p. 266-7.

STATEHOOD

37. Burnett, Peter. RECOLLECTIONS AND OPINIONS, p. 224.

CHAPTER VII

CONCLUSION

"Christianity is the most powerful factor in our society and the pillar of our institutions... Christianity is the only possible religion for the American people, and with Christianity are bound up all our hopes for the future." (CHRISTIAN HISTORY OF THE CONSTITUTION, Vol. II, p. 40.)

HOW THE EAST VIEWED THE WEST

After California had been acquired by the United States, what was the attitude of the people of the United States toward the newly acquired "Queen of the Pacific"? An article published in THE AMERICAN REVIEW, April of 1849, gives us an inkling of their feelings. There was no author's name attached to the article so it probably was an editorial. The following are excerpts from "**California**."

> "At a time when the golden treasures of California are attracting nearly all regards and absorbing nearly all interest, it is important not to neglect other aspects of the case which are even more remarkable and wonderful. It is no ordinary position, that in which these acquisitions (our new territorial acquisitions on the Pacific) have placed us."

Centralization Shifts to America by Acquisitions

> "Its significance is in fact that it contains the elements, the principles, the forces of A NEW CENTRALIZATION OF THE NATIONS OF THE EARTH. It is the beginning of a great American epoch in the history of the world. Just as certainly as there was a period when Asia was historically the centre of the world; and subsequently a period when Europe became so; just so certainly the acquisition of these territories on the Pacific seems destined to make our country the world's historical centre...and America the mediator between both sides of the Old World.

> But what has hitherto been our Great West must cease to be so now. Our true West has passed over the Rocky Mts. and lies along the shores of the Pacific from Oregon to California... As to the rapid settlement of the country, this seems likely to be secured by the golden attractions that are drawing thousands and thousands....

> But this alone, the mere filling up of the country by settlers, going, even the great majority of them, from among ourselves, and carrying the spirit and the love of our institutions and the desire to remain in political union with us; this will not of itself be enough to make those territories a permanent integral portion of the United States, and to secure those stupendous, world-embracing historical consequences of which we have spoken."

Physically

> "For if communication is to be maintained between the Atlantic and Pacific shores only by long voyages around Cape Horn, or even by the shorter route through a

foreign state, across the Isthmus by Chagres to Panama, it seems scarcely possible that a permanent political union can be preserved. The great Rocky Mountains, the deserts said to lie between the two sides of the nation, will form a barrier to prevent the sense of oneness, the preservation of national feeling, and of true social and political union. But let the...great projected lines of railroad communication connect the two sides of the continent; let the telegraph wires electrically unite them; and how different the case... And how easily then, under God, is the problem solved of binding and keeping together, in a living social and civil union, the eastern and the western shores of the continent....

Add again to this the sameness of language, institutions and laws, which will prevail throughout the States; the effect of the reserved sovereign rights of the several States in securing all local interests and satisfying, all local sense of importance; while, at the same time, membership in the Union secures innumerable advantages not other-wise attained, and gratifies the larger sense of national importance. Put these things together, and we do not see why, under God, we may not remain centrally united as a nation, though we grow to be fifty states and 300 millions of people."

Commercially

"...it must work a change in the whole commercial relations of the globe. The trade of China, and of a large portion of Asia, must find its way across the western ocean to our Pacific shores, building up great towns and cities there, and thence across the continent to the Atlantic coast, there to meet the trade of Europe coming over the Atlantic on its western route. And thus for Europe the old problem of a western passage to the Indies will be solved in a way that Columbus never dreamed of, when he set out to find it across the trackless, unknown seas."

Spiritual Purpose of California

"America must become the centre of the world; and that not in a merely physical or commercial way, but in a deeper, true historical sense – a sense not to gratify an overweening national pride and vain-gloriousness, whereof we have already more than enough, but a sense full of momentous responsibilities, involving infinite possibilities of evil as well as of good.

Now for what purpose has the **providence of God** conducted our nation unconsciously through the events of the last three years (1846-1849), to the edge and prospect of such a stupendous, startling future?

We say the providence of God; and we say this, not as mere words of course – a customary phrase, without meaning. For as certainly as **Divine Providence** is recognized for a truth at all, it must be recognized that there are two elements in history, a Divine element as well as a human element; that a Divine idea is ever realizing itself in the historical life of humanity, as truly as in the life of nature; in the events of human history, as in the phenomena of the material world; an idea not realized, nor to be apprehended, in the developments of a day or a year, but in the flow of generations and ages. The disciplinary education of the human race – this,

274

we believe, is the divine idea that underlies the whole history of the world... (The most ancient historical records) disclose to us the **providence of God**, interposing with a special moral purpose in events which, to all outward appearance, were the mere results of the ordinary laws of nature and of the working of ordinary historical causes... Beyond question, the great purpose for which these historical records...have come down to us, is to teach impressively, for all nations and for all times, **the great truth that the providence of God is the genius of human history."**

Of Good Purpose

"...it seems no less clear that God intends to give here, on this continent a scope for human energies of thought and will, such as has never yet been seen since the days before the flood; to let here be seen the freest, widest, most diversified and powerful display of what man's science and skill can accomplish, in subduing the elements, in controlling and applying the tremendous forces of nature; in overcoming and annihilating the old limitations of human endeavor; in unfolding the physical resources of the earth; in the creation of boundless wealth and a boundless sphere for action and enjoyment, a movement that shall draw the whole world around it and along with it in its gigantic march."

Of Evil Purpose

"But here the great and solemn question springs up, is this boundless physical development to subserve the moral and spiritual perfectionment of man and of society; or is it, on the contrary, to lead to a godless, self-willed, gigantic wickedness?

...it is not in mere forms of government; not in the fullest, world-wide development of democratic institutions, to save and regenerate the world. Men must learn to reverence something higher than money and themselves; they must learn that the spirit of self-will is not the genius of true freedom. It is not in popular education, as it is called – mere intellectual culture, and the diffusion of knowledge; men must be wise and good as well as sharp and knowing. No widest extension of suffrage, and largest possession of political rights; no marvels of scientific discovery and application; no increase of wealth; no multiplication of the means and refinements of earthly enjoyment, can work the regeneration and perfection of the social state, and secure the permanent well-being of humanity. A godless self-willed world, armed with the more than gigantic powers over nature which modern science gives, may rear heaven-climbing towers, only in the end to be crushed in the fall of their own toppling erections. Nothing, in the long run, can save our country and the world from a fate worse than that of the old Titans – nothing but the living power embodied in the constitution of Christianity permeating and sanctifying this prodigious material, civilization."

Christianity, the Answer

"No competent historical philosopher but admits the principle, that the fates and fortunes of nations are determined, not merely by material, but by moral causes; causes lying in the inmost mind and heart, in the character and spirit of the people;

and that, of all these causes, the religious convictions and systems of a people resting as they do upon one of the most deep-seated sentiments of human nature, are the most powerful. Equally undeniable and undenied is the fact that Christianity, considered as a special constitution of religion not only has had an historical existence for near 2000 years, but in nearly all that time has been one of the most significant facts in the history of the world.

...if Christianity is to exist to any good purpose in the new and grand career of development on which the world is entering, it must exist not as a mere formula, not as a mere outward institute, but as a true moral power, an organic life power in the historical life of the world. It must exist as a counteracting power to the naturally destructive tendencies resulting from any prodigious, unchecked overgrowth of the mere intellectual and physical elements in the life of the people.

Grandeur and wealth, luxury and corruption, dissolution and ruin, this is the brief but accurate summary of the history of the extinct but once powerful empires of the ancient world...without some adequate conservative moral power, our national history will sooner or later be summed up in the same words... Christianity, in the proper working of its spirit and principles, is that adequate conservative power."

Practical Christianity Needed

"(It is) not enough that Christianity be acknowledged as a formula, and exist as a visible institute, deferentially recognized while practically disregarded or resisted. Yet here precisely lies the danger to be apprehended. The spirit of the age is a spirit of hard worldliness and self-willed pride – not announcing itself in any theoretic rejection of the ideas of God and the divine constitution of religion, but in a disposition to resist and overbear the practical force of those ideas. The natural tendency of the prodigious multiplication of material interests, of the prodigious extension of man's sphere of activity, and of the prodigious intensity of the outward life that is everywhere going on, is to increase this spirit more and more. It may be quite willing to allow the ideas of God and his Church, provided it may shape and bend them after its own way.

...No political contrivances, no balance-of-power systems, no commercial relations, can effect the fraternization of the nations of the earth and bring humanity up to a state of true social perfectionment, independently of those more purely moral influences which, if they come not from Christianity, cannot be looked for from any other source. We may get on after a sort; we may get on for a long time to come; but we cannot get well on in the best sense, and in the long run, unless Christianity becomes a true, living power, incorporated into the social organization, and permeating the historical life of the world."

California

"(Our thoughts)...spring naturally from a consideration of the true historical significance of our new acquisitions on the Pacific – the immense consequences for our country and the world those acquisitions involve... The circumstances under which

276

those territories are destined to be filled rapidly up, makes the problem of our future fortunes as a nation infinitely momentous. The foundations of new states, of a new social order, are being laid there. What a hell upon earth, if the boundless lust of gold be unrestrained, unsanctified by better influences!... By the immense significance, the world-embracing issues that depend on the settlement of that land; by every pulse that beats for our country's true glory and the world's true welfare, should we endeavor to pour the highest and purest moral influence into the new-forming life that is to spring up on those shores." ▫

CALIFORNIA: THEN (1846) AND NOW (1850)

In the Appendix to his THREE YEARS IN CALIFORNIA, Reverend Walter Colton poetically chronicles for us the changes that occurred in California between the years of 1846 and 1850.

"Three years ago the white population of California could not have exceeded ten thousand souls. She has now a population of two hundred thousand, and a resistless tide of emigration rolling in through the heart of Mexico, over the Isthmus of Panama, around Cape Horn, and over the steeps of the Rocky Mountains. Then the great staple of the country was confined to wild cattle; now it is found in exhaustless mines of quicksilver and gold. Then the shipping which frequented her waters was confined to a few drogers, that waddled along her coast in quest of hides and tallow; now the richest argosies of the commercial world are bound to her ports.

Three years ago the dwellings of her citizens were reared under the hands of Indians, from sun-baked adobes of mud and straw; now a thousand hammers are ringing on rafter and roof over walls of iron and brick. Then the plough which furrowed her fields was the crotch of a tree, which a stone or a root might shiver; now the shares of the New England farmer glitter in her soil. Then the wheels of her carts were cut from the butts of trees, with a hole in the centre for the rude axle; now the iron-bound wheel of the finished mechanic rolls over her hills and valleys. Then only the canoe of the Indian disturbed the sleeping surface of her waters; now a fleet of steamers travers her ample rivers and bays. Then not a schoolhouse, public teacher, magazine, or newspaper, could be found in the whole territory; now they are met with in most of the larger towns. Then the tastes and passions of an idle throng rang on the guitar and the fandango; now the calculations of the busy multitudes turn to the cultured field and productive mine. Then California was a dependency of Mexico, and subject to revolution with the success of every daring military chieftain; now she is an independent state, with an enlightened constitution, which guarantees equal rights and privileges to all. Then she was in arms against our flag; now she unrolls it on the breeze, with the star of her own being and pride glowing in the constellation which blazes on its folds.

Three years ago and San Francisco contained only three hundred souls; now she has a population of twenty-seven thousand. Then a building lot within her limits cost fifteen dollars; now the same lot cannot be purchased at a less sum than fifteen thousand. Then her commerce was confined to a few Indian blankets, and Mexican reboses and beads; now from two to three hundred merchantmen are unloading their costly cargoes on her quay. Then the famished whaler could hardly find a temporary relief in her markets; now she has phrensied the world with her wealth. Then Benicia was a pasture covered with lowing herds; now she is a commercial mart, threatening to rival her sister nearer the sea. Then Stockton and Sacramento City were covered with wild oats, where the elk and deer gambolled at will; now they are laced with streets, and walled with warehouses, through which the great tide of commerce rolls off into a hundred mountain glens. Then the banks of the Sacramento and San Joaquin were cheered only by the curling smoke of the Indian's hut; now they throw on the eye at every bend the cheerful aspect of some new hamlet or town. Then the silence of the Sierra Nevada was broken only by the voice of its streams; now every cavern and cliff is echoing under the blows of the sturdy miner. The wild horse, startled in his glen, leaves on the hill the clatter of his hoofs, while the huge bear, roused from his matrimonial jungle, grimly retires to some new mountain fastness." ▫

BETWEEN CONSTITUTIONS (1849-1879)

California continued to grow under its first constitution which remained as the state's fundamental law for thirty years. It fulfilled Daniel Webster's prophecy that "to whatever region an American citizen carries himself, he takes with him, fully developed in his own understanding and experience, our American principles and opinions, and becomes ready at once, in cooperation with others, to apply them to the formation of new governments." California thrived under this new government.

What happened to this Child of America? Her foundation, built upon the Providence of God and upon the political system of America, was so sure. However, little-by-little, "reform-after-reform," the character of the State has lost its American Christian basis. To mention Christian principles in government now is often to "offend" those who are not believers. Therefore, its Christian influence is muffled wherever possible. The liberty of the individual, as Christianity teaches, is slowly succumbing to the good of the masses, as socialism advocates. How could this have happened? Perhaps, as the people enjoyed their freedom, they slowly relaxed their principles.

Without going into detail, the following historical events are reviewed from the time of California's first constitution (1849) to her second constitution (1879).

In February of 1851, the Committee of Vigilance of San Francisco was first organized. The leading citizens of San Francisco organized a group outside the law to protect the lives and property of its citizens against the lawless hoodlums, called "Hounds," who found they could get away with almost anything in that city of such instant growth. Hence, these Committees of 1851 and 1856 were formed. There was much controversy about the Committees of Vigilance.

After the prosperous times of the gold rush days, the depression of 1854 hit California. Prices and wages had been too high and their extravagant levels could no longer be maintained. Business houses closed, the banks were rushed, and people became afraid.

In 1859, the discovery in Nevada of the fabulously rich silver mine known as The Comstock Lode brought a remarkable wildness among fortune hunters to flock to western Nevada. It brought business to California as tons of freight were carried daily between Placerville, California and Carson

278

City, Nevada, amounting to $5,250,000 in one year. The Wells Fargo Express had been formed in 1852 and it transported more than 200,000 pounds of silver bullion.

Iron manufacturing started early in California with the Union Iron Works in 1849. In 1876 there were forty-seven foundries and similar businesses in San Francisco. But the lack of satisfactory transportation to the eastern centers was a drawback. To some, it was beginning to be apparent that manufacturing would eventually surpass both mining and agriculture.

Gold dust as a medium of exchange was replaced by coins, at first minted by private companies. In 1854 in San Francisco, a branch of the United States Mint was established.

The colorful stage coach was an important link with the States to California. Congress passed the Overland California Mail Bill, which resulted in the Butterfield Overland Mail Company in 1858. This provided better communication between Missouri and San Francisco and Los Angeles. Then the Pony Express started as a mail carrier between the Missouri River and the Pacific shores. It operated for eighteen months, 1859 to October of 1861. It was replaced by the electric telegraph.

During the Civil War, California's wealth played a significant factor. Due to the influence of Thomas Starr King, who has already been mentioned, California's contribution of gold to the Union cause proved to be one of the reasons the Union was successful.

A transcontinental railroad had been the dream of an engineer, Theodore D. Judah. He made the first survey over the Sierras for the Central Pacific Railroad. The financial backing came from four Californians, Leland Stanford, Collis P. Huntington, Charles Crocker, and Mark Hopkins, known as "The Big Four." The railroad was started in January 1863, the year Theodore Judah died. The railroad connecting East with West was completed May 10, 1869. A "golden spike" commemorating the event was driven at Promontory, Utah, when the Union Pacific of the East met the Central Pacific of the West.

To build the railroads, thousands of Chinese laborers were imported into California. By 1876, there were 116,000 Chinese "coolies" in California. They were a cause of concern because they worked for less wages than the white workers; all of their earnings were returned to China. This resulted in the Exclusion Act of May 6, 1882, forbidding immigration of Chinese laborers for a ten year period, renewable by the Geary Act. In 1902 it became a permanent policy of our national government.

The Chinese question in 1867, however, became the leading issue of political contenders. The political thought was divided between the railroad monopoly and the rights of farmers and the laboring "class." Dennis Kearney, from Ireland, was a leading agitator for the working class and was against the Chinese. On September 23, 1877 he organized The Workingmen's Party. On the political platform, Kearney's Party demanded that the government of California be taken out of the hands of the rich and be placed in the hands of the people. Kearney brought strange ideas to California as he referred to the "robber capitalists."

THE CONSTITUTION OF 1879

Demands for a new state constitution resulted in the second constitutional convention held in June of 1878. Kearney's Workingmen's Party was sufficiently well organized by April of 1878 to nominate a full ticket of delegates to the convention in every part of the state. The convention was more than three times as large as the Monterey convention of 1849, with 152 delegates as compared with 48. Of the delegates a majority were Non-Partisans (Republicans and Democrats); 51 were Workingmen, or one-third of the convention.

One writer says:

"The result of the election of June 19 was that a relatively small number of men of conspicuous ability were selected as delegates: viewed as a whole the delegates would not compare very favorably with the men of '49, nor can it be said that they were as free from the scheming of political leaders. Republicans and Democrats generally agreed to oppose the radicalism of the Workingmen's Party."[1]

The second constitutional convention lasted nearly six months, as compared to six weeks of the 1849 convention. The Constitution of 1879 was seven times as long as the United States Constitution. It was a great deal more liberal than the first California Constitution of 1849. It was at this time that "a State Board of Equalization was created, to consist of one member from each Congressional district, whose duty was to be 'to equalize the valuation of taxable property in the several counties, and also to assess the franchise, roadway, road-bed, rails and rolling stock of all railroads operated in more than one county in the state.'"[2]

A CHALLENGE

The foregoing gives a few of the trends of California between constitutions, some good and some footsteps away from our original premise.

It is up to us all to reclaim our American Constitutional Republic. It is up to a generation of American Christians here in California to remember the Providence of God in the background of our State. We have learned that California is the Child of America. What can we do to reforge her place on the Chain of Christianity? Could we not individually take a stand for a policy of "Back to Basics" in Christian living, law, and liberty? Could we not insist upon Christian criteria in electing our political representatives, our school officials, and our church government? "The price of liberty is eternal vigilance." To that end, God worketh with us.

II TIMOTHY 2:1,2.

"Thou therefore, my son, be strong in the grace that is in Christ Jesus.

And the things that thou hast heard of me among many witnesses,
the same commit thou to faithful men, who shall be able to teach others also."

References

1. Hunt, Rockwell D. and Nellie Van De Grift Sanchez. A SHORT HISTORY OF CALIFORNIA, p. 547.
2. Ibid., p. 549.

APPENDIX

THE HAND OF GOD IN AMERICAN HISTORY

ENGLISH PREPARATION

by Verna M. Hall

(Note: The following are excerpts from the address Miss Hall gave to the Second Pilgrim Seminar in Plymouth, Massachusetts on November 19, 1971. These quotations are taken from THE JOURNAL, Volume I, 1989, pages 37-48, published by The Foundation for American Christian Education in San Francisco, California, with their permission. I believe this article is appropriate to our study, as Miss Hall mentions The Hand of God in the role that Portugal, Spain, and specifically that which England played in the background of America's Christian History, and consequently, that of California.)

"The particular preparation in England for the launching of our Mayflower Pilgrims, with which I am concerned in this paper, is the dramatic period from Wycliffe to the going forth of the Pilgrims from England to Holland. These years (1382-1608), a little over two hundred and twenty-five years, see the Hand of God literally overturning mankind's centuries-old concepts of sovereignty, government, liberty, freedom, property, unity, and voluntary union, in both the ecclesiastical and the civil spheres. It was a Christian miracle, the evidence of the power of Christ in the lives of a comparatively small number of individuals, who believed in the wholeness of Christ in every activity of their lives, be that life ever so lowly or the work ever so menial by worldly standards...

ST. AUGUSTINE

While the contest between external church and state was waging (during the Reformation), there were those sincere Christians endeavoring to see the relation between the 'internal' world of the individual and the 'external.' God is never without His witnesses in this regard. As an example, I refer to St. Augustine and his 'City of God.' In the turbulent fifth century, he was stating a fact which twentieth-century Christians seem to have forgotten, that God rules in all affairs of men, whether man knows it or not. The Pilgrims understood this and achieved that wonderful Christian balance – between the two extremes as presented by the monastic attitude, to avoid the world, or the Puritan who tries to legislate good for the world...

EXCHANGES TO BE MADE

What Biblical, Christian ideas of man and government had to be thought through before the seed of American Constitutional government could be planted on these shores by the Pilgrims? To name a few: 1) the centuries-old infallibility of the church organization had to be exchanged for the infallibility of the Bible; 2) the sovereignty of the king or pope had to be exchanged for the sovereignty of the individual governed by God; 3) class structure had to be exchanged for the equality of all under God's law and civil law; 4) the centralized church had to be exchanged for the independent church; 5) the limited liberty and freedom of the individual, as being granted, had to be exchanged for the concept of the inalienable God-given rights of the individual – life, liberty, and property; 6) the flow of power had to change from the king to the people, to the people choosing their representatives; 7) and compulsory uniformity had to be exchanged for diversity with unity in all areas of activity. While the Word of God is slowly permeating in the lives of individuals in

England, helping them think through the above-mentioned concepts, let us glance at the ways and means by which God now opened up North and South America.

EXPLORATIONS

Most historians will describe the opening as 'The discovery of the New World was in a sense an accident of the search for a sea-route to Asia, a search which Portugal led and which gave her the initial advantage.'[5] From the Christian position, this is the secondary cause for the explorations, not the primary.

PORTUGAL began to push down the west coast of Africa under the guiding hand of Prince Henry, the Navigator, prior to 1460. God used this man for the particular purpose of increasing man's geographical knowledge through maritime activities. Portugal, in sailing around Africa, went in an eastward direction.

SPAIN begins its major explorations with Columbus in 1492, sailing westward. Portugal, upon learning of the new discovery, claimed it, for since the middle of the fifteenth century, the papacy had been issuing bulls confirming Portuguese possessions. Ferdinand and Isabella appealed to Pope Alexander VI, a Spaniard, and during 1493, a series of papal bulls drew a boundary line between Spanish and Portuguese claims 100 leagues west of the Cape Verde Islands and granted the Spanish monarchs all the land they might find by sailing south and west until they reached India. Portugal was granted all land eastward. The loot of the Spaniards from Mexico and Peru became the ultimate source of weakness and decay for Spain. (Viewing all things from our theme, the Hand of God, I find it fascinating that the discovery of gold and silver in the hot regions of the New World merely confirmed a medieval theory that gold occurs only where the sun's rays are the hottest, thus keeping materialistic nations of that time focused on Central and South America. Also, vast resources of gold and silver in North America were reserved for the United States – another instance of God's loving care for America.)

What is ENGLAND doing about explorations? In 1496, John Cabot, a Genoese who had become a citizen of Venice, but who was then a resident of Bristol, got a grant from Henry VII. Cabot, a vassal and lieutenant of the king, was given all the lands he could find to the north, west, and east, and a monopoly of commerce. Cabot set forth from Bristol in 1497 and found the St. Lawrence River. On his return, Henry VII granted him 10 pounds. England's claims to North America were thus based upon one individual's voyage, Cabot's of 1497[6]...

I have called your attention to the directions each of these nations took in their early exploration. Notice...how the area of the thirteen colonies is protected. Is this happenstance, or the Hand of God? What would have happened if England, instead of Spain, had gone to the southwest and found gold? Would we have had the Pilgrims?...

QUEEN ELIZABETH

The long reign of Elizabeth, 1558-1603, forty-five years, is a period for the young college Christian to study in detail from the Hand of God concept. No novel of intrigue and adventure can compare with the actual happenings of this time. Nothing but the Hand of God could have produced the Pilgrims out of such human chaos. There is now the explosion of human energy because persecutions have somewhat ceased; economic activities are expanding; pinnacles of literature are reached – all midst the rule of a tyrannical and utterly selfish queen; uncouth and sordid actions in the court; intrigues almost beyond comprehension between England, France, Spain, Rome; trouble with Ireland and Scotland; the pleadings and warnings of the United Netherlands, and last but not least, the Spanish Armada in 1588. Yet out of this crucible, with its potpourri of mixed ingredients, comes the lesson clearly illustrated and recorded, that God will have His way with His people, in spite of the machinations of human wills. Only God saved England, only God saved the Pilgrims, only God saved and will save America.

The Pilgrim would be ready in 1606 to be used of God for Christ and America, with all the resultant freedoms for the individual we know today. Therefore, in 1588, the greatest effort was made by those forces which would keep mankind forever in bondage, to destroy England where the babe of Christian civil and religious liberty was born. From a human point of view, it did not seem possible for England to remain free from either Rome or Europe – she was so tiny by comparison with the combined forces of Europe. Emperor Charles the Fifth of Austria saw the possibility of bringing all western Europe and England together under the rule of a single family. Philip II of Spain and the Duke of Parma were to be his tools.

SPANISH ARMADA

Noah Webster says, 'The Supreme Being is the rightful disposer of all events, and of all creatures.'[9] The Spanish Armada is a classic example.

Time does not allow for the recounting of all the details, but if you have not read or taught the Spanish Armada recently, may I suggest you acquire a copy of one of the first accounts written by Richard Hackluyt in 1589, now available in several editions. Samuel Eliot Morrison calls it the prose epic of the English nation. Hackluyt says,

> Whereupon it is most apparent, that God miraculously preserved the English nation. For the L. Admirall wrote unto her Majestie that in all humane reason, and according to the judgement of all men (every circumstance being duly considered) the English men were not of any such force, whereby they might, without a miracle, dare once to approach within sight of the Spanish Fleet: insomuch that they freely ascribed all the honour of their victory unto God, who had confounded the enemy, and had brought his counsels to none effect.[10]

We know that England was being armed internally because of the Geneva Bible in the hands of the individual, but to emphasize the power of God, let us consider very briefly the external situation.

1. Elizabeth and her statesmen, influenced by the falsehood deliberately circulated by the Jesuit Spanish emissaries, did not believe, even as late as May 1588, that the armaments, notoriously preparing in Spain and Flanders, were intended against England. Elizabeth still believed in the possibility of averting the danger by negotiation. Even in the middle of July, just ten days before the fleet was to appear off Plymouth, the leading statesman, Walsingham, believed it had dispersed and returned to Spain.

2. Both the army and navy of England were quite unprepared, and the queen was reluctant to incur the expense necessary to the defense of her kingdom. The little nation of four million seemed oblivious to its dangers.

3. The Armada left Lisbon the end of May, after having been duly blessed by the Cardinal Archduke Albert, Viceroy of Portugal. There were more than 130 ships, divided into ten squadrons, with a total personnel of about 30,000. The plan was simple. The fleet was to proceed straight from Lisbon to Calais roads, there to wait for the Duke of Parma, bringing his 17,000 veterans. They were to cross the channel to Dover, and with a combined force of 23,000 men, march at once upon London.

4. On Friday, July 29, after being beset with their first gale, they had their first glimpse of the land of promise presented them by Sixtus V., of which they had come to take possession. On the same day and night, the blaze and smoke of ten thousand beacon-fires from Land's End to Margate, and from the Isle of Wight to Cumberland, gave warning to every Englishman that the enemy was at last upon them. Almost at that very instant, intelligence had been brought from the court to the Lord-Admiral at Plymouth that the Armada, dispersed and shattered by the gales, was not likely to make its appearance that year; and orders had subsequently been given to disarm the four largest ships.

5. On July 31, the fleets had their first meeting. There were 130 sail of the Spaniards, of which ninety were large ships, and sixty-seven of the English. Motley gives a dramatic picture:

> It was a solemn moment. The long-expected Armada presented a pompous, almost a theatrical appearance. The ships seemed arranged for a pageant, in honor of a victory already won. Disposed in form of a crescent, the horns of which were seven miles asunder, those gilded, towered, floating castles, with their gaudy standards and their martial music, moved slowly along the channel, with an air of indolent pomp.[11]

6. On Saturday, August 6, the great fleet anchored in Calais roads. Never since England was England had such a sight been seen between Dover and Calais. Along that long sandy shore, one hundred and thirty-odd Spanish ships – some of the largest and most heavily armed in the world, lay face to face with one hundred and fifty English sloops and frigates and commanded by men whose exploits had rung through the world – Howard, Drake, Hawkins, and Frobisher. The Dutch were protecting the Flemish coasts. Motley describes this scene:

> It was a pompous spectacle, that midsummer night, upon those narrow seas. The moon, which was at the full, was rising calmly upon a scene of anxious expectation. Would she not be looking, by the morrow's night, upon a subjugated England, a re-enslaved Holland – upon the downfall of civil and religious liberty?[12]

7. What was England doing? On the fifth of August, no army had been assembled – not even the bodyguard of the queen, and on the fifth the Armada was at Calais ready to land. There were no fortresses, no regular army, no population trained to any weapon.

8. But God dispelled the enemy through the actions of Admiral Howard, and the gales and storms. God answered the prayers of the people and protected those to be known as Pilgrims. At this time,

1588, William Bradford is born, William Brewster is about thirty, and John Robinson is a youth of about thirteen.

> Richard Hackluyt tells us, While this woonderful and puissant Navie was sayling along the English coastes, and all men did now plainely see and heare that which before they would not be perswaded of, all people thorowout England prostrated themselves with humble prayers and supplications unto God: but especially the outlandish Churches (who had greatest cause to feare, and against whom by name, the Spaniards had threatened most grievous torments) enjoyned to their people continuall fastings and supplications, that they might turne away Gods wrath and fury now imminent upon them for their sinnes; knowing right well, that prayer was the onely refuge against all enemies, calamities, and necessities, and that it was the onely solace and reliefe for mankind, being visited with affliction and misery.[13]

Hackluyt also tells us,

> A while after the Spanish Fleet was departed, there was in England, by the commandement of her Majestie, and in the united Provinces, by the direction of the Statyes, a solemne festivall day publikely appointed, wherein all persons were enjoyned to resort unto the Church, and there to render thanks and praises unto God: and the Preachers were commanded to exhort the people thereunto. The foresayd solemnity was observed upon the 19 of November; which day was wholly spent in fasting, prayer, and giving of thanks.... Her Majestie being entered into the Church, together with her Clergie and Nobles gave thanks unto God, and caused a publike Sermon to be preached before her at Pauls crosse; wherein none other argument was handled, but that praise, honour, and glory might be rendered unto God, and that Gods name might be extolled by thanksgiving...[14]

I should like to conclude by giving an example how Holland commemorated her deliverance: A Spanish galleon, the St. Matthew, was captured by the Zelanders, and Hackluyt tells us,

> For the memory of this exploit, the foresayd captaine Banderduess caused the banner of one of these shippes to be set up in the great Church of Leiden in Holland, which is of so great a length, that being fastened to the very roofe, it reached downe to the ground... Thus almighty God would have the Spaniards huge ships to be presented, not onely to the view of the English, but also of the Zelanders; that at the sight of them they might acknowledge of what small ability they had beene to resist such impregnable forces, had not God endued them with courage, providence, and fortitude, yea, and fought for them in many places with his owne arme.[15]

Holland struck a coin, which epitomizes my theme, the Hand of God in American History.

...Upon the one side whereof was represented a ship flee-ing, and a ship sincking: on the other side foure men making prayers and giving thanks unto God upon their knees; with this sentence: Man purposeth: God disposeth. 1588."[16] ▫

NOTES

5 English Historical Documents, Vol. IX, American Colonial Documents to 1776, edited by Merrill Jensen, Oxford University Press (1969), p. 9.

6 Ibid., p. 9-11.

9 Noah Webster, The American Dictionary of the English Language, Facsimile 1828 Edition, including Webster's Biography by Rosalie J. Slater, Foundation for American Christian Education, San Francisco, (1967).

10 Richard Hakluyt, Voyages, J. M. Dent & Sons, Ltd., Everyman's Library, London (1907), Vol. 2, p. 393.

11 John Lothrop Motley, History of the United Netherlands, Harper & Bros., New York (1888), Vol. 2, p. 474.

12 Ibid., Vol. 2, p. 485.

13 Op. Cit., Hakluyt, Vol. 2, pp. 399-400.

14 Ibid., p. 400.

15 Ibid., p. 395.

16 Ibid., p. 399.

THE STORY OF YOSEMITE

From SCENES OF WONDER AND CURIOSITY IN CALIFORNIA published by J. M. Hutchings & Co., San Francisco, 1861.

The Mariposa Indian War (March 1851) led to the discovery of Yosemite Valley. The following is an eye-witness account of Dr. L. H. Bunnell of the Mariposa Battalion. Dr. Bunnell is the historian of a detachment of volunteers sent into the mountains to seek the hiding place of renegade Indians. He records that when he beheld the Valley for the first time, "his eyes became suffused with tears and his whole being swelled with exalted emotions, such as he never felt before or afterward." This first view was from the present-day *Inspiration Point*.

"Preparations were being made for defence when the news came of the sack of Savage's place on the Frezno, and of two men killed, and one wounded...and the murder of four men at Doctor Thomas Payne's place, at the Four Creeks; one of the bodies being found skinned.

These occurrences so exasperated the people that a company was at once raised and despatched to chastise the Indians.

In a few days it was ascertained that some four or five hundred Indians had assembled on a round mountain, lying between the north branches of the San Joaquin, and that they invited attack.

...volunteers were called for,...thirty-six offered, and at daylight the storming commenced with such fury as is seldom witnessed in Indian warfare... The battle checked the Indians in their career of murder and robbery, and did more to save the blood of the whites, as well as of Indians, than any or all other circumstances combined.

In a subsequent expedition into that region after the organization of the battalion,...in January 1851, the remains of Jose (the Indian Chief killed in battle) were found still burning among the coals of the funeral pyre.

It was during the occurrence of the events mentioned...that the existence of an Indian stronghold was brought to light."

Dr. Bunnell goes on to tell us that "when the Indians were told that they would all be killed if they did not make peace, they would laugh in derision, and say that they had many places to flee to, where the whites could not follow them..."

Two companies of the Battalion started in search of the Indians. They had orders to "in no case shed blood unnecessarily," and Dr. Bunnell said: "and to the credit of our race, it was strictly obeyed throughout the campaign, except in one individual instance."

Orders were given at Bishop's Camp for the chief of the tribe living in the then unknown valley to bring his tribe to headquarters of the Mariposa Battlion. The chief, Ten-ie-ya, appeared alone. He promised peace and the appearance of his tribe, but none came.

Under the guidance of Ten-ie-ya, the men who volunteered for this duty, marched toward the valley. Seventy-two Indians met the soldiers and Ten-ie-ya said there were no more and these had been delayed because of the snow which was eight feet deep. Ten-ie-ya was returned to headquarters and a young Indian guide replaced him. Ten-ie-ya said these were the first white men ever in the valley.

The Battalion made another trip to the Yo-Semite Valley, established headquarters there determined to learn the country. Dr. Bunnell: "On our arrival in the valley, a short distance above the prominent bluff known as El Capitan, or as the Indians call it, Tu-toch-ah-nu-lah, which signifies in their language, The Captain, five Indians were seen and heard on the opposite side of the river, taunting us." The company crossed the cold river on their horses, and took two of the sons of Ten-ie-ya prisoners. Back at headquarters, while trying to escape, the prisoners undid their bonds, rushed to their feet, and the youngest son of Ten-ie-ya was shot and killed trying to escape.

Ten-ie-ya was again captured. Dr. Bunnell: "Upon his entrance into the camp of the volunteers, the first object that met his gaze was the dead body of his son. Not a word did he speak, but the workings of his soul were frightfully manifested in the deep and silent gloom that overspread his countenance... Captain Boling explained to him the occurrence and expressed his regrets..."

By means of a mission Indian who spoke Spanish and the various Indian tongues of the region, it was communicated to Ten-ie-ya that if he would call in his people, they would not be harmed. Ten-ie-ya agreed, but had no intention of doing so.

"While waiting for provisions, the Chief became tired of his food, said it was the season for grass and clover, and that it was tantalizing for him to be in sight of such abundance, and not be permitted to taste it... Captain Boling said that he should have a ton if he desired it. Mr. Cameron attached a rope to the old man's body and led him out to graze! A wonderful improvement took place in his condition, and in a few days he looked like a new man."

Ten-ie-ya was allowed to return home to his valley. Later a report came of him and a band of his pillager Indians who attacked a party of whites visiting the valley in 1852. Two men of the party were killed and one wounded.

After the murder, Ten-ie-ya and his Tribe fled to the Mono Indians, on the eastern side of the Sierra. As a reward for the hospitality shown them they stole a lot of horses from the Monos, and ran them into the Yo-Semite. The furious Monos retaliated and killed all but eight braves and a few old men and women of the Yo-Semite tribe. The Yo-Semite tribe became extinct.

Dr. Bunnell: "It is proper to say...that the Yo-Semite Indians were a composite race, consisting of the disaffected of the various tribes from the Tuolumne to Kings River, and hence the difficulty in our understanding of the name; but that name, upon the writer's suggestion, was finally approved and applied to the valley..."

"It is acknowledged that Ah-wah-ne is the old Indian name for the valley, and that Ah-wah-ne-chee is the name of its original occupants..." □

JOHN CHARLES FREMONT (1813-1890)

There have been a great many books written about John Charles Fremont, Pathmarker of the West. He is an American hero, and our country needs "heros" these days. He was deeply devoted to America and spent a good portion of his life in bringing California into the nation.

Fremont was not only an extraordinary explorer, but mapped the new country of his explorations; made astronomical observations; and noted the specimens of plant and animal life, of soils and rocks. Many plants have the classification, *Fremontia*.

Providentially, a copy of Fremont's original MEMOIRS OF MY LIFE was given to me, copyrighted in 1886. It was written by Fremont, in which he tells of his rugged and rough explorations, and privations, crossing the mountains and streams into the new territory of the West. Again, providentially, a little book came into my possession about Fremont: LIFE AND EXPLORATIONS AND PUBLIC SERVICES OF JOHN CHARLES FREMONT, 1856. In this book is the first-hand account of his teacher, a Dr. Roberton, a "learned instructor," of his experience teaching the young John Fremont. This is a remarkable account for it gives us an inward glance at the keen intellect of the man Fremont.

Fremont's mother was widowed when Fremont was very young. He had a brother and a sister, both younger than he, and there was very little money to be had. When Charles was about thirteen years old, Mr. John W. Mitchell, a lawyer in Charleston, South Carolina, recognized the "bright promise" of the youngster and took him into his office to prepare him for the study of law. Mr. Mitchell also wished Fremont to prepare himself for the ministry of the church. At the age of seventeen, he was confirmed as a member of the Protestant Episcopal Church, but his free disposition was not compatible with the ministry.

The following account is from the Preface of Dr. Roberton's edition of Xenophon's Anabasis, published in 1850:

"In the year 1827, after I had returned to Charleston from Scotland, and my classes were going on, a very respectable lawyer came to my school, I think some time in the month of October, with a youth, apparently about sixteen, or perhaps not so much, (fourteen) of middle size, graceful in manners, rather slender, but well formed, and, upon the whole, what I should call handsome; of a keen, piercing eye, and a noble forehead, seemingly the very seat of genius. The gentleman stated that he found him given to study, that he had been about three weeks learning the Latin rudiments, and (hoping, I suppose, to turn the youth's attention from the law to the ministry) had resolved to place him under my care for the purpose of learning Greek, Latin, and Mathematics, sufficient to enter Charleston College. I very gladly received him, for I immediately perceived he was no common youth, as intelligence beamed in his dark eye, and shone brightly on his countenance, indicating great ability, and an assurance of his future progress. I at once put him in the highest class, just beginning to read Caesar's Commentaries, and, although at first inferior, his prodigious memory and enthusiastic application soon enabled him to surpass the best. He began Greek at the same time, and read with some who had been long at it, in which he also soon excelled. In short, in the space of one year he had with the class, and at odd hours with myself, read four books of Caesar, Cornelius Nepos, Sallust, six books of Virgil, nearly all Horace, and two books of Livy; and in Greek, all Graeca Minora, about the half of the first volume of Graeca Majora, and four books of

Homer's Illiad. And whatever he read, he retained. It seemed to me, in fact, as if he learned by mere intuition. I was myself utterly astonished, and at the same time delighted with his progress.

I have hinted that he was designed for the Church, but when I contemplated his bold, fearless disposition, his powerful inventive genius, his admiration of warlike exploits, and his love of heroic and adventurous deeds, I did not think it likely he would be a minister of the Gospel. He had not, however, the least appearance of any vice whatever. On the contrary, he was always the very pattern of virtue and modesty. I could not help loving him, so much did he captivate me by his gentlemanly conduct and extraordinary progress. It was easy to see that he would one day raise himself to eminence.

Whilst under my instruction, I discovered his early genius for poetic composition in the following manner. When the Greek class read the account that Herodotus gives of the battle of Marathon, the bravery of Miltiades and his ten thousand Greeks raised his patriotic feelings to enthusiasm, and drew from him expressions which I thought were embodied, a few days afterward, in some well-written verses in a Charleston paper, on that far-famed unequal but successful conflict against tyranny and oppression; and suspecting my talented scholar to be the author, I went to his desk and asked him if he did not write them; and hesitating at first, rather blushingly, he confessed he did. I then said: 'I knew you could do such things, and suppose you have some such pieces by you, which I should like to see. Do bring them to me.' He consented, and in a day or two brought me a number, which I read with pleasure and admiration at the strong marks of genius stamped on all, but here and there requiring, as I thought, a very slight amendment.

I had hired a mathematician to teach both him and myself, (for I could not then teach that science,) and in this he also made such wonderful progress, that at the end of one year he entered the Junior Class in Charleston College triumphantly, while others who had been studying four years and more, were obliged to take the Sophomore Class. About the end of the year 1828, I left Charleston. After that he taught Mathematics for some time. His career afterwards has been one of heroic adventure, of hair-breadth escapes by flood and field, and of scientific explorations, which have made him world-wide renowned.

In a letter I received from him very lately, he expresses his gratitude to me in the following words: 'I am very far from either forgetting you or neglecting you, or in any way losing the old regard I had for you. There is no time to which I go back with more pleasure than that spent with you, for there was no time so thoroughly well spent; and of any thing I may have learned, I remember nothing so well, and so distinctly, as what I acquired with you.' Here I cannot help saying that the merit was almost all his own. It is true that I encouraged and cheered him on, but if the soil into which I put the seeds of learning had not been of the richest quality, they would never have sprung up to a hundred-fold in the full ear. Such, my young friends, is but an imperfect sketch of my once beloved and favorite pupil, now a senator, and who may yet rise to be at the head of this great and growing Republic. My prayer is that he may ever be opposed to war, injustice, and oppression of every kind, a blessing to his country and an example of every noble virtue to the whole world."

The author of my little book*, Charles Wentworth Upham, goes on to say:

"By the influence of Mr. Poinsett, afterwards Secretary of War, and others friendly to his family, young Fremont obtained the situation of teacher of mathematics and instructor of the midshipmen on board the Natchez (1833), and sailed in her, in that capacity, to the Brazilian station. At the termination of her cruise, she returned to New York. After appearing before a board of examiners, in Baltimore, Mr. Fremont was regularly commissioned as a professor of mathematics in the navy, and assigned to the Frigate Independence. The distinguished manner in which he passed the examination coming to the ears of the Faculty of the College in Charleston, they instantly conferred upon him both the academic degrees, of Bachelor and Master of Arts." ▫

*Upham, Charles Wentworth. LIFE, EXPLORATIONS AND PUBLIC SERVICES OF JOHN CHARLES FREMONT. Boston: Ticknor and Fields, 1856.

MINER'S TEN COMMANDMENTS, BY J. M. HUTCHINGS, 1854

THE MINER'S TEN COMMANDMENTS

A man spake these words, and said: I am a miner, who wandered "from away down east," and came to sojourn in a strange land, and "see the elephant." And behold I saw him, and bear witness, that from the key of his trunk to the end of his tail, his whole body has passed before me; and I followed him until his huge feet stood still before a clapboard shanty; then with his trunk extended, he pointed to a candle-card tacked upon a shingle, as though he would say Read, and I read the

MINER'S TEN COMMANDMENTS

I.

Thou shalt have no other claim than one.

II.

Thou shalt not make unto thyself any false claim, nor any likeness to a mean man, by jumping one; whatever thou findest on the top above or on the rock beneath, or in a crevice underneath the rock; – or I will visit the miners around to invite them on my side, and when they decide against thee, thou shalt take thy pick and thy pan, thy shovel and thy blankets, with all that thou hast, and "go prospecting" to seek good diggings; but thou shalt find none. Then, when thou hast returned, in sorrow shalt thou find that thine old claim is worked out, and yet no pile made thee to hide in the ground, or in an old boot beneath thy bunk, or in buckskin or bottle underneath thy cabin; but has paid all that was in thy purse away, worn out thy boots and thy garments, so that there is nothing good about them but the pockets, and thy patience is likened unto thy garments; and at last thou shalt hire thy body out to make thy board and save thy bacon.

III.

Thou shalt not go prospecting before thy claim gives out. Neither shalt thou take thy money, nor thy gold dust, nor thy good name, to the gaming table in vain; for monte, twenty-one, roulette, faro, lansquenet and poker, will prove to thee that the more thou puttest down the less thou shalt take up; and when thou thinkest of thy wife and children, thou shalt not hold thyself guiltless – but insane.

IV.

Thou shalt not remember what thy friends do at home on the Sabbath day, lest the remembrance may not compare favorably with what thou doest here. – Six days thou mayest dig or pick all that thy body can stand under; but the other day is Sunday; yet thou washest all thy dirty shirts, darnest all thy stockings, tap thy boots, mend thy clothing, chop thy whole week's firewood, make up and bake thy bread, and boil thy pork and beans, that thou wait not when thou returnest from thy long-tom weary. For in six days' labor only thou canst not work enough to wear out thy body in two years; but if thou workest hard on Sunday also, thou canst do it in six months; and thou, and thy son, and thy daughter, thy male friend and thy female friend, thy morals and thy conscience, be none the better for it; but reproach thee, shouldst thou ever return with thy worn-out body to thy mother's fireside; and thou shalt not strive to justify thyself, because the trader and the blacksmith, the carpenter and the merchant, the tailors, Jews, and buccaneers, defy God and civilization, by keeping not the Sabbath day, nor wish for a day of rest, such as memory, youth and home, made hallowed.

V.

Thou shalt not think more of all thy gold, and how thou canst make it fastest, than how thou wilt enjoy it, after thou hast ridden rough-shod over thy good old parents' precepts and examples, that thou mayest have nothing to reproach and sting thee, when thou are left ALONE in the land where thy father's blessing and thy mother's love hath sent thee.

VI.

Thou shalt not kill thy body by working in the rain, even though thou shalt make enough to buy physic and attendance with. Neither shalt thou kill thy neighbor's body in a duel; for by "keeping cool," thou canst save his life and thy conscience. Neither shalt thou destroy thyself by getting "tight," nor "stewed," nor "high," nor "corned," nor "half-seas over," nor "three sheets in the wind," by drinking smoothly down – "brandy slings," "gin cocktails," "whisky punches," "rum-toddies," nor "egg nogs." Neither shalt thou suck "mint-julips," nor "sherry-cobblers," through a straw, nor gurgle from a bottle the "raw material," nor "take it neat" from a decanter; for, while thou art swallowing down thy purse, and thy coat from off thy back, thou art burning the coat from off thy stomach; and, if thou couldst see the houses and lands, and gold dust, and home comforts already lying there – "a huge pile" – thou shouldst feel a choking in thy throat; and when to that thou addest thy crooked walkings and hiccuping talkings, of lodgings in the gutter, of broilings in the sun, of prospect-holes half full of water, and of shafts and ditches, from which thou hast emerged like a drowning rat, thou wilt feel disgusted with thyself, and inquire, "Is thy servant a dog that he doeth these things?" Verily I will say, Farewell, old bottle, I will kiss thy gurgling lips no more. And thou, slings, cocktails, punches, smashes, cobblers, nogs, toddies, sangarecs, and julips, forever farewell. Thy remembrance shames me; henceforth, "I cut thy acquaintance," and headaches, tremblings, heart burnings, blue devils, and all the unholy catalogue of evils that follow in thy train. My wife's smiles and my children's merry-hearted laugh, shall charm and reward me for having the manly firmness and courage to say NO. I wish thee an eternal farewell.

VII.

Thou shalt not grow discouraged, nor think of going home before thou hast made thy "pile," because thou hast not "struck a lead," nor found a "rich crevice," nor sunk a hole upon a "pocket," lest in going home thou shalt leave four dollars a day, and go to work, ashamed, at fifty cents, and serve thee right: for thou knowest by staying here, thou mightest strike a lead and fifty dollars a day, and keep thy manly self-respsect, and then go home with enough to make thyself and others happy.

VIII.

Thou shalt not steal a pick, or a shovel, or a pan from thy fellow miner; nor take away his tools without his leave; nor borrow those he cannot spare; nor return them broken, nor trouble him to fetch them back again, nor talk with him while his water rent is running on, nor remove his stake to enlarge thy claim, nor undermine his bank in following a lead, nor pan out gold from his "riffle box," nor wash the "tailings" from his sluice's mouth. Neither shalt thou pick out specimens from the company's pan to put them in thy mouth, or in thy purse; nor cheat thy partner of his share: nor steal

296

from thy cabin-mate his gold dust, to add to thine, for he will be sure to discover what thou hast done, and will straightway call his fellow miners together, and if the law hinder them not, they will hang thee, or give thee fifty lashes, or shave thy head and brand thee, like a horse thief, with "R" upon thy cheek, to be known and read of all men, Californians in particular.

IX.

Thou shalt not tell any false tales about "good diggings in the mountains," to thy neighbor, that thou mayest benefit a friend who hath mules, and provisions, and tools and blankets, he cannot sell, – lest in deceiving thy neighbor, when he returneth through the snow with naught save his rifle, he present thee with the contents thereof, and like a dog, thou shalt fall down and die.

X.

Thou shalt not commit unsuitable matrimony, nor covet "single blessedness;" nor forget absent maidens; nor neglect thy "first love," – but thou shalt consider how faithfully and patiently she awaiteth thy return; yea, and covet each epistle that thou sendest with kisses of kindly welcome – until she hath thyself. Neither shalt thou covet thy neighbor's wife, nor trifle with the affections of his daughter; yet, if thy heart be free, and thou dost love and covet each other, thou shalt "pop the question" like a man, lest another, more manly than thou art, should step in before thee, and thou love her in vain; and in the anguish of thy heart's disappointment, thou shalt quote the language of the great, and say, "sich is life;" and thy future lot be that of a poor, lonely, despised and comfortless bachelor. A new Commandment give I unto thee – if thou hast a wife and little ones, that thou lovest dearer than thy life, – that thou keep them continually before thee, to cheer and urge thee onward until thou canst say, "I have enough – God bless them – I will return." Then as thou journiest towards thy much loved home with open arms shall they come forth to welcome thee, and falling upon thy neck weep tears of unutterable joy that thou art come; then in the fullness of thy heart's gratitude, thou shalt kneel together before thy Heavenly Father, to thank Him for thy safe return. AMEN – So mote it be.

— FORTY-NINE ¤

James H. Hutchings, THE MINER'S TEN COMMANDMENTS (San Francisco, 1853)

"Perhaps no song of the gold days quite equalled 'The California Emigrant' in wide-spread popularity. This song, which later found many imitators, came from Salem, Massachusetts, with the bark ELIZA. Following is a favorite version set to the tune, 'Oh! Susannah!' by 'One of 'Em'":
(From Rockwell Hunt: CALIFORNIA AND CALIFORNIANS, Vol. II, pp. 164-165.)

"I come from Salem City,
       With my wash bowl on my knee;
I'm going to California
       The gold dust for to see.
It rained all night, the day I left,
       The weather it was dry,
The sun so hot I froze to death –
       Oh! brothers! don't you cry!

       O! California!
       That's the land for me,
       I'm going to Sacramento,
       With my wash bowl on my knee!

I jumped aboard the 'liza ship,
       And traveled on the sea,
And everytime I thought of home,
       I wished it wasn't me!
The vessel reared like my horse
       That had of oats a wealth;
It found it couldn't throw me, so
       I thought I'd throw myself!

I thought of all the pleasant times
       We've had together here;
I thought I ort to cry a bit,
       But couldn't find a tear.
The pilot bread was in my mouth,
       The golddust in my eye,
And though I'm going far away,
       Dear brothers, don't you cry!

I soon shall be in Francisco,
       And then I'll look around,
And when I see the gold lumps there,
       I'll pick them off the ground.
I'll scrape the mountains clean, my boys,
       I'll drain the rivers dry,
A 'pocket full of rocks' bring home –
       So brothers, don't you cry!

       Oh! California!
       That's the land for me!
       I'm going to Sacramento,
       With my wash bowl on my knee!" ▢

SUTTER'S MILL, COLOMA STATE PARK
Beulah Macdonald, Rosalie Slater, Verna Hall, Dorothy Dimmick
Picture taken by Walter Dimmick

Dorothy Dimmick, near Sutter's Mill with
"Giant" Hydraulic Nozzle used in hydraulic gold mining

MARIANO GUADALUPE VALLEJO'S REPORT

ON THE DERIVATION AND DEFINITION OF THE NAMES OF

THE SEVERAL COUNTIES OF CALIFORNIA

From: JOURNAL OF THE SENATE OF THE STATE OF CALIFORNIA
AT THEIR FIRST SESSION BEGUN AND HELD AT
PUEBLO DE SAN JOSE, ON THE
FIFTEENTH DAY OF DECEMBER, 1849.

[Y.]

Report of Mr. Vallejó, on the Derivation and Definition of the Names of the several Counties of California.

IN SENATE.

April 10, 1850.

TO THE SENATE OF THE STATE OF CALIFORNIA:

The Select Committee appointed by your honorable body in the latter part of January last, "to report to the Senate the derivation and definition of the names of the several Counties of the State," as established by the bill, entitled "An Act subdividing the State into Counties, and establishing the Seats of Justice therein," would

RESPECTFULLY REPORT:

That at the time of the appointment of the Committee the said bill had passed one branch of the Legislature only, nor did the same receive the approval of the Governor until the 18th day of February last. Upon the same day, however, another bill was introduced into the Senate, amendatory of no less than twelve sections of said Act; and shortly afterwards, another amendatory bill to the same Act was introduced into the lower branch of the Legislature. By the provisions of these two amendatory bills, a number of new Counties were created, the names of others changed, and the original bill materially altered in many particulars. As it was intended that the Report of the Committee thus appointed should contain the derivation and definition of the names of the Counties as created by law, they could not perfect their labors until these amendatory bills had been finally acted upon, and the names of the various Counties and their respective boundaries definitively settled. The last mentioned bill was not approved until the

5th instant, and consequently, but very little time has been allowed to your Committee to finish their labors and to prepare this Report.

Your Committee must also state that they have labored under great disadvantages in preparing their Report, from the absence of all books of reference on the subject committed to them. A resolution was adopted in your honorable body, directing the Secretary to procure certain works on the early history of California, and which, could they have been procured, would materially have assisted your Committee in the discharge of their duties. But the Secretary was unable to obtain them, and your Committee have been compelled to depend almost entirely upon recollection and upon oral information in the preparation of the following Report.

Your Committee would also ask the indulgence of the Senate for having introduced under the name of some of the Counties anecdotes and incidents of a personal character not properly belonging to "the derivation and definition" of the names of those Counties. But the circumstances mentioned have become so well known in those Counties, and some of them are so intimately connected with the family history of the compiler of this Report, that they have been permitted to find a place therein.

With these remarks, your Committee would most respectfully submit the following Report.

M. G. VALLEJO, Chairman.

April 15, 1850.

Report from the Select Committee on the Derivation and Definition of the Names of the several Counties of the State of California, &c.

SAN DIEGO.—This county (St. James) derives its name from its present chief town, named after the harbor, which is only three miles distant therefrom. This excellent harbor was discovered and so named by Sebastian Vizcayno, Admiral of the Spanish Royal Squadron, in the year 1603; and in 1768 His Catholic Majesty, by royal decree, determined upon its exploration and settlement. José Galvez, Royal Commissioner (Visitador General) of New Spain, was consequently intrusted with the undertaking; and for the purpose of successfully carrying it through, two expeditions were fitted out—one by land, the other by water; the latter was carried out in the San Carlos, Principe, and San José, commanded by Vicente Villa, two of which vessels having reached their destination respectively on the 11th of April and on the 1st of May, 1769, whilst the fate of the third (San José) still remains unknown. The land expedition was divided into two parts, the first being commanded by Fernando Rivera y Moncada, and the second by Captain Gaspar de Portala, Governor of the Province. The first division reached its destination on the 14th of May of said year 1769, and there found the two above-mentioned vessels at anchor. On the 1st of July the second division also arrived safely; and on the 16th of the same month and year, the land having been taken possession of with the accustomed formalities in the name of His Catholic Majesty, the establishment of the Mission of San Diego was at once started under the direction of the Rev. Father Junipero Serra—this being the first civilized settlement founded in the extensive and beautiful country known as Upper California.

San Diego presents an arid appearance, but it possesses nevertheless a pleasant and luxurious climate, with a clear, blue sky, enhanced by the sublime view of the Pacific Ocean.

There are no building materials or timber in its vicinity, but its water is of the best that is known in the country. It abounds in copper mines, whilst it produces the best olives and Indian pears; and although its vineyards have not increased in number, yet the fruit they bear is certainly of the very best quality which California yields.

Notwithstanding the departure of many families from San Diego, no part of the country maintains so high a claim for the amiable and sociable qualities of the fairer portion of its inhabitants. Here, indeed, the grace of person and amiability of disposition of the fair sex have attracted the young men of the North, and caused many of them to be led captive to the altar of Hymen, thus contributing to their moral subjection to the fair Dieguinas in the latters' native place, to whom the writer cannot but tender a tribute of admiration and respect.

ANGELES.—This County derives its name from the City of Los Angeles, which was founded in the latter part of the year 1781, by order of the viceroy of New Spain, Bailio Frey Antonio Bucareli y Ursua,

and is situated on the right bank of the "Porciuncula" river, which copiously waters the highly fertile plains whereon the city stands. Invited by the genial climate, the inhabitants have converted a large portion of this plain into a delightful garden, which is covered with all sorts of native fruit trees, but especially the vine, which is cultivated with care and extraordinary success.

This beautiful and extensive valley, famous for its excellent wines and liquors, contains within its limits the ex-Missions of San Juan Capistrano, San Gabriel, and San Fernando, which, to within the last few years, constituted the best and richest establishments of the kind. In 1832, including the environs, they numbered very nearly half a million head of cattle.

From the reasons above mentioned, as well as from its extent and natural advantages, the County of Los Angeles is destined to become the most populous of any in the South, and doubtless many men of business, both public and mercantile, tired of their avocations, will retire there to enjoy a life of Angels.

The white population of the County is from 12,000 to 15,000.

SANTA BARBARA.—There being a distance of more than five hundred miles between the military posts of San Diego and Monterey, and the Missions of San Antonio, San Luis Obispo, San Buenaventura, San Gabriel, and San Juan Capistrano, being situated in this intervening space, the Governor deemed it advisable, for the protection of these Missions, to establish another post or "presidio" at some suitable point somewhere in their vicinity; with this object in view, and with the requisite troops, and accompanied by the Rev. Presiding Father Junipero Serra, he bent his steps towards these Missions, until reaching a valley of delightful view and rich verdancy, in April, 1782, where the troops were stationed, and the new "presidio" called "Santa Barbara," which is the oldest and principal town of that immediate section of country. Hence the name of the County.

SAN LUIS OBISPO.—This County takes its name from its principal town, which is the so called Mission, founded on the 1st of September, 1772, by the Rev. Fathers Junipero Serra and José Cavaller, in the fertile and beautiful hollow named "Bears' Glen," by the troops of Monterey on the same day and year, from having there killed a number of bears, which, being cut up and dried, supplied them with meat for months. There is not in California a settlement that was more willingly and benignly received by the aborigines than the Mission of San Luis Obispo; indeed there was no reason for any other reception on the part of the Indians, since they were generously treated by the whites, and received from them the beneficial effects of their calling and the desirable extermination of dangerous wild beasts.

The following circumstance, which happened during the first months of the foundation of San Luis Obispo, is insignificant in itself, but the writer cannot but dwell upon it for a moment with the most tender feelings of the heart.

As a matter of course at that period, few families had as yet migrated to this country, and the female sex was an oasis in the desert. The writer's father was one of the many who emigrated here in bachelorship, and while sojourning in San Luis Obispo he unexpectedly met with a lady who was in travail, and about to bring a new being into the world; and as there was no one, save her husband, to assist her, he acted as holder (tenedor). The lady was safely delivered of a girl, whereupon the holder (then a young man) solicited the hand of the parents the hand of their child, and a formal agreement ensued between the parties, conditioned that if at mature age the girl should willingly consent to the union, the ceremony would be duly performed. . . . Time rolled by, and year after year transpired, until the *muchacha* had reached her fourteenth year, when the marriage took place, and the offspring of that union has now the honor to present his readers with this short biographical sketch.

MONTEREY.—This name is composed of the words monte and rey, and literally means "king of forests." The harbor of Monterey was discovered in 1603, by Admiral Sebastian Vizcayno, and so named in honor of Count Monterey, as well as from the neighboring forest of massive pines and other trees.

On being informed of this discovery, the King of Spain, at the instance of the Marquis of Croix, Viceroy of Mexico, and José Galvez, Most Illustrious Royal Commissioner, ordered a second naval expedition to act in concert with a land expedition, with a view to take possession of the harbor. The latter expedition, commanded by Captain Rivera y Moncada, reached its destination on the 23d of May; the former,

commanded by Captain Juan Perez, on the 31st May, 1770, when the banner of Spain was unfurled in token of possession.

Monterey has always been the residence of the superior authorities as the capital of Upper California. Since its foundation, fourteen duly appointed Governors of Upper California have discharged the duties of that office, viz Fages, Borica, Arrilaga, Arguillo 1st, Sola, Arguillo 2d, Echeandia, Victoria, Figueroa, Chico, Carillo, Alvarado, Micheltorena, and Pico.

The forest of Monterey, viewed from the bay, presents the most picturesque appearance imaginable. The surrounding hills of the city, crowned with tall pines and clothed in perpetual verdure, excite in the stranger a feeling at once of surprise and sympathy for the place. The native, as well as the foreign residents, are in constant admiration of it—at least such is the feeling of the writer, whenever he has the honor of being there,—his native place. On occasions like those, how fondly he recollects all the scenes of his childhood! Those of Monterey, born since the year 1807, to you this sincere sentiment of gratitude is addressed! The City of Monterey contains from 1500 to 2000 inhabitants.

In October, 1842, the American colors were hoisted there by Commodore Jones; 'tis said, through pretended mistake,—but he lowered them at the end of forty-eight hours. On the 7th of July, 1846, they were again unfolded to the breeze of Monterey by Commodore Sloate, and if the act was then done also through a convenient mistake, is a question of "*quien sabe*."

SANTA CRUZ.—The name of this County signifies "holy cross." The word cross, mystically speaking, is derived from the gibbet, which the Greeks, Romans, and other nations used to erect in that form, for the purpose of executing guilty slaves or persons of low condition. After the crucifixion of Christ the cross was sanctified, and has, since that period, been the distinguishing sign of the Christian religion.

The County of Santa Cruz is probably the richest in the State, as regards timber and irrigated soil. The mission of Santa Cruz, from which the County derives its name, was secularized in 1834, and has now a growing population. It is situated at the north of the bay of Monterey, and possesses an anchorage. Three vessels of ordinary size have been launched there.

SAN FRANCISCO.—The name of this County is famous throughout the Catholic world as being that of the creator of the religious order of the Franciscans in Europe and America, in whose name the mission of San Francisco de Asis (Dolores) was established in the year 1776, under the immediate superintendence of the Reverend Franciscan Father Junipero de Serra. In the same year and in the name of H. Catholic Majesty, the harbor of San Francisco was taken possession of, and a fort or a redoubt erected with the same name, which it still retains. The bay is also called San Francisco, and lately it was given to the town of Yerba Buena, by the municipal authorities of that place, doubtless so to harmonize the three places (distant one league from another, and forming a triangle), that they may amicably respond to the same name when the astounding activity and rapid growth of one will have united all three into an immense commercial city. In 1836 there were only two houses in San Francisco,—one belonging to Capt. Richardson, the other to J. P. Leese,—and up to 1846 the place had made little progress. In 1848, however, it received so wonderful an impulse from the discovery of the gold mines in the Sierra Nevada, that it can be said, San Francisco is an enchanted or magical city, built by spirits such as are spoken of in the Arabian Nights.

The town now contains a fluctuating population of from 20,000 to 40,000 inhabitants, made up in the short space of two years. The bay is large enough to accommodate the naval and commercial fleets of the world; there are now on its broad, magnificent bosom, five hundred vessels, and more than two thousand other craft, steamboats, scows, &c, actually engaged in all the ramifications of trade. San Francisco possesses theatres and good substantial wharves; it is the starting point of navigation to the Sacramento and San Joaquin rivers and their tributaries, which embrace an extent of two hundred leagues; it is the present seat of the Supreme Court of California, and the residence of the Collector of Customs, wherein more than two millions of dollars have been collected within two years.

SANTA CLARA.—According to the Roman Book of Martyrs or Martyrology, as Hortalana, the pious mother of Santa Clara, was once kneeling before a crucifix, praying earnestly that, being with child, she might be happily delivered, she heard a voice whispering, "Fear not, woman, thou wilt safely bring forth," whereupon a brilliant light

suddenly illumined the place, and the mother, inspired by the mysterious prediction, baptized her child Clara, which is the feminine of clear or bright. Clara was afterwards sanctified on account of her many eminent virtues, and accordingly venerated by the Catholics in all Roman Catholic churches.

The mission of Santa Clara, from which the County derives its name, was founded on the 12th day of January, 1777. The country is fertile, and abounds in timber and water, but particularly in quicksilver. Its inhabitants declare it to be the most advantageously situated for a large and flourishing city. Its chief town is the Pueblo of San José, the permanent seat of government until removed by law, as prescribed by the Constitution. Quien sabe?

CONTRA COSTA.—This name signifies "opposite coast," and the County is so called from its situation opposite San Francisco, in an easterly direction. It is, undoubtedly, one of the most fertile Counties in the State, possessing rich agricultural lands, which embrace an interior coast of thirty leagues, extending in the bays of Santa Clara, San Francisco, and San Pablo, the straits of Carquines, the bay of Suisun, and the San Joaquin river; a circumstance which, united to its mild climate, will render it very important. The Pueblo of Martinez is its chief town, and "New York of the Pacific," as well as other towns on the shores of the San Pablo and San Joaquin, will also very soon effectually contribute to its importance.

"Mount Diablo," which occupies a conspicuous place in modern maps, is in the centre of this County. It was intended so to call the County, but both branches of the Legislature, after warm debates on the subject (the representatives of the County opposing the proposed name), resolved upon the less profane name of "Contra Costa." The following is the history of "Mount Diablo" (Mount Devil): In 1806 a military expedition from San Francisco marched against the tribe "Bolgones," who were encamped at the foot of the Mount; the Indians were prepared to receive the expedition, and a hot engagement ensued in the large hollow fronting the western side of the Mount. As the victory was about to be decided in favor of the Indians, an unknown personage, decorated with the most extraordinary plumage, and making divers movements, suddenly appeared near the combatants. The Indians were victorious, and the incognito (Puy) departed towards the Mount.

The defeated soldiers, on ascertaining that the spirit went through the same ceremony daily and at all hours, named the mount "Diablo," in allusion to its mysterious inhabitant, that continued thus to make his strange appearance, until the tribe was subdued by the troops in command of Lieut. Gabriel Moraga, in a second campaign of the same year. In the aboriginal tongue "Puy" signifies Evil Spirit; in Spanish it means Diablo, and doubtless it signifies Devil in the Anglo-American language.

MARIN.—This is the name of the great chief of the tribe Licatiut, and the other tribes that inhabited this County and that of Sonoma. In Spanish "Licatiut" signifies "Arruzon," a favorite root or vegetable of these Indians, of which they made plentiful supplies to be used on great festival occasions. It affords them nourishment in great abundance in the valley of "Petaluma," their usual encampment. In the year 1815 or 1816 a military expedition proceeded to explore the country north of the bay of San Francisco, and on returning by the Petaluma valley an engagement ensued with Marin, in which he was made prisoner and conducted to the station of San Francisco, from which he escaped, and again reaching Petaluma, he united his scattered forces, and thenceforward dedicated his most strenuous efforts to harass the troops in their hostile incursions into that part of the country. He carried on hostilities until he was so closely pursued as to be compelled to take refuge in the Marin isles, situate at the mouth of the inlet San Rafael, so named from this circumstance. He there defended himself for some time, but was again taken captive to St. Francisco in 1824; whence being set at liberty, he retired to the mission of San Rafael, and there died in 1834.

SONOMA.—The name of this County is an Indian word, signifying "Valley of the Moon," by which the aborigines designated the valley wherein the town of that name is situated.

The tribe occupying this valley was called Chocuyen; but in 1824, on the arrival there of the first expedition for the purpose of establishing a mission, the name of "Sonoma" having been given to their chief by the paternal minister, Jose Altimira, the Chocuyenes then adopted the same, which they still retain. This, as well as the other tribes who occupied the tract which now composes the Counties of Sonoma and Marin, were dependent on a great chief who bore the heathen name of Marin de Licatiut, as mentioned in the history of the County of that name.

Sonoma is the most beautiful and picturesque valley in Upper California; and from its topographical situation, fronting the bay of San Pablo, from its delightful climate, fertile soil, abundant timber of all kinds close by, and from its pure and sweet waters, it is destined very soon to become one of the most populous parts of that valuable section of country. There are hot springs in its vicinity, which, from their medicinal virtues, may in future rival those of Arkansas.

Sonoma is at present the residence of the commander-in-chief of the western division of the army in California and Oregon.

In the Pueblo de Sonoma, in fine, there occurred an incident which will render the town celebrated in the history of the country, to wit. On the 14th day of June (of perpetual memory) a certain personage ordered a certain flag to be there hoisted, on whose white surface was conspicuously to be seen a certain animal; after other certain personages had taken the place by surprise, they took a certain personage prisoner to a certain fort, on the eastern bank of a certain river, in which they locked him for two months; during which he was overtaken by a certain disease which prevails there yearly, and from which he was set at liberty very nearly on the point or on the eve of settling accounts with a third personage, whose emblematic figure throughout the world is that of a skeleton armed with a scythe in his right hand.

SOLANO.—This is the second name of the celebrated missionary Francisco Solano, and was also borne by the great chief of the tribes originally denominated "Suisunes," and scattered over the western side of the river Jesus Maria (now Sacramento). The residence of this chief was the valley of Suisun, which is bounded by the hill near Suscol. Before receiving the baptismal name of Solano, the chief was called "Sem-yeto," which signifies the "brave or fierce hand."

In 1817 a military expedition (under command of Lieut. Jose Sanchez, and by order of the commandant of San Francisco, Jose Arguello), crossed the Straits of Carquines (on rafts made of rushes, as there were no ferries or regular boats in those days), for the double purpose of exploring the country and reducing it to Christianity. On crossing the river they were attacked by the Suisun tribe, then headed by their chief, Malaca, who caused them considerable loss; the Indians fought bravely and to the utmost extreme, but they were in turn attacked with such force and perseverance as to oblige them to retreat to their rancheria; where, being still hotly pursued and believing their fate sealed, these unfortunate people, incited by their chief, set fire to their own rush-built huts and perished in the flames with their families. The soldiers endeavored to stay their desperate resolution, in order to save the women and children; but even these preferred this doom to that which awaited them from the hands of their enemies. Thus perished this chief, and thus was his hearth and the home of his people destroyed.

The town of Benicia, situate in this County, is rapidly increasing in size and importance, and will soon rival the other towns that encircle the bay of San Francisco. The American squadron is stationed here, and many trading vessels lie at anchor. Here is the only passage to the interior; consequently there is, perhaps, no point from which the active trade of the bay can be better observed. There is in front of the town a bank or promontory extending out one mile, which precludes the necessity of wharves.

YOLO.—A corruption of the Indian word "Yoloy," signifying a place abounding with rushes (tular), with which the Indians composed the term "Toloytoy," Rushtown (Pueblo del Tule), situated on the western shore of the river Sacramento. The tribe occupying this Pueblo derived its name therefrom, and were the subjects of a great chief, who also ruled various other tribes with absolute sway. All these tribes were encamped on the western banks of the Sacramento and its tributaries. The Christian name of the chief was F. Solano, and his usual residence Sonoma. In 1835, Motti, captain of the Yoloy tribe, rebelled against the superior chief, and being unsuccessfully pursued, Solano applied to the commandant of Sonoma for assistance, pursued the tribe once more, and reduced it to submission. The rebellious leader was ordered to Sonoma, where he remained until the tribe and chief returned to their former hearths in 1846.

NAPA.—The name of the tribe who occupied the valley of the same name. The meaning of the word is not ascertained. Napa valley is fertile and beautiful in the extreme, possesses a very mild climate, and abounds throughout with timber of all kinds. The County, at the extreme north, contains the highlands of Mayacmas, famous as being the encampment of the Napa tribe, one of the bravest in California.

They greatly harassed the frontier posts, and were very numerous up to the year 1838, when they were mostly carried off by the small-pox. Napa city, situated on the stream that crosses the valley, will soon be a flourishing town; it is fifteen miles distant from the entrance of Napa bay. The creation of this County is attributable to the constant efforts of Capt. J. Brackett, member of the Assembly from the district of Sonoma. The writer is impressed with the belief that the subdivision is premature and will affect the interests of the people.

MENDOCINO.—In the year 1535 Antonio de Mendoza, first Viceroy of New Spain, appointed by the Emperor, arrived at the city of Mexico, fourteen years after its conquest or surrender, and ordered a survey of the coast of California, wherein Cape Mendocino was discovered, and so called in honor of the Viceroy. Mendocino, from which the County derives its name, is the patronymic of Mendoza.

SACRAMENTO.—Signifies Sacrament, or Lord's Supper. The streams known as Feather and Sacramento rivers, were first respectively named by Lieutenant Moraga "Sacramento" and "Jesus Maria;" but the latter now assumes the name of Sacramento, whilst the former is called Feather. Sacramento is the principal river in all that section of country, and gives name to the County. Several towns are springing up, but the chief one of the county is Sacramento City, situated on the eastern bank of the Sacramento. This rapidly growing and flourishing town, containing a permanent population of twelve thousand inhabitants, has sprung up in the short space of a year. It contains, besides, multitudes of transient residents, constantly going to and from the "Placeres;" steamboats and numerous vessels of light and heavy draught are safely moored immediately abreast of the town.

EL DORADO.—The far famed fabulous region of genial clime and never-fading verdure, where gold and precious stones are as common as rocks and pebbles, where wines gently flow from fountains, where wheat spontaneously grows overtopped with tiny loaves of bread, and pigeons fly about all ready roasted, where nature has converted the rudest things into harmony of shape and appearance, and where, in fine, a creature of the genus *mulier*, full of sympathy and grace, trips about in natural loveliness, the most beautiful of God's creations. Francis Orellana, a

present Legislature, in compliance with the wishes of the delegates from that portion of the State. It contains ten thousand inhabitants.

BUTTE.—This is purely a French word, signifying hill or mound of earth. The high hills or peaks situated in the valley of the Sacramento, and seen at a great distance, were so named by a detachment of hunters, headed by Michael Laframbeau, from the Hudson Bay Company at Columbia river, who visited this country in search of beaver in the year 1829. Nine years previous to this period they were denominated peaks (picachos) by Captain Luis A. Arguello, who headed an expedition to the Columbia river by order of the Governor of the Province. This County contains these peaks, and takes their name.

COLUSE.—Is purely an Indian word, being the original name of a numerous tribe on the western side of the Sacramento river; its meaning is not ascertained. The so called County is one of the new Counties created by the first Legislature of the State.

SHASTA.—Is the name of the tribe residing at the foot of the height or mountain, remarkable as being considerably higher than the range, and encircling the source of the Sacramento river. Upon the subdivision of the State into Counties, Mr. Walthall, member of Assembly of the delegation from the district of Sacramento, proposed this name for the County, and it was adopted by the Legislature. The mountain has likewise been so named.

TRINIDAD.—Signifies trinity. The Roman Catholics annually celebrate a certain Sunday in honor of the Most Holy Trinity. This festival has been observed since the year 1260, when it was so regulated by the Council of Arlez.

Trinity bay was so called from having been discovered on the anniversary of this festival, June 11, 1775, by the second naval exploring expedition, consisting of a frigate in command of Captain Bruno Ezeta, and a sloop commanded by Juan de la Quadra y Bodega. Hence the name of the County. The bay has been newly surveyed and found accessible. Since last January, rich gold "placeres" have been discovered there; and the surrounding fertile country, formerly known as New Albion, is now being settled.

companion of Pizarro first spread the account of the supposed existence of this province in South America.

As it is universally known how and when the discovery was made that has caused the star of the west to spring up as if by magic, given it the appropriate epithet of "golden," and will eventually revolutionize the world, more than the passing remark that gold was first discovered in this County at Sutter's mill, is here deemed unnecessary. The County derives its name from this circumstance.

SUTTER.—This County is named after Captain John Augustus Sutter, from Switzerland, and formerly a military officer under Charles X. He emigrated to this country in the latter part of the year 1839, for the purpose of forming a colony. With this object in view, he petitioned the Mexican Government for a grant of land, which he obtained, subject to the regulations prescribed by law. He then fixed the site of the colony on the eastern side of the Sacramento river, between its tributaries, known as the American Fork and Cosumnes, and named it New Helvetia. To inspire confidence in his colonists, as well as to protect them against the sudden attacks of the aborigines, who were very numerous at that period, or against any surprise whatsoever from any other power, he built a fort and manned it with several pieces of artillery. The building is well known as Sutter's Fort. Captain Sutter is the oldest settler in the valley of the rushes (valle de los tulares) on the banks of the Sacramento. His known enterprise, openness, and urbanity of manners, and characteristic hospitality towards all who approached his colony, have commanded public respect and gained for him the personal regard of friends. The former and present inhabitants of California, ever remembering the name of Sutter, as now borne by the County, will transmit it to future generations and thus immortalize it.

YUBA.—A corruption of the word uba, which, when pronounced in English, produces the sound Yuba. This pronunciation has been lately so generally adopted that the original word is now obsolete.

Yuba river is the chief tributary of Feather river, and was called Uba by an exploring expedition in 1824, from the immense quantities of vines that shaded its banks and the neighborhood, overloaded with wild grapes (properly called "uvas silvestres" in Spanish). The County which derives its name from the aforesaid river, was created by the

MEMORIAL.

To the Honorable the Senate and House of Representatives of the United States of America in Congress assembled:

The undersigned, Senators and Representatives elect from the State of California, have the honor, in pursuance of a requirement in the Constitution recently adopted by her people for her government as a State, to lay before your honorable bodies certified copies of said Constitution, together with their credentials, and to request "in the name of the people of California, the admission of the State of California into the American Union."

In performing this duty, the undersigned deem it but just to state that they have learned with astonishment and sincere regret, since their arrival in the City of Washington, of the existence of an organized, respectable, and talented opposition to the admission of the new State which they have the distinguished honor to represent. This opposition is so unexpected, so important in numbers and ability, and so decided in its sectional character, that they feel they should do injustice to their constituents, to the cause of good government, and to the progressive advance of freedom and civilization, did they not at least attempt an answer to the many arguments urged against the admission of California.

The undersigned, therefore, fully aware that much ignorance, misapprehension, and misconception exists in the public mind of the Atlantic States relative to their country, its citizens, and the proceedings by which a State Government has been recently formed there, and deeply sorrowful that false charges should have been made against the character, intelligence, and virtue of their constituents, have deemed it obligatory upon them, in presenting in a formal manner the request of the State of California for admission into the American Union, that they should, by a narration of facts, at once and forever silence those who have disregarded the obligations of courtesy and all the rules of justice, by ungenerous insinuations, unfair deductions, false premises, and unwarranted conclusions. They believe that in so doing they will carry out the wishes of those who have commissioned them, and contribute to the true history of this important political era; while they ardently desire and hope that they may thereby be enabled to exert a happy influence in allaying that intense excitement which now menaces the perpetuity of the Republic, and all the dearest hopes of freedom.

In pursuance of this determination, the undersigned have thought it proper to present, as briefly as possible, an outline of the history of the country, from its conquest by the American forces to the adoption of her present Constitution and the erection of a State Government. In order to do this satisfactorily, it is not believed to be necessary to dwell at length upon the details of the early history, but simply to state that the first emigration of Americans into California in any considerable numbers, occurred during the summer and fall of the year 1845. This emigration, which is believed not to have exceeded 600 persons, constituted the basis from which sprung the train of causes which led to the ultimate subjugation of the country. The particulars of those events are presumed to be familiar to the members of each of your honorable bodies, and generally understood by the public at large, and the undersigned therefore pass over the history of the revolutionary and military operations which resulted in the establishment of Col. Richard B. Mason as the military, and *ex officio* civil, Governor of the Department of Upper California, on the 31st day of May, 1847.

At that time the American forces held possession of the whole of what was then denominated Upper California, and were posted at different points, in small detachments, from Sutter's Fort in the north to the town of San Diego in the south. The Pacific squadron of the Navy of the United States, under the command of Commodore Shubrick, was then upon the coast, and its vessels were at anchor in the different harbors of the country. The country was quiet, and the population orderly, industrious, intelligent, and enterprising. From the time that the united forces of American emigrant volunteers under Col. Fremont, and the United States naval forces under Commodore Sloat had raised the American standard throughout the country, the supreme authorities had collected in all the ports of California a revenue from imports. This, with other slight cases of individual severity and infringement by the military and naval commandants during the war, upon what was regarded by the American emigrants as the inherent rights of the citizen, together with a natural jealousy of military rule, which is believed to be a national characteristic, could not fail to make the military authority, which had now devolved upon Col. Mason, a source of suspicion, disagreement, and discontent. This was more particularly the case in regard to the American inhabitants, who had now become quite numerous by continued arrivals of emigrants, both by sea and land; but the feeling was also participated in, to a great extent, by the native citizens of the country, who were further influenced by the chagrin, hatred, and uncertainty which is sure to fill the breasts of a subjugated but courageous people.

Even at this early day the subject of the establishment of a *Civil Territorial Government* had found advocates; but as the war was not yet ended, and as the country could not be regarded in any other light than that of a military conquest, and as such, subject to the government of the military power, and as the majority of the people felt that self-reliance which convinced them there was little danger of any serious attempt at usurpation on the part of the military authority, the matter was not seriously pressed, though generally approved. Nevertheless, it was becoming daily more and more a pervading sentiment, that the civil government, as then organized under the almost obsolete laws of Mexico, was totally inadequate to the changed circumstances of the country; and, as the undersigned believe, none were more fully convinced of that fact, than the executive officers of that Government. This sentiment finally became general; and the errors and difficulties that every day occurred, from the ignorance of Mexican law, or its inapplicability, induced the Governor to make a compilation and translation of all such Mexican regulations as could be found in the archives of the State Department at Monterey, with such additions as were thought advisable and necessary. These were printed in both the English and Spanish languages; but, unfortunately for the country, they were not quite ready for publication at the time news of peace reached California, and the Governor, therefore, never proclaimed nor issued them.

In the month of October, 1847, the Military Contribution Tariff, promulgated by the then President of the United States, was established in the ports of California. The custom-houses, which theretofore had remained in the hands of citizens who accounted to the Military Governor, or the Commodore of the Pacific Squadron, were now filled by army or navy officers. This tariff was justly but rigorously enforced; and, though its provisions bore so oppressively upon the country as to add slightly to the causes and feeling of discontent, no opposition was manifested. Indeed, during this whole time, although the evils and difficulties under which the country suffered were manifold, we believe no single instance can be found of unlawful or riotous resistance to the constituted authorities.

But the desire for a more congenial government went on steadily increasing in that portion of the country lying around and north of the district of San Francisco. To this feeling the arrival of the overland emigration in the fall of 1847 greatly contributed. In the meantime, the original citizens of California had become in a measure satisfied with their position, and as the conduct of the American officers and citizens was of a courteous and upright character they gradually became assured that there rights, property, and happiness were not likely to be destroyed by the conquerors. Still, a degree of solicitude and suspicion preyed upon the public mind. An uncertainty seemed to pervade the whole country, exercising a chilling and depressing effect upon its agricultural, commerce, mechanic arts, and general business relations. The military government had continued the collection of duties under the military contribution tariff, and as a parsimonious policy of expenditure was maintained, the whole circulating medium of the country was gradually locked up in the military chest. This exerted a paralyzing effect on the industrial and business pursuits of the whole community, and gave rise to complaints that the military power was taxing the people without allowing them a voice in the matter, and that at the same time they failed to give to the country a government in consonance with its wishes or commensurate to its wants; in other words, that after taxing the inhabitants of the country in contravention of all right, they committed the greater injustice of refusing or neglecting to expend the money so obtained in such a manner as would provide a government that would give protection to the citizen and security to his property. California, however, went on steadily increasing in population, wealth, industry and commercial and political importance.

Such was the condition of California in April, 1848. In that month was made the extraordinary discovery of the gold mines, and instantly the whole territory was in a blaze. The towns were deserted by their male population, and a complete cessation of the whole industrial pursuits of the country was the consequence. Commerce, agriculture, mechanical pursuits, professions—all were abandoned for the purpose of gathering the glittering treasures which lay buried in the ravines, the gorges, and the rivers of the Sierra Nevada. The productive industry of the country was annihilated in a day. In some instances the moral perceptions were blunted, and men left their families unprovided, and soldiers deserted their colors. The desire for gold was not regulated by any of the ordinary processes of reasoning, and such was the disastrous effect of the discovery of the precious ore upon the social, business, and political interests of the country, that the high hopes which the far-seeing and patriotic had entertained of the future progress and greatness of California, were dashed at once to the ground. A pall seemed to settle upon the country; and even the bewildered miners wondered as the result.

But the peculiar energy and the utilitarian predisposition of the American character could not long be diverted from its natural and accustomed channels, even by the glitter of gold. Commerce slowly revived, and mechanical and professional pursuits began to assume their wonted importance, as the novelty of gold digging was dispelled by a correct understanding of the difficult and laborious nature of the pursuit. The large emigration which was now pouring into the country from Oregon, Mexico, and the Sandwich Islands, though it added to the number of miners, contributed to the necessities which had made a diversion in favor of the sober pursuits of every day life, and a more healthy and staid condition of public opinion and business ensued.

310

At about this time (on the 7th of August, 1848) the news of peace between the republics of the United States and Mexico reached the country, and was communicated to the people in a proclamation by Governor Mason. This proclamation, after reciting so much of the treaty as applied to California, stated that the existing laws would remain in force, and the existing officers would administer them as heretofore ; and it did not fail to express the confident hope that the Congress of the United States, which was in session at the time of the ratification of the treaty, had already organised a Territorial Government, which might be expected to arrive at any moment. Governor Mason then abolished, in pursuance with treaty stipulations, the military contribution tariff ; but not deeming it advisable to abandon the collection of revenue entirely, and yet having no authority either in executive orders, law, or precedent, he declared the revenue laws of the United States in force throughout the Territory, appointed civilians to the post of collector, and received the duties into the military treasury of the department, under the distinctive appellation of the " civil fund of California."

There were those in the country at this time, and they were not few in numbers, who believed that it was the duty of Governor Mason, immediately after the reception of the news of peace, to have called upon the people to elect delegates to a Territorial Convention for the purpose of forming a *Civil Provisional Territorial Government* for California ; and that it was his duty, so soon as such form of government was ratified by the people of the Territory, to have delivered up to the appointed agent the powers he possessed as Civil Governor, and left to such appointee of the people the entire discharge of the duties appertaining to a civil Executive. It may be imagined then, that when, instead of doing this, the existing order of things was preserved and the United States revenue laws enforced, that great dissatisfaction ensued. To add to the general discontent, the daily arrival of large importations created so great a demand for coin with which to meet the custom house charges, that gold dust was depreciated so much in value as to be sold as low as seven dollars per ounce, at one time ; and finally such became the utter barrenness of the San Francisco money market, that the collector at that port was authorised to receive gold dust on deposit as collateral security for duties, at the rate of ten dollars per ounce. Other difficulties of a perplexing and serious character grew out of this sudden substitution of a new revenue system, by which foreign vessels were denied the privileges which they would have had under the military contribution tariff. But, suffice it to say, that again the public mind was disturbed and excited by taxation without representation, and by that falsely economical policy which continued to take money from the people without law, and yet would not appropriate the funds so obtained to the purpose of securing them a good government.

But the unsettled and unstable order of things which had ensued upon the discovery of the gold mines still existed ; and the dissatisfaction and discontent of the people, though quite general, failed, for this reason, to assume an organized or imposing form. The fact that four-fifths of the male population of the country were eagerly engaged in the mines, greatly contributed to this result, and the almost universal belief that the United States Congress had before its adjournment passed a law establishing a Territorial Government, satisfied the public mind that no action on its part was then necessary. So passed the summer and fall of 1848.

Upon the coming on of winter, the great majority of the miners returned to their homes in the towns. They came rich in gold dust ; but a single glance at the desolate and unthrifty appearance of the Territory convinced them that other pursuits than that of gold-digging must receive a proportion of their care and labor, if they wished to be really happy, and promote the true interests of the country. They felt, as all Americans feel, that the most important step they could take, and that most imperatively called for by the wants of the inhabitants, was the establishment of a stable system of government, which would command the respect and obedience of the people whose property it protected, and whose rights it preserved. Congress had adjourned without providing a Territorial Government, and the public had settled into the firm conviction that the *de facto* Government was radically defective and incapable of answering the public wants. The large increase in the emigration during the past year, the still greater prospective increase in the year to come, the increased wants which were daily growing from a rapidly rising and extending commerce, and the growing demands of an enterprising and progressive people, all required a new and compatible system of government. Recent murders, highway robberies, and other outrages in various portions of the country, had convinced the honest and the orderly that anarchy, misrule, and wrong were abroad in the land. For a moment doubt, fear, uncertainty and indecision seemed to paralyze the public energies ; but that love of order and justice which ever springs from the "still small voice," soon triumphed, and terrible indeed, was the retribution meted out to the offenders.

The opinions of the people, accelerated by the combined causes just enumerated, now, for the first time in the history of the country, assumed an organised form. On the 11th day of December 1848, a large meeting of the inhabitants of the district of San Jose was held at the town of that name, at which speeches were made, committees appointed, and resolutions unanimously adopted in favor of holding a convention for the purpose of forming a *Provisional Territorial Government*, to be put into immediate operation, and to remain in force until Congress should discharge its duty, and supersede it by a regular Territorial organization. The proceedings of this meeting were published and disseminated as rapidly as the means of communication would allow ; and its action met with the unanimous approval of the people of the northern and middle portions of California. On the 21st and 23d of December, 1848, two of the largest public meetings ever held in California convened at San Francisco, and unanimously declared their concurrence in the course of action recommended by the citizens of San Jose. On the 6th and 8th of January, 1849, meetings at Sacramento City were held concurring in the same purpose. In the district of Monterey a similar meeting was held on the 31st of January, 1849, and in the district of Sonoma a meeting of approval and concurrence was held on the 5th of February, 1849. These five districts elected delegates to the proposed convention, viz : The district of Sacramento 5, Sonoma 10, San Francisco 5, San Jose 3, Monterey 5. These districts comprised at that time more than three-fifths of the entire population of the country. But the five other districts, viz : San Joaquin in the north, and San Luis Obispo, Santa Barbara, Los Angelos, and San Diego in the south, failed to concur in this movement for the establishment of a Provisional Territorial Government. The reasons of this non-concurrence were substantially the following :

The meeting held at San Jose recommended that the Convention for forming a Provisional Government should assemble at San Jose, on the second Monday of January, 1849. The San Francisco meeting believing that day much too early to allow communication with the remote Districts—and deeming it of paramount importance that the whole Territory should be represented in the proposed Convention, recommended that it should meet on Monday, March 5. In this recommendation of the District of San Francisco the Districts of Sonoma and Sacramento concurred, as did tacitly the District of San Jose. The District of Monterey, also concurred therein, but constituted its elected Delegates a Committee to confer with the other Districts to obtain, if possible and advisable, a still further extension of the time of holding the Convention.

The Corresponding Committee appointed by the San Francisco meeting had taken great pains to spread the intelligence of the action of the people there and in San Jose, and to request that measures be adopted to promote the cause of Provisional Government in the surrounding Districts; but the inclemency of the weather and the impassable condition of the roads and streams in consequence of the severe winter rains, had, up to January 24, 1849, prevented all communication with the five Districts above named. The Committee received many letters and much verbal information from different sections, which finally decided them in issuing to the public on January 24, 1849, a recommendation "that the time for the proposed assembling of the Provisional Government Convention be changed from Monday, the 5th day of March, to Tuesday the 1st day of May, 1849."

As was to have been expected, this recommendation, though generally concurred in, and though the reasons by which it was supported were never attempted to be controverted, had a tendency, by creating an impression of uncertainty, to cool the ardor of those interested in the cause. In addition to this, the recent intelligence from the Atlantic coast had given some assurance that Congress would not again adjourn without the adoption of a Territorial Government for California, and the arrival of Gen. P. F. Smith, on the 28th day of February, at San Francisco, to assume the command of the Pacific Division of the U. S. Army, was considered a favorable omen of what might be expected from the action of the cabinet and the law-givers at Washington.

Notwithstanding all these obstacles, the cause of Provisional Government still progressed; and though it was now feared and foreseen that the attempt to assemble a Convention on the first of May would probably fail, yet twelve of the Delegates elected to that body met at San Francisco early in the month of March, 1849, and issued an address to the people of California. That address, after recounting the reasons which prevented the assembling of the Convention, as originally proposed, on the 5th of March, and after reasserting the truth, that the action of a Convention which did not consist of representatives from each and every district would not be likely to meet with approval or respect from the public at large, concluded with the suggestion that "new elections should be held in the several districts for delegates to meet in convention at Monterey, on the first Monday in August next ;" and that those delegates "should be vested with full power to frame a State Constitution to be submitted to the people of California ; and further staing their belief that the circumstances and wants of the country were "such as to requre the immediate formation of a State Constitution, and entitle us to a right to be admitted into that Union of sovereign States, which we trust will ever be 'distinct as the billows, but one as the ocean.'" There is no doubt that this was then the prevailing sentiment of the people of the Territory.

In order to provide for the immediate wants of their respective districts, the citizens of Sonoma and Sacramento had elected, early in the year 1849, District Legislative Assemblies. The district of San Francisco, in consequence of difficulties between their Alcalde and two Town Councils claiming jurisdiction, resorted to the same method, and elected a Legislative Assembly. These acts on the part of the people of the respective districts brought about various collisions between the people and the *de facto* government of which Gen. Riley, who arrived on the 13th of April, 1849, was now the head. It is not necessary for us to enter into details of these matters, further than to say that a very excited and bitter feeling of hostility to this *de facto* government was quite universal, and that this feeling was strengthened by the failure of Congress to pass a bill establishing a Territorial government in California, and the passage of a law for the collection of revenue. The intelligence of this failure to act in the one case, and action in the oth-

312

er, on the part of Congress, reached San Francisco on the 28th May, 1849, by the U. S. propeller Edith, which vessel had been despatched to Mazatlan by order of Gen. Smith, on the preceding 10th of April. No sooner was this intelligence disseminated throughout the country, than it became evident to all men that the political complexion which a great question had assumed in the Atlantic States had prevented Congress from establishing a Territorial government, or even authorizing the people of California to form a State government ; and there grew up at once a unanimous desire in the hearts of the citizens of the Territory, to adopt the only feasible scheme which promised them a government—that of a State organization. This sentiment daily gained ground until the beginning of June, 1849, when the Legislative Assembly of the District of San Francisco published an address to the people of California, asserting that they "believed it to be their duty to earnestly recommend to their fellow-citizens the propriety of electing at least twelve delegates from each district to attend a general convention to be held at the Puebla de San Jose on the third Monday in August next, for the purpose of organizing a government for the whole Territory of California ;" such "*conditional* or *temporary* State government to be put into operation at the earliest practicable moment" after "its ratification by the people," and "to become a *permanent* State government when admitted into the Union." This recomendation met with universal approval.

Simultaneous with this action on the part of the Legislative Assembly of the district of San Francisco, though without any knowledge thereof, Gov. Riley issued at Monterey, (130 miles distant,) on the 3d day of June, 1849, a proclamation recommending the election of delegates to a convention for forming a State Constitution, said body to convene at Monterey on the 1st day of September following. He also evinced a disposition, which had not been manifested before, to put in immediate, complete, and fair operation, the whole machinery of the *de facto* government, of which he claimed to be the head; he assured the people of his patriotic desire to accomplish his duty and their welfare by recommending them to elect all such officers as the existing laws authorized, whether it were provided that such officers should be elected by the people or appointed by the executive ; and he convinced them of his good faith by at once coming forward and appropriating the "civil fund of California," which had been collected upon the imports of the country without law or authority, to the payment of the current expenses of the *de facto* government, which he had determined to put fully into operation. Notwithstanding all this, however, the majority of the people of the Territory denied his right to issue a proclamation calling a convention, contending that in the default of the action of Congress, the right to pursue such a course was inherent in the people.

But the opposition of the people to the *de facto* government had sprung from patriotic motives and from experimental conviction that it was insufficient for the exigencies of the country. This opposition was confined in its public manifestations entirely to the American born population. The Californians proper, as a whole, had never participated in any of the popular exhibitions of discontent ; and the emigration that was now daily arriving in large numbers did not, of necessity, enter into the spirit of the grievances which were complained of by the older residents, nor espouse either side of a quarrel of which they could not distinctly comprehend the nature. All men, though, ardently desired a settled, Constitutional form of government ; and it became the duty of the patriotic to yield their prejudices and abstract opinions, and to unite in one common effort to promote the public good. Congress had abandoned the Territory to its own resources — had oppressed it by the passage of an unjust law—a large portion of its population were in determined and open hostility to the *de facto* government—petty governments had been established in several districts—and anarchy and civil discord impending over the land. It was a moment of uncertainty and fear for California ; but American patriotism and American love of law and order were superior to all other considerations, and the present and future prosperity of California was secured by a unanimous combination to form a State government

On the 7th of June, 1849, the citizens of San Jose, in a public meeting, concurred in the recommendations of Gen. Riley; and on the 11th of the same month the citizens of Monterey agreed thereto in a similar manner. On the 12th day of that month the largest mass meeting of the citizens of San Francisco ever held convened in Portsmouth square in that city. That meeting was addressed by Hon. T. Butler King, Wm. M. Gwin, Edward Gilbert, and other gentlemen ; but such was the excited state of feeling in that district that the meeting, by a direct vote, refused to concur in the recommendation of Gen. Riley's proclamation. A corresponding Committee was, however, appointed, which, on the 18th of June, in an address to the public, used the following language, viz :

"The Committee, not recognizing the least power, as matter of *right* in Brev. Brig. Gen. Riley to 'appoint' a time and place for the election of delegates and the assembling of the convention, yet as these matters are subordinate, and as the people of San Jose have, in public meeting, expressed their satisfaction with the times mentioned by Gen Riley, and as we are informed the districts below will accede to the same ; and as it is of the first importance that there be unanimity of action among the people of California in reference to the great leading object—the attempt to form a government for ourselves—we recommend to our fellow citizens of California the propriety, under existing circumstances, of acceding to the time and place mentioned by Gen. Riley in his proclamation, and acceded to by the people of other districts."

This is believed to have been the general sentiment.

In all the other districts of the Territory, public meetings of concurrence in Gen. Riley's proclamation were subsequently held. The election followed on the 1st of August, and the convention assembled at Monterey on the 1st of September, 1849.

The undersigned have not presumed to weary your patience by laying before you in full the proceedings and action of the public bodies to which they have made allusion ; nor have they thought it necessary to enter into a detail of minor particulars of difference and disagreement between the people and the *de facto* government. They, however, deem it their duty to assure you, that the persons who figured most conspicuously in the whole undertaking, enjoyed a high share of the public confidence and esteem ; and we believe that the best tribute to their worth and respectability is to be found in the fact that many of them were members of the convention which framed the Constitution, and now enjoy responsible and honorable positions under the government whose basis they so patriotically contributed to establish.

Such, in the opinion of the undersigned, is a brief and impartial history of the causes which have resulted in the formation of the present State government of California, and the presentation of her request for admission into the American Union. And the undersigned firmly and religiously believe that a perusal of the foregoing pages must lead irresistibly to the following conclusions, viz :

1. That a Territorial government, under the revisory power of Congress, would, so far from promoting the interests of California, so circumscribe its energies, prevent the development of its capacities, and impede its general advancement, as to be a source of discontent, difficulty, and ultimate ruin, either to the government or governed.

2. That the wonderful increase of the country in population, in wealth, and consequently in commercial, social, and political importance, renders imperatively necessary the adoption of such a system of measures as can only be enacted by a State Legislature and enforced by a State government.

3. That the neglect and oppression of the United States Congress, forced California to form a State government, if she desired to avoid civil strife and anarchy.

And, 4. That the people of that country did not adopt such form of government in obedience to dictation from the executive here, through Gen. Riley there ; but on the contrary, actually took the initiative in the movement, and only concurred in the suggestions of the *de facto* Governor as a matter of convenience, to save time, and with a patriotic resolution to merge all minor differences of opinion in one unanimous effort to avert impending ills and remedy existing evils.

Much misapprehension appears to have obtained in the Atlantic States relative to the question of slavery in California. The undersigned have no hesitation in saying that the provision in the Constitution excluding that institution, meets with the almost unanimous approval of that people. This unanimity is believed to result not so much from the prejudices against the system, which are quite general in the northern portion of the United States, as from a universal conviction that in no portion of California is the climate and soil of a character adapted to slave labor. Since the discovery of the mines, the feeling in opposition to the introduction of slavery is believed to have become, if possible, more unanimous than heretofore. The relation of master and slave has never existed in the country, and is there generally believed to be prohibited by Mexican law, consequently the original California population is utterly opposed to it. Slavery is a question little discussed in California, so settled appears the public mind relative thereto. Public meetings have scarcely ever considered it. The opinion put forward, that the decision of this question has been forestalled, has no foundation in truth. And no more conclusive proof of this can be found than the simple facts, that fifteen of the forty-eight members composing the convention which *unanimously* inserted the prohibtory clause in the Constitution, were from slaveholding States, while twelve were Californians proper, and twenty one northern men. Further than this, there is no doubt, that two-fifths of those who voted in favor of the Constitution were recent emigrants from slaveholding States, while it is known that many of the votes given against the instrument were so given in consequence of the failure of the messengers to distribute the printed copies in several mining localities. No debate upon the subject was had in the convention, though some "conversation" ensued upon a proposition to submit the provision to the people for a separate vote. This was suggested by northern men, and did not prevail.

Objections have been urged against the boundaries of California, as fixed by her Constitution. The convention which settled upon the proposed boundary, was engaged during three days in debate upon that subject. There were two parties, or rather two propositions : 1. To take in the whole of California as it existed when a department of Mexico ; but with a proviso that Congress and the State Legislature might limit the bounds of the State to the summit of the Sierra Nevada, and leaving it to Congress to establish Territorial governments over such portions of the country as it might see fit. 2. To divide the whole Territory on the 116th degree of west longitude, from the southern boundary of Oregon to the northern boundary of Mexico, that portion of said Territory lying west of the one hundred and sixteenth degree of West longitude, and between that line and the Pacific Ocean, to constitute the State of California. The opinion of the convention was so nearly divided between these two propositions, that both were supported by a majority at different times during the informal stages ; and on the final passage the present boundary was adopted as a

314

species of compromise. This question called out the most vehement and angry debate which was witnessed during the sitting of the convention. The project of fixing the southern boundary of the State on the parallel of 36° 30' was never entertained by that body. Indeed, when it is recollected that eleven of the delegates sitting in the convention, represented a large constituency south of that line, it is at once apparent that it would have been a most unjust and discourteous act to have listened to such a proposition, unless it came from them. The people of that southern portion of California most certainly did not wish, and probably never would consent to such a separation. In former years they constituted the great majority of the population—they have always been governed by the same laws—and they would be the last to sanction a division of California as they have always known it. In a political point of view, too, it would seem desirable that these original Mexican citizens should become as speedily as possible Americans in sentiment and language, and there certainly can be no more effectual mode of accomplishing this than by bringing them into that daily contact which an existence under the same laws and the same social, political, and commercial regulations must inevitably produce. In the extreme north, also, the adventurous miners had crossed the coast range, and penetrated to the head waters of the Trinity river, which finds its way through an unexplored and dangerous Indian country to the Pacific Ocean. As the abundance of gold found there rendered it probable that a large community would soon become permanently established in that region, the convention felt that it could not refuse them the benefits and protection of a government by circumscribing the limits of the State in that direction. The eastern boundary of the State, so far as explored and known, runs through a desert. A small portion of the eastern slope of the Sierra Nevada is said to be adapted to agricultural and grazing purposes, and as that country, when settled, must necessarily find an outlet across the mountains into the valleys of the Sacramento and San Joaquin Rivers, and as it could never have any natural connection with the country to the eastward of it, by reason of the great desert, it was thought advisable and proper to include that strip of territory within the bounds of the State. That portion of the State lying to the southward and eastward of the Sierra Nevada and the coast range, and between those mountains and the Colorado river, is believed to be an arid desert. So much as lies upon the usual emigrant trail from the Colorado to San Diego and that further north in the vicinity of the explorations of John Charles Fremont, is known to be of that character. The general impression therefore is, that that part of the Territory included in the State boundaries is of little or no value. The superficial area of the State of California, according to the boundaries prescribed in her Constitution, is 155,550 square miles, or 99,552,000 square acres, exclusive of the islands adjacent to her coast. A glance at the map prepared by order of the United States Senate, from the surveys of John C. Fremont and other authorities, upon which the above calculation is based, will at once satisfy all that the topographical characteristics of that country are peculiar and novel. Two great chains of mountains, the Sierra Nevada, and the coast range, traverse it in nearly its whole extent from north to south. The large valleys that lie between these two ranges, and the small lateral valleys that pierce their rugged sides in every direction, are the valuable arable portion of the land of California. Assuming then, that two-fourths of the whole superficial area of the State is covered by mountains, that another fourth is a desert waste, and we have left one fourth as useful for agricultural purposes, that is, 38,887½ square miles, or 24,888,000 square acres of arable and productive land. This estimate, in the opinion of the undersigned, is fully borne out by the topographical surveys of the country; but anxious as they are to avoid misstatement, they do not hesitate to assert their belief that it is quite apparent, after all due allowances, three-fifths of the whole Territory embraced in the State of California will never be susceptible of cultivation or useful to man. This, then, would give, as the remaining two-fifths, 62,220, square miles, or 39,820,800 square acres, which would constitute the sum total of valuable arable and grazing land embraced within the boundary fixed by the Constitution of the State of California, and distributed at intervals over the whole surface of the country, from its extreme northern to its extreme southern limit. The foregoing are believed to be substantially the reasons which led to the present proposed boundary of California.

The qualifications prescribed for voters by Gen. Riley's proclamation were carried out at the election of delegates to the convention. These qualifications were generally approved, and believed to be correct. By that proclamation, after requiring the voter to be twenty-one years of age and an actual resident of the district where he offered his vote, three classes of voters were declared eligible, viz: 1. American citizens; 2. Mexicans who had elected under the treaty to become American citizens; and 3. Mexican citizens who had been forced to leave their country in consequence of giving aid and succor to the American arms during the recent war. These requirements were faithfully complied with, beyond all doubt. Such would seem to be the undeniable fact, as no complaint was ever made of illegal voting.

Under the provision relative to the right of suffrage in the Constitution of California, white male American citizens twenty-one years of age, and white male citizens of Mexico of the same age, who had elected to become citizens of the United States under the treaty of peace, were permitted to vote, in the districts of their residence, upon the ratification of the Constitution, and for the various officers to be elected under it. No other persons were allowed to vote—no other persons did vote. The allegation, therefore, that foreigners, aliens, and adventurers adopted the Constitution, of California is not warranted by facts. That Constitution was ratified by over 12,000 votes in its favor, of which, it is firmly believed, not a single one was that of a foreigner, and from the best information, it is past doubt that there were only about some 1,300 Californian votes, while the remaining 10,700 were totally American.

The undersigned believe that they would fail to fulfil their duty if they did not, in connection with this subject, express the regret which they so strongly feel at the unjust attacks which have thus been made upon their constituents. They regard such assaults as not only ungenerous toward the citizens of California, but as direct offences against the nobility and sacredness of the American character itself. They look upon such insinuations as hurtful and injurious to the last degree, to a population than which none nobler and truer ever existed. You will search history in vain for an example of order under excitement like that which California has presented for the last two years. And it is the proud boast of every American, that to the republican education which that people has received, is due the extraordinary state of things which has heretofore rendered life and property secure where there was no law but the law of force. Yet this people, whose conduct has excited the admiration of every portion of the civilized world where their course is understood, are disparaged by a portion of their American brothers!

The Convention which formed the Constitution of California assembled at Monterey on the 1st day of September, 1849. Under the apportionment fixed by the Proclamation of General Riley, it would have consisted of 37 Delegates. This apportionment was based upon the Mexican law applicable to the country when it was a Department of Mexico ; but inasmuch as the recent large immigration had changed the relative importance of the Districts in regard to the number of population, Gen. Riley had recommended the election of such number of supernumerary Delegates from each District as the inhabitants thereof might deem proper. Most of the Districts acted on this suggestion ; and one of the first acts of the Convention was the settlement of the rights of membership, and the adoption of a new apportionment. Under the rule thereupon passed, the number of Delegates was fixed at 73, of whom 48 appeared, took their seats, and participated in the deliberations and action of the body. The Convention was in session from the 1st day of September till the 13th of October 1849. Its proceedings were characterized by order and a correct understanding and application of legislative rules. Every subject upon which diverse opinions were entertained was fully and ably debated ; and though the action of the body was unanimous to an extraordinary degree, it was a unanimity springing from reasoning and conviction, and not the effect of sycophancy, truckling, or fear. The men composing it were highly and justly esteemed among their immediate constituents for their independence, republican principles, ability, and honesty ; and it is confidently believed that the great and good qualities displayed by them in their action in the Convention have not only endeared them the more to their old and devoted friends, but have given them an enviable reputation and a flattering name coextensive with the boundaries of the State and perhaps of the American Union. Known among their fellow citizens by their social qualities and virtues ; appreciated for their industry, enterprise, and devotion to the interests of the masses, to liberty and law, they were elected without distinction of party ; and the Constitution which they prepared for the government of the new State in which they have cast their lot, and on whose soil many of them were born, and most of them have resided for several years, is an instrument which cannot fail for ever to bear testimony to the integrity, the capacity, and the patriotism of those who framed it. The insinuation that those men were awed or influenced by Gov. Riley, is an unjust assault not only upon their character and that of their constituents, but upon the fame and integrity of as brave a soldier and as good a man as the annals of American glory can boast.

The result of the labors of the Convention was submitted to the People of California for their consideration on the 13th day of October, 1849, on which day the Convention adjourned *sine die*. The Constitution was printed in the English and Spanish languages, and extraordinary efforts were made to circulate it in every portion of the Territory. In order that as full a vote as possible might be had both upon the Constitution and for the election of the officers under it, it was deemed absolutely necessary that the election should be fixed at a time anterior to the setting in of the winter rains. The impassable condition of the roads and rivers during the winter, it was well known, must inevitably detain large numbers of voters from the polls, if the election were too long postponed. Beside, it was deemed important that the admission of the State should be secured as speedily as possible, in order that her Senators and Representatives might early take their seats in Congress, and devote their energies to the promotion of the national legislation of which the country was so much in need. Accordingly the 13th of November, 1849, was fixed upon as the day of the election, and the 15th of December, 1849, as the day of the assembling of the State Legislature.

The anticipations which had caused the election to be held at an early day, proved not to be unfounded. The winter rains commenced several days before the 13th of November, and on that day one of the worst storms ever experienced raged throughout the whole country. The consequence was, notwithstanding the personal exertions of the friends of the different candidates for popular favor, that only about fifteen thousand votes were polled. Of these 12,061 were for the Constitution, 811 were against it, and from 1,200 to 1,500 were blanks, in consequence of the failure of the printer to place the words " For the Constitution" at the head of the ballots. It is believed that there never was an election attended with less excitement. The sentiment in favor of the Constitution was nearly unanimous, and was entirely the result of the unbiassed and deliberate opinions

316

of those who were most interested in it. No attempt was made to mislead or control public opinion in relation to the Constitution. No candidate sought success by either an ardent advocacy of its merits, or a broad denunciation of any of its provisions. The three newspapers published in the Territory did not feel called upon to aid it, further than to publish it with a simple recommendatory paragraph, and no member of the Convention urged its adoption with improper zeal. The truth is, that no political result in the history of any nation is more surely the honest expression of a public opinion founded in reason, reflection, and deliberate judgment, than the ratification afforded by the People of California to their Constitution.

The Legislature elected in November, assembled at San Jose, the Capitol of the State, on the 15th December last. The Governor elected by the People, PETER H. BURNETT, Esq. was inaugurated according to the requirements of the Constitution; and on the 20th of the same month, Gen Riley, by proclamation, delivered the Civil Government into the hands of the duly-elected agents of the newly-organized State. That State Government, complete in all its elemental parts, is now exercising the powers and performing the duties prescribed by the Constitution of the State of California. The legislation that is likely to ensue will be of such a character as is demanded by the public interests, but always in conformity to the Constitution of the United States and the laws of Congress. The intelligence and patriotism of those composing the State Government, are a warranty that no conflict of authority or interests is likely to occur, either from ignorance or design, between the Government of the United States and the Government of the State of California; and while it cannot be denied that the position of affairs is anomalous, it is not doubted that the legitimate channels of the two powers are so widely different that, running in a parallel direction, they never can come into collision. Such is believed to be the settled opinion of the People of California and of their Legislative and Executive authorities.

It was not from any desire to establish a State Government in opposition to or regardless of the wishes and rights of the people of the United States, that the people of California pursued this course. No improper motives, no ambitious impulses, no executive influence prompted their action. They believed that their brethren on the Atlantic appreciated their sufferings, admitted their patriotism, and would hail their action with joy. They thought that the Congress of the United States would instantly open its doors to their delegated representatives, and that the State would be immediately and gladly admitted. To this impression the tone of the public press, the dispatches of executive officers, and the speeches of distinguished statesmen in Congress had contributed in a very great degree; and as nothing of a contrary character had ever reached the Pacific shores, it is not surprising that the sentiment became a general one. The daily arriving emigration added their corroborative evidence to the already general belief, and it finally came to be credited that the great public of the Atlantic States were as ardently and unanimously in favor of the admission of California as were her own citizens. They did not anticipate delay, and consequently could not perceive or guard against a contingency arising from such a state of things. They believed their action to be eminently right and necessary, and sanctioned by the approving voice of the American people.

The population of California on the first day of January, 1850, is supposed to have been about 107,000 souls. There are no means of ascertaining with certainty the number and character of the large immigration which has poured into the country since the discovery of the gold mines, but the undersigned, having taken much pains to arrive at correct conclusions on this subject, submit the following estimates:

The population of California, exclusively of Indians and Africans, is supposed to have been, on the first day of January, 1849, as follows, viz:

Californians..13,000
Americans..8,000
Foreigners...5,000
                                                                          ————
    Total..26,000

From that time down to the 11th day of April, 1849, the arrivals by sea at the different ports is believed to have exceeded 6,000, and the arrivals by land from Sonora, Mexico, is estimated at 2,000. One-half of this increase, it is presumed, were Americans.

The following statistical table, compiled from the records of the Harbor-Master's Office at San Francisco, presents a more reliable and satisfactory account of the immigration which arrived there by sea from the 12th of April to the 31st of December, 1849, viz:

Months.	Americans.	Foreigners.	Males.	Females.	Totals.
April, May, June....	3,944	1,942	5,677	209	5,886
July....................	3,000	614	3,565	49	3,614
August................	3,384	509	3,806	87	3,893
September............	4,271	1,531	5,680	122	5,802
October................	2,655	1,414	3,950	119	4,069
November............	1,746	490	2,155	81	2,236
December............	3,069	500	3,436	133	3,569
Totals.......	22,069	7,000	28,269	800	29,069

In addition to the immigration thus arriving by sea at the port of San Francisco, it is believed that not less than 1,000 persons landed at other ports in California, during the same time. By the way of Santa Fe and the Gila the immigration was estimated at 8,000. From Mexico by land, from 6,000 to 8,000 were supposed to have arrived, of which only about 2,000 were believed to have remained in the country. Adding to these amounts the 3,000 sailors who have deserted from ships arriving in the country, and computing the great overland immigration (which was variously estimated from 30,000 to 40,000,) at 25,000, the following totals result, viz:

	Jan. 1, 1849.	Jan. 1, 1850.
Americans	8,000	76,069
Californians	13,000	13,000
Foreigners	5,000	18,000
Totals	26,000	107,069

The foregoing figures and estimates though known not to be strictly accurate, are thought to be a near approximation to the actual numbers of the inhabitants. The round numbers are presumed, in every case, to be below the mark.

The undersigned do not deem it their duty or province to urge upon your honorable bodies the many cogent reasons which in their opinion might be justly presented in favor of the admission of California as a State. Nor do they feel assured that it would be proper for them to lay before you any impressions which they may have of the history of the admission of new States, or the prescriptions, regulations, or laws of Congress relative thereto. Neither would they wish to overstep the bounds of true propriety by indelicately requesting a speedy decision of this question. Yet they cannot refrain from saying that great interests—interests of the highest importance to the Republic and to California—are suffering incalculably for want of action on the part of Congress. They will not attempt to particularize them, confident that the intelligent statesmen who compose your honorable bodies will at once understand to what they allude, and properly appreciate the suggestion.

The people of California are neither rebels, usurpers, nor anarchists. They have not sought to sow the seeds of revolution, that they might reap in the harvest of discord. They believe that the principles that guided them are true—they know that the motives which actuated them are pure and just—and they had hoped that their action would be acceptable to every portion of their common country. They did not expect that their admission as a State would be made the test question upon which would hang the preservation of the American Union, nor did they desire such a result; but urged by the imperative and extraordinary necessities of their country, they united in such action as they believed would secure them a government under and in conformity to the Constitution of their country.

In thus presenting the certified copies of their State Constitution and their credentials, and asking the admission of the State, and that they may be permitted to take their seats in your respective bodies, the undersigned feel that they would neglect an important duty if they failed to assure you of the anxious desire for the perpetuity of this Union which animates all classes of their constituents. Born and reared under its protecting influences, as most of them were, their patriotism is as broad as the Republic—it extends from the Atlantic to the Pacific—it is as deep as the current of their mighty rivers—as pure as the never-melting snows which crown their mountains, and as indestructible as the virgin gold extracted from their soil. Coming as they nearly all do from the different States composing the Union, deeply impressed, as most of them have been by passing through foreign lands, with the immeasurable superiority of American institutions and American character, it would be strange, indeed, if they did not turn with reverence and affection toward their country, its institutions, and its people. Possessed, too, in a remarkable degree, of intelligence, enterprise, and ability, rich in high moral qualities, industrious, energetic and honest, firm in their devotion to order and justice, they compose a community which has no superiors in the elements which constitute a citizen's glory, and a nation's greatness.

This people request admission into the American Union as a State. They understand and estimate the advantages which will accrue to them from such a connection, while they trust they do not too highly compute those which will be conferred upon their brethren. They do not present themselves as suppliants, nor do they bear themselves with arrogance or presumption. They come as free American citizens—citizens by treaty, by adoption, and by birth—and ask that they may be permitted to reap the common benefits, share the common ills, and promote the common welfare, as one of the United States of America!

WILLIAM M. GWIN,
JOHN C. FREMONT,
GEORGE W. WRIGHT,
EDWARD GILBERT.

Washington, D. C. March 12, 1850.

BIBLIOGRAPHY

THE MAKING OF AMERICAN CALIFORNIA: A PROVIDENTIAL APPROACH

BIBLIOGRAPHY

Bancroft, Hubert Howe. THE WORKS OF HUBERT HOWE BANCROFT. History of California, Vol. V., VI. San Francisco: The History Company, Publishers, 1886.

Bari, Valeska, Editor. THE COURSE OF EMPIRE, FIRST HAND ACCOUNTS OF CALIFORNIA IN THE DAYS OF THE GOLD RUSH OF '49. New York: Coward-McCann, Inc., 1931.

Bates, D. B. INCIDENTS ON LAND AND WATER. Boston, 1860.

Bean, Walton. CALIFORNIA, AN INTERPRETIVE HISTORY. New York: McGraw-Hill Book Company, 1968. Used with permission of McGraw-Hill Book Company.

Bidwell, John. "Life in California Before the Gold Discovery," THE CENTURY MAGAZINE, Dec. 1890 and Feb. 1891. Reprint: Palo Alto: Lewis Osborne, 1966.

Browne, J. Ross. REPORT OF THE DEBATES IN THE CONVENTION OF CALIFORNIA ON THE FORMATION OF THE STATE CONSTITUTION, IN SEPTEMBER AND OCTOBER, 1849. Washington, 1850. (Printed by John T. Towers.)

Bulmore, Laurence and Milton Lanyon. CINNABAR HILLS: THE QUICKSILVER DAYS OF NEW ALMADEN. Los Gatos: The Village Printers, 1967.

Burnett, Peter H. RECOLLECTIONS AND OPINIONS OF AN OLD PIONEER. New York: Appleton Edition, 1880. Reprint: Joseph A. Sullivan, Editor. PETER BURNETT, FIRST GOVERNOR OF THE STATE OF CALIFORNIA, AN OLD CALIFORNIA PIONEER. Oakland: Biobooks, 1946.

California. THE ORIGINAL CONSTITUTION OF THE STATE OF CALIFORNIA, 1849. Published by Telefact Foundation in cooperation with The California State Department of Education and The California State Archives, Sacramento, October 13, 1965.

California. JOURNAL OF THE SENATE OF THE STATE OF CALIFORNIA AT THEIR FIRST SESSION. San Jose: J. Winchester, State Printer, 1850. A copy may be obtained from the California State Library, Law Department, Sacramento.

"California," THE AMERICAN REVIEW. New York, April, 1849.

Caughey, John and Laree. "Take Your Bible in One Hand," CALIFORNIA HERITAGE. Los Angeles: The Ward Ritchie Press, 1962.

Chapman, Charles E. A HISTORY OF CALIFORNIA: THE SPANISH PERIOD. New York: The Macmillan Company, 1921.

Cleland, Robert Glass. THIS RECKLESS BREED OF MEN. New York: Alfred A. Knopf, 1963.

Colton, Walter. THREE YEARS IN CALIFORNIA. New York: A. S. Barnes & Co., 1850. (Reprint: Board of Trustees of Leland Stanford Jr. University. Stanford: Stanford University Press, 1949.)

Coy, Owen Cochrane. GOLD DAYS. San Francisco, Los Angeles, Chicago: Powell Publishing Co., 1929.

Dana, Julian. SUTTER OF CALIFORNIA: A BIOGRAPHY. New York: The Press of the Pioneers, 1934. Reprint: New York: The Macmillan Company, 1936.

Eldredge, Zoeth Skinner, Editor. HISTORY OF CALIFORNIA, Vol. I., New York: The Century History Company, 1915.

Ellison, William H. A SELF-GOVERNING DOMINION, CALIFORNIA, 1849-1860. Berkeley and Los Angeles, 1950.

ENCYCLOPEDIA BRITANNICA, Eleventh Edition 1910; Fourteenth Edition, 1929.

Fiske, John. THE DISCOVERY OF AMERICA, Vol. I and Vol. II. Boston and New York: Houghton, Mifflin and Company, 1892.

Fleming, Sandford. GOD'S GOLD, The Story of Baptist Beginnings in California, 1849-1860. Philadelphia: The Judson Press, 1949.

Fremont, John Charles. MEMOIRS OF MY LIFE. Chicago and New York: Belford, Clarke, and Co., 1887.

Gihon, John, James Nisbet, Frank Soule. THE ANNALS OF SAN FRANCISCO. New York: D. Appleton Co., 1855. Reprint: Dorothy H. Huggins, Compiler. Palo Alto: Lewis Osborne, 1966.

Gillespie, Charles B. "Marshall's Own Account of the Gold Discovery," THE CENTURY MAGAZINE, Feb. 1891, Vol. XLI (New Series XIX).

Grant, Blanche C., Editor. KIT CARSON'S OWN STORY OF HIS LIFE AS DICTATED TO COL. AND MRS. D. C. PETERS ABOUT 1856-57, AND NEVER BEFORE PUBLISHED. Taos: Santa Fe New Mexican Publishers Corp., 1926.

Gudde, Erwin G. SUTTER'S OWN STORY. New York: G. P. Putnams' Sons, 1936.

Hale, Edward Everett. "The Queen of California," Paper to the Antiquarian Society, 1863. THE ATLANTIC MONTHLY, Vol. XIII, No. LXXVII, March 1864. Reprint, Boston: THE ATLANTIC MONTHLY, April, 1949.

Hall, Verna M., Compiler. THE CHRISTIAN HISTORY OF THE CONSTITUTION OF THE UNITED STATES OF AMERICA: CHRISTIAN SELF-GOVERNMENT, Vol. I. American Revolution Bicentennial Edition. San Francisco: Foundation for American Christian Education, 1975.

THE CHRISTIAN HISTORY OF THE CONSTITUTION OF THE UNITED STATES OF AMERICA: SELF-GOVERNMENT WITH UNION, Vol. II. San Francisco: The Foundation for American Christian Education, 1962.

THE CHRISTIAN HISTORY OF THE AMERICAN REVOLUTION: CONSIDER AND PONDER. San Francisco: Foundation for American Christian Education, 1976.

Hall, Verna M. "The Hand of God in American History: English Preparation," THE JOURNAL OF THE FOUNDATION FOR AMERICAN CHRISTIAN EDUCATION, Vol. I. San Francisco: Foundation for American Christian Education, 1989.

Hall, Verna M. and Rosalie J. Slater. THE BIBLE AND THE CONSTITUTION OF THE UNITED STATES OF AMERICA. San Francisco: Foundation for American Christian Education, 1983.

THE HOLY BIBLE, King James Version.

Hunt, Aurora. MAJOR GENERAL JAMES HENRY CARLETON 1814-1873, WESTERN FRONTIER DRAGOON. Glendale: The Arthur H. Clark Company, 1958. Used with permission from The Arthur Clark Company.

Hunt, Rockwell D. CALIFORNIA'S STATELY HALL OF FAME. Stockton: College of the Pacific, 1950.

CALIFORNIA IN THE MAKING. Caldwell, Idaho: The Caxton Printers, Ltd., 1953.

NEW CALIFORNIA THE GOLDEN. Sacramento: California State Printing Office, 1937.

"The Genesis of California's First Constitution (1846–1849)," JOHNS HOPKINS UNIVERSITY STUDIES IN HISTORICAL AND POLITICAL SCIENCE. Baltimore: The John Hopkins Press, August 1895.

JOHN BIDWELL, PRINCE OF CALIFORNIA PIONEERS. Caldwell, Idaho: The Caxton Printers, Ltd., 1942.

"1850: A Year of Destiny," Fourteenth Annual Research Lecture, Graduate School. University of Southern California, April 1947.

Hunt, Rockwell D. and Nellie Van de Grift Sanchez. A SHORT HISTORY OF CALIFORNIA. New York: Thomas Y. Crowell Co., 1929.

CALIFORNIA AND THE CALIFORNIANS, Vol. I. (Hunt: The American Period; Sanchez: The Spanish Period) San Francisco: The Lewis Publishing Company, 1932.

Hutchings, J. M. SCENES OF WONDER AND CURIOSITY. San Francisco: J. M. Hutchings & Co., 1861.

Irving, Washington. LIFE AND WORKS OF WASHINGTON IRVING, Vol. I and Vol. II. New York: P. F. Collier, 1827; LIFE AND VOYAGES OF CHRISTOPHER COLUMBUS, Vol. VIII.

Johnston, Alexander. HISTORY OF THE UNITED STATES: New York, 1892.

Klotz, Edwin. "The Confluence of Cultures," THE ORIGINAL CONSTITUTION OF THE STATE OF CALIFORNIA, 1849. Telefact Foundation in cooperation with the California Department of Education and the California State Archives, October 1965.

Komroff, Manuel, Ed. THE TRAVELS OF MARCO POLO. Garden City Publishing Company, Inc., 1930.

Kroeber, A. L. ANTHROPOLOGY. New York: Harcourt, Brace & Co., 1923.

Lanyon, Milton and Laurence Bulmore. CINNABAR HILLS: THE QUICKSILVER DAYS OF NEW ALMADEN. Los Gatos: The Village Printers, 1967.

Loofbourow, Leon L. IN SEARCH OF GOD'S GOLD. San Francisco: The Historical Society of the California-Nevada Annual Conference of The Methodist Church; Stockton: The College of the Pacific, 1950. With permission by the Commission on Archives and History, The California-Nevada Conference of The United Methodist Church.

Morgan, Dale L. JEDEDIAH SMITH AND THE OPENING OF THE WEST. Lincoln, Nebraska: University of Nebraska, 1953.

Morrison, Samuel Eliot. ADMIRAL OF THE OCEAN SEA: A LIFE OF CHRISTOPHER COLUMBUS. Boston: Little, Brown and Co., 1942.

Muzzey, David Saville. AN AMERICAN HISTORY. Boston: Ginn and Company, 1920.

Nisbet, James, John Gihon, Frank Soule. THE ANNALS OF SAN FRANCISCO. New York: D. Appleton Co., 1855. Reprint: Dorothy H. Huggins, Compiler. Palo Alto: Lewis Osborne, 1966.

O'Dell, Scott. ISLAND OF THE BLUE DOLPHINS. Boston: Houghton, Mifflin Co., 1960.

OLD SOUTH LEAFLET NO. 29; "Discovery of America" by Ferdinand Columbus. Boston: Old South Association.

OLD SOUTH LEAFLET NO. 45; "First Ascent of Fremont's Peak." Boston: Old South Association.

Pond, William C. GOSPEL PIONEERING: Reminiscences of Early Congregationalism in California. Oberlin, Ohio: The News Printing Co., 1921.

THE PRESBYTERIAN LAYMAN, October 1971.

Prescott, William Hickling. HISTORY OF THE CONQUEST OF MEXICO AND HISTORY OF THE CONQUEST OF PERU. New York: Random House, Inc. Reprint, unabridged, Prescott's edition, 1843.

Revere, Joseph Warren. A TOUR OF DUTY IN CALIFORNIA. New York: C. S. Francis & Co.; Boston: J. S. Francis, 1849. Reprint: Joseph A. Sullivan, Editor. NAVAL DUTY IN CALIFORNIA. Oakland: Biobooks, 1947.

Rickets, A. H. "A Dissertation Upon The Origin, Development, and Establishment Of American Mining Law," ELEVENTH REPORT OF THE STATE MINEROLOGIST: Two Years Ending September 15, 1892. Sacramento: California State Printing Office, 1893.

Rose, James B. A GUIDE TO AMERICAN CHRISTIAN EDUCATION FOR THE HOME AND SCHOOL: THE PRINCIPLE APPROACH. Camarillo, CA: American Christian History Institute, 1987.

Sanchez, Nellie Van de Grift and Rockwell D. Hunt. A SHORT HISTORY OF CALIFORNIA. New York: Thomas Y. Crowell Co., 1929.

CALIFORNIA AND THE CALIFORNIANS, Vol. I. (Hunt: The American Period; Sanchez: The Spanish Period) San Francisco: The Lewis Publishing Company, 1932.

Shinn, Charles Howard. MINING CAMPS: A Study in American Frontier Government. New York: Alfred A. Knopf, 1948.

Slater, Rosalie J. TEACHING AND LEARNING AMERICA'S CHRISTIAN HISTORY: THE PRINCIPLE APPROACH. American Revolution Bicentennial Edition. San Francisco: The Foundation for American Christian Education, 1975.

"Introducing Teachers to the Christian History Program," unpublished article.

Slater, Rosalie J. and Verna M. Hall. THE BIBLE AND THE CONSTITUTION OF THE UNITED STATES OF AMERICA. San Francisco: Foundation for American Christian Education, 1983.

Soule, Frank, John Gihon, James Nisbet. THE ANNALS OF SAN FRANCISCO. New York: D. Appleton Co., 1855. Reprint: Dorothy H. Huggins, Compiler. Palo Alto: Lewis Osborne, 1966.

Stone, Irving. IMMORTAL WIFE. Garden City, New York: Doubleday, Doran & Co., Inc., 1944.

Taylor, Bayard. ELDORADO. New York: George P. Putnam, 1850.

Underhill, Reuben L. FROM COWHIDES TO GOLDEN FLEECE. Stanford: Stanford University Press, 1939.

Upham, Charles Wentworth. LIFE, EXPLORATIONS AND PUBLIC SERVICES OF JOHN CHARLES FREMONT. Boston: Ticknor and Fields, 1856.

Veniaminov, Ioann (Priest). TRAVEL JOURNAL OF TRIP TO CALIFORNIA AND BACK, JUNE 1 TO OCTOBER 13, 1836. This may be found in The Sacramento State Library, Sacramento, California.

Webster, Noah. AN AMERICAN DICTIONARY OF THE ENGLISH LANGUAGE. San Francisco: Foundation for American Christian Education, 1967. (Facsimile of Webster's First Edition of 1828.)

Wendt, Charles W. THOMAS STARR KING, PATRIOT AND PREACHER. Boston: The Beacon Press, 1921.

White, William F. A PICTURE: PIONEER TIMES IN CALIFORNIA. San Francisco: W. M. Hinton & Co., 1881.

Williams, Elisha. "The Essential Rights and Liberties of Protestants," 1744.

Wilson, Iris H. WILLIAM WOLFSKILL, 1798-1866. Glendale: The Arthur H. Clark Company, 1965. Used with permission from The Arthur H. Clark Company.

Winsor, Justin. CHRISTOPHER COLUMBUS. Boston and New York: Houghton, Mifflin and Company, 1892.

Wood, Eric. FAMOUS VOYAGES OF THE GREAT DISCOVERERS. New York: Thomas Y. Crowell and Company.

INDEX

SCRIPTURE REFERENCES
(*Implied References)